Cover art is from the journal of Eduard Harkort (1797-1836), a German engineer who as a young man worked as a surveyor, served his compulsory military service in a Prussian artillery regiment and then studied mining and mineralogy. In 1828, he was hired by a British mining firm to supervise their smelting operations in Mexico. Becoming involved in politics in 1832, he joined the revolutionary army of Antonio López de Santa Anna, and was captured at the Battle of Tolomé, imprisoned, and then escaped to rejoin Santa Anna's forces. After serving as a colonel in their artillery, Harkort switched sides to the federalists after Santa Anna turned dictator. In May 1835, he was captured at the Battle of Zacatecas, imprisoned yet again, and then deported in October to New Orleans (one month after Stephen F. Austin left Mexico under similar circumstances). While there, he met Stephen F. Austin, who interested him in joining the Texas Revolution against his old nemesis Santa Anna. His journal records his arrival at Velasco in Feb-1836, where he apparently made the drawing on our cover. He traveled up the Brazos valley, where Sam Houston was encamped with the Texas Revolutionary Army. The General appointed him Captain of Engineers in late March, with orders to return to the coast to fortify Velasco and Galveston Pass. These forts on land, together with the new "First Texas Navy" at sea, protected Houston's southern flank, helping him to prevail at San Jacinto and win the independence of Texas. Afterwards, while focusing on building Fort Travis on Galveston Island, Harkort sent his journal back to family in Germany. Tragically, he died at the Kokernot home at San Jacinto Bay on 11-Aug-1836. In the 1990's, Louis Brister, Professor of German at Southwest Texas State University, discovered Harkort's journal in an archive in Dortmund, Germany, and published a version of the drawing in 1999. In 2020, the Stiftung Westfälisches Wirtschaftsarchiv (Westphalian Business Archives Foundation) graciously provided modern high-resolution scans of ten drawings from the journal, two of which are of the mouth of the Brazos River and have been digitally spliced, proudly displayed on the cover.

1836 version of "Map of Texas With Parts of the Adjoining States" compiled by Stephen F. Austin, published by H. S. Tanner of Philadelphia, with observations of General Teran of the Mexican Army.
An early published map of Texas, versions exist from 1830 to 1840. Austin cannily emphasized Texas despite being "Coahuila y Tejas" at the time, & featured symbolism above title for Mexican federalism.

Here Rests the Brave
A Chronological and Archaeological History of the Forts Velasco

... an illustrated narrative by
Chris Kneupper

... published under the auspices of the
Old Fort Velasco Historical Association
a 501c3 non-profit organization

Library of Congress Catalog Number 2025921213

International Standard Book Number 979-8-9932899-1-5

DEDICATION

Dedicated to the memory of my great friend
Johnney Taylor Pollan Jr. (1947-2022)
who was a kind, humorous and wise mentor
for over four decades to the
avocational and professional archaeologists
of the Brazosport Archaeological Society
and Texas Archeological Society.

ACKNOWLEDGEMENTS

The study of early efforts to research and to build a replica Fort Velasco was greatly helped by reviewing the papers of the late George Kramig, which his two daughters graciously loaned to the author for an extended period. Johnney T. Pollan Jr., James L. Smith, Sue Gross, Clint Lacy and other members of the Brazosport Archaeological Society (BAS) provided invaluable assistance with old maps, records and knowledge of past archaeological efforts. Many local papers and images were obtained at the Adriance Library & Research Center at the Brazoria County Historical Museum, through the efforts of curators Michael Bailey and Abigail Martin. The Blueline Print Shop in Freeport Texas graciously provided professional copying and digitizing work for old documents at no or reduced cost. The librarians of the Brazoria County Library System (especially the Brazoria branch) helped me obtain numerous obscure titles through Interlibrary Loan. James Glover and Jennifer Parsley of the Brazoria County Parks Department reviewed the early stages of research, making helpful suggestions. The staff of the Dolph Briscoe Center for American History (CAH), the Texas State Library And Archives, the Texas General Land Office , the Catholic Archives of Texas (all in Austin, Texas), and the Galveston & Texas History Center (Rosenberg Library, Galveston, Texas) were also most helpful in locating old documents in their collections. Unless otherwise stated, the author made transcriptions and English translations of many of the handwritten Spanish-language documents obtained from these sources, with the assistance of James E. "Jake" Ivey, Xavier Sendejo, Sonia Bennett, Flor Leon, Paul-Michael Dusek and Gregg Dimmick. Many of the images used in the Figures are photographs taken by the author or obtained from the Internet under Title 17 U.S.C. Section 107. Others are the work of artists such as Fred Toler, Peter Rindlisbacher, Sherman A. Thompson II, Conrad Wise Chapman, Dan Parkinson and Bob Duke. Jeff Durst of the Texas Historical Commission has helped with archaeological counsel about this site for years. Tiffany Osburn (of THC) and Doug Boyd (then of Prewitt & Associates) have advised on use of remote-sensing techniques and contractors. George Nelson, Wade Dillon and Andy Hall have provided historical context and advice. Bart R. Forbes provided advice on the path to publication as a book. Last but not least, my family (wife Helen, daughters Elissa & Christiane, son Carl) have provided endless support through years of archaeological projects and research, and here with digital editing of images, formatting, pagination, and proof-reading. The author expresses gratitude for all of this invaluable help.

A key but previously under-used resource has been the Béxar Archives, due the fact that its documents of this era have not yet been translated, and their Calendar is a useful finding aid, although the Calendar is no longer maintained on-line by the Briscoe Center (instead use Wayback Machine link below).
https://web.archive.org/web/20160820043615/http:/www.cah.utexas.edu/projects/bexar/calendar.php

In general, we also owe a great debt to all the other here-unnamed historians, archivists, cartographers, authors, modelers, artists and history buffs who have created collections (such as the Béxar Archives, Austin Papers, Lamar Papers, Portal to Texas History, etc.), models, publications, drawings or maps, making it possible for us to build this illustrated story, tidbit-by-tidbit, brick-by-brick, to bring to life the events of the past at or near old Velasco.

Dios y Libertad

Don Christiano

AUTHOR'S PREFACE

Dear readers, please indulge me for a moment, as I lead you into a little thought experiment. What must it have been like at the mouth of the Brazos in the early days during the first attempts at settlement? Low-lying salt flats spread out as far as the eye could see, such that early Spanish explorers often failed to even see the *Rio de los Brazos de Dios* as it emptied directly into the *Seno Mexicano*. They created charts and maps that failed to show it, having sailed right past it without notice. The land was subject to inundation in storms, tides or hurricanes, with little to offer in the way of prairie for grazing, timber, game or healthful water. Hot and humid in the summer, only the almost-constant onshore wind kept plagues of mosquitos from driving everyone crazy. Rainfall, when it came, could be torrential. Winter "northers" could bring a quick change to freezing weather with little natural protection from the elements. Fresh water could only be obtained by collecting rainwater as runoff from the roofs of structures built hastily from drift logs. I can't imagine drinking such water that had washed bits of leaves, dirt and dust, mold and mildew, insects, seagull poop and God knows what, into a barrel or cistern to steep for a while before use. The occupants must have been hardy folks …… and Brave!

The main title of this book is taken from an obscure newspaper article in the **Arkansas Advocate** issue of 6-Feb-1833, which describes a late-1832 meeting in San Felipe de Austin where one item discussed was that the Texian militia fatalities in the 1832 Battle of Velasco were to be honored with a stone monument. Commemorative words there include the phrase "**Here Rests the Brave**".

This book is an illustrated narrative, including many maps, diagrams, photos and documents, and also many direct quotes, but we hope these add a touch of the times and lighten up some of the studious detail. Names and direct quotes use spellings and grammar as found, even when not up to modern English standards. The book has a rather narrow subject, focusing primarily on the small town of Velasco at the old mouth of the Brazos River, so we expect it will be of interest only to a limited audience. But it is also broad in some respects, trying to fit this story into the larger context of the creation of modern Texas. Effort has been made to thoroughly uncover and review contemporaneous or primary source material. Indeed, this book could also be called a literature survey. It also emphasizes maritime activities, as these are sometimes neglected in other treatments. References are listed together in one section at the end in the alphabetical style used in archaeological reports, in part to avoid cumbersome numbering and footnotes. The lay reader can blow past the [bracketed] reference listings, while the Reference section allow others to see the basis for our story or to dig deeper.

The forts referred to in the sub-title are a series of military fortifications and (later) other government posts that were at this strategic location, and which are used here as the spine of the story. Despite the early disadvantages of the mouth, the Brazos River offered a transportation artery right into the heart of Austin's Colony from the beginning, making it also critical for travel, commerce and military purposes. Thus, two rustic yet modestly prosperous towns grew up at the location, Quintana on the right bank and Velasco on the left bank, the latter taking its name from the first fort built there. They flourished from Republic of Texas days to the end of the Civil War. However, like Indianola, these two towns fell victim, in the last few decades of the 1800s, to nature's hazards of sandbars and storms, and competition from deeper and safer harbors nearby. By 1900, old Velasco was not much more than a ghost town. Reborn after World War II as the seaside resort community of Surfside Beach, the name of Velasco has now disappeared from the maps. But it had a significant impact on the development of the Republic and State of Texas, and I have endeavored to produce a scholarly work to add granularity to that story. I hope you enjoy my efforts to bring this Velasco-centric and under-told story out of the mists of the past.

TABLE OF CONTENTS

LIST OF ILLUSTRATIONS

PURPOSE

It is a thesis of the author, after researching this topic for over six years, that old Velasco played a more significant role in early Texas history than is generally recognized today, and that efforts should be made to redress the situation by historical interpretation of the area, to teach local residents, and promote heritage tourism for visitors. Francis White "Frank" Johnson, an early settler in Mexican Texas and leader during the Texas Revolution, wrote a manuscript before his death in 1884 (later published in 1914), where he wrote *"Perhaps no section of Texas has more landmarks and associations with early history than Brazoria County. Its area was included within the grant of the Austin colony, and settlement began early in the decade of the 20's. The Brazos River was the gateway by which immigration and commerce came to Texas by sea, and the prestige of such ports and towns as Velasco, Brazoria and Columbia is easily understood."* [Johnson 1914 p. 648]. Another historian, William C. Binkley, once wrote *"... the history of the Texas Revolution had not been written and that until a number of detailed studies of various phases of the struggle could be made, it would perhaps be unreasonable to expect an adequate synthesis."* [Binkley 1952 p. v]. So, better late than never, extensive research into primary sources and others has been accomplished for Velasco, to compile and tell that part of the Texas story. Believing that any interpretation should respect historical facts to the fullest extent possible, this detailed history of the Velasco area has been here assembled for public access. It focuses on the several forts built at Velasco, while trying to place these details within the context of the better-known history of the times. The work product also comprises an image-heavy "executive summary" (as a MS-PowerPoint document suitable as an audio-visual presentation to interested groups), and a website where obscure documents can be viewed:

https://velascohistoryarchaeology.weebly.com/

Readers are welcome, indeed eagerly requested, to provide corrections or additional information, especially from documented sources or for the first Fort Velasco. All statements in this document are the responsibility of the author only, and do not represent the position of the groups to which he is a member. Thus, amendments should be requested directly from the author.

INTRODUCTION

As the 1830s dawned in southeast Texas, significant but mostly rural settlement had been underway for almost a decade in this previously undeveloped area of Mexican Texas, through the colony established by Stephen Fuller Austin known as Austin's Colony, with his original settlers known as the Old Three Hundred. By 1835, it has been estimated that 25,000 settlers had arrived through the mouth of the Brazos [Texas 1969, Weir 1976]. However, the only towns of note were the rustic hamlets of San Felipe de Austin, Brazoria, Matagorda and Harrisburg, each only a few years old, as shown in the 1830 version of a map created and commissioned by the empresario himself (Figure 1 below). Please note, aside from a road from Brazoria down the right bank, no development is shown at the mouth of the Brazos River.

Figure 1: Portion of 1830 version of Austin and Terán map published by H. S. Tanner

Although some unimproved roads existed, much of the transportation and commerce occurred via waterways, such as shallow-draft schooners in the Gulf of Mexico, bays and lower portions of major rivers; as well as sloops, packet boats and small steamers in the inland rivers and canals [Puryear & Winfield 1976, Francaviglia 1998, Meed 2001 pp. 4-6]. Since developed harbors or port towns had yet to be created, the mouth of the Brazos became a chief port of entry, in part since it was navigable for some distance inland. In the period of 1823-1824, a landing was established by Josiah H. Bell known as Bell's Landing (later known as Marion and then East Columbia), where the smaller ships of the era could dock. Brazoria was laid out later (circa 1828), also to receive ships. To assist commerce, the colonists had been granted a reprieve from customs duties for seven years by a decree from the Mexican Congress on 29-Sep-1823 [Supremo Gobierno 1825], stating "*The Mexican Sovereign Congress, taking into consideration*

Figure 2: Portrait of Asa Mitchell
Courtesy of Dolph Briscoe
Center for American History

the pitiful and deplorable state to which the hostilities of the barbarians have reduced the province of Texas, and in part to the misery of its civilized inhabitants, has come to direct and decree. - That all the effects of any kind, national or foreign that are introduced in the province of Texas for the consumption of its inhabitants, be free of duties; This exemption lasts for seven years counted from its publication in that capital". No attempt was made to establish customs posts for Austin's Colony until near the expiration date in 1830 [Morton 1945 p. 508]. So, free trade practices became the norm, unlike other portions of Mexico.

Although the mouth of the Brazos River was a key port of entry for Austin's Colony [Hardy & Roberts 1910 p. 356], the adjacent low "salt flats" were mostly barren of fresh water, timber and game, vulnerable to tides and storms, and only a few settlers eked out an existence there. One of the few was Asa Mitchell (Figure 2), who had settled there in the early 1820s with family, obtained a land grant in 1824 in the unnamed area on the left bank or east side, and established a salt works in about 1826 [Mitchell 1826, Mauermann 1950].

An early description of the area was made by Stephen F. Austin while visiting in late 1825 for a fishing trip, perhaps at the Mitchell homestead. He wrote *"This river mouths into the wild ocean without any bay, and the breakers are roaring within Eighty yards of me – there is a good two story frame house and some cabins here, and there is at this time 8 feet water over the bar. Salt water is produced here by digging 10 feet so strong that 5 gallons of it will make one of salt, …"* [Austin Dec-1825]. By 1830, it was estimated that two vessels per month arrived at the Brazos from New Orleans over the prior ten months, with a combined capacity of 1200 tons [Fisher 21-Jul-1830a, Barker 1926 p. 183, Letts 1928 p. 46], usually tacking upriver to Brazoria to dock. However, despite these modest beginnings, major developments in the history of Texas would occur at the mouth, primarily due to its strategic location for transportation, military and commercial purposes.

Alarmed by Austin's success at colonization, and skeptical of his colonists' assimilation of Mexican customs/laws/religion/language, the Mexican national government established a customs post at the location, soon joined by a small military fort initially named as *"Fortaleza de Velasco"*, which later gave its name to the area. Soon after its construction in 1832, this fort was the site of a skirmish called the Battle of Velasco, sometimes memorialized as the *"first battle of the Texas Revolution"* or its version of the *"Boston Tea Party"* or *"Lexington and Concord"*, after which the rustic fort was largely abandoned.

Although many accounts have been published about the Battle of Velasco, very few details (size or dimensions) were mentioned about the 1832 fort's actual construction. Due to the strategic location of the mouth of the Brazos, other later forts were also built during the Texas Revolution and the Civil War at almost but not the same location [Hardy & Roberts 1910 p. 359]. Since the history of the several "Forts Velasco" can be very confusing, this illustrated narrative is intended to sort and align all the chronological and archaeological facts to describe the several military emplacements and posts on the left bank of the Brazos River at its original mouth, now the entrance to Freeport Harbor near Surfside Beach. Thus, this history of the site can inform and enable any historical interpretation or archaeological projects in coming years.

BACKGROUND

Lest we think old Velasco was the first attempt to establish a port on the upper Texas coast, our story needs to start a little earlier, to get some inkling of prior efforts at and near the mouth of the Brazos. Before Mexico won its independence from Spain in 1821, the King of Spain authorized Bahía de San Bernardo (a broad area currently known as Matagorda, Lavaca and perhaps Espiritu Santo and San Antonio Bays) for free trade [Soler 1805], and this was recognized again by the Eastern Interior Provinces of Mexico in 1821 [Barker 1926 p. 179-180]. This was probably due to the fact that these bays provided the closest deep-water harbor to the settlements, ranchos and missions along the lower San Antonio River near La Bahía (modern Goliad), and their incomplete knowledge of other harbor options along the middle and upper Texas coast. Interestingly, the original name for Goliad was La Bahía, taken from the name of the presidio which moved there in 1749, Presidio Nuestra Señora de Loreto de la Bahía. The term "La Bahía" ("The Bay" in English) harkens back to the original location for this presidio on Garcitas Creek just above Bahía de San Bernardo (Lavaca Bay) in the period of 1721-1726. So, this area had been explored and known for some time. Some sign of the state of geographical knowledge of

the time can be seen in an 1807 map, drawn by a Franciscan friar at Nacogdoches, Fray José Maria Puelles. Figure 3 is a digital copy of the Puelles map found among Stephen F. Austin's papers (the original is now at the Texas Map Collection at the Dolph Briscoe Center for American History). This map was probably the best map of Texas for its time, although it was never publicly released by Spanish authorities.

Figure 3: Stephen F. Austin's copy of the Puelles 1807 map, aka "Mapa Geografica de las Provinciales Septentrionales de Esta Nueva Espana"
Courtesy of Dolph Briscoe Center for American History

Published maps, such as the Humboldt map of New Spain (drawn 1804, published 1810) and the Zebulon Pike map of the Internal Provinces of New Spain (visited 1807, published 1810) were less accurate for the Texas interior and its rivers, although they were similar for coastal geography. On these maps, the series of bays known today as Matagorda and Lavaca Bays is labeled as *"Bahía (or Lago) de San Bernardo"*, San Antonio/Aransas/Copano Bays as *"Bahia de San Jose"* and Galveston/Trinity Bays as *"Bahía de Galveston"*. Galveston Island was labeled as *"Isla de San Luis"* and its northeast end was *"Punta de Culebras"*, and the island was shown reaching all the way southwest to the entrance of Bahía de San Bernardo. Except for the Puelles map, the Brazos River is poorly represented as a minor river emptying into an intervening bay. With this state of knowledge, it is little wonder that Bahía de San Bernardo was considered the best choice for a Texas port. The Colorado River is shown to empty into Lavaca Bay, although it in fact emptied into the northeast end of Matagorda Bay. This bay and East Matagorda Bay were once a single bay until about 1929 when the Colorado "raft" was finally dislodged and a new delta formed into the bay. In 1934, a 200' wide x 9' deep channel was cut through this delta and across Matagorda Peninsula to empty directly into the Gulf. Thus, to reach the mouth of the Colorado in the early years, sailors had to enter Bahía de San Bernardo, and then turn northeast to travel some distance up the bay to the mouth. However, at the time, the "raft" prevented further navigation up the Colorado River itself much past the modern location of the town of Matagorda [Clay 1949], so this river never developed the early commerce that the Brazos River did.

Among the first Americans to visit Texas by sea was George Graham, who was given a special commission in the summer of 1818 to visit the area of Galveston Bay, to contact a group of French exiles who had settled on the lower Trinity River. Charles Lallemand had led a group, mostly Bonapartist military men unwelcome in France, to Galveston Island in early 1818, where Jean Laffite assisted them to form Champ d'Asile, reported to be at or near the current town of Liberty. Rumors of this settlement caused U. S. Secretary of State John Quincy Adams to send George Graham to disabuse Lallemand from such an idea, since the French group had never sought official permission. After traveling overland from Washington DC as far as the Sabine River, Graham learned the French had left their settlement and departed for Galveston Island. He traveled south to Calcasieu Lake, where he hired passage on a smuggler's vessel to Galveston Island, arriving on 24-Aug-1818. There he met with Laffite and the retreating Lallemand, convincing Lallemand to fully quit the project. His commission accomplished, Graham began his return trip, dispatching an undated report to Adams from Bayou Rapides. He writes he was impressed with Galveston Island and its strategic location, despite being low, without timber or good water, claiming that only it and Matagorda were suitable inlets on the Texas coast. He mentions *"the Brassos"* and other rivers *"... affording good navigation, & watering the best part of the province of Texas. At the mouth of each of these rivers is a bar which does not afford more than four feet of water, & the only pass into the Bay which admits the entrance of large vessels is that at Galveston."* He recommended the immediate occupation of Galveston Island by the U. S. military, to stop widespread smuggling and help U. S. claims to Texas *"... when the people will settle the question of title to the province of Texas, by silently & quietly occupying it without the immediate or direct interference of the Government ..."*, despite the possibility of war with Spain [Prichard 1937]. At the time, Texas was disputed between the U. S. and Spain; the Americans claiming Texas was theirs due to the Louisiana Purchase. Back in Washington DC by Nov-1818, Graham even suggested to Adams and President James Monroe to negotiate for the Brazos as the border. Graham's report helped spur the Adams-Onis Treaty the following year, where the U. S. agreed to the Sabine and Red Rivers as the boundary, in favor of Spain giving up *the Floridas*. Jean Laffite and other privateers had established a base on Galveston Island in 1817, in cahoots with rebel elements in Mexico; Laffite's residence and fort made of red brick and famously named Maison Rouge, before burning the buildings and leaving for Yucatan in about 1820. He is reported to have died there in 1825 although that has recently been challenged [Oliphant & Yarbrough 2021].

Perhaps, we can also infer why Moses Austin and his son Stephen F. Austin sought a grant of land to the east of the Spanish settlements and authorized bay, and southwest from Nacogdoches and the Spanish missions of east Texas, in what was a larger-than-mapped poorly known and undeveloped "wilderness". In 1822, Stephen F. Austin prepared the first of a series of maps for Austin's Colony (a version found in the Library of Congress is shown in Figure 4), which continued to display poor knowledge of coastal geography, although it is rich with inland information about roads, Indian villages and names, and the extent of forested lands (in green). Many rivers are represented, flowing correctly to the southeast, but he seems to have left out naming the Brazos River [Martin 1982, Reinhartz 2015]. The coastal areas are not much improved from the Puelles, Humboldt or Pike maps.

Figure 4: Hand-drawn map by Stephen F. Austin, showing forested areas, circa 1822

Library of Congress

An apparent copy of this map by or for a Mexican army officer, José Dominguez Manso, is found in the U. S. National Archives (illustrated in [Reinhartz 2015] Figure 9) that was captured during the Mexican-American War, and another hand-drawn version by Austin can be found at the Briscoe Center for American History (CAH), both of which clearly label the Brazos River. Notably, these maps display the early unimproved roads of the time, and a detailed discussion of these roads can be found in a book by Robert W. Shook, a retired history professor at the University of Houston-Victoria [Shook 2007]. Still-another map was also prepared in 1822 by Nicholas Rightor for the area between the Brazos and Lavaca Rivers, held at the CAH (Figure 5). Again, no improvement of coastal geography is apparent, but there is accurate information about rivers and roads, as well as extensive "prairie" areas.

**Figure 5: "A Map of the Country between the Brassos & La Baca Rivers",
N. Rightor, 1822**

Courtesy of Dolph Briscoe Center for American History

The first (of four) land contracts to Stephen F. Austin extended from the Lavaca River on the southwest to the San Jacinto River on the northeast, bounded by the coast and the "El Camino Real" or "San Antonio Road" (between San Antonio de Béxar and Nacogdoches), the boundaries of which can be seen in Figure 1. Although the background and history of Austin's Colony is beyond the scope of this document, Stephen F. Austin wrote a concise summary of his efforts up to 1829 [Austin 1829], and the eminent Austin-era historian and professor, Eugene Campbell Barker, wrote an excellent synopsis [Barker Jun-1918]. Another brief but excellent review can be found in Gambrell's biography of Anson Jones [Gambrell 1948], the chapter entitled "Mr. Austin's Texas". The very first effort to actually bring colonists there involved the voyage of the schooner **Lively**, intended for "Bahía de San Bernardo"- at the time, the only authorized port in Texas. A model can be seen in the Figure below.

It sailed from New Orleans on or about 23-Nov-1821 with about twenty colonists and important supplies steering for the mouth of the Colorado River to meet Stephen F. Austin, but instead dropped them at the mouth of the Brazos River after a difficult month-long trip [Lewis 1899]. Upon returning to Texas on a second voyage with more colonists and supplies in 1822, the **Lively** was lost on Galveston Island, although the passengers were rescued and continued on to the mouth of the Colorado [Bugbee 1899]. Ships and colonists continued to arrive, and by the summer of 1824, most of the Old Three Hundred had arrived and taken title to much of the prime property along the lower Brazos and Colorado Rivers. Stephen F. Austin foresaw the need for an authorized port, and wrote to the military commander of the Eastern Interior Provinces (which included Texas) on 27-May-1823, asking for authorization on several points, including a port of entry and authority to issue clearances for vessels [Austin 1823], apparently without success.

Figure 6: Hand-made Model of Schooner "Lively" by Michael Seright at Surfside City Hall

After the Mexican federal legislature passed a national colonization law on 18-Aug-1824 that forbade settlement in a 10-league band along the coast, Stephen F. Austin must have felt some urgency to legalize a port, and he formally requested permission to establish "*el puerto de Galvezton*" in a petition also asking to extend his empresario contract to an additional 300 (then 500) families [Austin 1824, White 1839 p. 582]. Although the land contract was successfully authorized by the new state of "Coahuila y Tejas" on 27-April and 20-May-1825 [White 1839 pp. 610-613], the port was separately authorized in a modest decree by the federal legislature on 17-Oct-1825 [Arévalo 1829 p. 6], which was also published as a circular [Pedraza 1825]. This decree anticipated creation of a customs house (*aduana marítima*), but did not specify the location of the port - please see Figure 7. Thus, "*el puerto de Galvezton*" became the second authorized port on the Texas coast.

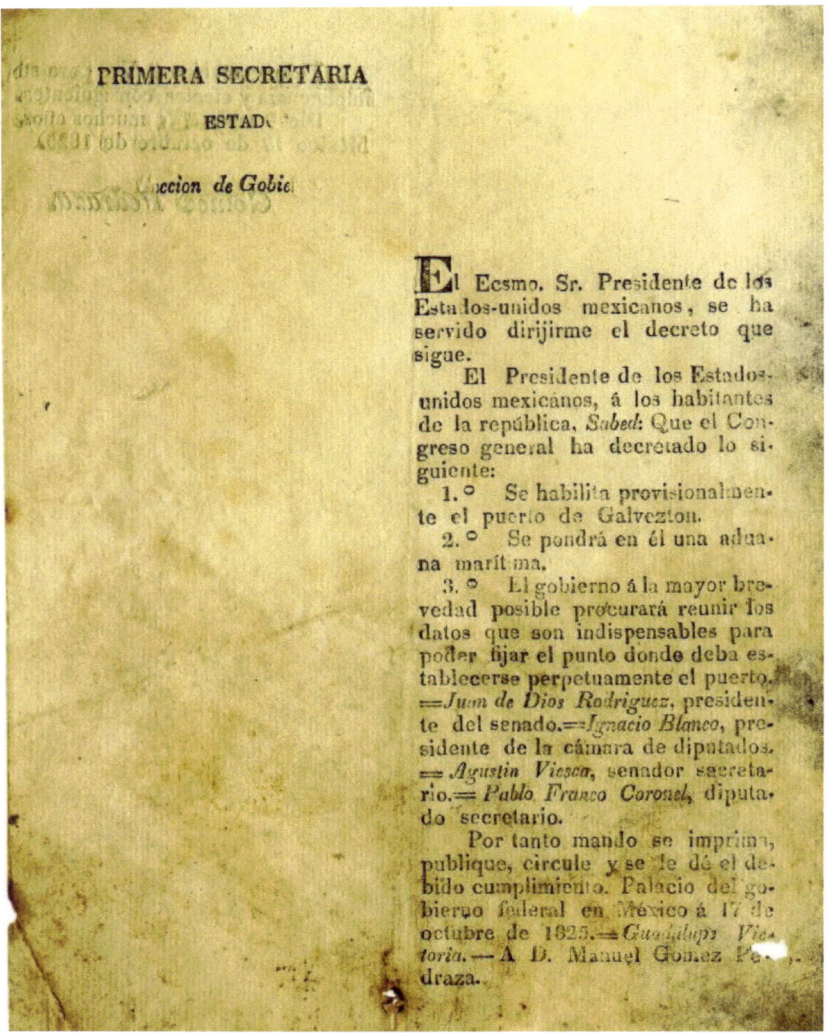

After inspection and survey of Galveston Bay and Island, probably over 16 days in Feb-1826 using the rented sloop **Mexicana** and a rowboat, Austin realized the island was without timber or freshwater, subject to inundation, and isolated from the mainland [Austin 1826a, Martin 1982 p. 384] - so he favored the existing port at the mouth of the Brazos River [Austin 1826a, Austin Dec-1829, Barker 1926 p. 180]. Austin's survey resulted in an improved chart of Galveston Bay and Island [Austin 1826a], although the chart was forwarded on to the governor of Coahuila y Tejas in Saltillo, and from there to Mexico City, and no surviving copy is known to exist. Since Austin had been asked earlier by Mexican authorities to seek boats for use by their detachments on the middle Texas coast, he then purchased the two boats he had used in Galveston Bay, initially suggesting they be delivered to Balandra Point (along current San Antonio Bay) complete with sails and tools [Austin 1826b, Ahumada 1826]. However, later dispatches reveal they were

Figure 7: Decree of Mexican federal legislature authorizing "el puerto de Galvezton"

Samuel May Williams Collection, MS 23-0022,
Galveston & Texas History Center, Rosenberg Library

delivered to *"Sabino"* or *"destacamento de la Balandra"* on 24-July-1826, and were to be used from a newly staffed satellite post of La Bahia called "Matagorda" [Manchola 1826] – probably on the shore of Lavaca or Matagorda Bay, near the location later known as Port O'Connor.

Not long after, advocates for a new town at the mouth of the Colorado tried to make their case as a main port [League et al 1826], and in 1827 this town was laid out, also using the name "Matagorda". No significant port or town was established on Galveston Island in this period, and the Brazos continued to be used instead, under the authority of *"puerto de Galvezton"*. Mary Wightman Helm, widow of Elias R. Wightman who was surveyor for Stephen F. Austin and founder of Matagorda, wrote later of her first arrival at Matagorda in 1829 that *"... All immigrants heretofore having landed at the mouth of the Brazos."* [Helm 1884 p. 45]. Although not completely true, it probably indicates that most of the settlers were indeed entering at the Brazos River.

Once Mexico had achieved independence in 1821, the new country went through a few years attempting to be the Mexican Empire. Soon though, inspired by the example of the Spanish and American constitutions, the liberal element of Mexico succeeded in writing a federal-style constitution in 1824. Also in 1824, a Mexican federal decree had combined the provinces of Coahuila and Texas, and its state congress began meeting in August in Saltillo, with the Baron de Bastrop representing the "Department of Texas" until his death in early 1827. This congress of the new province of Coahuila y Tejas had issued its own state constitution soon after on 11-Mar-1827. It provided for a one-house legislature consisting of twelve members serving two-year terms. The executive was known as the governor, and separate "departments" were administered by a political chief appointed by the governor for four-year terms. The entirety of what was then known as Texas was originally made the department of Béxar, with its capital at San Antonio de Béxar. In Jan-1831, the eastern part of Texas was made the

department of Nacogdoches, with its capital at the town of Nacogdoches. In Mar-1834, a third department was carved out of both jurisdictions as the Department of Brazos, capital at San Felipe de Austin, as indicated in Figure 8. In turn, each department was divided into municipalities, consisting of a town and a large area surrounding it, much like modern Texas counties. Each municipality was governed by an ayuntamiento (a district council), headed by an alcalde, who combined the roles of mayor, magistrate and militia commander [Johnson 1914 pp. 51-54].

Figure 8: Political departments employed in Mexican Texas beginning in 1834
Map 2750, Courtesy of Texas State Library & Archives Commission

10

A Mexican general, Manuel de Mier y Terán visited Texas as leader of a boundary-commission expedition and inspection tour from late 1827 to early 1829 (Comisión de Límites), visiting Laredo, San Antonio de Béxar, Gonzales, San Felipe de Austin, Nacogdoches and the east Texas border area (boundary line set by the Adams-Onis Treaty of 1819) while inbound to the Sabine [Morton 1945, Terán 2000]. Terán was considered *"... one of the most admirable men of the Mexican revolutionary era ... a brilliant tactician, a broadly interested scholar, a sympathetic leader, and an outstanding patriot"* [Berlandier 1980 p. xii]. Terán's journal indicates he stopped at San Felipe de Austin from 27-Apr- to 9-May-1828, and mentions casual conversation with Stephen F. Austin (such as the discovery of mammoth skulls at the Brazos) but shares no deeper discussions [Terán 2000 pp. 55-61], despite being the first time the two met face-to-face. The return trip started back from Nacogdoches on 16-Jan-1829 via the Coushatta Trace to the Brazos crossing near Groce's Plantation (29 Jan- to 1-Feb-1829, bypassing San Felipe), Guadalupe Victoria and La Bahía to Matamoros. A brief on-line biography of Terán can be found at the website of The Sons of DeWitt Colony. After his visit to Texas, and alarmed at what he had seen, Terán became one of the advocates for a revised immigration policy and stronger military presence, later writing an influential report about his visit that was delivered to the government on 6-Jan-1830 [Howren 1913 p. 403]; the full report (translated into English) is given in [Howren 1913 pp. 407-413]. In the meantime, he played a pivotal role in repelling a Spanish expeditionary force at Tampico in Aug-1829, and afterwards was promoted to "General of Division" with the post of Commander General of the Eastern Interior Provinces (which included Texas), eventually establishing his headquarters at Matamoros in Mar-1830. In this role, Terán initially had plans to gather a large military force at Matamoros to be used in Texas as necessary [Morton 1944 pp. 194-196]. Stephen F. Austin, hearing of these plans, published a notice and editorial in the **Texas Gazette** to assure his colonists this was in their best interests [Austin 13-Mar-1830]. However, these plans were altered somewhat by a new law enacted by the Mexican federal legislature.

Based on Terán's report, Lucas Alamán (Mexican minister of foreign relations) and others created the infamous Law of 6-Apr-1830, sometimes exceeding Terán's advice. An excellent and still-authoritative review of the precursors and complex formation process for this law, especially Terán's plan for Texas, was written in 1913 [Howren 1913] by a graduate student at the University of Texas, Alleine Howren (Mrs. Reuben R. Nunn, 1881-1952) born at Georgetown, Texas. One provision of the new law called for the military occupation of Texas using, in part, convicts as soldiers and laborers. Another important aspect of the law was that authority for colonization in frontier states was vested in federal commissioners, removing such from the individual states. This latter article directly opposed Stephen F. Austin's stated opinions [Austin 29-Mar-1830]. For Texas, the post of colonization commissioner was added to Terán's duties in late Apr-1830 [Morton 1944 p. 199]. Another provision of the law was Article 12, which stated, *"Coastwise trade shall be free to all foreigners for the term of four years, with the object of turning colonial trade to the ports of Matamoros, Tampico and Veracruz."* [Howren 1913 p. 416, Johnson 1914 pp. 65-66]. This law, justified from the Mexican government's perspective, had a negative and galvanizing effect on the loyalty of the Anglo-American colonists in Texas [Hardy & Roberts 1910 p. 91-92], and its effect is often equated with the *"Stamp Act"* in catalyzing the American Revolution. However, this law's immediate effect was to give birth to the first efforts at a military site at the mouth of the Brazos River, to enforce its customs and immigration provisions.

Accompanying Terán's expedition had been the naturalist Jean Louis Berlandier, whose journal also confirms he detoured (on the return trip) from San Antonio de Béxar, starting to La Bahía on 25-Feb-1829. There he met the captain of the **Paumone** (probably **Pomona**); they traveled to Cópano (northwest end of Copano Bay) from which they departed by sea on 11-Mar-1829. They sailed southeast through the mouth of Copano Bay, then turning northeast they traversed (modern) Aransas, Carlos, Mesquite, Ayres and Espiritu Santo Bays, and then out through Paso Cavallo (the entrance of Bahía de San Bernardo) for New Orleans, returning on 13-May-1829 the same way [Berlandier 1980 pp. 390-408]. Apparently, during this trip, Berlandier gained knowledge of the coastal geography and drew at least two maps, one of which is shown below in Figure 9, still indicating very poor conception of the local bays [Berlandier 1829a]. Although some great detail about the entrance to Bahía de San Bernardo appears correct, the adjacent bays and rivers are badly inaccurate, especially the Brazos shown in the lower right corner. Obviously, however, local sailors knew well how to use these adjacent bays, and they must have been considered part of Bahía de San Bernardo.

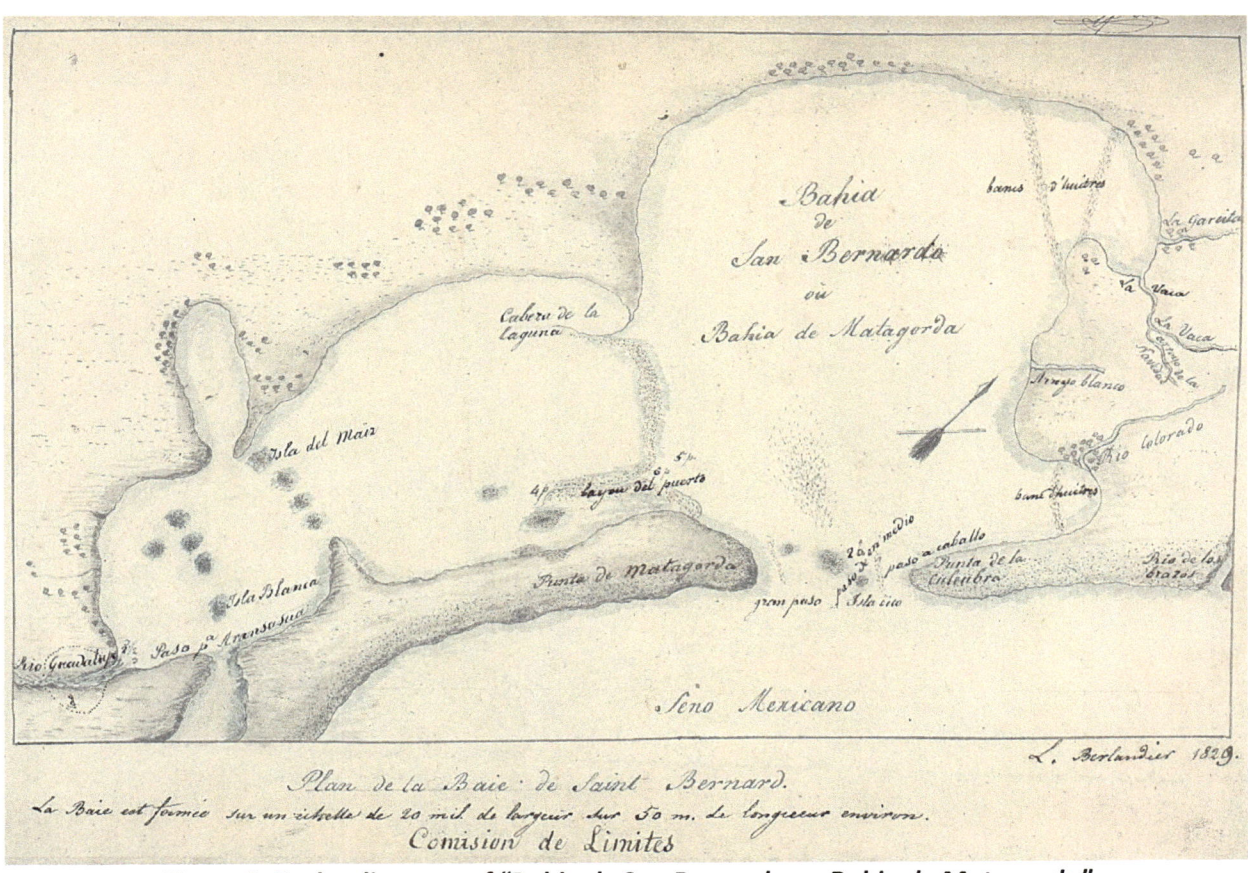

Figure 9: Berlandier map of "Bahia de San Bernardo ou Bahia de Matagorda"
Beinecke Rare Book & Manuscript Library, Yale University

On 13-May-1829, the Congress of Coahuila y Tejas had issued Decree No. 94, setting conditions for customs officers to be placed at the ports of Galveston and Bahía de San Bernardo, including mention that the salary was $500 annually, and duties due to the state were to be two reales per ton [White 1839 p. 548]. José Antonio Navarro received an appointment from the government to become Administrator for the port of Galveston, but Stephen F. Austin advised him *"... that for some time it will not produce sufficient to live upon."* [Austin Dec-1829], and he apparently never took such a position.

So, as the 1830s began, it can be seen that geographic knowledge of the upper Texas Coast was still very limited, but improving, and only with Stephen F. Austin's 1830 map (Figure 1) did an accurate widely available representation occur. Apparently, Austin drew on information collected by the Comisión de Límites (such as Figure 9), provided to him by Terán, to improve on his 1822 maps. For example, another Berlandier sketch of Matagorda, Lavaca, Espiritu Santo and Aransazu Bays [Berlandier 1829b] bears great resemblance to those same bays drawn on the 1830 Austin/Terán/Tanner map (although still not completely accurate). Only with the 1839 Hunt-Randel map did a reasonably accurate representation of these lower bays occur [Hunt & Randel 1839]. Tanner published several updates of the 1830 map through 1840, usually adding new towns and landmarks to the base map. It can also be seen that several previous efforts have occurred to authorize ports and/or customs.

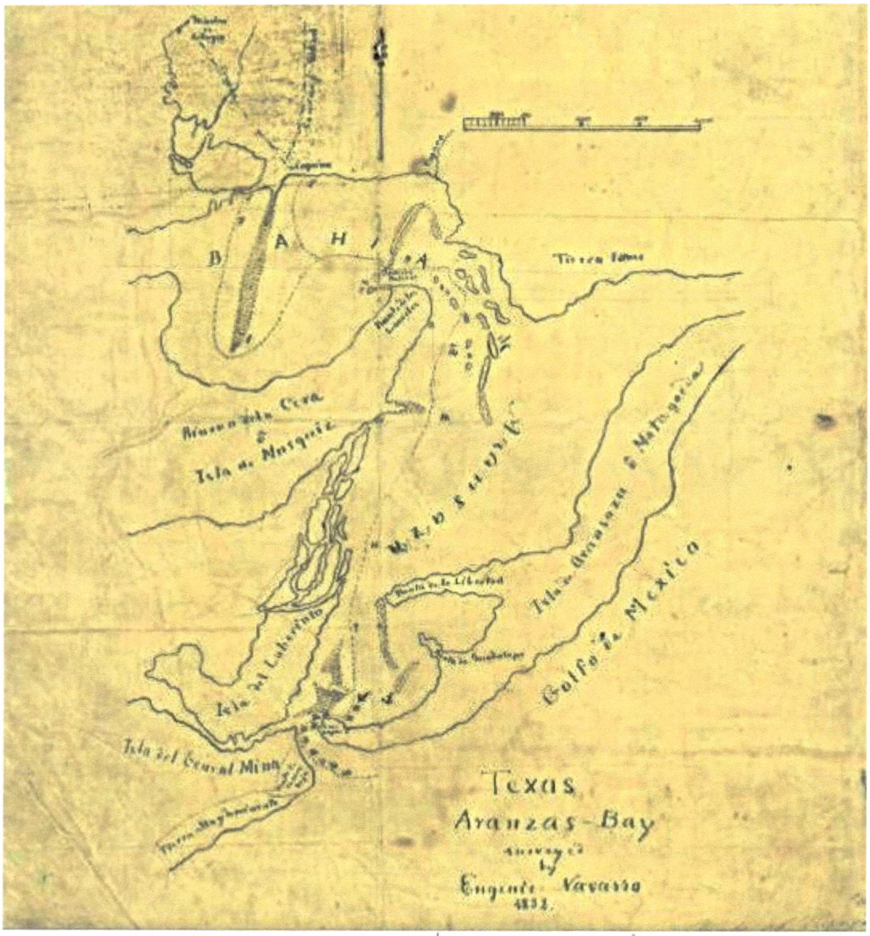

**Figure 10: Sketch of Aranzas Bay
surveyed by Eugenio Navarro, 1832**
Courtesy of Texas General Land Office (Map #145)

José Antonio Navarro's brother, José Eugenio Navarro, while an Alférez (2nd Lieutenant) in the Second Flying Company of San Carlos de Alamo de Parras, produced a sketch in 1832 of "Aranzas Bay" (today's Aransas and Copano Bays) and the navigable path to the early port of Cópano, today found in the records of the Texas General Land Office as Map #145 (see Figure 10). This may illustrate the path of the *Pomona* in taking Jean Louis Berlandier to and from New Orleans a few years earlier, and was one part of the improving knowledge of coastal geography.

So, it seems apparent that Spanish and then Mexican efforts on the coast of Texas had focused more on the Matagorda Bay area, ever since the late 1600s when LaSalle came to that area, and caused a great deal of Spanish searching and investigation. Other efforts had existed for Galveston Bay. It seems that in the beginning, the Brazos River was almost overlooked, although Austin's Colony brought it into prominence. The saga of old Velasco begins ……….

HISTORY OF THE FORTS

Mexican Republic (1830-1835) ... or Fort Velasco #1

The first public development at the mouth of the Brazos involved creation of a customs house; however, it was a very strange beginning due to the appearance of a talented, officious, self-promoting adventurer and schemer named George "Jorge" Fisher. The year 1830, and a few years afterwards, would involve a very unusual interlude in Austin's Colony with this man. Perhaps the authoritative work on Fisher's time in Texas is a biographical Master's Thesis from 1928 written by Bessie Lucille Letts from Marlin, Falls Co., Texas (later Mrs. Clark Wright, 1901-1996), a student at the University of Texas under Professor Eugene C. Barker [Letts 1928]. The document is extremely rare, with the only known copies existing at the Dolph Briscoe Center for American History in Austin, another copy in storage in the University of Texas Library system and a photostat copy in the Margaret Swett Henson Papers at the Rosenberg Library in Galveston.

Fisher arrived in San Felipe de Austin in early May-1830, being announced in a small notice in the hometown weekly *Texas Gazette* newspaper as "*Col. Fisher, Administrador, for the port of Galveston, arrived in our town a few days since, from New Orleans – and will enter on the duties of his office in a short time.*" [Cotten 8-May-1830, Barker 1926 p. 327].

Image representing Mexican Constitution of 1824 & its Republic (Coahuila y Tejas nopal highlighted) [Primera 1824]
similar to Austin/Terán maps of 1830-1840 (see Frontispiece);
coded message for Mexican federalism,
includes Phrygian cap at top symbolizing freedom and liberty

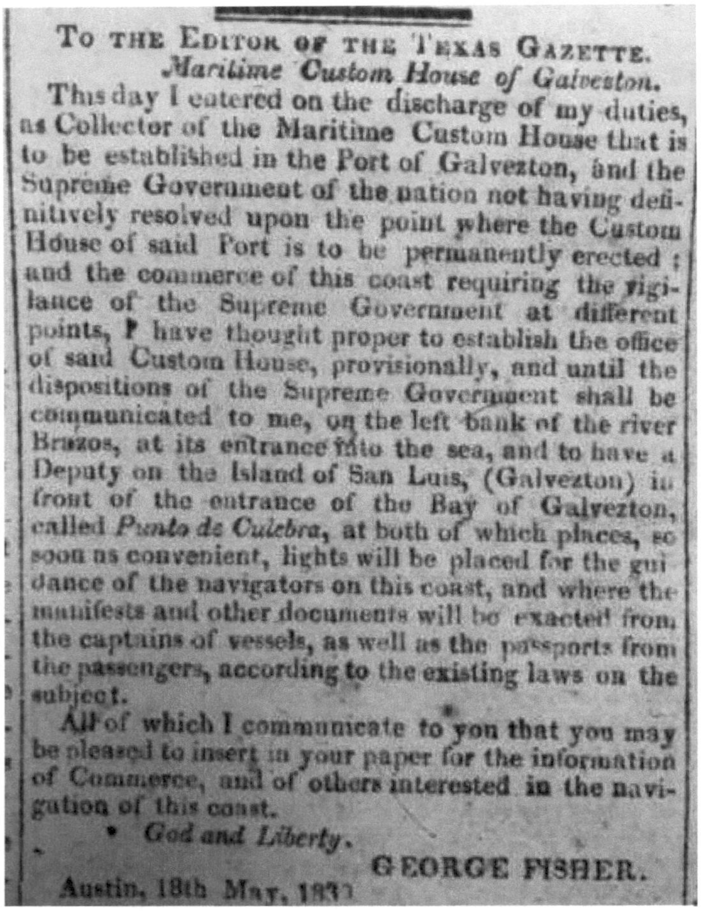

TO THE EDITOR OF THE TEXAS GAZETTE.

Maritime Custom House of Galveston.

This day I entered on the discharge of my duties, as Collector of the Maritime Custom House that is to be established in the Port of Galvezton, and the Supreme Government of the nation not having definitively resolved upon the point where the Custom House of said Port is to be permanently erected; and the commerce of this coast requiring the vigilance of the Supreme Government at different points, I have thought proper to establish the office of said Custom House, provisionally, and until the dispositions of the Supreme Government shall be communicated to me, on the left bank of the river Brazos, at its entrance into the sea, and to have a Deputy on the Island of San Luis, (Galvezton) in front of the entrance of the Bay of Galvezton, called *Punto de Culebra*, at both of which places, so soon as convenient, lights will be placed for the guidance of the navigators on this coast, and where the manifests and other documents will be exacted from the captains of vessels, as well as the passports from the passengers, according to the existing laws on the subject.

All of which I communicate to you that you may be pleased to insert in your paper for the information of Commerce, and of others interested in the navigation of this coast.

God and Liberty.

GEORGE FISHER.

Austin, 18th May, 1830

Figure 11: Notice in Texas Gazette issues of 22-May-1830 (p. 2 col. 2)

On May 18th, Fisher wrote a letter (in Spanish) to Stephen F. Austin declaring that he had assumed his duties that day as Collector for the Galveston Maritime Customs [Fisher 18-May-1830a]. The letter was subsequently published (in both English and Spanish) in the local newspaper [Cotton 22-May-1830] – see Figure 11 for the English version. Fisher stated he would establish a <u>provisional customs house at the mouth of the Brazos River on the left bank</u>, and post a deputy collector at *"Punto de Culebra"*, the northeast end of *"Isla de San Luis"* (Galveston Island). Fisher also sent a letter on May 18th to the local militia commander (also Austin) requesting support for his new role [Fisher 18-May-1830b] – already revealing Fisher's officious manner. Perhaps prompted by Fisher, the Alcalde of San Felipe de Austin (Thomas Barnett) also published a letter to Austin (as a circular) the same day [Barnett May-1830]. The next day, Austin sent formal responses to Fisher, Barnett, and a *"Battalion Order"* to the militia to accept Fisher in his new role [Austin May-1830]. In the response to Fisher, Austin used his best diplomatic and loquacious manner, but one gets the feeling Austin had sized up the man, and was cagily "putting Fisher in his place" by warning him about *"foreign adventurers"*, and also pridefully citing the significant work already done to create the colony and its value to the Mexican nation. The Battalion Order was also published in the local newspaper [Cotten 22-May-1830]. So, in a significant way, Fisher was recognizing the Brazos as the main port, representing the *"port of Galvezton"*; Fisher himself defined it to include *"... an extensive coast, from the Sabine River to Matagorda Bay ..."* [Fisher 5-Jun-1830]. Although Fisher was presuming much in claiming this position, the local authorities originally accepted his word without question. In one letter to Terán, though, Stephen F. Austin wrote Fisher did possess a *"despacho"* (dispatch) from Lorenzo de Zavala granting his assignment [Austin 13-Jul-1830], and this point was sufficiently important that Terán forwarded this portion of Austin's letter on to the Secretary of Relations in Mexico City, while clarifying the date of Austin's letter as 13-Jul-1830 [Terán Aug-1830].

Fisher had apparently been appointed by the Federalist government of Vicente Guerrero in Mexico City in 1829 by Lorenzo de Zavala (then Secretary of the Treasury and head of the cabinet) [Fisher 10-Feb-1830a, Parmenter et al 1959], perhaps expecting cessation of the customs exemption and/or legislative actions arising from Terán's report. But the Guerrero government was overthrown in the period of Dec-1829 to Jan-1830, and Fisher never obtained official credentials, instructions or funds from either the old or new governments. Suddenly being a part of the "out-of-power party", he judiciously left Mexico in self-exile for New Orleans, staying there and visiting his abandoned family in Mississippi for some months, before traveling overland through Nacogdoches to San Felipe.

Soon after his arrival in New Orleans in early Feb-1830, Fisher had written two letters back to Mexico City, one to Anastasio Zerecero and another to Lorenzo de Zavala [Fisher 10-Feb-1830a & b]. Both express similar sentiments, including referring to North American emigrants to Texas as numerous and "… *like locusts*", and that they used the many river systems as unauthorized seaports. He also seemed to verify his intent to become administrator for the Galveston customs house, as if repeating it in these letters would help make it so, and by "dropping names" of other important Mexican officials. To Zavala, he also seemed to volunteer to be his agent for Zavala's land grant in east Texas, and his trip through Nacogdoches was to include checking on his own grant of 20 sitios (over 85,000 acres) within Zavala's grant. Readers can readily sense Fisher's motives and state-of-mind, before even reaching Texas, as he was already plotting, apparently based on information he had picked up in Mexico and New Orleans, to establish for himself a position of power, influence, land and wealth by "getting in early" on the rising population and development of eastern Texas.

After reaching San Felipe, Fisher soon departed for the mouth of the Brazos. However, hearing of Fisher's activities in Texas (probably by receiving an issue of the *Texas Gazette* by mail), Terán wrote an open letter to him from Matamoros on 24-May-1830 that establishment of a customs house was premature, agreed to by Stephen F. Austin, so this plan was postponed [Terán May-1830, Morton 1945 p. 509]. A copy of this letter was sent to Erasmo Seguin at Béxar, which he forwarded on to Samuel May Williams on 24-Jun-1830. At the same time, Stephen F. Austin wrote *"The custom house at Galveston is suspended by order of Govt. and the reason given is that the exemptions from duties in favor of the colonists of Texas has rendered it unnecessary to establish any custom houses here for the present ..."* [Austin Jul-1830], although Terán was also probably concerned that Fisher had been dispatched by now-deposed civil authorities (so, then his political opponents) in Mexico City, into his jurisdiction. Terán was apparently referring to Article 12 of the Law of 6-Apr-1830, which opened coastal trade for four years [Howren 1913 p. 416].

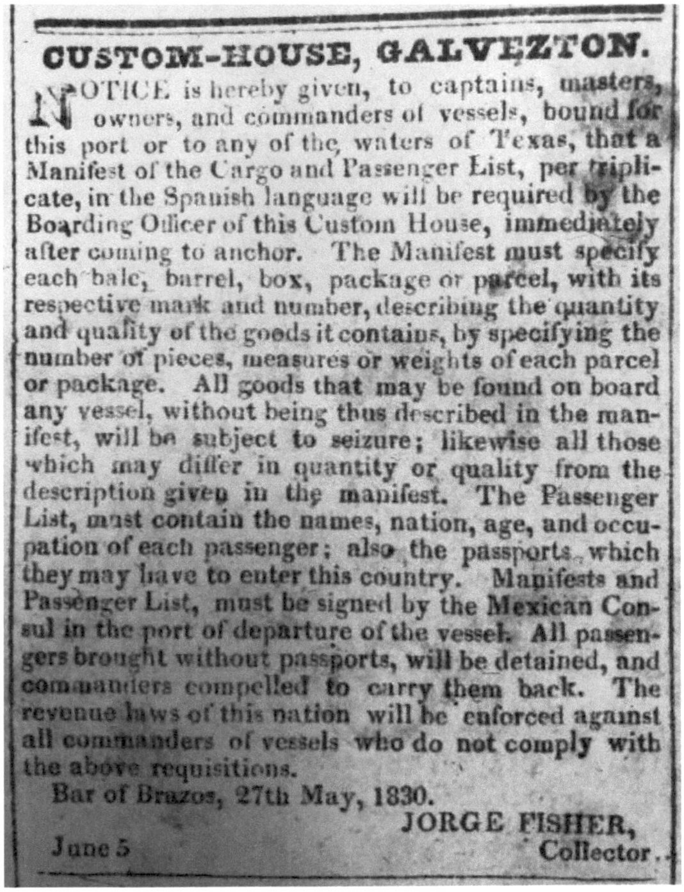

CUSTOM-HOUSE, GALVEZTON.

NOTICE is hereby given, to captains, masters, owners, and commanders of vessels, bound for this port or to any of the waters of Texas, that a Manifest of the Cargo and Passenger List, per triplicate, in the Spanish language will be required by the Boarding Officer of this Custom House, immediately after coming to anchor. The Manifest must specify each bale, barrel, box, package or parcel, with its respective mark and number, describing the quantity and quality of the goods it contains, by specifying the number of pieces, measures or weights of each parcel or package. All goods that may be found on board any vessel, without being thus described in the manifest, will be subject to seizure; likewise all those which may differ in quantity or quality from the description given in the manifest. The Passenger List, must contain the names, nation, age, and occupation of each passenger; also the passports which they may have to enter this country. Manifests and Passenger List, must be signed by the Mexican Consul in the port of departure of the vessel. All passengers brought without passports, will be detained, and commanders compelled to carry them back. The revenue laws of this nation will be enforced against all commanders of vessels who do not comply with the above requisitions.

Bar of Brazos, 27th May, 1830.

JORGE FISHER,
June 5   Collector.

Figure 12: Notice in Texas Gazette issues of 5-Jun-1830 (p. 3 col. 2) and 12-Jun-1830 (p. 4 col. 2)

However, even in this short interval, Fisher had already initiated many plans, apparently of his own invention, including several newspaper announcements and many actions and letters. He was especially keen to enforce the outright prohibition on importation of tobacco, passed by the legislature of Coahuila y Tejas on 2-Nov-1827 as Decree No. 28 [White 1839 p. 501]. One of Fisher's notices involved instructions to ship owners and captains, as shown in Figure 12, which was published twice. It was dated 27-May-1830 at "Bar of Brazos", indicating that Fisher was there by that time.

CUSTOM-HOUSE, GALVEZTON.

SEALED PROPOSALS, will be received until the first day of August next, at this Custom-House, for building a brick house at Brazos Bar, of best materials and workmanship, of the dimensions and construction according to the plot, which may be seen at the Post-Offices at Austin, and Brazoria, and at Harrisburg at the store of Mr. Dunlap.

Propositions must be forwarded by mail, post paid, and endorsed "Proposals." Also, for building a Light-House at Brazos Bar, and one on Galveston Island, according to the model to be seen at the same places. Proposals for each Light-House to be made out separate. Bond and security will be required from builders for the execution of the contracts.

Bar of Brazos, 27th May, 1830.

June 5. JORGE FISHER, Colr.

Figure 13: Notice published in Texas Gazette issues of 5-Jun (p. 3, col. 2), 12-Jun (p. 4, col. 2), 19-Jun (p. 4, col. 2), 26-Jun (p. 4, col. 3) and 3-Jul-1830 (p. 4, col. 3)

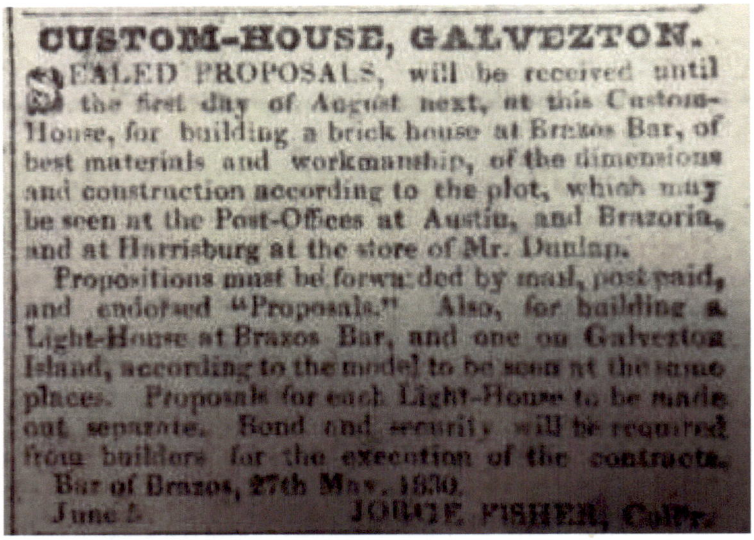

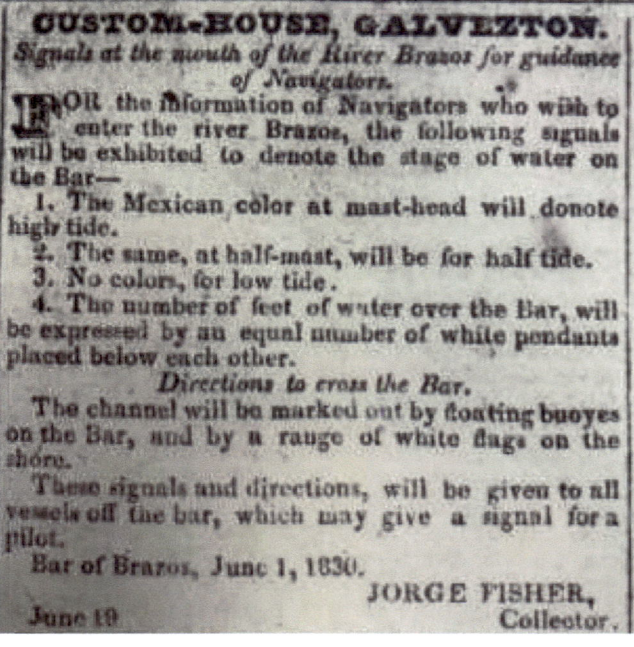

Fisher also advertised for "*SEALED PROPOSALS*" to build a brick customs house at the mouth of the Brazos, and a "*Light-House at Brazos Bar and one on Galveston Island*" [Cotten 5-Jun-1830, Ward 1962 pp. 214-215], as shown in Figure 13. It was published in five consecutive issues in the ***Texas Gazette***.

A little later (dated 1-Jun-1830 at Bar of Brazos), he added a notice about pilot instructions over the Brazos Bar, shown in Figure 14 below, which was published three times. The "*pilot*" mentioned may have been Asa Mitchell.

Fisher led the seizure of the schooner ***Cañon*** at the Brazos bar in the late evening of 1-Jun-1830 [Fisher 2-Jun-1830], which was found to be importing a cargo of contraband tobacco (162 bales of high-quality and 45 bales of low-quality, each bale weighing about a *quintal* - a *quintal* was an approximate term equivalent to a *hundredweight*, or one hundred pounds), which was unloaded upon seizure into a thrice-locked warehouse at Brazoria [Fisher 2-Jun-1830, Barnett & Fisher 1830]. This ship (also listed as the ***Cannon***) had left New Orleans on or about 25-May-1830, being certified for commerce to Mexico by James W. Breedlove, the Vice-Consul at the Mexican Consulate of New Orleans [Breedlove 1830]. The fine imposed by Decree No. 28 was twenty-five dollars per *arroba* for high-quality tobacco (an *arroba* was one-fourth of a *quintal*, or about 25 pounds) [Terán May-1831, White

CUSTOM-HOUSE, GALVEZTON.

Signals at the mouth of the River Brazos for guidance of Navigators.

FOR the information of Navigators who wish to enter the river Brazos, the following signals will be exhibited to denote the stage of water on the Bar—

1. The Mexican color at mast-head will denote high tide.

2. The same, at half-mast, will be for half tide.

3. No colors, for low tide.

4. The number of feet of water over the Bar, will be expressed by an equal number of white pendants placed below each other.

Directions to cross the Bar.

The channel will be marked out by floating buoyes on the Bar, and by a range of white flags on the shore.

These signals and directions, will be given to all vessels off the bar, which may give a signal for a pilot.

Bar of Brazos, June 1, 1830.

JORGE FISHER, Collector.

June 19

Figure 14: Notice to Navigators in Texas Gazette issues of 19-Jun-1830 (p. 3, col. 3), 26-June-1830 (p. 4, col. 2) and 3-Jul-1830 (p. 4, col. 2)

1839 p. 501], for a total cost of about $16,000 [McKinstry 1832], which was enough money at the time to purchase an entirely new schooner! Fisher wrote letters reporting the seizure to Samuel May Williams on the 5th and Thomas Barnett on the 7th [Fisher 5-Jun-1830]. On 12-Jun-1830, a small news item was published in the **Texas Gazette** *"... that some smuggled tobacco has been seized on the coast by the Collector of Galvezton – this is as it should be!"* [Cotten 12-Jun-1830 p. 3 col. 1]. Fisher sought help from the local authorities such as Samuel May Williams, Thomas Barnett and George McKinstry to adjudicate the seizure and impose the fine, but their response was slow.

Local authorities provided a few militiamen to help guard the **Cañon** lying at Brazoria, who Fisher described as *"... bad armed, worse disciplined y pesimamente subordinados (terrible subordinates) ..."*, where he also stood guard every few hours and where he got ill with a fever [Williams 12-Jul-1830, Fisher 21-Jul-1830b, Letts p. 35]. Indeed, notice of his suspension only reached Fisher on 1-Jul-1830 while aboard the embargoed schooner, still awaiting a final decision about it by local authorities. Apparently, Fisher never received Téran's original letter of suspension, but found out when Samuel May Williams forwarded a copy of the Erasmo Seguin copy to Fisher on 30-Jun-1830 [Williams 12- & 27-Jul-1830, Letts 1928 p. 36]. Afterwards, Fisher notified Williams by letter that he was reluctantly suspending operations, and wanted to see Williams and Stephen F. Austin to settle the **Cañon** affair [Fisher 6-Jul-1830]. He followed up with a second letter on the 15th, mentioning he would travel to San Felipe de Austin to await further instructions [Williams 27-Jul-1830]. Once there, Fisher received messages from George McKinstry (at Brazoria) and W. D. Dunlap (at Harrisburg) about ship arrivals; they were apparently working in his stead as deputy collectors in the period after Fisher's dismissal [Dunlap Jul-1830, McKinstry 21-Jul-1830, McKinstry 1832]. The political chief at Béxar, Ramón Músquiz, perhaps aware of Fisher's suspension, apparently tried to organize these deputy collectors to coordinate their gathering of tonnage duties through officials at San Felipe [Músquiz 20-Jun-1830]. At some point, the **Cañon** was sailed to Matagorda Bay, loaded there with corn and other products, headed to Tampico and Veracruz, saying the *"... schooner was seized to partially assure the solvency of the fine that should be imposed on the smuggler..."* [Fisher Apr-1831]. Eventually, the matter was turned over to Samuel May Williams, who became *de-facto* administrator of the port. Later, in 1832, the **Cañon** was apparently lost at the entrance to Matagorda Bay [Cosío 30-May-1832].

Fisher had also commissioned Asa Mitchell as a *"boarding officer"* or pilot for the Brazos, as indicated in letters of unmentioned date from Fisher to Mitchell which were examined in a meeting of the San Felipe ayuntamiento (district committee) on 2-Nov-1830 [Barker 1919 p. 69]. A good possibility for such letters may be documents found in the Samuel May Williams Papers, in which Fisher asks Mitchell whether the grounded schooner **True Blue** was illegally importing tobacco consigned to John Austin – the Alcalde of Brazoria! A notice of the stranding appeared in the **Texas Gazette** issue of 9-Oct-1830 (see Figure 15).

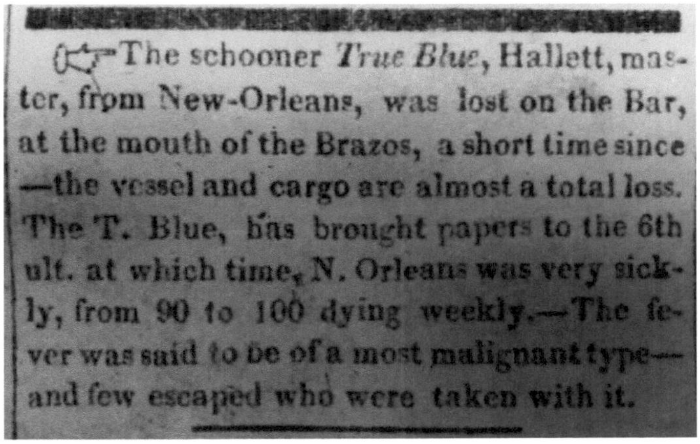

☞ The schooner *True Blue*, Hallett, master, from New-Orleans, was lost on the Bar, at the mouth of the Brazos, a short time since —the vessel and cargo are almost a total loss. The T. Blue, has brought papers to the 6th ult. at which time, N. Orleans was very sickly, from 90 to 100 dying weekly.—The fever was said to be of a most malignant type— and few escaped who were taken with it.

Figure 15: Article found in Texas Gazette issue of 9-Oct-1830, Page 2, Column 2

Mitchell's response indicates that John Austin and others sold some of the salvaged cargo from the ship that had stranded at the Brazos Bar on 18-Sep-1830, and his belief the ship had deliberately been stranded to collect the insurance [Fisher Sep-1830].

Despite all these plans and activities, no permanent customs facilities are known to have been constructed at this time. Fisher found himself in an embarrassing position, believing the suspension must be an error in judgement and thinking there was still a need to interdict contraband such as then-illegal tobacco and also to control immigration. He lingered in Austin's Colony, expecting some kind of counter order. He wrote from San Felipe to Terán and others to maintain the customs house [Fisher 21-Jul-1830a & b, Fisher 27-Jul-1830, McKinstry 2-Aug-1830, Letts 1928 pp. 37-50] by mentioning that smuggling of contraband (usually tobacco) occurs in Texas, but without success. The letter to Terán (27-Jul-1830) was lengthy, and mostly consisted of a defense against claims in Mexican newspapers that Fisher was working with Lorenzo de Zavala to sell off pieces of Texas, but also included a plea that the customs house should be maintained, while also asking that the letters be shared with other Mexican federal officials. Eventually, Fisher was rebuked by Terán in a letter on 22-Oct-1830 saying *"... I say to You, that for no reason do you elude any of my orders, under pretext of giving account to other authorities. I expect, without any excuse, that my said note of 21st August, will be complied with; and consequently, you deliver the object of contraband of the schooner Cañon, in the state in which it was, to the Comisario of (San Felipe de) Austin, citizen Samuel Williams ..."* [Terán Oct-1830]. One can imagine how all these activities did not endear him to the Texian colonists used to unfettered trade, and which was technically before expiration of their seven-year exemption. Terán's suspension of Fisher's activities probably saved him much personal distress, and wider dissatisfaction among the colonists. But in the end, all of Fisher's activities to that point were for naught. It is also notable that the *"Port of Galvezton"* was first established at the mouth of the Brazos several years before *"Punto de Culebra"* was developed as such!

Ironically, due to their need for bilingual skills, the San Felipe ayuntamiento then hired Fisher as secretary, perhaps as early as 27-Jul-1830 [League 1830], and the ayuntamiento's notices were published over Fisher's name in the *Texas Gazette* issues on 6-Sep, 25-Sep and 2-Oct-1830. He was soon suspected of spying for Mexican government officials, and was found to be hiding both originals and copies of the municipality's correspondence, so he was dismissed at the meeting of the ayuntamiento on 5-Oct-1830, which was reported fully in the local newspaper [Cotten 23-Oct-1830]. Five days later, Fisher wrote from San Felipe to Terán about the *True Blue* affair, claiming also that John Austin threatened him, telling him to leave Austin's Colony, and also accused James W. Breedlove of complicity in the smuggling [Fisher Oct-1830]. So, Fisher continued to earn the enmity of the Texians, and left quickly for Mexico in a cloud of distrust. As they said at the time, he *"... took French leave"* [McKinstry 1832], showing up at Matamoros by 1-Nov-1830. Later that month, the thrice-locked warehouse containing the tobacco seized from the *Cañon* was reported by John Austin as *"broken into"*, since its door remained locked, and its keys had been taken away by George Fisher [John Austin 1830].

The usually affable Stephen F. Austin had meanwhile developed an especially dim view of Fisher, writing in the very first words of a long letter to Lucas Alamán, *"We have had the misfortune to receive a visit here from one of those miserable and shameless adventurers who have neither country nor principles of honesty – George Fisher"* [Austin Oct-1830 p. 512]. Austin then gives a detailed account of Fisher's duplicity with and termination from the San Felipe ayuntamiento. Later, Austin wrote to Samuel May Williams (about the Law of 6-Apr-1830) that *"... you and I know that emigration to the colony could have been stopped, and that all the ports could have been closed, or a George Fisher with a guard put at each."* [Austin Feb-1831, Bacarisse 1952, Parmenter et al 1959]. In the years following, the ever-practical Austin was officially asked, and often took the public stance, to accept Fisher into later assignments [Terán Oct & Nov-1831, Austin 29-Jul-1832], but his personal animus for the man remained, shared only as necessary [Fisher 1833 enclosure#2].

After his return to Mexico, Fisher began vigorous attempts to rehabilitate his reputation, especially in the eyes of Terán. On 11-Nov-1830, Terán himself wrote to ask for any documents on the seizure of the *Cañon* [Seguin 1830]. Fisher wrote a brief rebuttal to the *Texas Gazette*'s issue of 23-Oct-1830, in a letter to its editor [Fisher Nov-1830], indicating *"... a full detail of the transactions in question shall appear in due course of time"* and also *"This detailed account, is now ready for the press, and will be published as soon as circumstances will permit."* Although any such follow-up document has not been found, Fisher wrote a letter to the governor of Coahuila y Tejas on 14-Feb-1831, claiming he'd been falsely accused by the *Texas Gazette* and the Ayuntamiento, as he was only trying to document illegal

behavior in Austin's Colony. He claimed retaliation, and seemed to blame everyone in Texas except himself, asking that the governor order the return of documents seized from him by the Ayuntamiento of San Felipe de Austin, to bolster his defense [Fisher Feb-1831]. This effort was seconded by Terán himself in a follow-up letter to the same governor and also the federal secretary of interior and exterior relations [Terán Feb-1831]. Fisher did eventually publish a certificate (see Figure 16) from Terán indicating retroactive approval of Fisher's actions in regards to seizure of the *Cañon*, and also indicating this was not the reason for his suspension as administrator of the customs house [Terán May-1831]. All of this created a flurry of document gathering and copying, many of which were sent to Samuel May Williams, and they have come down to us in his personal papers (now known as the Samuel May Williams Collection at the Rosenberg Library in Galveston, Texas). In the aftermath of this period, Stephen F. Austin continued to fear that Fisher would harm him or Austin's Colony by publishing Fisher's *"detailed account"*, by exaggerating or generalizing unlawful but uncommon occurrences [Austin Sep-1830, Jan, Mar & Apr-1831].

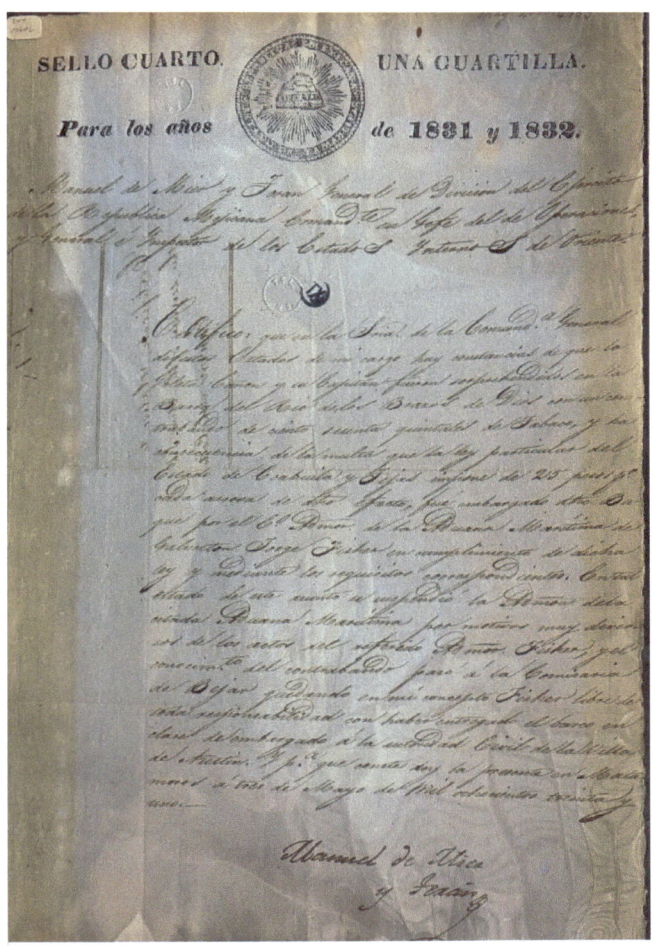

Figure 16: Original certificate by Terán about George Fisher's lawful seizure of Cañon
George Fisher Collection, Texas State Library & Archives

At the same time as Fisher's activities occurred on the Brazos in the summer of 1830, Terán was also busy commanding forces to establish new forts on the upper Brazos (Tenoxtitlán) and the lower Lavaca River (Barranco Colorado). And, as the episode with Fisher at the Brazos seemed to close in the fall of 1830, a third "Terán fort" was also being started over in Galveston Bay, and this one portended future activity with "Colonel" George Fisher. His unsuccessful efforts at the Brazos, though, following Terán's prior visit to Texas, further convinced Terán that military forces were also needed at the Brazos to enforce the customs and immigration provisions of the Law of 6-Apr-1830.

Figure 17: Galveston Bay inset from
David H. Burr 1833 Map of "Texas"

Unlike Fisher's efforts, this more-successful step in implementation of the new law was the creation of a fort near Perry's Point (an elevated prominence atop a bluff at the northeast corner of Galveston Bay, at the mouth of the Trinity River), which came to be known as Fort Anahuac. Colonel Juan Davis Bradburn, three lieutenants (Ignacio Domínguez, Juan María Pacho and José Rincón) and about forty soldiers were the first to arrive for this purpose on the shallow-draft sloop **Alabama Packet** from Matamoros to Galveston Bay on 26-Oct-1830, relying on Bradburn's previous knowledge of the area to select a good location [Bradburn 1830, Henson 1982 p.52]. The site of Anahuac can be seen in Figure 17, which is from an inset in the lower left corner on David H. Burr's 1833 map of "Texas", and which was based on soundings made by Alexander Thompson of the Mexican Navy in 1828.

The location was chosen to exert control over the somewhat-lawless Trinity River valley and border area [Morton 1945 p. 503], including many illegal settlers from across the Sabine River, and which was not part of Stephen F. Austin's well-managed colony to the west [Barker Jan-1918]. The adjacent town of Anahuac was laid out and established by Mar-1831, and a permanent brick fort was completed over the next year. The garrison grew to as many as 285 soldiers, although typically less at most times. In total, six new forts were to be constructed to enforce the new law, including also Fort Terán, Fort Tenoxtitlán, Fort Lipantitlán, and at the mouths of the Lavaca and Brazos Rivers, adding to existing garrisons at San Antonio de Béxar, Presidio La Bahía, and Nacogdoches, (as illustrated in Figure 18), along with a war frigate to serve the coastal forts [Filisola 1848 pp. 65-66]. Although Terán requested such a vessel, also to act as a coast guard, it was never obtained due to lack of funds [Morton 1945 pp. 499-500]. Some of these forts also included smaller satellite posts, often as a very temporary camp but also some were more substantial (for example, customs houses on Galveston Island and the mouth of the Brazos as early adjuncts to Fort Anahuac). The first of these new forts to be established was Fort Tenoxtitlán beginning in Apr-1830, followed quickly by the fort near the mouth of the Lavaca River (known as "Barranco Colorado"). Fort Velasco was to be the last.

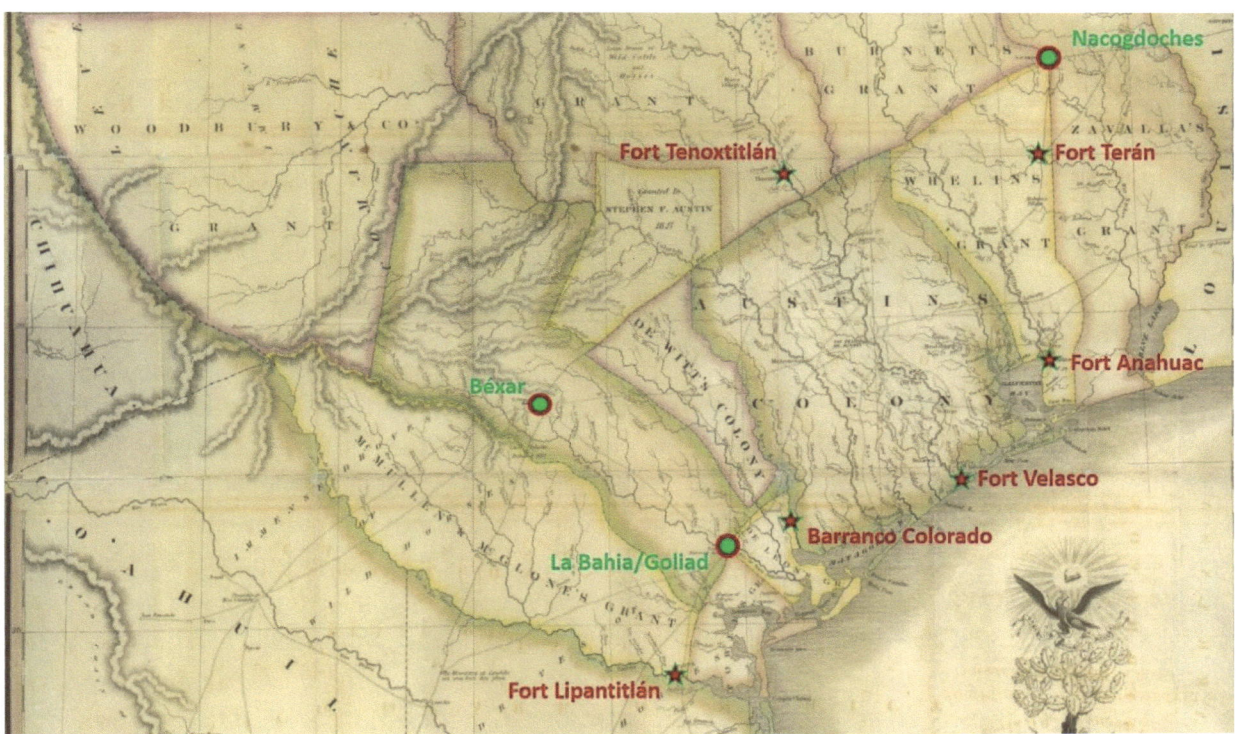

Figure 18: Mexican Forts in Texas 1830-1832 (drawn atop 1836 version of Austin/Terán/Tanner map)

Anahuac was otherwise an odd choice due to shallows and oyster reefs (originally called Barra de las Pescador Encarnador, later as La Barra del Pescado Colorado, Barra Pescado, or Redfish Bar or Reef) stretching across the bay between (what is now called) Eagle Point and Smith Point (this bar or reef can easily be seen in Figure 17). A visitor in 1831 described its depth as *"On that bar, at low tides there is but three or four feet, and at the highest tides not more than five feet eight inches"* [Fiske 1836 p. 97]. Another visitor who traveled in a small rowboat from Galveston Island to New Washington on 24-Mar-1837 wrote *"At sundown we reached Redfish Bar, composed almost entirely of shells which extend from bank to bank the distance of several miles and appear to be formed by the confluence of the tide and the waters of the San Jacinto and Trinity, which unite a short distance above. The water upon the bar does not exceed three or four feet in depth but at some seasons of the year is found as much as six. This point is undoubtedly the head of navigation for vessels of heavy burden …."* [Muir 1958 p. 12]. Charles Hooton arrived at Galveston in March 1841, and described the bay this way *"Sprinkled with wrecks of various appearances and sizes – all alike gloomy, however, in their looks and associations – it strikes the heart of a stranger as a sort of ocean-cemetery, a sea churchyard, in which broken masts and shattered timbers, half-buried in quicksands, seem to remain above the surface of the treacherous waters only to remind the living, like dead camels on a level desert, of the destruction that has gone before, and yet awaits many who may come after. … The remaining mass of water, at least three miles across from Galveston to Pelican Island opposite, is so shallow, that, under the influence of particular winds, combined perhaps with other causes, it may in certain places be waded across in safety.*" [Hooton 1847 p. 6]. Other stories exist about cattle or horses being driven across the bay on this reef, in the days before mining of oyster shell destroyed much of it [Glass 1986, Roper & Linton 2019 p. 18, 40 & 82]. Indeed, later troubles with the residents of Austin's Colony and other Texians were, in no small measure, due to the difficulty in reaching this location, as only ships of very shallow draft could reach the place by sea, and land routes were lengthy and often impassable due to lack of roads and wet conditions.

As an outpost of Fort Anahuac, a customs-house was soon established on the northeast end of Isla de San Luis (Galveston Island), which involved a few soldiers living in a crude dwelling [Hayes 1879 1:130, Henson 1982 p.56]. George Willich, an immigrant and visitor to the island in the summer of 1834 described the building as "… *A house made out of raw cedar logs laid one over the other, the spaces between stuffed with pretty, pleasant smelling tree moss, several yards long; the roof out of crudely split pine shingles nailed one over the other; in every corner of the single communal room a pure cotton mattress beside an overhang of coarse net or curtain for protection against mosquitos; a few iron pots and tin or earthen bowls and plates; a tea kettle, and a coffee mill screwed to the wall for grinding coffee and wheat specifically for bread; a number of gourds for funnels; dippers for milk, water, brandy, fats and fish oils; and around on the walls a quantity of hides of buffalo, oxen, horses, calves, deer, panthers, tiger cats, wolves, racoons, and other; a good stock of kiln-dried cow and deer meat strung up by strings; rifles, muskets, snake-sticks, axes, hoes and shovels. That was the furnishment and decor of the house in which also in the corner under a chimney of mud and wooden blocks laid one over the other, a big fire was blazing. Outside in from the door slowly smoldered another fire of green wood against the mosquitos and around which a number of hogs were nibbling at rinds of watermelon and mushmelons which had just eaten, as well as a heap of half eaten fish, etc. Also some hens, ducks, geese, and pigeons were running around, each left completely to his own resources. Beside the fenced corn field, planted with a kind of military precision, grazed a number of oxen, cows and calves, all mixed together, ass as pretty and slender as deer but as fat as the eel; also a dozen mustangs or captured wild horses of which two or three had been broken to the saddle …*" [Willich 1834, Epperson 1986]. Mirabeau Lamar made notes indicating that this first customs-house at Galveston Island lasted through about 1836 when it "… *has subsequently been consumed as fuel for the* **Yellow-Stone**" [Lamar 1836], a Brazos-River steamer which operated in Galveston Bay during the period of the Battle of San Jacinto in 1836.

Plans for a similar establishment at the Brazos followed quickly, also using Anahuac as a staging point. Although no specific description has been found, it was probably similar to Willich's description of the Galveston Island post, since it was built and manned about the same time and by the same people. The Brazos post was then manned or built up in stages over a period from early 1831 to Jun-1832 by an ever-increasing garrison of Mexican soldiers (ultimately under the command of Lt. Colonel Domingo de Ugartechea (beginning in Apr 1832).

Bradburn, acting in his role as commander of Fort Anahuac, reported that at some point in early 1831 he *"... sent Captain James Lindsay with a sergeant and 10 soldiers (to the Brazos)... Señor Lindsay remained as Captain Of The Port and Don Juan Austin as administrator .... In September, Lieutenant (Ignacio) Domínguez went to take Lindsay's place until Señor George Fisher should arrive"* [Bradburn Memorial 1832 pp. 132-133]. Presumably, Lindsay took over the customs duties from Asa Mitchell and Samuel May Williams. Although Bradburn does not specify a date, this posting was probably before mid-Mar 1831, when a visitor *"from the Northern States"* aboard the sloop **Majesty** (out of New Orleans) landed at the beach near the Brazos by rowboat and, after overturning in the surf, reported *"... we soon reached the house of Captain Cotton (Godwin Brown M. Cotten), where a flag was flying. It stands on the bank of the Brazos river, and is an inn, for the accommodation of passengers landing here, though a mere log house. The owner was formerly the editor of a Mexican gazette. ... There were ten or twelve puny, dark-complexioned men, at Captain Cotton's in uniform, who I learnt were Mexican soldiers, stationed there to enforce the revenue laws."* [Fiske 1836 pp. 3-5]. Cotten was formerly editor of the **Texas Gazette**, from Sep-1829 to Jan-1831, published at San Felipe de Austin [Bacarisse 1952], indeed the publisher of Fisher's earlier notices. Terán also reported that he had ordered a detachment to the *"punto de Brazoria"* in a letter to Ramón Músquiz to stop the clandestine trade in settlers and slaves [Terán 26-Mar-1831].

As of 2-Mar-1831, William Dobie (under alias of W. D. Dunlap, formerly of Harrisburg) was employed by Bradburn as a customs collector instead at Brazoria, and he notified Samuel May Williams to confirm his support and obtained clarification that tonnage duties were to be collected on all ships [Williams 10-Mar-1831]. Interestingly, this man was the great-grandfather of J. Frank Dobie. Later that summer, Williams made formal report indicating that 74 pesos and 4 reales had been collected to date as tonnage duties at Brazoria, among other ports, with a 5% surcharge for the collector [Williams 30-Jun-1831]. Ramón Músquiz then wrote to the Governor, asking for guidance that resulted in a series of letters clarifying that tonnage duties were to be centralized through Goliad and San Felipe, and that the revenue employees could keep a percentage to be determined by the legislature [Músquiz 31-Jul-1831].

A record from this period has been preserved in the Samuel May Williams Collection which shows the ships that entered the Brazos River between 1-Mar- and 20-Aug-1831 [Bradburn Aug-1831], perhaps indicating that the post began operations at this point (see Figure 19).

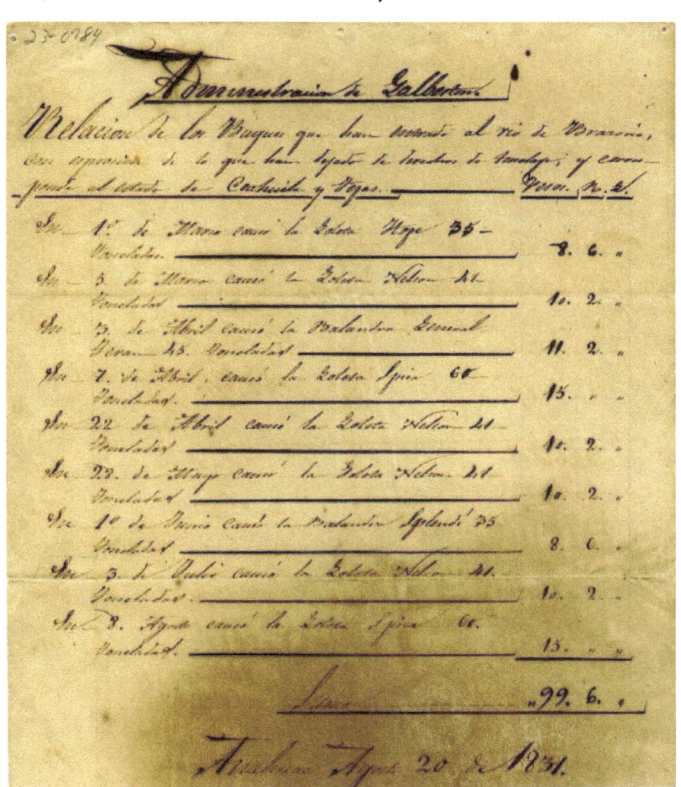

Figure 19: List by Bradburn of ships entering "el rio de Brazoria" between 1-Mar and 20-Aug-1831
Samuel May Williams Collection, MS 23-0784, Galveston & Texas History Center, Rosenberg Library

A total of 9 ships (7 schooners, 2 sloops) were listed during this period of almost 6 months, carrying a total of 399 tons of cargo, earning 99 pesos and 6 reales in duties (rate = 2 reales per ton). The same documents include a similar report from Anahuac for Galveston Bay arrivals, listing 195 pesos of tonnage duties, for a total of 294 pesos and 6 reales.

Another document from the Béxar Archives, dated about the same time (1-Sep-1831) and presumably composed by Bradburn, is a census or count of military personnel in the "Detachment of Anahuac" (see Figure 20 below). One line is of interest here as it says "Detachment in Brazoria", listing 1 Sub-Lieutenant and 13 soldiers [Bradburn Sep-1831], highlighted with a red oval, showing these personnel were probably posted at the mouth of the Brazos.

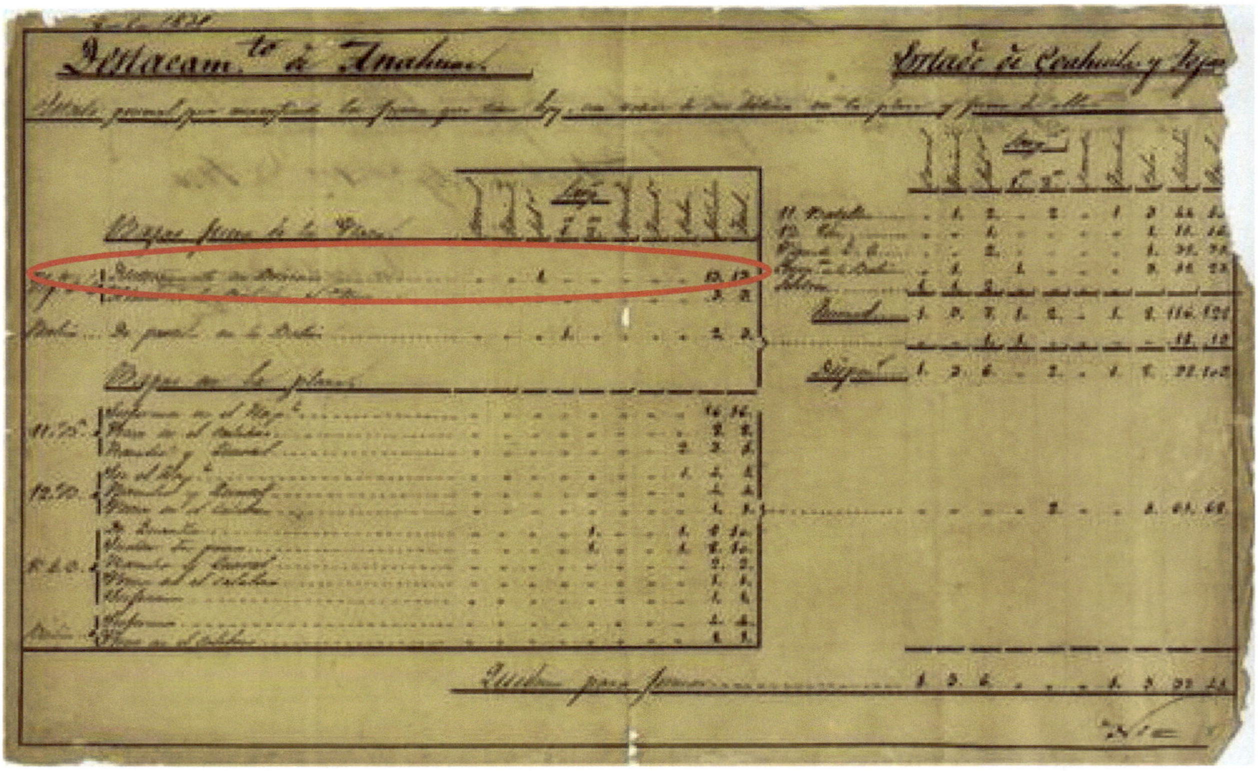
Destacam.to de Anahuac
Estado de Coahuila y Tejas

Figure 20: Military census report – Detachment of Anahuac, 1-Sep-1831 [Bradburn Sep-1831]

Courtesy of Dolph Briscoe Center for American History

Mary Austin Holley described the post on 22-Oct-1831 at the mouth of the Brazos aboard the ship ***Spica***: *"... Here there is a Mexican garrison, and the tri-colored flag is hoisted, the first signal of our approach to a foreign land On our right, in front of their palmetto-roofed, and windowless barracks, the lazy sentinels were 'walking their lonely rounds,' without excessive martial parade; nor did the unturretted quarters of the commanding officer, show forth much of the blazonry of a Spanish Don."* After a while, she further writes *"We came to, before the door of the pilot's house, which fronts the stream. The officer of the garrison boarded us, to examine our passports; a ceremony, the Mexicans are very tenacious of, from their known jealousy of foreigners. He was a young man, dark and rather handsome, in a neat Mexican uniform, probably his dress suit; for occasions of so much company, are not of every day occurrence, on this station"* [Holley 1833 p. 24-25, 29]. This may have been Lt. Ignacio Domínguez.

Mrs. Holley was the widowed cousin of Stephen F. Austin, and the two would later make plans to marry and settle down at Durazno Plantation (near modern Jones Creek, Texas), but this never occurred due to Stephen's death at age 43 in late 1836. It may have been during or after her 1831 trip that she composed a short three-verse song with piano accompaniment, entitled the "Brazos Boat Song" [Holley 1831]. This tune is confirmed in an 1831 letter [Mooney 2008], and reported to be the first English-language song of Texas (and about the Brazos!); the first (of two) pages are shown in Figure 21. Perhaps she tried to put down a tune or verses she heard from boatmen on her 1831 trip.

George Fisher's efforts in Matamoros at his rehabilitation were apparently successful, as Terán reinstated him on 27-Sep-1831 as the civilian customs collector for the Galveston area, but under his control, and also named Lt. Juan Pacho (Bradburn's paymaster at Anahuac) to become his assistant, and Juan Landavaco as head of the military guard [Terán Sep-1831]. Fisher then named Francisco Duclor to be his assistant and customs collector for the Brazos [Henson 1982 p.73]. Terán wrote to Stephen F.

Figure 21: "Brazos Boat Song" by Mary Austin Holley, first page [Holley 1831]
Courtesy of Dolph Briscoe Center for American History

Austin on 3-Oct-1831, notifying him of this development, and asked Austin to forget past difficulties with Fisher [Terán Oct-1831, Fisher Oct-1831]. Similar sentiments were repeated in a second letter [Terán 20-Nov-1831], in which Terán also staunchly defended Fisher. The October letters specifically mention the "*Aduana Marítima de Galvezton*" was to be partnered with the "*Receptoría Subalterna á ella de Brazoria*" (Subordinate Reception to it at Brazoria), clearly indicating their intention to establish the main customs house on Galveston Bay at Anahuac, and there would be a secondary receiving office for the Brazos. Thus, as of late 1831, management of "*el puerto de Galvezton*" switched over to Anahuac.

Terán and Fisher later went by sea to Anahuac on the brig ***Constante***, arriving there on 9-Nov-1831, but without Duclor who had to finish his job at the Matamoros customs house till the end of 1831 [Henson 1982 pp. 73-74]. Terán approved Fisher's plan to have customs houses built at Bolivar Point and the Brazos Bar made of lumber "*... with the greatest diligence and at least cost*" [Terán 19-Nov-1831], and twenty soldiers were added to the few soldiers already at the Brazos post [Ugartechea 1835, Lamar 1836, Letts p. 84. Morton 1945 p. 513, Boddie 1978 p. 10], in the absence of a dedicated civilian collector. Funds already collected at Anahuac and the Brazos were to be turned over to Fisher [Terán 22-Nov-1831].

Upon attempting to return with Terán to Matamoros on 24-Nov-1831, the **Constante** became lost in fog, grounded on Redfish Reef, and ultimately had to be abandoned [Lamar 1836, Henson 1982 pp. 78-79]. Terán and crew were rescued by Fisher on the port's schooner, but Terán then commissioned Capt. Nicholas Rider and his American schooner **Topaz** (late of Harrisburg) to carry him back to Matamoros in early Dec-1831. The cannons from the **Constante** were recovered in early 1832 and mounted at Anahuac. Upon reaching Matamoros, the **Topaz** was to return to Anahuac with Ugartechea and approximately 100 soldiers and supplies, acting as a base to create a true military fort at the mouth of the Brazos [Henson 1982 p. 91]. Fisher issued an order (also on 24-Nov-1831- the same day that Terán originally left) to the newly reinforced Brazos post *"to require all masters of vessels arriving at this port to go to Anahuac to enter and clear their vessels and merchants to visit that place to Bond their goods"* [McKinstry 1832], apparently for Fisher's personal convenience, effectively closing the area's main port (the Brazos) and others to open commerce, and this was met with great disagreement by the settlers of Austin's Colony.

Unusually, the original or complete decree by Fisher on 24-Nov-1831 has apparently not survived, especially given Fisher's penchant for keeping copies of correspondence, although some hints about it can be found in a letter from Stephen F. Austin to Horatio Chriesman [Austin 19-Jun-1832 pp. 785-786] suggesting it was not just a brief or casual note. Austin writes *"... the appointment of Fisher ... was obnoxious and unpopular - it must have been known that his order or decree of 24 Novr. last relative to the commerce of the Brazos River was highly vexatious – one fixing the custom house at Anahuac, instead of Galveston where the law really placed it – also the 20th article of that decree which subjected all vessells then in the river to its vexatious restrictions was retroactive and illegal from the face of it – a vessell may have been six months in the river, with cargo all distributed over the country and sold six months before the custom house was established, and still by that article it could not have gone to sea until the master owners etc. went to Anahuac and presented manifests, and paid the duties which were not due nor collectable when the vessel came in and discharged."*

It remains unclear why customs duties were now being implemented (as shown in Figure 19, and as intended by Terán and Fisher at Anahuac), considering Terán's earlier suspension of Fisher under the claim that the Law of 6-Apr-1830 had extended duty-free privileges to the Texians until 1834. As Eugene C. Barker wrote *"The early history of Mexico's fiscal administration has been neglected by writers of its political history, so that it is very difficult for foreign students to obtain an intelligent conception of it."* [Barker 1926 p. 179]. It would seem that "tonnage duties" were still being collected, while duties on the monetary value of imported goods were in abeyance until 1834.

On the Brazos, and disgruntled with the new requirement to travel overland to Anahuac for customs clearance, owners Edwin Waller and William H. Wharton attempted to sail their schooners **Sabine** (captained by Jeremiah Brown) and **Nelson** past the customs post on or about 15-Dec-1831. The ships were fired upon by the Mexican commander (Lt. Ignacio Domínguez) and his few troops (with muskets, as no artillery is mentioned) wounding Capt. Fuller on the **Nelson**, and a passenger (Spencer Jack) returned the fire, injuring one Mexican soldier - arguably the very first anti-government bloodshed in a series of events that led to the Texas Revolution. Waller and Wharton were arrested and imprisoned at the "fort" (probably then a group of crude buildings) but soon released [Peareson 1900 p. 35, Henson

1982 p. 82]. The ships **William A. Tyson**, **Spica** and others had also passed without customs clearance [Rowe 1903 p. 275, Morton 1945 p. 513, Henson 1982 p. 82 and 134]. Stephen F. Austin wrote on 30-Dec-1831 that *"The Officer at the mouth of the River has done his duty, so far as it was possible."* [Austin Dec-1831]. After entreaties to Bradburn at Anahuac, the Brazos port was reopened by posting an authorizing customs collector there, Lt. Juan Pacho (till then, Fisher's assistant at Anahuac). Pacho established his office at Brazoria on 22-Jan-1832, as Stephen F. Austin and others had been suggesting, since Velasco lacked wharves and warehouses, but found immediately that he was not welcomed by some colonists [Rowe 1903 pp. 276-277]. Duclor had been further delayed by contrary winds which took his ship to Tampico instead of Texas [Terán Jan-1832]. Stephen F. Austin had written to Terán complaining about Fisher's original edict [Austin Jan & Feb-1832]. Austin's letter of 5-Feb-1832 was written immediately following a visit to Anahuac, and in which he boldly suggested Fisher's removal. Terán replied sternly that he had already granted many favors to Austin's Colony, but agreed that a collector should also exist at the Brazos [Terán Jan-1832, Perez y Calleja 1834 #5]. During the recriminations, Fisher claimed he had issued the decree of 24-Nov-1831 under Terán's direct order [McKinstry 1832, Austin 28-Jul-1832], but Terán himself denied this later and scolded Fisher in a letter on 9-Feb-1832 [Perez y Calleja 1834 #4]. Apparently, perhaps due to friction between colonists and Pacho or Fisher, Samuel May Williams was again solicited to act as collector of duties, but declined due to the distances to Anahuac and Brazoria [Williams 7-Feb-1832].

Bradburn and Fisher did not let the matter drop, though. In letters to the Mexican Consul at New Orleans, who passed them onto the Mexican Chargé d'Affaires in Washington DC and the Mexican Secretary of Relations in Mexico City, they exaggerated the incident to some degree, even claiming that the **Tyson** and **Sabine** returned to the Brazos from New Orleans heavily armed with cannon, to continue violating the custom laws, asking the Consul to investigate. The Consul recommended to the Secretary of Relations that the Brazos be fortified, saying *"I believe it my duty to add that if the mouth of said river is not well garrisoned, the foreigners will continue to carry out the scandalous clandestine traffic ..."* [Martinez 1832]. One such trip of the **Sabine** from New Orleans to Velasco in about Apr-1832 was later mentioned in the reminiscences of a young Englishwoman, Ann Raney. She, with her mother and sister, then traveled on to Brazoria and Bailey's Prairie to join the father where he was teacher for the family of Britt Bailey. She describes being courted and almost marrying the captain, Jeremiah Brown [Coleman 1971].

Edna Rowe cited the troubles surrounding the **Sabine/Nelson** incident as a reason for Ugartechea's posting to the mouth of the Brazos, apparently based on reading *"Memorias para la historia de la guerra de Tejas"* by Vicente Filisola. She writes it was Terán's reaction to the **Sabine/Nelson** incident (presumably after Terán returned to Matamoros) that caused him to order Ugartechea to create and command a Brazos fort under Bradburn's overall command [Rowe 1903 p. 277]. However, in the same book, Filisola clarifies that some type of fort had been a part of Terán's overall plan for some time [Filisola 1848]. In light of the fact that the Brazos was probably the single busiest port on the upper Texas coast, it is also tempting to conclude that Terán recognized the issue with Anahuac's location (and that the Brazos was just its subordinate outpost), and rectified the problem by belatedly establishing a full military fortification at Velasco. This may explain why the 1832 Fort Velasco was established last, almost two years after he began with Fort Tenoxtitlán and Barranco Colorado.

From his base at Anahuac, Fisher implemented Terán's instructions about outposts at Galveston Island (apparently deciding against the location at Bolivar Point) and also the Brazos, as indicated in a letter from Fisher to William P. Harris and Robert Wilson, owners of a steam-operated sawmill at Harrisburg, who were hired to build customs-houses, warehouses and ferry boats for both locations in Jan-1832 [Fisher 1832]. The building on Galveston Island was later described by Amasa Turner after his arrival at Galveston with his family on 7-Feb-1837, to assume his duties as commander of Post Galveston, as: *"The old custom-house was an excellent frame building of cypress timber. Its sides and roof were covered. There was no joist or floor above or below – no windows or doors; but with the lumber I had brought I soon made it into a comfortable, if not elegant, residence. The house was about twenty-five by thirty-five feet, one story and a half high, and stood on the highest ground on the bay-shore of the island."* [Hayes 1879 1:275]. As with the first customs-house at Galveston Island, this description may also provide some clues to any building erected at the Brazos by Harris and Wilson.

During the return journey to Anahuac, bringing Ugartechea and his troops from Matamoros, the **Topaz** was the site of some turmoil which might have ended this first attempt to create a military fort on the Brazos - a mutiny in mid Feb-1832 offshore of Galveston Island to steal the ship's cash box, resulting in the death of Captain Rider and a Mexican sentry at the hands of the crew, with the soldiers locked below decks and doomed to drowning if the ship was scuttled. But, hearing the cries of their officers being attacked, the Mexican soldiers broke out and ultimately defeated the few mutinous crew. The surviving mutineers were imprisoned at Anahuac, and Bradburn took possession of the ship [Bryant 1832, Filisola 1848 I pp. 73-74, Henson 1982 p. 91-92, Epperson 1995], no doubt to transport Ugartechea on to the Brazos. Ugartechea reported he had successfully disembarked at Anahuac on or about 6-Mar-1832 *"... with 86 men and two pieces of 18 at the disposition of .... Bradburn"* [Ugartechea 13-Mar-1832]. Mirabeau Lamar also writes *"The Vessel reached Anahuac in safety, landed the soldiers; and then <u>filling her with pickets to build a fort at Velasco</u>, she sailed with Col. Ugartechea aboard to the mouth of the Brazos, where she was wrecked and lost."* [Lamar 1836, Bradburn Memorial 1832 p. 138-139]. The letter by Ugartechea also states that he was *"... getting myself ready for marching, within eight days, with one cannon of 6 (un cañón á 6.) and 100 infantrymen, carrying at the same time aboard, all of the utensils for fortifying myself at the mouth of the Brazos River, carrying with me the receiver named by the government for that point, Don Francisco Duclor ..."*.

However, Ugartechea was still at Anahuac on 26-Mar-1832, when he wrote another letter from there to José de las Piedras, commander at Nacogdoches, stating slightly different facts (arrival on the **5th**, carrying *"dos piezas de á **16**"* for Anahuac, and twice mentions his own *"cañón de á **8/ocho**"*). Further, he writes he had no gunpowder cartridges for his "cannon of eight" <u>that he had brought</u>, but he will make 100 cartridges from Anahuac's supply of gunpowder, and asks Piedras to replace it, and also that he needs some sergeants and corporals [Ugartechea 26-Mar-1832]. José de las Piedras responded he had sent 8 arrobas (about 200 pounds) of gunpowder but could not provide any officers or sergeants [De Las Piedras May-1832]. Thus, it seems likely the cannon came not from the **Constante** but was purposely brought by Ugartechea from Mexico on the **Topaz**, and that some staging and preparations were obviously being done first at Anahuac. The plans are further detailed in a letter from Bradburn on 4-Apr-1832 which mentions that Ugartechea was planning to leave with 100 infantrymen, 17 artillerymen and a cannon to establish a fort at the Brazos to be named *"Fortaleza de Velasco"* (Fortress of Velasco) [Bradburn 4-Apr-1832, Rowe 1903 p. 277]. This is the first known mention of the site as

Velasco, perhaps named after José María Cervantes y Velasco, a Mexican army officer and signer of the Act of Independence of the Empire of Mexico, and thus was probably known to Terán, Bradburn or Ugartechea. Terán's wife also came from a family whose paternal surname was Velasco. A railroad engineer and author, James Llewellyn Allhands, that built the original St. Louis, Brownsville & Mexico Railway (aka the "Brownsville Line" or "Brownie") through Brazoria County in 1905-1906, published a book in 1931 that states that Velasco was *"... named after Louis de Velasco, a Spanish viceroy in Mexico"* [Allhands 1931 p. 224], but cites no primary source. He apparently collected quite a bit of local history, as this rail line was extended from Bay City to Sweeny, Brazoria, Angleton, Algoa and eventually Houston in the period of 1905-1906, and which later joined the Missouri-Pacific rail network. J. P. Bryan surmised later that it was Terán who chose the name and also favored the possibility it was after Luis de Velasco, an early viceroy of New Spain [Holley 1965 p. 73].

The letter from George Fisher to William P. Harris was written on 20-Mar-1832, indicating that Harris was late in providing the buildings and ferry boats, and this was a problem especially at the Brazos since Ugartechea was planning to arrive soon, so Fisher urged him to finish by writing *"In few day a vessel goes from here to the mouth of the river Brazos with 100 men and a 8 pounder, under command of Leut. Colonel Domingo Ugartechea, with all the necessaries for a fortification at the entrance of said River, accompanied by two other officers and two customhouse officers; in consequence of these preparations, it is necessary that you should with possible despach place said buildings and the ferry boat, also sufficient lumber to make the sheds to the warehouse, and in case of need, to put some repairs to Mitchells house. The officers of the **Constante** accompany the expedition, on board the **Topaz**. The hull of the **Constante** is for sale, at $200 for the whole, with the copper on it. Should you wish to buy it let me know it."* [Fisher 1832]. So, apparently, the construction of the 1832 fort may have involved workers of Harris and Wilson working to build buildings at the site, alongside the Mexican soldiers building the fort itself.

Significant developments would now occur at the mouth of the Brazos over the next few months; however, before relating these, it is notable that Stephen F. Austin (and his peacekeeping counsel) would be absent from Texas in this critical period, attending the legislature in Saltillo. He left San Felipe for Béxar in mid-March 1832, meeting there with their ayuntamiento to secure their approval of a *Memorial* to the legislature, asking for some revisions in laws [Austin Mar-1832], reaching Saltillo by 9-Apr-1832. Austin's intention was to travel to meet with Terán during a summer break of the legislature, perhaps occasioned by a plaintive invitation from Terán (then at Matamoros) [Terán Apr-1832], but return to Saltillo in time for its short session starting in late August, before returning to Texas. But as they say, things happen – and events at Anahuac and the Brazos that same summer of 1832 would alter both Austin's schedule and that of Texas history.

The actual date of Ugartechea's departure from Anahuac to the Brazos was further delayed by bad weather but was about 12-Apr-1832 [Bradburn 12-Apr-1832]; ([Filisola 1848 p. 81] reports it as 2-Apr). Another letter from Ugartechea on 15-May-1832 (now at the mouth of the Brazos) mentions that he had disembarked there on 19-Apr-1832 and began work on the fort, that the cannon was mounted nine days after arrival, and that the fort was mostly complete [Ugartechea 15-May-1832a]. Apparently, the men, artillery and other supplies were successfully removed from the grounded **Topaz**, and the fort was built quickly with pickets scavenged from the wreck and perhaps also available drift logs, in a short period between 19-Apr and 15-May-1832. It is also possible, given that the **Topaz** was available, that it made more than one trip ferrying men and supplies to the site, before its final demise. The labor force could have been up to about 150 men - or probably less as there was trouble with many desertions [Ugartechea 15-May-1832b & 7-Jun-1832b] and only 100 men were reported present by early June [Ugartechea 7-Jun-1832c]. One of Ugartechea's dispatches mentioned 17 desertions on the date of the fort's completion [Ugartechea 15-May-1832b] to the military commander of the Mexican state of Coahuila y Tejas, Col. José Antonio Elosúa (also spelled Elozúa) based at San Antonio de Béxar, and Elosúa responded to other nearby commanders with a directive to arrest these deserters [Elosúa 5-Jun-1832].

Given the short time period and limited manpower, the 1832 fort was probably a fairly modest structure. In the past, significant comparisons have been made to a circular fort design of 60-vara radius (about 330 feet diameter), found in the papers of Stephen F. Austin [Austin 1822] shown in Figure 22. While a remarkable similarity does exist, detailed analysis shows it was not the design for Fort Velasco. This design was a significant departure from typical Spanish forts (presidios) of the era, which were usually rectangular structures with corner bastions (as found at Anahuac). The two-sided Austin 1822 diagram was suggested for connection to Fort Velasco and Ugartechea in 1982, when found by James E. "Jake" Ivey (co-author of [Fox et al 1981]) in the Stephen F. Austin Map Collection at the University of Texas at Austin at the Barker Center for American History, but was apparently known locally earlier [Fox 1991]. But it is NOT labeled as to location or author, and has substantial Spanish hand-written descriptions. The Briscoe card catalog does describe it might be for Velasco, which may derive from this 1982 rediscovery. A note in the hand of Stephen F. Austin indicates it was from Mexico in 1822. The drawing is mentioned in a 1961 article simply as "A Fort, 1822" without any mention of Fort Velasco [Sharp 1961 p. 388]. Our conclusion is that this document was created much earlier than 1832 for other purposes, but somehow was given or sent to Stephen F. Austin for some reason. Copies (in the form of photographic negatives of a microfilm copy) were provided to the Brazoria County Historical Museum (BCHM) in late 1982. High-resolution photo duplicates of the original document in Austin were made in Sep-2019, to decipher any and all writing on the document (revealing some faintly written words), to better understand its origin. However, finding no labeling connecting it to Fort Velasco, along with the fact that it involves an excavated perimeter, with stakes ("tala" in Spanish) pointing inward (perhaps to contain cattle), suggests it cannot really be a direct design for the fort at the mouth of the Brazos. The words on the new photo-duplicate have been transcribed and (when in Spanish) translated, and are shown in Appendix 1. In 1982, when this diagram was made known in Brazoria County, the story was that it was drawn by Ugartechea himself in 1822, thus making it more likely to be connected to Fort Velasco [Barnett 1982]. However, the 2019 high-resolution photos show no such name or signature. Our hypothesis is that someone might have mistakenly "saw" his name in the Spanish writing in the poor-quality microfilm copies available in 1982.

Difficulties continued to fester between Fisher and the colonists at Anahuac, and rumors reached the Political Chief of Texas (Ramón Músquiz, stationed at Béxar) that Brazos River merchants were continuing to resist Fisher, so Músquiz wrote a letter to the new Alcalde at San Felipe (Horatio Chriesman) on 24-Apr-1832 inquiring about conditions [Músquiz Apr-1832]. Chriesman requested that Samuel May Williams travel to Brazoria and the mouth of the Brazos to investigate, meeting with Ugartechea and the merchants. They responded Fisher was the problem, and the merchants were otherwise agreeable to paying the lawful customs duties, and even had built a customs warehouse on their own at Brazoria [Chriesman May-1832].

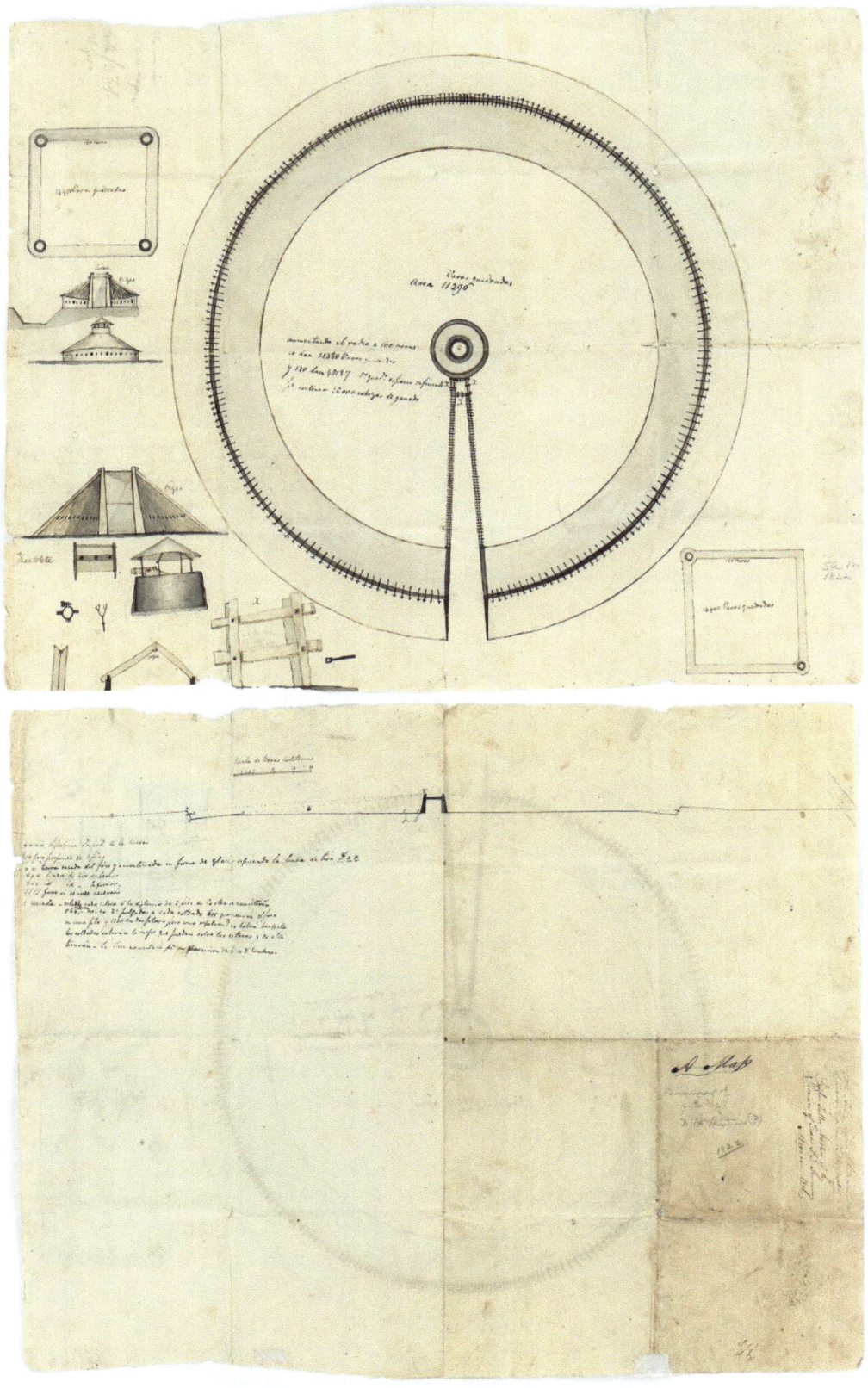

Figure 22: Two-sided diagram from Stephen F. Austin Map Collection, circa 1822

Stephen F. Austin Map Collection, Dolph Briscoe Center for American History

During this period, Fisher also quarreled with Bradburn, so he moved to the outpost on Galveston Island on 22-Apr-1832 [Lamar 1836, Letts p. 99], so we might assume the new customs house there was completed by then. He eventually failed in his intended role as administrator of customs in the Galveston Bay region. Terán ordered him to turn over his duties [Perez y Calleja 1834 #'s 6, 8 & 9] and he returned to Matamoros by 6-Jun-1832 [Perez y Calleja 1834 #6], just ahead of impending trouble at Anahuac and the Brazos, in events for which Fisher had had a role in creating some of the antecedents for these conflicts.

These disagreements over customs and other matters with the officious Fisher and the autocratic Bradburn had been developing in early 1832, known to history as the Anahuac Disturbances, which came to a head when Bradburn imprisoned five or more civilians, one of which was the hot-headed William Barret Travis, as related by one of the Texian leaders in a first-hand account [Johnson 1914 pp. 69-75]. Ugartechea noticed the Brazoria colonists' involvement in the Anahuac dispute while visiting Brazoria and, perhaps expecting trouble on the Brazos too, had written from there seeking extra reinforcements especially cavalry [Ugartechea 7-Jun-1832a & b] and also reported the situation to Bradburn and the regional commander, Antonio Elosúa [Ugartechea 7-Jun-1832c]. The commander of Barranco Colorado on the lower Lavaca River (Capt. Aniceto Arteaga), though, initially declined to endanger his troops in the "Caney Swamp" [Linn 1986 p. 21-22], who had suffered for months without proper provisions (see many letters in Béxar Archives).

Ugartechea further indicated that he had met with John Austin (Alcalde of Brazoria) and tactfully proffered for Austin to travel to Anahuac to act as civilian judge to defuse the issue, but also said that he could only spare up to 60 of his 100 troops (and apparently, himself) to reinforce Bradburn [Ugartechea 7-Jun-1832c]. A response from Elosúa on 18-Jun-1832 complimented his diplomatic approach but also ordered him to assist Bradburn "... *in everything that may be in your means and authorities in shielding him from any insult that with such scandal is to be feared ...*" [Elosúa 18-Jun-1832a]. Elosúa wrote other letters the same day, to Ramón Músquiz (at Béxar) and José de las Piedras (at Nacogdoches), summoning aid for the Anahuac Disturbances, also notifying Ugartechea and Bradburn of these orders [Elosúa 18-Jun-1832b]. After a dispatch was received in Béxar from the Alcalde of San Felipe on or about the 19th which confirmed the "*unfortunate occurrences that were to be feared in the military post of Anahuac*", Ramón Músquiz wrote to announce his new plans. The next day, Elosúa wrote again to de las Piedras, Bradburn and Ugartechea, stating that Músquiz proposed to travel over to San Felipe "*to restore order*" and that Piedras and Ugartechea were to assist Bradburn [Elosúa 20-Jun-1832]. Músquiz arrived at San Felipe on 24-Jun-1832 [Músquiz 26-Jun-1832]. The dispatches to and from Músquiz on the 19th are not apparently found in the Béxar Archives, but are quoted in Elosua's letters of the 20th although his drafts (in the Béxar Archives) copy nothing but the first sentence of Músquiz's message.

Before the Battle of Velasco, apparently in response to the Anahuac Disturbances, José Mariano Guerra (substituting for Terán) issued orders from Matamoros to Elosúa for Tenoxtitlán, Lipantitlán and Goliad to reinforce Fort Velasco. A week later, Guerra rescinded those orders, apparently after hearing from Terán, who thought Stephen F. Austin should preferentially handle the matter [Guerra 20-Jun-1832]. Apparently, the original order also went directly to Lavaca, which caused Aniceto Arteaga to stand by with 1 officer and 24 men to join with forces from Goliad on their way to Velasco [Arteaga 28-Jun-1832 frames 107-108]. The commander at Goliad had sent a troop of 37 infantry and 10 cavalry, which arrived at Barranco Colorado on July 1st on their way to Velasco [Arteaga 1-Jul-1832] – and the combined force left in that direction, but this would be too late. Belatedly, and perhaps against his better judgement (since he may have become aware of the Battle of Velasco), Mariano Cosío obeyed the superior order from Guerra and issued an express mail to recall troops from Velasco [Cosío 3-Jul-1832].

No settlement was reached at Anahuac, primarily because of Bradburn's reneging on a tentative agreement to release the prisoners. John Austin returned to Brazoria, and prepared by gathering militia and some artillery to reclaim by force the prisoners from Fort Anahuac [Johnson 1914 pp. 73-75]. A more-substantial reprise of the *Sabine*/*Nelson* incident then occurred involving the forced passage of the schooner *Brazoria* (under William J. Russell) to take two cannon and militia from Brazoria to Anahuac for this dispute, made problematic now by the existence of a heavily armed Fort Velasco, guarding and blocking the mouth of the river. The *Brazoria* (see Figure 23) had sailed from New Orleans to Brazoria with a load of sundries under Capt. John G. Rowland, arriving there on 14-Jun-1832, and was commandeered by John Austin on the 21st to carry cannon and militia to Anahuac [Rowland et al 1832]. Curiously, the two cannon put aboard the *Brazoria* had arrived in the period of Aug-1830 from the Rio Grande on the steamboat *Ariel* but had been left at the town of

Figure 23: Hand-made Model of the Schooner "Brazoria" by Michael Seright at Surfside City Hall

Brazoria so the ship (after taking on wood) could pass the Brazos Bar [Puryear & Winfield 1976 pp. 41-42]. Bradburn had apparently sought to purchase the cannons, and Stephen F. Austin also suggested they be might be delivered to the customs officer at Brazoria [Letona 1832, Austin Mar-1832, Chriesman Mar-1832].

Ugartechea's refusal to allow passage of the *Brazoria* (in compliance with his orders) led to the Battle Of Velasco over several days in late Jun 1832; the battle itself occurring mostly in the overnight period of 26-Jun-1832. The Texian battle plan was to sail the schooner down the Brazos under cover of darkness, engage the fort with cannon fire, while land forces stealthily encircled the fort. An attack at dawn was to overwhelm the fort, but the Texians were discovered in the night, and firing began. The *Brazoria* was hit by the Mexican 9-pounder, and became grounded. The morning light saw improved accuracy and, after a mid-morning rain shower, the Mexicans surrendered since their ammunition was exhausted. Several first-hand or contemporaneous accounts of the battle are available, most notably an "after-action report" by the Mexican commander [Ugartechea 1-Jul-1832].

William J. Russell wrote that "... *The plan and structure of the fort were well understood, of circular form, of logs and sand, with strong stakes, sharpened, and placed close together, all around the embankment. In the center, stood a bastion, in height considerably above the outer wall, on top of which was mounted a long nine-pounder, worked on a pivot, and around which, on top of the bastion, was a parapet made of wood, about two feet in height.*" [Russell 1872].

John H. Brown (whose father Henry S. Brown was at the battle of Velasco) wrote "... *The fort at Velasco stood about a hundred and fifty yards both from the river and the Gulf shore which formed a right angle. It consisted of parallel rows of posts six feet apart, filled between with sand, earth and shells, for the outer walls. Inside of the walls was an embankment on which musketeers could stand and shoot over without exposing anything but their heads. In the center was an elevation of the same material, inclosed by higher posts, on which the artillery was planted and protected by bulwarks.*" [Brown 1892].

Henry Smith wrote in 1836 that "*It will be recollected that there was a strong fortress at the mouth of the river Brazos garrisoned by about one hundred and fifty men, well armed and provisioned with one long brass nine mounted on a carriage and one (swivel gun) on a pivot ..... The fort was a complete circle enclosing but a small area so that it was full and completely manned. The nine-pounder was planted on an elevation in the center of perhaps ten feet above the musquetry. As soon as our company opened on the fort, it seemed to ignite instantaneously and flame like a volcano. And from that time until the battle ended, the fort seemed to emit one continued blaze of fire. They had burned all the houses but two, one was used as a custom house, and the other a small office. .... We ... learned one thing, and that was in some measure to escape the shot of the nine-pounder. .... (we) planted the palisades within thirty paces of the fort so that their nine-pounder could not be depressed enough to bear upon us, but [we] were compelled to stand the (swivel gun) and the musquetry.*" [Smith 1836].

Edwin Waller said "... *fort of circular form, having in the center a mound or raised platform of earth, whereon the artillery was placed <u>en barbette</u>, so as to fire over the outer wall, and command a range on every side. This outer wall was surrounded by a fosse or ditch, and perhaps something intended for <u>chevaux de frize</u> or <u>abattis</u>.*" [Peareson 1900].

<u>The few precise details of the as-built 1832 fort mentioned in various references are reproduced and summarized in Appendix 2.</u>

There have also been many retellings [Fry 1832, Newell 1838 pp. 26-28, Foote 1841, Kennedy 1841, Willson 1847, Yoakum 1855 I:290-297, Thrall 1883, Bancroft 1889, Rowe 1903 pp. 289-292, Johnson 1914 pp. 77-81, Hill 1937 pp. 14-17, Gambrell 1948 pp. 32-33, House 1960, Dow 1961, Ward 1962 pp. 272-308, Cotton 1968, Brazosport 1970, Freeport 1971, Creighton 1975 pp. 58-72, Boddie 1978, Henson 1982 pp. 107-108, Linn 1986 pp. 17-23, Meed 2001 pp. 11-16, Jordan 2006 pp. 4-5] and even an entire historical novel [Hicks & Parkinson 1980]. The Newell account [Newell 1838 p. 28] seems to be the origin of the story that Domingo de Ugartechea, once his artillerymen had been depleted by Texian rifle fire, had bravely manned the cannon bastion himself to great acclaim even from the opposing forces; however, this seems to have later been embellished to the fact that he actually fired the cannon by himself [House 1960 p. 94] and to Texian applause [Hicks & Parkinson 1980 p. 228-9]. Another account said that "*During the 20 hours of battle Colonel Ugartechea was successively gunner and gunsmith, private soldier, the leading spirit of his men, and Commander. He attended to everything, and had his hat pierced by two balls while pointing a gun.*" [Unknown 1832]. As reported by Ugartechea, the Texians taunted his forces by shouting "*Long Live Santa Anna!*", to which they replied "*Long Live the Mexican Republic, Its Constitution and Laws, and Long Live the Supreme Government*" [Ugartechea 1-Jul-1832]. Newell had spent a year interviewing participants in the Texas Revolution in the year following the contest, his book being published in 1838, so his book was virtually contemporaneous and the first authoritative account of Texas independence to reach print. His exact words about Ugartechea were "*... Those who manned the cannon were repeatedly shot away till, at length, Ugartechea, having in vain endeavored to force his men to ascend the bastion, heroically set the example himself, and directed the gun. Upon this the Texans, though they might have shot an eye out of his head, respecting Ugartechea as a man and admiring his courage as a soldier, generously ceased their fire.*" [Newell p. 28].

Another re-telling closed by saying "*While the battle of Velasco has not received much of a place in Texas history there is no denying this was the same funnel-shaped war cloud that a few years hence was to sweep over the swamps of San Jacinto.*" [Allhands 1931 p. 227]. The battle was heard down the coast at Matagorda, where Mary Wightman Helm recollected that "*... in June, 1832, we distinctly heard the sound of cannons for six or eight hours, we living 25 miles west, at the head of Matagorda Bay.*" [Helm 1884 p. 49].

On the day after the overnight battle, Britt Bailey had written to David Shelby of Austin County for reinforcements, anticipating a further siege, but this proved unnecessary due to the Mexican surrender. A copy of his letter [Bailey 1832, Creighton 1975 p. 67] soon found its way to Arteaga which he then sent on to the regional commander. Accounts vary, but the Texian casualties have been given as 2 to 23 killed and 2 to 40 wounded, with Mexican casualties of 7 to 42 killed and 7 to 70 wounded. Edna Rowe evaluated several accounts, but felt a reliable number was 7 killed and 27 wounded for the Texians, and 35 killed and 15 wounded for the Mexicans [Rowe 1903 p. 292]. However, it was also reported that two additional Texians died from their wounds later, and a mate was killed aboard the ***Brazoria***. An extensive discussion of the casualties can be found in [Ward 1962] and [Boddie 1978]. History does not record all the individual names of the Texian dead, but they are thought to include Aylett C. "Strap" Buckner, Antonio "Jose" Buckner (Strap Buckner's Mexican foster child), Andrew Castleman, Mathew Thomas Hinds, mate of schooner, Edward Robertson, William C. Smith, Leander Woods and Isaac Jamieson [Boddie 1975 p. 26], with most of these names recorded on the Brazoria Fallen Heroes Memorial. A capitulation agreement was signed on 29-Jun-1832, one copy of which can be found in the Béxar Archives [Ugartechea 29-Jun-1832], also published in the local Brazoria newspaper [Cotten 1832] and in Mary Austin Holley's 1833 book [Holley 1833 pp. 157-158].

However, by the time the battle was over, the prisoner issue at Anahuac had been resolved by the arrival from Nacogdoches of Bradburn's superior (José de las Piedras) who negotiated with the locals, released the prisoners, and then later relieved Bradburn of command on 2-Jul-1832 [Johnson 1914 pp. 73-76, 165-166]. Bradburn left Anahuac on the evening of 13-Jul-1832 by a land route, narrowly escaping pursuit by eight men while losing his horse and swimming the Sabine River, then heading to New Orleans [Morse 1832, Rowe 1903 p. 297], where he took ship back to Mexico. Bradburn then lived on his ranch in what is now Hidalgo County, Texas, serving sporadically in the military, but died in Matamoros in 1842 and was buried on his ranch.

Interestingly, Ugartechea identified the ordnance used during the Battle of Velasco as 4600 musket rounds (with 400 remaining), 96 rounds (with 14 or 15 remaining) for the *"canon de a ocho"* (usually interpreted as 8-pound cannon) and as 76 rounds (with none remaining) using the *"cañonsito (or pedrero) de cuatro onzas"* (often misinterpreted as 4-pound cannon, but more likely a large flintlock smoothbore for four-ounce cast-iron shot of 1.231" diameter, mounted on a swivel) [Ugartechea 1-Jul-1832]. The Lamar Papers include a report by the Brazoria Militia on 22-Jun-1832 of their preparations, including that they had made 4' x 20' barricades of 2-inch thick pine boards [Lamar 1832], so it was these parapets that were penetrated by the swivel gun and caused many of the Texian casualties, among John Austin's division outside the north wall. This document also pinpoints the date the attack began as the night of 26-Jun-1832. Secondary references, though, gave conflicting (probably less correct) details about the barricades: 2" cypress planks supplied by Wharton, 10-12' long and 4' high [Smith 1836 p. 39, Brown 1970 p. 184, Boddie 1978 p. 20], or 6" x 10" oak planks 20' long obtained at Wharton's Eagle Island Plantation [Hicks & Parkinson 1980 p. 207]. Ann Raney also recalled that she had helped mold bullets and make patches for the battle, carrying them 15 miles on horseback (from Bailey's Prairie?) to drop them at the Bertrand place upstream of Velasco, being chased by two Mexican spies [Coleman 1971].

As news of the battle reached San Felipe, Ramón Músquiz wrote to Arteaga, suggesting that he send troops to relieve Ugartechea [Músquiz 30-Jun & 2-Jul-1832a], with help also coming from Goliad and Lavaca [Arteaga 9-Jul-1832]. Músquiz also wrote directly to Ugartechea, inviting his troops to come to San Felipe [Músquiz 2-Jul-1832b]. Troops were even dispatched from Matamoros by order of José Mariano Guerra [Guerra 7-Jul-1832a]. Eventually, as news of Ugartechea's abandonment of Fort Velasco became known, these troops were recalled [Arteaga 10-Jul-1832, Elosúa 13-Jul-1832].

After the Battle of Velasco, the Mexican and (at least some of the) Texian dead were buried in the fort's vicinity [Ugartechea 1-Jul-1832, Holley 1965 p. 54]. the **Arkansas Advocate** newspaper on 6-Feb-1833 published some proceedings of a meeting at San Felipe de Austin in late 1832, under the headline ""Monument – (to be erected at the mouth of the River Brazos.)", shown in Figure 24. The article has commemorative words and specific details for the monument [Bertrand 1833]. Although it says the monument was to be immediately obtained, no evidence of its actual placement at Velasco is known. Given that the area was devastated by a cholera epidemic in 1833 (for example, that killed John Austin), the area became heavily involved in the Texas Revolution of 1835-1836, and the 1837 hurricane called Racer's Storm hit the area, the concept was probably forgotten, among a local population then struggling to just survive.

The monument is also briefly mentioned in an issue of the **Texas Republican** newspaper during the beginning of the Texas Revolution in late 1835, which repeated some of the exact words intended for inscription *"... We will remind Santa Ana of the lines designed for the monument at Velasco -- Here fought, here fell, in freedom's cause – the Brave. Tyrants beware! Man will not be a slave."* [Gray 10-Oct-1835 p. 3]. It is also mentioned in the 1869 Texas Almanac, referring to an early 1833 issue of **The Constitutional Advocate** newspaper of Brazoria [Unknown 1869 p. 38]. Unfortunately, very few issues of that newspaper have survived, and that one has not been found.

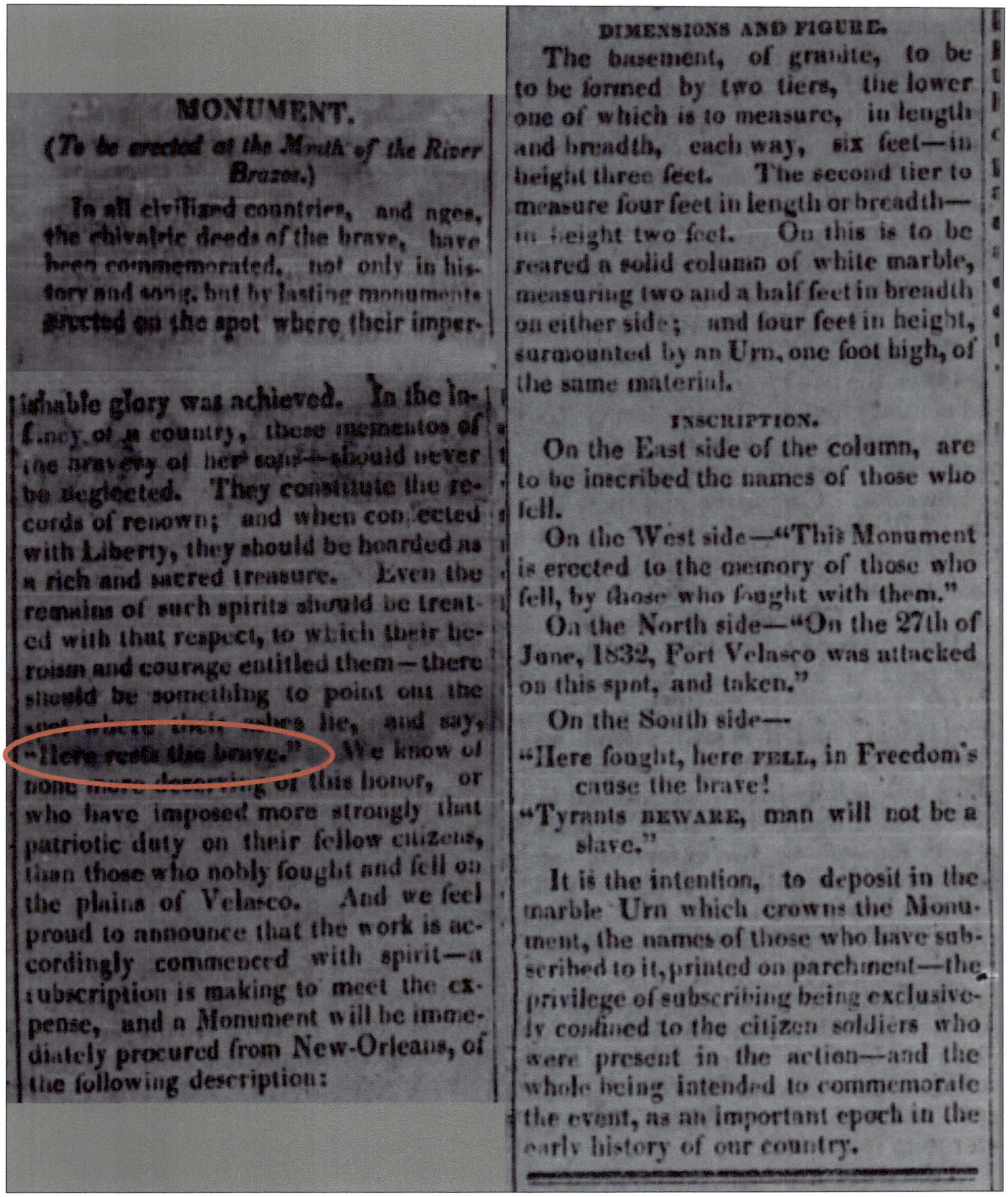

MONUMENT.

(To be erected at the Mouth of the River Brazos.)

In all civilized countries, and ages, the chivalric deeds of the brave, have been commemorated, not only in history and song, but by lasting monuments erected on the spot where their imperishable glory was achieved. In the infancy of a country, these mementos of the bravery of her sons—should never be neglected. They constitute the records of renown; and when connected with Liberty, they should be hoarded as a rich and sacred treasure. Even the remains of such spirits should be treated with that respect, to which their heroism and courage entitled them—there should be something to point out the spot where their ashes lie, and say, "Here rests the brave." We know of none more deserving of this honor, or who have imposed more strongly that patriotic duty on their fellow citizens, than those who nobly fought and fell on the plains of Velasco. And we feel proud to announce that the work is accordingly commenced with spirit—a subscription is making to meet the expense, and a Monument will be immediately procured from New-Orleans, of the following description:

DIMENSIONS AND FIGURE.

The basement, of granite, to be to be formed by two tiers, the lower one of which is to measure, in length and breadth, each way, six feet—in height three feet. The second tier to measure four feet in length or breadth—in height two feet. On this is to be reared a solid column of white marble, measuring two and a half feet in breadth on either side; and four feet in height, surmounted by an Urn, one foot high, of the same material.

INSCRIPTION.

On the East side of the column, are to be inscribed the names of those who fell.

On the West side—"This Monument is erected to the memory of those who fell, by those who fought with them."

On the North side—"On the 27th of June, 1832, Fort Velasco was attacked on this spot, and taken."

On the South side—

"Here fought, here FELL, in Freedom's cause the brave!

"Tyrants BEWARE, man will not be a slave."

It is the intention, to deposit in the marble Urn which crowns the Monument, the names of those who have subscribed to it, printed on parchment—the privilege of subscribing being exclusively confined to the citizen soldiers who were present in the action—and the whole being intended to commemorate the event, as an important epoch in the early history of our country.

Figure 24 – Monument article spliced from Arkansas Advocate, 6-Feb-1833, page 2, columns 1 & 2

In 1838, Mary Austin Holley wrote in her diary *"We crossed over to Velasco. Went shopping (they have one store), visited the Archer House, a fine hotel. Large 2 story with gallery painted, white, looks well. Had a commanding view. Met with Gen. Green* (Thomas Jefferson Green) *the master spirit here who attended us in our walk – pointed to the graves of those who fell in the first battle for Independence – looked at the old fort – the work of the Mexicans – Velasco looks like quite a place."* [Holley 1965 p. 54].

Soon after the battle, Samuel May Williams called for Texians to remain faithful to Mexico, and that Stephen F. Austin would soon return from Matamoros [Williams 1-Jul-1832], as had been suggested in letters from Austin while there [Austin 19- & 20-Jun-1832]. The surviving Mexican soldiers were paroled back to Matamoros, and the fort was apparently occupied by the victorious Texians for a short period, as William H. Wharton and others penned a defiant letter on 4-Jul-1832 from the fort, in which they mention having "… *kept 80 rounds of powder for the 9 pounder and all the shots and slugs*", and not displaying the nuance of support for the Mexican constitution or the Santa Anna Party [Wharton 1832]. These letters of divergent opinion show the predicament the Texians felt in the battle's aftermath. Other Texian individuals and communities expressed various opinions on the matter. The Ayish Bayou community near San Augustine met on 29-Jun-1832, and resolved for neutrality, but supported constitutional and civil authority above the military [Ayish 1832]. In Matagorda, a meeting on 2-Jul-1832 expressed disapproval of the attacks at Anahuac and Brazoria (Velasco) and resolved support for the Mexican government and constitution [Matagorda 1832]. An unknown author (apparently at San Felipe) was very critical of the attack on Fort Velasco, and John Austin in particular, suggesting they sought rebellion with assistance from the United States [Unknown 1832], also reporting Ugartechea arrived there on 7-Jun-1832 with some details of the battle. The ayuntamiento of San Felipe reported on a large meeting on 7-Jun-1832 which declared allegiance to the Mexican constitution and desiring peace and order, which was transferred to Ramón Músquiz [San Felipe 1832]. For his part, Ramón Músquiz (still at San Felipe) wrote a conciliatory letter to the people of Austin's Colony, urging peace, harmony and friendship, and for them to return to their normal occupations [Músquiz 7-Jul-1832]. In a bold and shrewd move to avoid difficulties, Austin plays offense and writes back to Músquiz, restating that his colonists were not seeking rebellion and independence, but fought Bradburn and Fisher since they favored the Santa Anna Party, and forcibly argued that the path forward should be separate statehood for Texas (away from Coahuila) within the Mexican federal system [Austin 28-Jul-1832].

Although the surrender terms [Cotten 1832, Holley 1833 p. 158-159] indicated that Ugartechea and troops would be carried back to Matamoros by sea, the **Brazoria** was so damaged in the battle that it was not seaworthy; the owners abandoned her to the underwriters, who eventually billed the Mexican government $7215 [Rowland et al 1832]. However, it was aboard the schooner that Ugartechea wrote a lengthy "after action report" and explanation to the regional commander [Ugartechea 1-Jul-1832], which mentions many details about the fort and battle.

During these same few weeks, Terán had been involved in a rebellion in Mexico fighting against the forces of Antonio López de Santa Anna, having to move his command afield to Hacienda de Buena Vista del Cojo and then to Croix (now Casas) further south in Tamaulipas, leaving José Mariano Guerra in charge of the command at Matamoros. During the summer break in the legislature, Stephen F. Austin left Saltillo on 12-May-1832 to make a hot arduous journey through Monterrey, Pilón (current Montemorelos), Linares, Victoria (current Ciudad Victoria) to meet briefly with Terán at Buena Vista on 30-May-1832 [Morton 1945 p. 536, Barker 1926 p. 336] – probably only the second (and last) time they met in person (after Terán's 1828 visit to San Felipe). For reasons yet unclear, Austin then continued north to Matamoros in the summer heat, arriving there by mid-June, with plans to still return to Saltillo. After writing some letters back to Texas [Austin 20-Jun-1832], he reports learning of the Anahuac Disturbances and counsels peaceful explanations, and his plans change. Terán also hears of the trouble at Anahuac, and issues orders to have Ugartechea replace Bradburn at Anahuac, for Juan Cortina to take over the Galveston customs office, and for Francisco Duclor to move the Brazos customs office to Brazoria [Terán Jun-1832] – apparently not yet aware of the Battle of Velasco. Austin, still at Matamoros, is informed by Terán of these orders in a letter of the 27th, and he mentions it in additional letters back to Texas [Austin 29-Jun-1832, 1-Jul-1832] – all too late as the Battle of Velasco had already occurred. This was one of Terán's last official acts, as he committed suicide on 3-Jul-1832 behind a church in Padilla, Tamaulipas near his new headquarters, already ill and overworked, despondent over Mexican politics (since he had sided with the unsuccessful centralist regime that had just fallen to Santa Anna) and his belief that Texas was lost. Terán was replaced by Ignacio de Mora and then Vicente Filisola, who later wrote in his memoirs that he believed Terán had instead been assassinated by agents of Santa Anna. In Matamoros, Austin learned about the Battle of Velasco, and had also observed the arrival of José Antonio Mexía and troops from Tampico (in what has been termed Mexía's Expedition). The news from Texas prompted a truce with José Mariano Guerra of the Matamoros garrison [Mexía & Guerra 6-Jul-1832]. The letters from Texas mentioned in this reference most likely included Ugartechea's after-action report [Ugartechea 1-Jul-1832, Turner 1903 pp. 6-7]; the copy in the Beinecke Library is addressed directly to Terán, and may have been the one Mexía found when he "*overhauled a mail packet from Brazoria*". All agreed that Austin should then travel with Mexía and his troops by sea to Texas to help restore order [Guerra 7-Jul-1832b, Mexía 8-Jul-1832 & Austin 8-Jul-1832]. In Austin's letters, he boldly (and at length in his letter to Guerra) defended the Texians, saying they were actually defending the Mexican flag and constitution against corrupt officials violating them, and were not rebels or insurrectionists. Given Austin's character and track record, it is almost certain that he lobbied Mexía on the subject all the way to Texas. Mexía and Austin left the harbor of Matamoros (Brazos Santiago) on 14-Jul-1832 and arrived forty hours later at the mouth of the Brazos [Turner 1903, pp. 12-13].

Not yet having received Terán's now-obsolete orders, Ugartechea and his surviving troops seem to have detoured quickly to San Felipe de Austin, probably based on Músquiz's invitation, and he was reported to have arrived there on 8-Jul-1832 [Castaneda 1832], and he wrote letters from there on 8- and 10-Jul-1832, prior to their return overland to Matamoros [Ugartechea 8- & 10-Jul-1832a]. Moses Austin Bryan wrote about his uncle, Stephen F. Austin, being in San Felipe as well, and "*... the soldiers captured at Velasco being present, Austin embraced the officers and all sat down to a banquet of barbecued meat and had a joyous time ...*" [Bryan 1897 p. 105]. Since Austin has been reported to have only arrived back in Texas with Mexía on 16-Jul-1832 at the Brazos, Austin's presence in San Felipe would only be possible some days later, so perhaps Ugartechea and his troops lingered for some time at San Felipe, and were part of the welcome-back celebrations for Austin and general support for Mexican troops that had also declared for Santa Anna. Indeed, Lt. Juan Moret, an officer from Velasco that was directly mentioned several times by Ugartechea in his "after action report", was reported as toasting "*May the Supreme Being preserve the life of Colonel Austin to the citizens of Texas for twenty years and longer, so that they may have the benefit of his exertions to separate Texas from Coahuila, and form it into a state of the great Mexican Confederation, as the only means of securing its prosperity, and the true interests of the Mexican Republic.*" [Anthony 1832]. Austin apparently had reached San Felipe by 22-Jul-1832, as he wrote a letter from there asking Samuel May Williams to provide wagons and money to Ugartechea for travel on to La Bahía (Goliad) [Austin 22-Jul-1832], and this plan was followed a week later [Williams Jul-1832, McQueen 1832]. Land fees from Austin's Colony were used to finance the trip [Chriesman Oct-1832]. John J. Linn recollected the wounded troops passing through Guadalupe Victoria, apparently traveling south, writing "*I saw the Mexican soldiers as they passed through Victoria on the retreat to*

Matamoras. Many of them had received gun-shot wounds in the wrist, which were inflicted by the Americans while they were loading the cannon, which was mounted on a parapet above the walls of the fort. Colonel Ugartechea discovered after daylight that every one of his men that appeared exposed above the fort was instantly shot dead. He therefore ordered his gunners to cease firing, and in a short time made an overture of capitulation, which was accepted." [Linn 1986 p. 18].

Antonio Elosúa and José de las Piedras apparently had other ideas, perhaps even trying to follow Terán's last orders, as they had sent dispatches, respectively, on 7- and 16-Jul-1832 ordering Ugartechea to Anahuac to assume command after Bradburn's ignominious departure, and even mentions that Fort Velasco might be restored [Elosúa 7-Jul-1832, De las Piedras Jul-1832]. Terán's immediate successor, Ignacio de Mora, also wrote to support Ugartechea as replacement for Bradburn [de Mora 21-Jul-1832]. However, after receiving the letter of 7-Jul-1832 from Elosúa, Ugartechea argues from San Felipe in his letter of the 10th that he and his troops should return to Matamoros [Ugartechea 10-Jul-1832]. Elosúa agreed troops were needed back in Mexico to fight the rebellious forces of the Federalists from Veracruz and Tampico (i.e., Santa Anna) [Elosúa 17-Jul-1832].

After fighting rebels in Mexico, Ugartechea returned later to Texas by 1835 as military commander at San Antonio de Béxar presidio (replacing Elosúa) and was involved in the Texas Revolution. For example, it was under his orders that a cavalry unit from San Antonio de Béxar was sent to Gonzales to reclaim a small cannon in Oct-1835, resulting in the Battle Of Gonzales and the "Come and Take It" slogan, which has been considered the "first shot" of the Texas Revolution. He was also directly involved in the Battle of Concepcion and the Siege of Béxar, but had rear-line assignments during the rest of the Texas Revolution. After he returned again to Mexico, he was killed in action at Saltillo in 1839 during a federalist uprising.

The 1832 fort itself with arms, supplies and also the wounded were enumerated after the attack listing a brass 8-pound cannon and an "*iron swivle*" gun [Cotten 1832, Holley 1833 pp. 157-158], with a slightly different version listing a brass long nine pounder on a carriage, and an iron swivel (gun) on a block [Breedlove 1832]. The items were returned to General José Antonio Mexía after he arrived with five ships and 400 men (and Stephen F. Austin) at the mouth of the Brazos on 16-Jul-1832. The Texians received Mexía warmly, and convinced him they were not rebels against Mexico, but (like Mexía) were supporters of Santa Anna and the Mexican Constitution [Cotten 1832, Holley 1833]. Indeed, one part of the effort to convince Mexía was an evening "public dinner and ball" held at Brazoria in honor of Santa Anna (not present) on 22-Jul-1832, which has been revived in recent years as an annual costume ball and fund-raising program for the Brazoria Heritage Foundation called the Santa Anna Ball (the name of which has not been without controversy since Santa Anna became such an archenemy of Texans in the years after 1832). Indeed, the ever-faithful federalist Mexía fought against Santa Anna in 1834-1835 in Mexico once the latter assumed dictatorial power, ending in what is known as the unsuccessful Tampico Expedition, retreating by sea to the mouth of the Brazos in Dec-1835 and then to New Orleans for a few years. He returned to Mexico, suffering further military defeat, and was executed by Santa Anna near Puebla in 1839. The town of Mexia (in east Texas) was named in 1871 in honor of the Mexía family, at the site of their 1833 land grant.

Stephen F. Austin's sister (Emily Austin Bryan Perry) and her second husband (James F. Perry) had emigrated from Missouri to Texas in 1831, and James mentioned in one of his letters dated 6-Sep-1832 that "…. *the withdrawing of all the troops from our frontiers by the Santa Anna party has deprived us of another source for money but that change we are very willing to put up with as we were never very anxious to have troops quartered among us*" [Perry 1832]. A biographical Master's Thesis of James F. Perry was written in 1934 by another graduate student at the University of Texas, from Frio County, Lela Ethel McKinley (1905-1978), entitled "Life of James F. Perry" [McKinley 1934].

The civilian customs collector (Francisco Duclor) remained until 27-Sep-1832, transferring his office from Velasco to Brazoria soon after the battle [Duclor Jun-1832] where, like Pacho, he was made to feel unwelcome. Duclor had originally indicated his desire to return to Matamoros soon after the battle, asking Samuel May Williams to yet again assume the responsibility for collection of customs duties, which Williams (again) declined since he lived and worked at San Felipe [Duclor Jul-1832]. Duclor was ordered to stay at his post at Brazoria by José Antonio Mexía on the day after the "Santa Anna Ball", using Sub-Lieutenant Ignacio Domínguez as an assistant [Mexía 23-Jul-1832]. Duclor and Domínguez ultimately departed by sea to Tampico, though, frustrated in their efforts to continue collection of customs duties [Filisola 1848 I p. 126, Duclor Sep-1832]. Duclor must have traveled by way of New Orleans, as we find him writing from there in mid-November to Santa Anna, claiming that the "*Brazorianos*" (Texas colonists) were seeking full independence and prevented him from his customs duties, and he asks for further orders [Duclor Nov-1832]. Later, Stephen F. Austin thought Duclor's departure had been a bad move, as he said "*It would take a sheet or two of paper to tell you the extent of the injury that was done to all Texas by the departure of Duclor from Brazoria. He was a Santa Anna officer*" [Austin 1833].

Later, in Dec-1832, a feud developed between John Austin and William H. Wharton over Wharton's claim that he "*planned the whole attack at Velasco*" and Austin's counter-claim that Wharton wasn't even present for much of the engagement, when they competed against each other in an election for Brigadier General of the militia [John Austin 1832]. Although Austin won the election, he died the following year on 11-Aug-1833 during a serious cholera epidemic which struck the area.

There does not appear to be any direct evidence that the 1832 fort was ever used again, and it was probably robbed gradually of its wood and other materials as the town of Velasco grew up around the location beginning in the period of the Texas Revolution. It is believed that the site of the fort was set aside as an open block called Monument Square (commemorating either the fort and the battle, OR the Texian graves there), adjacent to Fort Street, as shown in two early plat maps of Velasco, shown in Figures 45 and 46 [Mesier 1837, Hunt 1838]. The former hypothesis might be understood by an advertisement by the Velasco Association for a ball and oration on the first anniversary of the victory, published in **The Constitutional Advocate And Texas Public Advertiser** newspaper on 15-Jun-1833, reproduced below in Figure 25.

Some credence to the latter hypothesis (about Monument Square being instead the site of Texian graves) is to be had from the previously mentioned article in the **Arkansas Advocate** newspaper, since it also mentioned the creation of a granite and marble Monument at the mouth of the Brazos to the men that perished at the Battle of Velasco [Bertrand 1833].

THE CONSTI TUTIONAL
ADVO CATE
AND TEXAS PUBLIC ADVERTISER.

VOL. I. NO. 36. BRAZORIA, SATURDAY, JUNE 15, 1833.

VELASCO ASSOCIATION
BALL.
[In commemoration of the capture of Fort Velasco.]

A *Splendid Anniversary Ball* will be given by the Proprietors, on the E-VENING OF THE **27TH JUNE** NEXT, in the Town of Velasco—to the participation of which, the friends of the Association, and the public generally, are respectfully invited.

By order of the Association,
  L. C. MANSON, Sec.
March 9, 1823—25tf

ORATION AT VELASCO.

An Oration will be delivered by B. T. Archer Esqr. on the 27 th of June, the anniversary of the victory gained at Velasco, by the constitutional forces, in 1832.

Figure 25: Newspaper advertisement published on first anniversary of Battle of Velasco
Courtesy of James L. Smith

Jeremiah Brown apparently continued to captain the schooner **Sabine**, as he is reported to have used this vessel to rescue people from a Brazos flood above Columbia in 1832. One family included that of Isaac C. Hoskins and his wife Nancy Spragins, living near Columbia, as well as her sixteen-year-old sister Francis Spragins. In a typescript manuscript dictated to her granddaughter in 1903, Francis recollected that Captain Brown rescued about 50 people from high water, anchoring to a large oak tree opposite Columbia. Later, they were married in Fall 1832 by "Judge Smith" until a Catholic priest (Father Aguentimienta) could sanctify the marriage, as required by Mexican law. They lived in Brazoria until 1833 and then in Velasco until 1835. She described it: "*Velasco was a small place with two hotels and three private houses.*" Later, she described her husband as captain of the **Invincible**, as well as evacuating Velasco aboard a sloop to New Orleans ahead of the Mexican army during 1836, and travel on to New York and Providence (home of the Brown family) before returning to Texas in Oct-1837. Here, Captain Brown resigned from the Texas Navy, and became collector for the Port of Velasco. She states "*In 1839, Capt. Brown died and is buried in Texas, on the banks of the Brazos River.*" – this is believed by the author to be the old Velasco Cemetery (later known as the Shannon Family Cemetery). She stayed in Texas, living with the Hoskins family again until 1844 when she traveled back east, eventually marrying Mr. Charles Raine [Raine 1903].

Another episode of Jeremiah Brown as captain of the **Sabine** involved a voyage from New Orleans to Velasco in Apr-1833 carrying some notable passengers, Alexander Somervell, David Ayres and George Bernard Erath [Erath 1923]. Erath, a native of Vienna and later a Texas surveyor, soldier and legislator, recollected that *"Brazoria at this time was perhaps the most prominent shipping point in Texas. Galveston had no inhabitants. Harrisburg was a little town to which schooners and small craft brought goods from New Orleans. Neither Houston nor Galveston was laid off until after the battle of San Jacinto. Matagorda on the Colorado and Anahuac on the Trinity were smaller shipping points. The Brazos was deemed navigable to Bell's Landing, ten miles above Brazoria. During the revolution of the year 1832 the Texans took sides with Santa Anna, and expelled the Mexican garrison at the mouth of the Brazos, as well as all others in Texas east of the San Antonio River. After this engagement in June, 1832, the town of Velasco was laid off near the site of the battle, and now it had about fifty inhabitants. The houses were mere shanties <u>with one unfinished two-story building</u> – its sides half open. The making of salt from water obtained from salt wells near the beach comprised its business, and this was conducted on a very small scale by the two brothers Porter."* The two-story building is likely to have become the hotel and tavern owned by brothers-in-law and partners Jeremiah Brown and Isaac C. Hoskins, later known as the American Hotel.

The man who would later serve the fourth and last term as President of the Republic of Texas, Anson Jones, arrived in Texas at Velasco on 20-Oct-1833, traveling aboard yet-another trip of the **Sabine** from New Orleans under Jeremiah Brown [Jones 1859 p. 8-9 & 104, Gambrell 1948 p. 1]. Originally from New England and trained as a doctor, he had met Jeremiah Brown in New Orleans and had been persuaded to come to Texas, with the aim of opening an office in Brazoria. Initially, he did not take a favorable impression of the area and wished to return to New Orleans, but was convinced to stay for a while, and ending up staying the rest of his life. He wrote in his Private Memoirs *"... and finally abandoning myself to a fate which appeared I could not control or direct, I passively floated as it were upon a tide which bore me to Texas; and the sixteen following years have been to me comparatively prosperous and successful ones. ... I have succeeded in every thing I attempted, and accomplished every thing I undertook. ... In Texas, therefore, I commenced the world anew, profiting by my severe experience in its roughest ways. I have also had constantly before my eyes a conviction from which I have been unable to escape, that somehow or other the destiny of Texas was interwoven with my own, that they were indissoluble, and that the one materially depended on the other."*

After Terán's death, Vicente Filisola served as Commander General of the Eastern Interior Provinces, and was ordered to re-establish customs houses in 1833 with George Fisher as collector [Austin 1833, Pavón 1832, Perez y Calleja 1834 #'s 12-16, Parmenter et al 1959, Filisola 1848 I p. 134-136], but this customs house appears to have never been implemented due to lack of resources (especially troops), and free-trade practices became the norm again until early 1835, when the Mexican government made still another attempt to establish customs houses at Anahuac, Galveston Island and at the Brazos. The mystery about Fisher's missing *"detailed account"* of Texian misdeeds from 1830 to 1831 might be explained by a letter he wrote to Austin in this period of 1833, obviously bitter about his lack of success as administrator of customs, and estrangement from Texas. He accused Austin of leading efforts against him, and tried to blackmail Austin to stop maligning his reputation [Fisher 1833]. It almost seems Fisher really wanted to settle in Texas, so withheld doing maximum harm there, but seemed to threaten Austin at the same time. Fisher continued unsuccessfully to become Administrator of Galveston customs into 1834 [Perez y Calleja 1834 #'s 17-19] while occupying a number of government posts and then publishing a newspaper in Matamoros [Fisher 1830s]. Based on Fisher's federalist sympathies, which were then out of favor with Santa Anna's government, he was eventually expelled from the Republic of

Mexico in Sep-1835, leaving aboard the schooner *Henrrique* [Cos 1835] to New Orleans, where he assisted his old supporter, Lorenzo de Zavala, in the Tampico Expedition.

During the summer of 1834, Col. Juan Almonte was dispatched to make an inspection of Texas, and he wrote a thorough but secret statistical report. A modern translation is available [Almonte 2005]. In this report, he describes the Department of Brazos, enumerating each "municipalidad" (a term for the district administered by its main town). One interesting statistic is a general census of the towns and districts (Velasco was then part of the Columbia *municipalidad* and administered by their *ayuntamiento*), originally the Brazoria *municipalidad* before 1834 [Hardy & Roberts 1910 p. 356-357]. The modern reference [Almonte 2005 p. 245] has a table of the results:

Districts and towns	District Population	Town Population
+San Felipe	2500	400
+Columbia (aka Brazoria)	2100	150
+Matagorda	1400	250
+Gonzales	900	340
+Mina (aka Bastrop)	1100	210
	--------	--------
	8000	1350

Amos A. Parker visited Texas, passing down the Brazos in late 1834, and wrote *"A small town called Velasco is situated on the sandy beach, at the river's mouth—containing one public house, two stores, four or five dwelling houses, and* the ruins of an old Spanish fort. *The mouth of the Brazos, and a long distance on the seashore, is lined with large masses of trees; and from this source the inhabitants of Velasco obtain their fuel."* [Parker 1836 pp. 220-222].

Another customs collector, José Gonzalez, was appointed by the government of Santa Anna as the new administrator for Galveston customs; he arrived from Tampico to New Orleans on 19-Nov-1834, and then took ship aboard the *San Felipe* for Brazoria [Martinez 1834]. He is reported to have arrived at Velasco in early 1835 [Filisola 1848 II p. 35, Johnson 1914 pp. 200-201] moving to Brazoria by Aug- 1835, but he was no more successful than Pacho, Duclor or Antonio Tenorio [Gray Aug-1835 p. 1, Barker Jan-1901 p. 194, Barker 1905].

Mary Austin Holley visited Velasco again while coming and going on a May-Jun 1835 trip up the Brazos River [Holley 1965]. She had initially traveled from New Orleans aboard the schooner *San Felipe* under Capt. Fuller of Sandwich, Massachusetts, arriving at Velasco in early May. In her diary entry of 10-May-1835, she wrote about how Velasco had changed since her last visit in 1831 *"Then it was a garrison with a few ragged looking Mexican troops, presenting little appearance of comfort. Now it has two good boarding houses for the accommodation of travellers with a domestic look & air of comfort – nothing military in the aspect - no one to demand passports. On the opposite point ... stands McKenney's ware house to increase the show of prosperity."* [Holley 1965 p. 14]. Apparently, upon her return to the mouth of the Brazos on or about 10-Jun-1835, while awaiting favorable tides and winds aboard the same vessel, she drew a series of four sketches of Velasco and Quintana [Holley 1965 pp. 16-18, Earls et al

1996 pp. 302-307]. In the latter reference, the researchers concluded that three of the images could be combined into a panoramic view of Velasco and the river mouth, and indeed this composite image was used for the cover art of that report, and is shown in Figure 26 below. The researchers also surmised that the two left-most buildings were to the left of posts that might be the ruins of the 1832 fort, as seen in the background (red ring).

Figure 26: Panoramic compilation of Mary Austin Holley sketches
Courtesy of Prewitt & Associates

In 1845, the property involving the Archer House (Lots 4, 5, 6 and 7 of Block 13 and Lots 1 and 10 of Block 29 – *see Figure 45 or 46 for lot numbers*) was sold with the comment "*...... all that certain parcel of property lying and situated in the Town of Velasco known as the 'Archer House' with the four lots immediately adjoining said 'Archer House' and not including the two lots near what was called the 'Old Fort'.*" [Brazoria 1845, Smith Sep-2014]. Since the Republic of Texas battery was located in Block 61, this seemingly can only refer to the 1832 fort. Lots 4 and 7 were on the river side of the Archer House, so may have been the ones not sold, and may be nearest the "Old Fort". Lots 8 and 9 of Block 13 were purchased by James Thompson Shannon (1818-1883) in 1856 [Smith Dec-2014], immediately adjacent to Lot 7. The "Archer House" was bought in 1855 by John H. Herndon, and was known afterwards as the "Archer-Herndon House" or simply the "Herndon Beach Home" [Smith Sep-2014].

In 1898, Adele B. Looscan (1848-1935) published a seminal article entitled "The Old Mexican Fort at Velasco" [Looscan 1898], apparently after interviewing several lifelong residents of the area. In this article, the second wife of James T. Shannon (Mrs. Ellen Adele Wilcox Shannon, m. 12-Jun-1862) claimed her residence (in Lots 8 and 9 of Velasco Block 13, fronting on the southeast side of <u>Fort</u> Street) as the site of the Mexican fort. To quote Mrs. Looscan "*The exact location of the old fort is attended with difficulty, on account of the changes wrought by winds and waves. In the course of sixty-six years accretions of land on the eastern shore of the river have been so marked, that a certain locality known to old residents as the site of the old fort, and which was quite near the river bank and gulf shore, is now several hundred feet from the former, while the gulf shore line extends a full quarter of a mile or more beyond its original boundary. These changes were effected chiefly by the destructive storms of 1875 and 1886, which submerged nearly all of this low lying coast section. ... Mrs. Ellen A. Shannon, who was born at Velasco in 1841, her parents, Henry C. and Pamela Wilcox, having moved there in 1837, gives a reliable account of the old fort, which, she says, is now marked by her own residence. She lived continuously at Velasco until August, 1863, when she and her husband, James T. Shannon, moved away, not returning until June, 1867. Before their departure, her husband had often called her attention to one of the posts or upright logs of the old fort, with muskets stuck in it.*" Mr. Alexander Glass Follett, Sr. (1822-1906) agreed, and also added that Mrs. Shannon's house was newly built in 1887, after the previous structure was damaged in the 1886 hurricane. In 1852 (when Ellen Wilcox was 11 years old), the U. S. Coast Survey (USCS) charted the upper Texas coast, producing a series of drawings, one of which was known as T-Sheet or Chart# T00375 for the area from San Luis Pass southwest to a watch station called Jupiter (today's Bryan Beach). A detail of Velasco from this map is shown below in Figure 27, with the location highlighted (red oval) of the house that James T. Shannon would buy in 1855 – please notice the unusual circle next to the structure (perhaps a remnant of the central mound and cannon bastion? – or that upright log?).

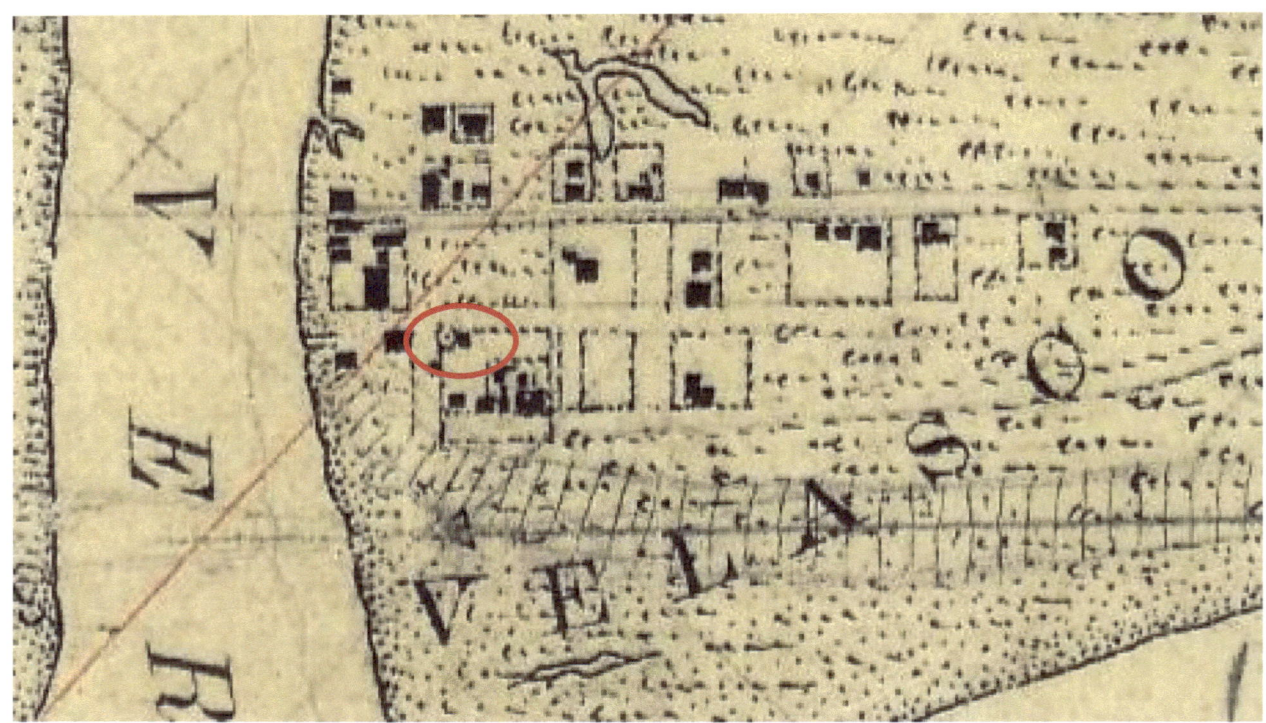

Figure 27: Detail from 1852 USCS Chart T00375

NOAA's Historical Map & Chart Collection

Frontispiece found in [Dienst 1909]; original source is unknown

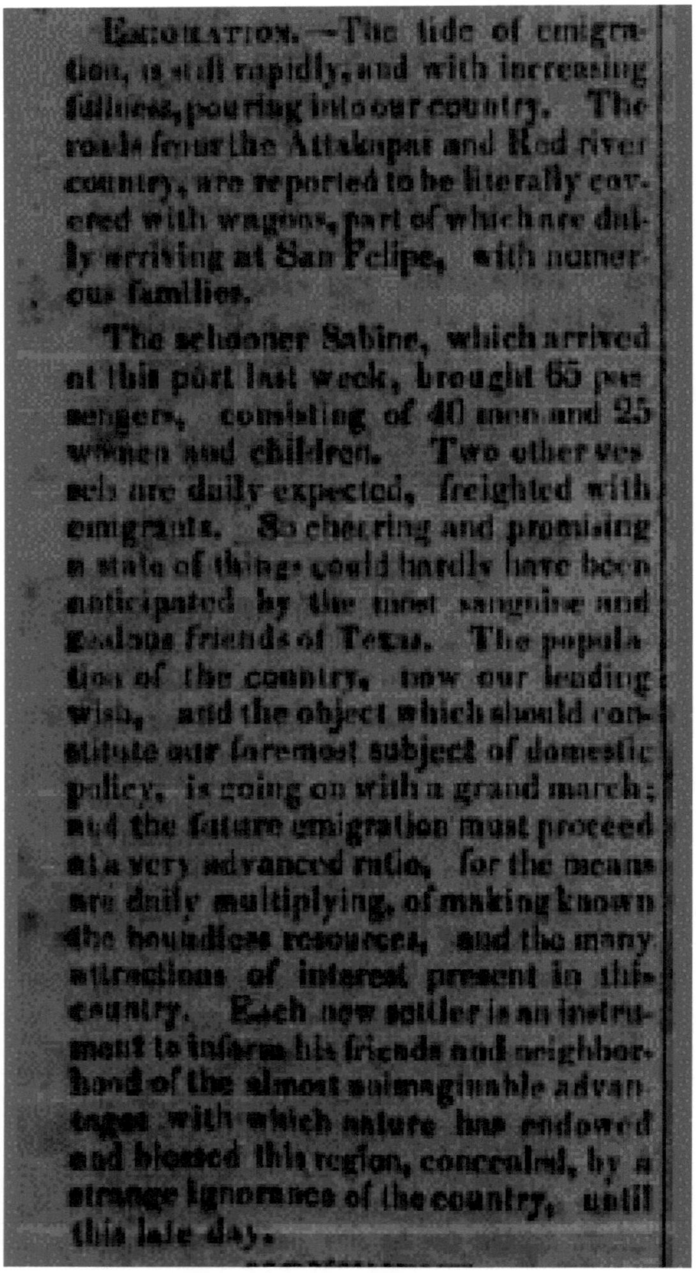

EMIGRATION.—The tide of emigration, is still rapidly, and with increasing fullness, pouring into our country. The roads from the Attakapas and Red river country, are reported to be literally covered with wagons, part of which are daily arriving at San Felipe, with numerous families.

The schooner Sabine, which arrived at this port last week, brought 65 passengers, consisting of 40 men and 25 women and children. Two other vessels are daily expected, freighted with emigrants. So cheering and promising a state of things could hardly have been anticipated by the most sanguine and zealous friends of Texas. The population of the country, now our leading wish, and the object which should constitute our foremost subject of domestic policy, is going on with a grand march; and the future emigration must proceed at a very advanced ratio, for the means are daily multiplying, of making known the boundless resources, and the many attractions of interest present in this country. Each new settler is an instrument to inform his friends and neighborhood of the almost unimaginable advantages with which nature has endowed and blessed this region, concealed, by a strange ignorance of the country, until this late day.

Figure 28: Emigration article in Arkansas Advocate, 6-Apr-1833, page 2, column 1

In the period after Terán's "six-fort plan" had failed, and Mexican troops had abandoned eastern and southeastern Texas, immigration and trade with the United States continued and even increased, as is mentioned in an article in the *Arkansas Advocate*, reprinted from a New Orleans newspaper about a meeting at San Felipe, citing both overland routes and arrivals on the schooner *Sabine* at Velasco [Bertrand 1833], see Figure 28.

The mouth of the Brazos continued to be the major port of Texas, as revealed in a comment made by Samuel May Williams on 31-Mar-1835 to Stephen F. Austin "*In Jany and Feby 2000 persons arrived in at the mouth of the Brazos. Emigration has been tremendous this year, and still continues.*" [Williams 1835, Cantrell 1999 p. 299]. This was largely ignored by the Mexican federal government, as Santa Anna was preoccupied with uprisings in various Mexican provinces against his increasingly centralist rule. However, as these rebellions were put down, Santa Anna decided it was time to return his attention to the unruly northern province of Texas.

Captain Antonio Tenorio arrived with two officers and thirty-four soldiers at Anahuac on or about 23-Jan-1835, although these efforts were not very successful due to increasing opposition from the Texas colonists [Filisola 1848 II pp. 34-36, Barker Jan-1901, Dienst 1909 pp. 1-2], causing a second round of the Anahuac Disturbances, in which a group of about 30 Texians commanded by William Barret Travis ejected Tenorio from Anahuac on or about 20-Jun-1835 [Johnson 1914 pp. 209-211]. This same reference has many details about the ferment that followed this event on pages 199-262, by a direct participant, which appear to have laid the tinder for the Texas Revolution of 1835-1836.

The Mexican naval presence along the Texas coast was also increased, including the lightly armed schooner *Correo Mexicano* and the schooner *Montezuma* (later renamed *Bravo*), with orders to enforce immigration and customs provisions which had been laxly enforced for several years [Powers 2006 p.

18]. Mexico was also in the process of acquiring and deploying even larger vessels within the next year or two [Thompson 2020], such as the *Libertador*. The *Montezuma* captured an American merchant ship arriving near Galveston Bay, the *Martha* (on 7-May-1835) and the McKinney & Williams schooner *Columbia* at anchor off Velasco ten days later, taking passengers as prisoners and seizing their personal property [Lamar 1836, McKinney 1870, Wells 1998] – a step that had not before been practiced. Another version has the *Correo* capturing the *Columbia* off Quintana [Powers 2006 p. 18]. The new customs collector at the Brazos (Gonzalez) is reported to have come aboard the *Montezuma* to accompany the captured ships when they were taken south to Veracruz or Matamoros [Lamar 1836]. In reaction (especially to Americans being taken prisoner), the U.S. revenue cutter *Ingham* was dispatched from New Orleans, found *Montezuma* near Brazos Santiago in Jun-1835, and exchanged fire in what is known as the Ingham Incident. *Ingham* was later to be sold to Texas interests and rechristened *Independence*. After the ejection of Tenorio, the Mexican ships were additionally ordered to blockade the Texas coast by General Martín Perfecto de Cos, who then landed at Cópano at the head of 300 troops, marching them to La Bahía and then San Antonio de Béxar, to put down any resistance in Texas.

These newly harsh conditions helped shift public opinion in Texas to believe, first in rebellion against Santa Anna to reclaim their rights under the Mexican Constitution of 1824 [Hancock 2020] but, as Santa Anna's "scorched earth" practices became clear in early 1836, this struggle blossomed into a blood fight for full independence. An excellent summary of these political developments in (what would become) Brazoria County was written by Forrest Elmer Ward [Ward 1960, Ward 1962]. He describes that this area was originally part of Austin's Colony, later organized by the Mexican Government Of Texas in 1834 as the Department of the Brazos, and played an important role in the change of attitudes leading to the Texas Revolution. The origin of the "Lone Star" in the emerging Texas flags has even been ascribed to the fact that Texas was, at this point, the sole remaining Mexican state fighting for federalism [Hancock 2020].

In this period, one Francis J. Haskins advertised as a harbor pilot for the mouth of the Brazos, as indicated in a notice dated 9-May-1835 (Figure 29) in the *Texas Republican* newspaper, and later as a shipwright at Velasco. The notice was published in many issues including those of 9-May-1835 (p. 3), 6-

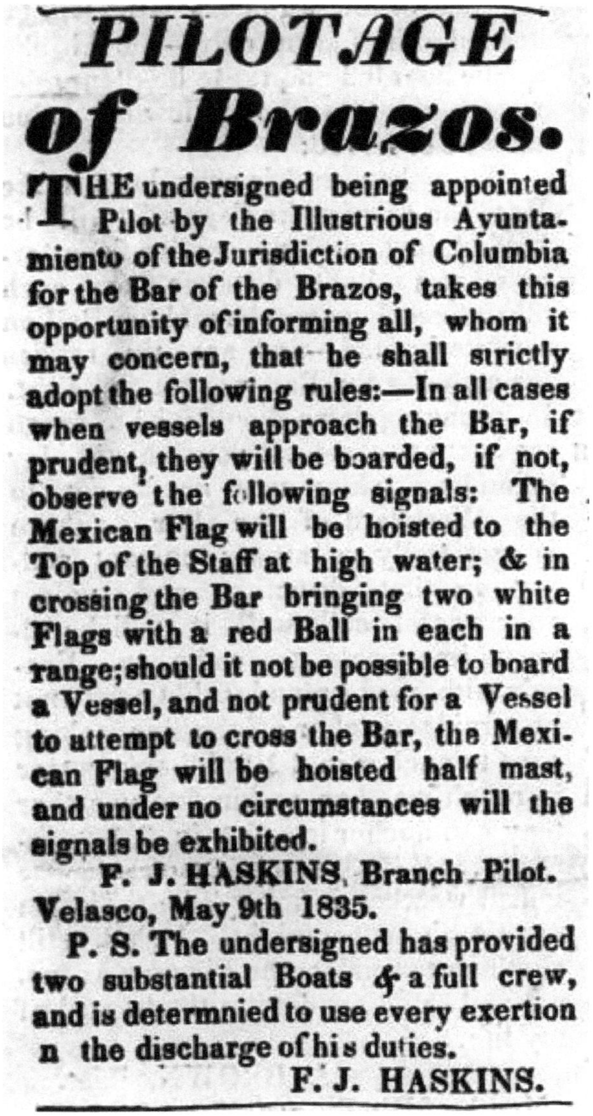

PILOTAGE of Brazos.

THE undersigned being appointed Pilot by the Illustrious Ayuntamiento of the Jurisdiction of Columbia for the Bar of the Brazos, takes this opportunity of informing all, whom it may concern, that he shall strictly adopt the following rules:—In all cases when vessels approach the Bar, if prudent, they will be boarded, if not, observe the following signals: The Mexican Flag will be hoisted to the Top of the Staff at high water; & in crossing the Bar bringing two white Flags with a red Ball in each in a range; should it not be possible to board a Vessel, and not prudent for a Vessel to attempt to cross the Bar, the Mexican Flag will be hoisted half mast, and under no circumstances will the signals be exhibited.

F. J. HASKINS, Branch Pilot.
Velasco, May 9th 1835.

P. S. The undersigned has provided two substantial Boats & a full crew, and is determnied to use every exertion n the discharge of his duties.

F. J. HASKINS.

Figure 29: Notice in Texas Republican issue of 25-Jul-1835 (page 4, column 1)

Jun-1835 (p. 1), 20-Jun-1835 (p. 1), 27-Jun-1835 (p. 1), 4-Jul-1835 (p. 1), 18-Jul-1835 (p. 1), 25-Jul-1835 (p. 4), 8-Aug-1835 (p. 3), 22-Aug-1835 (p. 3), 19-Sep-1835 (p. 4), 26-Sep-1835 (p. 4), 3-Oct-1835 (p. 4), 10-Oct-1835 (p. 4), 17-Oct-1835 (p. 4), 24-Oct-1835 (p. 1), 31-Oct-1835 (p. 4), 14-Nov-1835 (p. 3) and probably others.

At the same time, Jeremiah Brown had apparently settled down at Velasco, no longer the captain of commercial schooners, and was also acting as pilot for the mouth of the Brazos, as indicated in a notice dated 23-May-1835 (Figure 30) also in the ***Texas Republican*** newspaper issues of 20-Jun-1835 (p. 4), 27-Jun-1835 (p. 4), 4-Jul-1835 (p. 2), 25-Jul-1835 (p. 3). Circumstances are not clear, but he may have been working with or in competition with Francis J. Haskins. Sometimes, these Haskins and Brown notices appeared (separately) in the same issue of the newspaper. As we shall see, though, Jeremiah Brown was soon destined to go back to sea, in a heavily armed vessel.

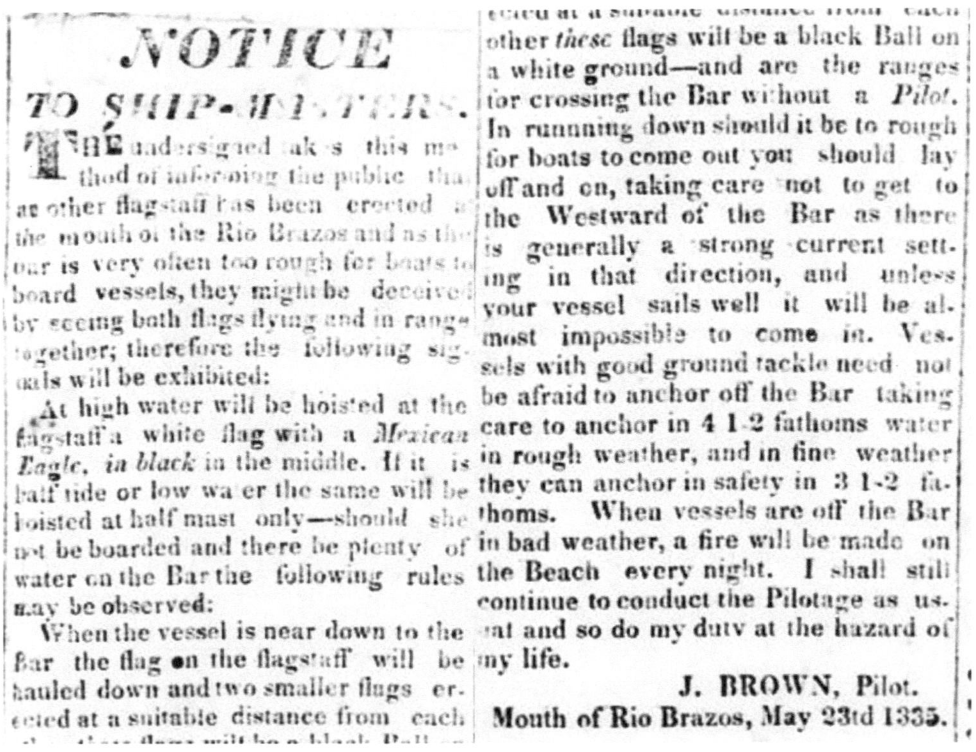

NOTICE

TO SHIP-MASTERS.

THE undersigned takes this method of informing the public that another flagstaff has been erected at the mouth of the Rio Brazos and as the bar is very often too rough for boats to board vessels, they might be deceived by seeing both flags flying and in range together; therefore the following signals will be exhibited:

At high water will be hoisted at the flagstaff a white flag with a *Mexican Eagle, in black* in the middle. If it is half tide or low water the same will be hoisted at half mast only—should she not be boarded and there be plenty of water on the Bar the following rules may be observed:

When the vessel is near down to the Bar the flag on the flagstaff will be hauled down and two smaller flags erected at a suitable distance from each other *these* flags will be a black Ball on a white ground—and are the ranges for crossing the Bar without a *Pilot*.

In running down should it be to rough for boats to come out you should lay off and on, taking care not to get to the Westward of the Bar as there is generally a strong current setting in that direction, and unless your vessel sails well it will be almost impossible to come in. Vessels with good ground tackle need not be afraid to anchor off the Bar taking care to anchor in 4 1-2 fathoms water in rough weather, and in fine weather they can anchor in safety in 3 1-2 fathoms. When vessels are off the Bar in bad weather, a fire will be made on the Beach every night. I shall still continue to conduct the Pilotage as usual and so do my duty at the hazard of my life.

J. BROWN, Pilot.

Mouth of Rio Brazos, May 23td 1835.

Figure 30: Notice in Texas Republican issue of 27-Jun-1835 (page 4, column 3)

As mentioned previously, the Battle of Gonzales has often been presented as the first significant event or "First Shot" of the Texas Revolution, yet more-serious happenings at Velasco presaged even this event. The leading sentence of the book "**Thunder on the Gulf**" leads off with "*The merchant schooner **San Felipe** under full sail and with a fair wind behind, was beating in for Velasco, the Texas trading port at the mouth of the Brazos River*." [Douglas 1936]. The ship was carrying trade goods, munitions and two important passengers, Stephen F. Austin (returning from twenty months of imprisonment in Mexico City via Veracruz and New Orleans) and Lorenzo de Zavala (former minister for Santa Anna, now a political refugee). Captain William A. Hurd had armed the ship in New Orleans with two six-pound waist guns and small arms for the crew, and armored it with bales of cotton. Waiting at anchor off Velasco was the blockading gunboat ***Correo Mexicano*** of the Mexican navy, captained by the notorious Thomas M. "Mexico" Thompson, who had just captured the American brig ***Tremont*** earlier in the day without apparent justification [Hayes 1879 1:133 & 2:818-819, Bryan 1897 pp. 107-108, Dienst 1909 pp. 2-4, Underwood 1927 p. 24, Francaviglia 1998 pp. 108-109]. The ***Correo*** is variously listed as a sloop-of-war [Dienst 1909 p. 2, Hooton 1847 p. 17] and as a schooner [Winthrop 1835, Brown 1887 p. 62, Underwood

1927 p. 24]. Although the *San Felipe* appeared to have slipped past the Mexican warship into the Brazos bar on 1-Sep-1835, the owner Thomas F. McKinney observed the situation from land (seeing the *San Felipe* was the *Correo*'s next target), and then loaded some armed volunteers aboard his steamer *Laura* to challenge the *Correo*. First swapping out the passengers for the volunteers, the *San Felipe* assisted by the *Laura* went after the becalmed *Correo* and captured her after a cannon duel and overnight sea chase, eventually sending its officers (in irons) and the ship to New Orleans to be charged with piracy [Gray 19-Sep-1835, p.2, 17-Oct-1835 pp. 1-2 & 24-Oct-1835 p. 4, Winthrop 1835, Parker 1836 pp. 330-331, Yoakum 1855 I:356-361, McKinney 1870, Wooten 1898 pp. I:177-178, Dienst 1909, Weems 1971 pp. 39-40, Puryear & Winfield 1976 pp. 44-46, Hill 1987 pp. 26-29, Cantrell 1999 pp. 308-310, Meed 2001 pp. 32-35, Jordan 2006 pp. 10-18, Thompson 2020 pp. 49-53,218-223]. Perhaps the most thorough version of this episode, including the complex series of preceding and causative events, is given by John Powers in his book "**The First Texas Navy**" [Powers 2006 pp. 28-33]. Author and artist Sherman Allen "Al" Thompson II, rendered a pencil drawing of the incident, shown in Figure 31.

Figure 31: Image found in [Thompson 2020, p. 51] - Original caption below:
"The early morning engagement between the Texas San Felipe and the Mexican revenue cutter Correo, signaling the start of the Texas Revolution, September 1 and 2, 1835

Courtesy of Sherman A. Thompson III

Among the "munitions" in the hold of the *San Felipe* were one or two 18-pound cannon, one of which was soon unloaded at Velasco, intended for mounting in a shore battery there [Johnson 2015 pp. 340-

348] – more on that later. It was no wonder that Thomas McKinney did not want the *San Felipe* captured by any of the Mexican blockading vessels.

The episode has been described as the San Felipe Incident, and was the last step in convincing Stephen F. Austin in favor of Texas rebellion [Humphries 1932, Binkley 1952 p. 63, Weems 1971 pp. 39-40]. One might imagine his confused state of mind as he left Mexico after being imprisoned, and gone from Texas for over two years. One clue comes from a striking letter he wrote to his cousin, Mary Austin Holley, from New Orleans once his mail was safe from Mexican postal thieves [Austin 21-Aug-1835, Johnson 1914 pp. 145-147, Cantrell 1999 pp. 307-308]. In this letter, he seems to unburden himself of Texas political thoughts as he states "... *Texas should be effectually, and fully Americanized ...*", while pleading for increased immigration to help force the matter. He never writes the word "*revolution*", but slyly writes "*A gentle breeze shakes off a ripe peach.*" - he knows not whether it can be a strong politically American province of Mexico, or perhaps bought by the U.S., or indeed its own land. This is not the same Stephen F. Austin, who once held to the motto "Fidelity to Mexico". Another rendition of this incident is shown below, a painting by famed maritime artist Peter Rindlisbacher.

Figure 32: Painting by Peter Rindlisbacher "Night Battle: San Felipe Vs. Correo, 1835"
Courtesy of Peter Rindlisbacher

As Austin's nephew recollected on that first evening back on Texas soil, "... *he walked the beach until late at night, hoping to hear or see something of the vessels. Next day the **Laura** returned with the intelligence of the capture of the **Correo**. Austin saw in this the beginning of trouble.*" [Bryan 1897 p. 108]. William Binkley's little volume of four speeches is perhaps the best starting point for any student of the Texas Revolution, where he concluded that Austin "... *was gradually coming to the conclusion that the ultimate solution to the problem must be complete separation from Mexico ...*" [Binkley 1952 p. 62]. Gregg Cantrell also wrote in his biography of Austin "*But in his own mind he had already reached the most critical conclusion: Texas must be free from Mexico .... The question was no longer one of ends, but of means.*" [Cantrell 1999 p. 309]. John Powers also wrote that "*.... Within days of the episode Stephen F.*

Austin ... called publicly at Brazoria for a general consultation of the people to decide what course Texas should now pursue in the mounting political process. The convening of the General Consultation followed." [Powers 2006 p. 33]. Writing of the incident some years later, Charles W. Hayes claimed the circumstances of the San Felipe Incident were known in advance by Thomas McKinney and Samuel May Williams, but wrote "*This was the first naval triumph, and was one of the principal causes that led to the proclamation of war, and its success is justly due to the boldness and daring of Col. McKinney*" [Hayes 1879 2:818-819]. Chester Newell described this period as "*... the event which, more than anything else, operated to change the public sentiment of Texas, was the arrival of their respected commissioner, Stephen F. Austin, early in September, 1835.*" and he quotes Austin's entire address to the citizens of Brazoria on 8-Sep-1835 (perhaps from the Brazoria **Texas Republican** newspaper issue of 19-Sep-1835), followed by the comment "*This advice of Austin worked like leaven; the people rapidly came over in sentiment to the rescue of their rights.*" [Newell 1838 pp. 45-48; pp. 54-55 in 2015 edition]. Careful reading of Austin's address, though, reveals no call for the <u>independence</u> of Texas from Mexico, only revolution against Santa Anna's government to protect Texans' rights. As Ruby Cumby Smith wrote, "*Their revolution passed through two distinct phases: (1) a defence of the Mexican Republic Constitution of 1824, in an effort to secure the cooperation of Mexican Liberals who opposed military despotism; (2) a struggle for absolute independence.*" [Ruby Smith 1919, p. I-79].

In the Brazoria newspaper (**Texas Republican**) issue of 26-Sep-1835, notices were published over the names of Branch T. Archer and Stephen F. Austin, clearing calling for revolution and war, as well as militia orders to assemble [Gray 26-Sep-1835 pp. 2-3]. One excerpt from this newspaper was from a circular published by Stephen F. Austin at San Felipe on 22-Sep-1835 in response to the San Felipe Incident and Cos' landing of troops at Cópano on 20-Sep-1835 (and Cos' demand that some Texians be turned over to him), stating "*An expedition is now raising in the lower country to take the field at once. They are called upon to rendezvous at League's old place on the Colorado on the 28th of this month. Every man in Texas is called upon to take up arms in defence of his country and his rights. Those who can join the expedition are requested to do so or they can join it at James Kerr's on the Lavaca which will the principal rendezvous. A Corps of reserve will be formed to march on and sustain the advance. Those who cannot join the advance are requested to unite with the reserve and report themselves to the Committee of Safety in this place.*" Thus, the San Felipe Incident was important not only as a <u>sign</u> that the Texas Revolution was already underway but, more profoundly, was also a major proximate <u>cause</u> of it, since it convinced "The Father of Texas", perhaps the most influential man among the Texians, to rebel against the government of Santa Anna in Sep-1835, after which things moved rapidly to open revolt [Binkley 1952 pp. 65-67]. No less an authority than the Texas State Library and Archives agrees, as their web page for the San Felipe Incident accurately describes it as the "**Opening Shot of the Texas Revolution**", which occurred about one month prior to the Battle of Gonzales.

An engraving (Figure 33) often cited as the **Laura** is captioned only as "*Navigating Buffalo Bayou in Early Days*" in a 1926 pamphlet [Farrar 1926], and appears to be specifically mentioned as the **Laura** in a 1951 newspaper supplement as "*The actual history of Port Houston began late in 1836 or early 1837 when the first steamboat operated above Harrisburg. The **Laura**, fated to go down as the first steamboat into Houston, took four days to make the eight-mile trip from Harrisburg to Houston, because of sunken logs, overhanging trees and thick foliage. She had to stop for hours while overhanging trees and vines were cut down or log jams blown up. An old woodcut shows passengers passing the long hours of unforced delays by shooting alligators.*" [Citizen 1951]. The original image is also reported to actually be from Florida, but is found in a Texas book of 1883 describing a ride up Buffalo Bayou from Galveston to Houston, captioned as "*Coming Up The Bayou.*" [Sweet & Knox 1883, p. 40-41].

Figure 33: Drawing of an early steamer on Buffalo Bayou, sometimes attributed as the Laura

This connection may be why a model of great resemblance was created by Burton D. Reckles (included below as Figure 34) as the *Laura*, now found at the Houston Maritime Museum.

Figure 34: Model of steamboat Laura at the Houston Maritime Museum

The maritime artist Peter Rindlisbacher has made a painting of a slightly different design for the *Laura*, featured at its arrival at (what would become) Houston, illustrated below in Figure 35.

Figure 35: "First Arrival: Steamboat Laura at the Port of Houston, January 1837"
Courtesy of Peter Rindlisbacher

This scene was based on a drawing by Edward Johns (circa 1840), as shown in his journal [Johns 1841 p. 1], shown in Figure 36 – please note the name on the sidewheel.

Thompson had previously earned the ire of the Texians by threatening the citizens of Anahuac not to form a militia [Thompson 1835], apparently in response to Tenorio's surrender in June. In an 1847 book, based on a visit to Galveston in the early 1840s, Charles Hooton wrote *"On inquiry, I found that Thompson (an Englishman, I believe by birth) had several years previously been a*

Figure 36: Detail from Edward Johns journal, apparently labeled as Laura

captain of a sloop-of-war in the Mexican service. During the latter end of the year 1835, he was ordered to Galveston Bay for the purpose, it was stated, of ascertaining the facts connected with certain troubles that had previously taken place at Anahuac between the Mexican Government and the people there. Thompson, however, improved upon these orders (if they were his orders), and at once attacked, captured, and carried off an American vessel, then engaged in the Texas trade, and which at the time chanced by ill luck to fall in his way. This act was regarded by the inhabitants as a virtual declaration of war on the part of Mexico, and the highest indignation was expressed toward the individual aggressor himself." [Hooton 1847 p. 17]. Thompson also refused to grant a permit and then later seized a schooner bound for Velasco, and "*... declared the port of Brazos in a state of Blockade, and should take all vessels entering there as prizes ...*" and also "*... that all vessels and persons on board thereof, found sailing in the waters of Texas or on its coast without a permit from him or in his absence from the Captain of the port, when found, were liable to be seized and pressed into the Mexican service.*" [Yates et al 1835]. John H. Brown described him as "*... the notorious scoundrel known as 'English Thompson' was on the coast as a naval officer in command of the Mexican war schooner **Correo**. He was both a ruffian and a tyrant, and had, as assumed commander of all the ports on the Texas coast, made him odious to the people.*" [Brown 1887 p. 62]. However, in 1837 while at Matamoros, Thompson assisted William H. Wharton and George Wheelwright (among others) in escaping captivity, and fled to Texas, apparently wishing to switch sides [Hill 1987 pp. 78-79]. According to Thompson's entry in the Handbook of Texas, Sam Houston rewarded him by naming him commander at Velasco (not yet confirmed with period documents), and George Wheelwright then appointed him commander of the new Texas Navy Yard at Galveston as of 2-Feb-1838 [Thompson 18-May-1838], perhaps as a reward for helping Wheelwright and Wharton's escape from a Matamoros prison. At that point, he wrote that the Galveston property was "*... not a Navy yard, but an open space of ground staked out only, but without any fence or partition whatever nor any building except that known as the armory which was then used as a bedroom for the Carpenter.*" About this same time, Andrew Neill described it as "*... a navy-yard of no mean pretensions had sprung up near the foot of Twenty-eighth street, on the bay side. Here a marine depot was established, a powder-house built and the nucleus of a navy yard commenced.*" [Hayes 1879, pp. 293-294]. Thompson served in the Texas Navy only until 9-May-1838 [Thompson 26-May-1838], and, while in Galveston, was often the center of controversy [Hayes 1879 1:392-393, Epperson 1991]. In 1841, he died in a drunken brawl in a Tampico bar when his pistol misfired, and instead he suffered a blast from a double-barreled shotgun [Hooton 1847 pp. 18-19, Jordan 2006 p. 114, Powers 2006 p. 126].

A visitor to Texas who would figure prominently in Republic of Texas politics, Mirabeau B. Lamar, arrived in Velasco on 26-Sep-1835, after having traveled overland through Austin's Colony from Nacogdoches to Washington-on-the-Brazos to San Felipe to Velasco. He attempted to leave by sea to travel back to his Georgia home to settle his affairs. He had the intention to return and make Texas his home, but got ill and retreated to Brazoria, finding suitable lodgings at Jane Long's tavern and boarding house, until he took ship in Nov-1835 to Mobile. But in his journal, he left us a few choice words when he first arrived at Velasco – "*Tarried there at Brown's, Mrs. Brown a dam'd hansome woman, & sensible enough. Brown himself morose, selfish, & prone to dictatorial violence. I liked him not. Hawkins (really Hoskins), barkeeper who married an older sister of Mrs. Brown, I liked better. The female portion of the family treated me with much neglect. Kept damd nasty table & as scanty in variety & quantity as it was filthily prepared. A pretty woman to keep a dirty table! Oh! Hell! The lady did not like the boarders of 'low degree' tho' they paid their dollar a day, to eat too much of the stinking beef; as for butter and milk &*

such things, scarce as hen's teeth." Lamar also stated, "*After subscribing $5.00 to erect a fort at Valascoe, left the place in the steamboat Laura, & arrived at Brazoria on Thursday 8th Octr ....*" [Parker 1981 pp. 323-325].

Thomas F. McKinney had established the trading firm of McKinney, Williams and Company in 1834 at Quintana, along with his personal residence. As the Texas Revolution began, one step was the creation of the Texas Consultation. Election of delegates from the Columbia municipality included William H. Wharton, Henry Smith, Branch T. Archer, John A. Wharton, John Byrom and Warren D. C. Hall [Gray 10-Oct-1835, p. 3] – all advocates for full Texas independence from Mexico. McKinney took exception to their election, as he felt that voters in the Velasco/Quintana area had been disenfranchised by shenanigans with the date of the election in late September and early October 1835 [Gray 3-Oct-1835 pp. 2-3]. A rebuttal by William H. Wharton was published in the next issue [Gray 10-Oct-1835 p. 4], as was a reply by McKinney two weeks following [Gray 24-Oct-1835 p. 2] which included many witness accounts of a rigged ballot. As it turned out, delegates from other areas merely favored restoration of the 1824 Constitution, and the Consultation ultimately voted for this option.

The **Texas Republican** issue of 17-Oct-1835 also printed a letter from Gail Borden, R. R. Royal and Isaac Batterson (at San Felipe) to the Committee of Safety at Columbia, stating "*... we think it highly important that the cannon should be mounted, and Velasco put in a state of defence as speedily as possible, and should an enemy appear, every precaution should be used to prevent a landing .... A gentleman by the name of Poe, proposes to mount the cannon, &c.*" [Gray 17-Oct-1835 p. 1]. In the same issue is printed a report from Thomas McKinney dated 11-Oct-1835 at Quintana that the schooner **Lady Madison** arrived with seven pieces of cannon, ammunition, muskets, etc.

Soon after, McKinney wrote on 24-Oct-1835 that "*... we have this evening completed the mounting on our fort at Velasco a most superior long 18 pounder besides some other smaller pieces ...*" and again on 29-Oct-1835 that "*The Mexican cruiser is off this place, has been seen yesterday & the day previous fired one shot at Velasco which fell short of the shore, four at her were fired from shore, none however took effect, it has made her less bold in her movements ... You would doubtless say by all means go and take her, so we say and so we will endeavor to do at all hazards.*" [McKinney 1835a & b]. The Mexican cruiser was probably the **Bravo,** formerly the **Montezuma** [Gray 7-Nov-1835, Powers 2006 pp. 33-34, Thompson 2020 p. 260]. Velasco's cannon was that brought by the **San Felipe** in early September. Since no fortifications other than the 1832 fort are known to have existed yet at Velasco, it is entirely possible that McKinney mounted this cannon in the now-abandoned fort. The letters also indicate that men and supplies were arriving on ships from New Orleans, and were being forwarded on to the camp of the Texas Revolutionary Army. Indeed, a second 18-pounder was soon sent on to the army, leaving the "smaller pieces" at Velasco [McKinney 1835c]. On the very day the **Bravo** first engaged the Velasco battery (27-Oct-1835), McKinney and Williams were authorized by the Permanent Council at San Felipe to travel to New Orleans and quietly negotiate a $100,000 loan. Although these efforts were unsuccessful as a loan, land scrip was instead offered successfully [McKinney 1870, Barker 1904 pp. 274-276]. Although ships and vessels are not mentioned as the purpose of the loan, the council also provided blank letters of marque on 31-Oct-1835. Interestingly, this authorization also added "*You will be particular at all times to carry the flag of the Mexican Republic.*" [Barker 1904 p. 278] and, indeed, Texian ships were reported to fly the 1824 tri-color for some months thereafter. So, significant revolutionary activity was well underway at Velasco in the period of Sep-Oct 1835.

McKinney was true to his word to chase the "*Mexican cruiser*", as the **San Felipe** was soon pressed into official service on 1-Nov-1835 by the Columbia Committee of Safety [Dinsmore & McNeel 1835], making her the first ship of a new and growing fleet of Texian privateers, privately owned ships and official navy vessels. Under existing Capt. William Hurd, McKinney took her to sea the same day, armed with seven cannon and seventy men, chasing the **Bravo** down the Texas coast. As they neared Paso Cavallo on 3-Nov-1835, they spotted her at anchor and, in attempting to gain an advantageous wind position overnight, they ran ashore at dawn the next morning 6-8 miles east of the pass [Gray 7-Nov-1835]. As some tried to hike up the beach toward the town of Matagorda, they found the merchant schooner **William Robbins** at anchor, which was then sought by both the Matagorda Committee of Safety and McKinney, to continue chasing Mexican vessels. Capt. Hurd was put in charge of the **William Robbins** which was first used to recover the cannon from the **San Felipe** to arm itself. One key piece of "hollow-ware" cargo was that other 18-pounder, which was first removed to Bird Island, then found its way to Dimmit's Landing. From there, the family of Bailey Hardeman was involved in its transport from Dimmit's Landing to the Battle of Béxar in early December, and is thought to have been the cannon of this size used on the southwest corner at the Battle of the Alamo [Hall 1835, Johnson 2015 pp. 340-348].

Figure 37: Painting by Peter Rindlisbacher "Take it Back; William Robbins on Matagorda Bay, 1835"
Courtesy of Peter Rindlisbacher

The web page from the Texas State Library and Archives indicates that the **San Felipe** may have been refloated by Dec-1835, but was soon lost again at Paso Cavallo [Thompson 2020 p. 223]. An artist's rendition by Peter Rindlisbacher of the *Williams Robbins* is shown below, as it sails away from its anchorage in Matagorda Bay, while a coasting schooner against Dog Island Reef (in the background) is shown lightering off cargo to smaller boats (necessary to cross the shallow water to reach the town).

Soon afterwards, the *William Robbins* also attempted to recover munitions and goods from the schooner *Hannah Elizabeth* (grounded and captured on 19-Nov-1835 at Paso Cavallo by the *Bravo*), with an armed force under S. Rhoads Fisher. At some point, the crew of the *Hannah Elizabeth* had thrown the munitions overboard before a Mexican prize crew could arrive, although some passengers were removed to the *Bravo*, before a norther drove the *Bravo* into the Gulf. A group of three Texians, including one named Somers and apparently present at Paso Cavallo, captured a Mexican prize crew from the *Bravo* as they came ashore in a small boat and capsized in the breakers, holding them for two days [Dienst 1909 p. 22]. When the **William Robbins** arrived, the Mexican officer surrendered officially, but the arms had already been lost, although the remaining cargo was auctioned off quickly, fearing the return of the *Bravo* [S.R. Fisher 1836, Dienst 1909 pp. 20-21]. Although Fisher submitted an official report [S.R. Fisher 1835], James W. Fannin took exception to the recovery [Fannin 11-Dec-1835], which alarmed Governor Henry Smith [Smith Dec-1835], causing a cloud of suspicion over Hurd and Fisher until the matter was resolved [Barrett 1835, Dienst 1909 p. 23-24]. A shipwreck located in modern times off the eastern tip of Matagorda Island (southwest side of Paso Cavallo) has tentatively been identified as the *Hannah Elizabeth* [Borgens 2004]. Peter Rindlisbacher has also rendered the moment when the crew of the *William Robbins* re-captures the grounded *Hannah Elizabeth* from the Mexican prize crew.

Figure 38: Painting by Peter Rindlisbacher "Re-Capture of the Hannah Elizabeth, 1835"

Courtesy of Peter Rindlisbacher

After all this trouble with the *Correo* and the *Bravo*, James F. Perry and 11 other citizens of Brazoria wrote to the provisional Texas government in Nov-1835 that the sea coast was defenseless and unprotected, suggesting the building of forts at the east end of Galveston Island, at the mouth of the Brazos, and at the entrance to Matagorda Bay. They also suggested a naval force to drive away these cruisers [McKinley 1934]. Similar sentiments had been expressed by Thomas F. McKinney [McKinney 1835b] and the newly named governor Henry Smith in a letter on 15-Nov-1835 [Smith Nov-1835]. At first, this took the form of the provisional Texas government authorizing privateers. On 25-Nov-1835, over three months before Texas actually declared its independence, the provisional Texas government at the General Council of the Republic of Texas at San Felipe decreed creation of a navy (two schooners, to rendezvous at Galveston Bay) [Robinson et al 1835]. Such thoughts about a naval force were not unusual and soon acted upon to actually create the first Republic Of Texas Navy, primarily through the ongoing efforts of the Quintana merchants Thomas F. McKinney and Samuel May Williams of the trading firm of McKinney, Williams and Company, who put up cash and personal credit required to obtain two of four existing topsail "Baltimore schooners" (also known as "Baltimore Clippers") in a short period [Riggan & Blocker 2019 pp. 104-106]. The official navy would soon include the *Liberty* (60-80 tons), *Independence* (112 tons), *Brutus* (125-127 tons) and *Invincible* (130 tons). These schooners were maneuverable and fast, fitted out and heavily armed, also notably having one (sometimes two) heavy guns mounted amidships on a rotating carriage modeled on the U.S. Navy schooners of 1820-1821 [Chapelle 1949], to fire in any direction and called "pivot guns".

Although the Matagorda Committee of Safety had agreed to buy the *William Robbins* on McKinney's credit for use as a privateer [Lewis 1835, S.R. Fisher 1836], thus making her the second ship to join the fleet, McKinney preferred her to be an official government-owned ship in the new navy. He sent her to Velasco where she was fitted out in Dec-1835 by Jeremiah Brown (formerly captain of the *Sabine* and a business owner in Velasco) who then sailed it to New Orleans carrying the new Commissioners to the United States (Stephen F. Austin, Branch T. Archer and William H. Wharton) and also José Antonio Mexía [Powers 2006 pp. 34-39]. There, the vessel was converted to a war schooner, purchased by the Commissioners on the credit of McKinney, Williams & Co., renamed *Liberty*, and a crew was recruited by Jeremiah's brother William S. Brown [Powers 2006 p. 56]. One such recruit wrote of the scene at Slaughter-House Point in Algiers, that the ship *"... was being transformed from a peaceful merchantman into a man-of-war ... the armament, consisting of one medium twelve-pounder for a pivot-gun, two long sixes, and two twelve-pound carronades ..."*, departing there on 12-Jan-1836 in convoy with several merchant schooners laden with munitions for Texas. At the mouth of the Mississippi River, S. W. Cushing also wrote *"Here our colors were first hoisted, under a salute of thirteen guns. The flag was that of the Mexican republic – red, white, and green, with the addition of the figures 1824 in the centre, expressive of the determination of the Texans to sustain the constitution of the Federal government, which the usurper Santa Anna had overthrown."*. Stopping a week at Galveston Harbor, he observed *"Where now stands an opulent city, one solitary presented itself to the eye ... dignified with the title of custom-house."* [Cushing 1857 pp. 4-7]. *Liberty* arrived back at Velasco on 25-Jan-1836, together with the convoy ships. After early and gallant action during the Texas Revolution (more on that below), the *Liberty* was refitting in New Orleans but was claimed there by creditors later in 1836.

The *Invincible* had had been built in 1835 in Baltimore, and purchased there for McKinney, Williams & Co. by Henry W. Williams (Samuel May's brother), arriving at Velasco on 2-Jan-1836 laden with arms and supplies [Powers 2006 pp. 56-57]. She was still there when the *Liberty* arrived. A painting of the *Invincible* by Fred Toler is shown below in Figure 39, in a scene depicting its loss at the entrance to Galveston Bay in late 1837; the image shows the clean lines, gaff rigging, and topsails on the foremast of the topsail schooner type known as a "Baltimore Clipper". Please notice the "pivot gun" amidship in the act of firing.

Figure 39: Painting of "Loss of the Invincible" by Fred Toler
Courtesy of The San Jacinto Museum and Battlefield Association

The merchant schooner *Brutus* was purchased in New Orleans by Augustus C. Allen [Allen 1835], fitted out as a privateer in Dec-1835 with William A. Hurd as captain, and stopped at Velasco in mid-Jan 1836 with about 100 passengers (Alabama Red Rovers) on their way to Dimitt's Landing where they disembarked. Upon return to New Orleans, Allen instead sold the vessel to the Provisional Government [Powers 2006 pp. 46-47]. The schooner *Independence* (formerly the U. S. revenue cutter *Samuel D. Ingham*) was similarly purchased in New Orleans [Powers 2006 pp. 47-48], both vessels arriving at Velasco about 5-Mar-1836, and then continuing on to Paso Cavallo [Powers 2006 p. 57].

These government-owned "navy" vessels were also joined by several privately owned ships, which are sometimes also considered as part of the First Texas Navy, such as the steamers *Cayuga*, *Laura*, *Yellowstone* and *Ocean*, and also the schooners *San Felipe* (as already discussed), *Thomas Toby* and *Flash*. Together with other privateers, such as the *Terrible*, this hastily assembled "fleet" helped defend the coast during the Texas Revolution and the dangerous months following the victory at San Jacinto [Thompson 2020]. Many times, these vessels did not survive long. During this period, Quintana and Velasco served as a principal base of the First Texas Navy, due to its position at the mouth of the Brazos River and easy access to areas settled as part of Austin's Colony [Andy Hall, personal communication]. One of the first written histories of the First Texas Navy (in the *Texas Almanac for 1860*) put it this way: *"For the purposes of facilitating the supply and control of the vessels, the Government commissioned Thomas F. McKinney, a Captain in the Navy, with authority similar to that vested in a Secretary of the Navy; he then resided at the mouth of the Brazos de Dios, the usual naval rendezvous, and most frequented port of entry for Texas."* [Haugh 1960 pp. 572-573]. McKinney was originally suggested to captain the **Invincible**, but appointed Jeremiah Brown instead, and his brother William S. Brown to take over the **Liberty** [Wharton 1836, McKinney 1870], so that McKinney could act as an agent for the cause.

Back on land ….. it was also in this period that one company of the New Orleans Greys arrived by sea at Velasco aboard the schooner **Columbus**, where they organized themselves and elected officers, including Robert C. Morris as captain and William Gordon Cooke as first lieutenant – indeed the first volunteer unit from the United States to arrive for the Texas Revolution. They stayed two days after their arrival on 22-Oct-1835 while being supported by Thomas McKinney, before being transported upriver to Brazoria aboard his steamboat **Laura**, from which they marched onto San Antonio for the Siege Of Béxar [Brown 1999] and their later fates, many of which would die at Goliad. Another company of the Greys had marched overland to Nacogdoches and then San Antonio, and included Thomas S. Lubbock and Herman Ehrenberg [Crisp 2022]. Lubbock would later travel afoot (in Jan-1836) back to the Brazos, where he would join Thomas W. Grayson (a family friend) aboard the steamboat **Yellowstone**, being aboard when the vessel helped Sam Houston's army cross the Brazos, and then ran downstream past Santa Anna's army and then Velasco, arriving at Galveston Bay on 24-Apr-1836. There, he observed President David G. Burnet *"camping on Galveston Island"*, the announcement of the San Jacinto victory the next day, and the return trip of Burnet and *"part of his cabinet"* to the site of the battle [Lubbock 1900 pp. 33]. Burnet had barely escaped Mexican troops at New Washington a few days earlier by just 30 yards, fleeing in a rowboat to Galveston Island; famously, Col. Juan Almonte had ordered soldiers not to fire on Burnet (although standing at the tiller), since his wife and two children were also in the boat [Almonte 2005 pp. 403-404, Clarke 1969 pp. 84-86]. Both Lubbock and Ehrenberg would survive the revolution and return to Velasco afterwards - Lubbock would work briefly for McKinney, Williams & Co., and Ehrenberg would escort the Mexican prisoner Johann Josef Holzinger to the government at Velasco in late May-1836 and there be discharged from the Texas Army on 2-Jun-1836, where he observed the imprisoned Santa Anna [Crisp 2022 pp. 253, 337n9, 515-520].

As the Texas Revolution began in earnest in late 1835, Velasco also became a staging and training area for about 250 volunteers under the command of Col. James W. Fannin, known as the Georgia Battalion Of Permanent Volunteers. It was this group that brought the Troutman flag, and the flag was flown over the American Hotel on 8-Jan-1836, alongside William S. Brown's Independence flag. Their military training under their adjutant, Capt. John Sowers Brooks, occurred in camps near Velasco named Camp Independence and Camp Fannin [Roller 1906]. Fannin had moved with his family from Georgia to Velasco in late 1834. He was present for Austin's address in Brazoria on 8-Sep-1835, even giving a toast [Ruby Smith 1919 pp. 82-83]. He apparently responded to Austin's call to arms in late Sep-1835, and was present for the Battle of Gonzales and the Battle of Concepcion, leading a group referred to as the

"Brazos Guards" [Fannin 25-Dec-1835, Ruby Smith 1919 p. 84]. After duty near San Antonio, he was discharged from Austin's command on 22-Nov-1835, assumed the role of Colonel offered by Sam Houston, to be stationed at La Bahía, but later returned to Velasco where he was placed in command of the newly arrived Georgia volunteers.

Another group of volunteers included John C. Duval and his two brothers of the Kentucky Mustangs who arrived at Quintana in late Dec-1835. In a book published in 1892, Duval described his first view of the area *"The country in the immediate vicinity of Velasco is low, and back of it a dead level prairie extending as far as the eye could reach; consequently, I must confess I was not much pleased with the first view of the 'promised land'. Velasco was a miserable little village consisting of two stores and a hotel, so called, and five or six grog shops, dignified with the name of 'saloons.'"* [Duval 1892 p. 20]. Duval was soon enrolled in the Texas Revolutionary Army, and for a short period was posted aboard the **Invincible** as *"a kind of marine corps"*. In late Jan-1836, both groups had been ferried on the schooners **Columbus** and **Flora** down the coast to Cópano [Fannin 1836, Helm 1884 p. 54], and then marched to Presidio La Bahía (at Goliad), which they called Fort Defiance [Roller 1906]. Fannin, Brooks and most of these men died in the Goliad Massacre on 27-Mar-1836, although Duval was among the few escapees.

Mary Austin Holley had a more favorable view of Velasco, perhaps wishing to publicize her cousin's colony, mentioning it in her guidebook entitled "Texas" published in 1836, writing *"Excellent accommodations can always be obtained at boarding houses, which, among other attractions, are always furnished with supplies of oysters and fish of the first quality. Musquetoe bars are not often needed here, and, altogether, it is one of the most delightful places in the country. A Mexican garrison was formerly situated at Velasco; at present, it is a rendezvous of the patriot troops"* [Holley 1836a].

Christmas of 1835 found Stephen F. Austin at Velasco and Quintana, apparently on his way to the United States, since he had been appointed as one of three commissioners at the Texas Consultation in Nov-1835, to seek aid for Texas in the U. S., the others being William H. Wharton and Branch T. Archer. While at Quintana, Austin met with Thomas McKinney, to plan for laying out town lots, next to McKinney, Williams & Co.'s warehouse. The commissioners left the area on the 26th [Barker 1926 p. 425, Cantrell 1999 p. 332] aboard the **Liberty**, bound for New Orleans and then overland to Washington DC and New York. Austin sent an interesting series of four letters before leaving Texas, stating his official opposition to independence for Texas, and dread of serving with Wharton who was lobbying for independence, unscrupulously in Austin's opinion [Austin 22- & 25-Dec-1835]. Yet, less than two weeks later, while in New Orleans, he confessed his personal opinion, and that he had changed his official position, writing glowingly of independence since he had apparently seen evidence of much aid coming to Texas [Austin 7-Jan-1836]. Austin would be gone from Texas for seven momentous months.

The Texian battery of artillery at Velasco was apparently placed in a new more-substantial earthen embankment or fort after Feb-1836, when an address was published by the Brazoria Committee of Safety calling for aid in erecting a new fort at Velasco [Streeter 1955 #119 p. 71], and which has been called the Texan Fort Velasco, sometimes confused with the 1832 fort. A meeting was held on 6-Mar-1836 at Velasco of the "Committee for Vigilance and Safety", where a resolution was passed for *"... purchase of ammunition, reconstruction of the battery, and the mounting of guns ..."* [Potter & Wells 1836] – please see Figure 40.

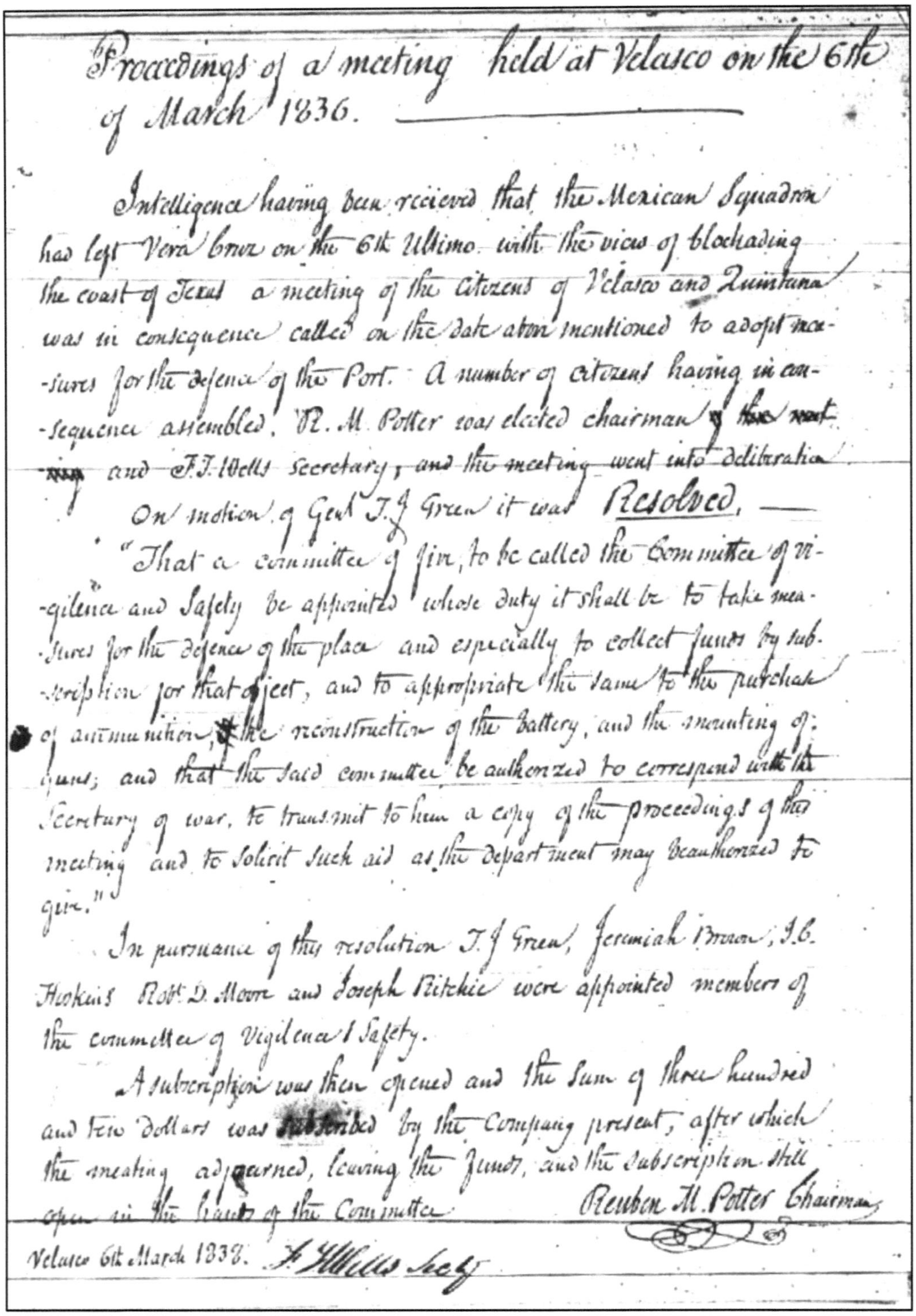

Proceedings of a meeting held at Velasco on the 6th of March 1836.

Intelligence having been recieved that the Mexican Squadron has left Vera Cruz on the 6th Ultimo with the view of blockading the coast of Texas a meeting of the citizens of Velasco and Quintana was in consequence called on the date above mentioned to adopt measures for the defence of the Port. A number of citizens having in consequence assembled, R. M. Potter was elected chairman ~~of the meeting~~ and F. J. Wells Secretary, and the meeting went into deliberation.

On motion of Genl T. J. Green it was Resolved, —

"That a committee of five, to be called the Committee of Vigilence and Safety be appointed whose duty it shall be to take measures for the defence of the place and especially to collect funds by subscription for that object, and to appropriate the same to the purchase of ammunition, the reconstruction of the Battery, and the mounting of guns; and that the said committee be authorized to correspond with the Secretary of war, to transmit to him a copy of the proceedings of this meeting and to solicit such aid as the department may be authorized to give."

In pursuance of this resolution T. J. Green, Jeremiah Brown, F. J. Haskins Robt. D. Moore and Joseph Ritchie were appointed members of the committee of Vigilence & Safety.

A subscription was then opened and the sum of three hundred and ten Dollars was subscribed by the company present, after which the meeting adjourned, leaving the funds, and the subscription still open in the hands of the Committee.

Reuben M. Potter Chairman

Velasco 6th March 1836. F. J. Wells Secy

Figure 40: Proceedings of a meeting held at Velasco on the 6th of March 1836

Thomas Jefferson Green Papers, Southern Historical Collection, University of North Carolina Library

Another document shows expenses from Francis J. Haskins for *"... mounting two 6 pounders at Velasco"* and *"... servicing caissons & repairing carriages"* on 19-Feb-1836, and also for *"... Services rendered in getting on Shore & mounting one 9 pounder from the wreck of the Schooner **America**"* and *"... blocks & rigging for same"* on 14-Mar-1836, for a total of $90.00 [Haskins Mar-1836].

In early March, Capt. George W. Poe commanded troops at Velasco, consisting of Amasa Turner's company of regulars and Richard Roman's company of volunteers. Initially, Poe recommended they stay to defend the area, writing on 3-Mar-1836 that *"I have received letters from the Citizens beseeching me not to remove the troops from here ... they have offered to work with hands and oxen in the Construction of Batteries & mounting the Cannon – moreover there is a large supply of arms ammunition & Clothing here which without troops cannot be protected ..."* [Poe 1836]. These troops apparently left soon after to join the army under Sam Houston, as it retreated from Santa Anna's advance after the defeats in revolutionary battles at the Alamo and Goliad. The civilian population also retreated, abandoning their settlements in the Runaway Scrape, and Velasco was no different.

During this same time, Edwin Morehouse and his New York Battalion arrived at Velasco aboard the *Matawamkeag*, escorted by *Independence* and *Brutus* about 5-Mar-1836 [Powers 2006 pp. 56-57] before continuing on to Paso Cavallo where this unit disembarked at Cox's Point. This unit was initially assigned the duty of assisting civilians west of the Brazos to escape to safety during the Runaway Scrape, serving at Matagorda, Columbia and Brazoria, before joining Houston's army after San Jacinto. Afterwards, as part of the new Army of the Republic of Texas under Thomas J. Rusk, this group followed the Mexican Army out of Texas and assisted in the burial of the burned remains from the Goliad Massacre in Jun-1836 [Morehouse 1836, Daniell 1892, Huson 1953 I:391].

At sea, the First Texas Navy had also become active. Velasco was often the place where seamen and provisions were boarded upon the vessels. As stated previously, the *Liberty* joined the newly purchased *Invincible* at Velasco, after which the *Invincible* helped transport Fannin's troops to Cópano. The *Liberty* departed Velasco on 13-Feb-1836, stopped at Galveston Bay before departing for Yucatan where she captured the Mexican schooner *Pelicano* on 5-Mar-1836, including eight of its crew as prisoners (this capture is shown in the painting in the Figure 41 below). The *Liberty* returned her prize to Texas at the entrance to Matagorda Bay, encountering the *Matawamkeag*, but where the heavily laden *Pelicano* foundered on the bar, although its supplies of flour and gunpowder were of use to the Texas Army [Cushing 1857 pp. 22-24, Powers 2006 pp. 67-71]. The *Liberty* sailed up the bay toward the town of Matagorda to a point described by Cushing as *"... in sight of the anchorage, nine miles below the town of Matagorda."*, joining the *Independence*, *Brutus*, and merchantman *Durango* [Cushing p. 24]. The eight prisoners were transferred to Velasco, where they stayed at the Brown-Hoskins hotel and tavern, before being allowed to travel on to New Orleans [Brown 19-Jun-1836].

This was also the tumultuous time when the Convention for the aborning Republic of Texas hurriedly formed at Washington-on-the-Brazos from 1-17 Mar 1836, issuing the Declaration of Independence on 2-Mar-1836 and the Constitution over the following two weeks, while also hearing of the loss of the Alamo. The aforementioned arrival of the *Invincible* and *Brutus* at Velasco seems to have spurred the Convention on navy matters, as they named Robert Potter (chairman), Stephen H. Everett and S. Rhoads Fisher to a "select committee on naval affairs" on 10-Mar-1836, then named S. Rhoads Fisher, Robert Hamilton, Lorenzo de Zavala, Thomas J. Gazley and Samuel P. Carson to a "standing committee of five on naval affairs" two days later [Ellis 1838 pp. 61-64, 75]. In the late evening of May 16th, the delegates elected an *ad interim* government: David G. Burnet (President), Lorenzo de Zavala (Vice Pres.), Samuel P. Carson (Sec. of State), Bailey Hardeman (Sec. of Treasury), Thomas J. Rusk (Sec. of War), Robert Potter (Sec. of Navy), and David Thomas (Attorney General) [Gray 1997 p.123, Wortham 1924 III-227].

Figure 41: Painting of "Capture of the Pelicano" by Fred Toler. Pelicano is on the left, and the Liberty on the right flying the 1824 tricolor flag, which was used by the Texas Navy up to about this point.

Courtesy of The San Jacinto Museum and Battlefield Association

As mentioned above, several incidents with ships of the Texas and Mexican Navies are reported at Matagorda or Matagorda Bay; however, there seems to be some confusion with these place names. The Spanish and then Mexican "*puerto de Matagorda*" (literally, the "door of Matagorda") referred to the deep-water channel on the western side of Paso Cavallo (once, the area later known as Calhoun or Saluria, and today, the area of Port O'Connor), while the Anglo-American town of Matagorda at the mouth of the Colorado was established later (about 1828) at almost the opposite (east) end of the bay. As often as not, the use of the singular term "Matagorda" in the days of Mexican Texas actually applied to the port/coast/bay of Matagorda (e.g., especially in the Béxar Archives). It is hard to imagine the ships of the Texas Navy could have made port at the <u>town</u> of Matagorda, due to the shallow water and oyster reefs at that end of the bay. It seems more likely that passage was limited to the deeper water of Paso Cavallo toward Mad Island Reef, and lightering was used for transport to and from the town of Matagorda. The Cushing quote (on the previous page) indicated the anchorage was nine miles from town. Modern nautical charts indicate water depth can be 6' about 75% of the way across the bay from Mad Island Reef, but shallower (or blocked by Dog Island Reef) towards the mouth of the Colorado.

On 3-Apr-1836, the *Invincible* searched for, grounded and destroyed the heavier-armed *Bravo* near the mouth of the Rio Grande, after gaining supplies and personnel at Velasco [Hoskins 11-Jul-1836, Powers 2006 pp. 78-82]. Peter Rindlisbacher has also interpreted this scene, below.

Figure 42: Painting by Peter Rindlisbacher "Invincible Vs. Bravo, 1836"

Courtesy of Peter Rindlisbacher

In the summer of 1836, the *Invincible* took on water at Marion (Columbia), and then traveled downriver to Velasco, joining the steamer *Ocean* and the privateer *Terrible* to travel down the coast. They found the heavily armed Mexican brig *Vencedor del Alamo* trapping the *Brutus* in Matagorda Bay, and chased her all the way to Veracruz. The *Invincible* returned to Velasco, where she discharged her marines and some sailors, before traveling to New York for repairs [Powers 2006 pp. 106-108]. Although some state that Velasco became the "*homeport*" of the steamboat *Yellowstone* and the war schooners *Invincible* and *Independence* [Stahman 2008 p. 14], it was probably not in the full sense of that word. Refitting had to be done at New Orleans or even New York, although provisioning was apparently done at the Brazos.

After his victories at the Alamo and Goliad, Santa Anna apparently believed the revolution was defeated, and had scattered his forces (in part, to forage for supplies), before he came to understand that Sam Houston had gathered a large surviving force, and both maneuvered for a final fight. Robert Potter, the elected Secretary Of The Navy by the *ad interim* Texas government, instead moved to the coast to help organize defenses there, where Col. Warren D. C. Hall was ordered to defend Velasco and Galveston Island at some point after mid-March but, noticing Velasco was abandoned, he initially consolidated his defense only at Galveston [Shearer 1951 pp. 67-69]. However, a group of volunteers under Thomas B. Bell arrived in late March and agreed to defend Velasco. Robert Potter wrote to Bell on 31-Mar-1836, saying *"The offer of service by yourself and friends to fortify and defend Velasco is accepted, and as soon as communication can be had with other members of the Government, a Captain's commission will be sent to you to authorise you to organize your friends into a company and be constituted a part of the army of the Republic of Texas. Genl. Hall will return to Velasco as soon as he is informed of the stand you have taken; but in the meantime you are requested and authorised to take command and proceed immediately to collect laborers, teams &c for constructing fortifications .... Col. Edwd. Harcourt an experienced and scientific engineer has been ordered to Velasco and Galveston to superintend the construction of fortifications at those respective points – in all matters therefore relating to that branch of the public service at Velasco, Col. Harcourt will have the command."* Eduard Harkort (sometimes Anglicized as Harcourt) was a German national and engineer recruited in New Orleans to the cause of Texas independence by Stephen F. Austin, and who Sam Houston appointed on 28-Mar-1836, writing *"I sent Colonel Harcourt, as principal engineer of the army, down to the coast, to erect fortifications at the most eligible point of defence. I placed at his disposal the resources of the lower country for its defence and protection."* [Houston 1836 pp. 384-386]. Bell responded on 12-Apr-1836, writing *"We are pressing forward, in the operation of the Fort ..."* [Potter 1836, Myers & Smith].

During this same period, one notable arrival from New Orleans was the schooner **Flash** under Capt. Luke A. Falvel (also spelled Falwell), which arrived at Velasco on 25-Mar-1836, and which had stopped a few days earlier at Galveston Harbor, learning the latest news of the Texas Revolution [Barber 2009]. James Morgan had ordered the vessel on to Velasco, to evacuate citizens fleeing from the Brazos. On board was the returning Mirabeau B. Lamar, who then traveled north from Velasco to Groce's Ferry to join Sam Houston's army as a private (the army was there from 31-Mar to 14-Apr-1836). The day before the Battle of San Jacinto, he was promoted to colonel of cavalry, and commanded the 61-member unit in the battle.

Upon leaving Velasco, and to avoid the advancing enemy, the **Flash** carried Robert Potter, Eduard Harkort (among others) and the "Twin Sisters" to New Washington (current Morgan's Point) [Dienst 1909 p. 30, Meed 2001 p. 52, Barber 2009 p. 22]. Many documents are found in the pension claim of Capt. Luke A. Falvel, but one is an affidavit by David G. Burnet (dated 23-May-1868 at Galveston) stating *"This is to certify that Luke A. Falvel held a Commission as Captain in the Navy of the Republic of Texas ..."*, and another is an "Oath of Identity" (dated 22-Oct-1870) which states *"... The said Schooner **Flash** being under his command when the celebrated "Twin Sisters" were transported on board of her, for service, in the Memorable battle of San Jacinto"* [Falvel 1870]. The "Twin Sisters" were a brace of field cannon donated by the citizens of Cincinnati, that had been transported down the Mississippi River to New Orleans, and then by sea aboard the schooner **Pennsylvania** to Brazoria in Mar-1836 [Winkler 1917]. However, the lack of oxen or horses to haul them, and the muddy roads, prevented further progress. John M. Allen reported from Brazoria on 31-Mar-1836 to Sam Houston *"I have been now three days at this place with forty men – two fine field pieces – and one Howitzer with 160 shells and 880 round shot .... Col'n Houston (Almanzon Huston??) ... informed me that he had orders from the Governm't to send back everything in the shape of arms and ammunition - and to proceed forthwith to Galveston Bay ... have therefore concluded to march my men onto the army and send everything else back to Velasco."* [Allen 1836]. In his new assignment, Eduard Harkort traveled through Bell's Landing and Brazoria, organizing the building of breastworks there. He also initiated fortifications at Velasco the day (3-Apr-1836) he wrote to Sam Houston, also saying *"I found two complete field pieces with ammunition and a howitzer on board the **Pensilvania** which has order to take them down again and bring them over to Galveston. I would not opose to this order, and have them unloaded here, because I think that in case you wish them with the army, I could easier find means to send them by Harrisburg than from Brazoria where even we could not find team for bringing up the provisions. Please to send me your orders by the war department of Harrisburg with respect to these canons which in the meanwhile I shall place at the entrance of the harbor of Galveston."* [Harkort 1836b]. The **Flash** delivered the cannon to New Washington on 6-Apr-1836, which were then carried to Harrisburg on the sloop **Ohio** and then overland to the Texas army at Groce's Ferry, reaching there on 11-Apr-1836 [Morgan 1836, Huston 1836, Winkler 1917 p. 22, Barber 2009 p. 22, Powers undated]. The Morgan reference indicates that one mate and three soldiers were detached for three days *"... to go to Harrisburg"*, indicating they may have been needed on the **Ohio** to help carry the cannons there. Finally, the "Twin Sisters" returned with the army toward San Jacinto, where this brace of field artillery was the heavy ordnance used by the Texians.

On the very day of the battle, the **Independence** anchored offshore of Velasco, unable to enter the river due to a stiff offshore wind caused by a "norther". Charles DeMorse, Lieutenant of Marines, along with the 2nd Mate and four gunners, were ordered to take a small boat to shore to gain intelligence about the revolution. Later, in DeMorse's pension claim of 1870, he wrote *"... we found at Velasco, Col."* Thos. F. McKinney, and Captain Bell from Tennessee with 6 men, holding <u>the little fort on which one gun was mounted</u>." [DeMorse 1870].

As mentioned previously, president David G. Burnet was encamped on Galveston Island during this same period of the Battle of San Jacinto. The Texas Almanac of 1869 had this reminiscence: *"The armed schooner **Liberty** was lying at what is now known as the Strand. There was but one small building, the Mexican Custom-House, on the island. The President and some of the Cabinet and a large number of citizens, with their families, (fugitives from the enemy,) and about sixty organized soldiers, under the command of Col. James Morgan, were encamped on the extreme eastern point of the island. The ground thus occupied has been since washed away."* [Unknown 1869 p. 58]. Some days after the battle, a curious incident occurred with the stalwart mariner of Velasco, Jeremiah Brown (former captain of the **Sabine**, hotel owner and pilot at Velasco, outfitter of the **William Robbins/Liberty**, and current captain of the **Invincible)**, now also anchored in the Galveston Harbor channel. A group of four men including Robert J. Calder and Benjamin C. Franklin traveled from the San Jacinto battleground to Galveston Island in a leaky dingy with the news of the victory, taking four days. Arriving first at the **Invincible**, they announced their news to Capt. Brown. Calder later wrote *"... his men literally lifted us on board, and in the midst of the wildest excitement Brown took off his hat and gave us three cheers, and threw it as far as he could into the bay. He then shouted to his men, 'Turn loose Long Tom* (the large "pivot gun"). *' After three discharges, he suddenly stopped and said: 'Hold on, boys, or old Hawkins* (the senior commodore) *will put me in irons again.' "* [Thrall 1883 pp. 519n-522n, Dienst 1909 p. 57-58, Shearer 1951 pp. 73-74]. Charles E. Hawkins, anchored nearby in the **Independence**, fired thirteen cannon salutes next upon being informed of the news, and hosted Calder's group to a sumptuous dinner. Finally, president Burnet, ashore on the island, was informed some hours later, but was miffed since he was about the last one to be told of the victory [Thrall 1883 pp. 519-521n, Thompson 2020 pp. 82-83]. Peter Rindlisbacher has also commemorated one of those cannon salutes in his painting (Figure 43) below.

Figure 43: Painting by Peter Rindlisbacher "San Jacinto Victory Salute"

Courtesy of Peter Rindlisbacher

It was also here on Galveston Island, that Burnet must have seen the value of the Galveston Harbor Channel, as he decreed on the very day of the Battle of San Jacinto for the island and bay to be a naval depot for the Texas Navy under control of the Secretary of the Navy [Burnet 1836], then Robert Potter. Later in 1836, the Texas government (perhaps strapped for cash) sold most of the eastern end of Galveston Island, reserving 15 acres for a Navy Yard [Ingram et al 1836]. These documents are an early sign that the home base of the Republic of Texas Navy would eventually swap from the Brazos over to Galveston, ultimately beginning in early 1838 with the "Galveston Navy Yard" and the "Second Texas Navy". Burnet also issued an executive order on 25-Apr-1836 declaring martial law on the island, and marshalling all able-bodied men, due to fear of a new Mexican invasion [Unknown 1869, pp. 59-60].

James F. Perry (while traveling to the mouth of the Brazos) had written from Galveston Island on 15-Apr-1836 to wife Emily (then at William Scott's plantation known as Point Pleasant with the family while escaping during the Runaway Scrape) that *"Mr. Grason (*probably Thomas Wigg Grayson, captain of the *Laura) is here he left Velasco yesterday morning and says there is a fort there and one at Columbia"*. In a second letter to his wife, written on 26-Apr-1836 from aboard the *Laura* (then at Galveston Harbor), he mentioned being sent to Velasco for tools to build a fort (at Galveston?, since the fort at Velasco was complete?) but that it had not been started yet [Perry 1836]. Francis J. Haskins wrote on 13-Jul-1836 to Col. James Morgan, asking that his account and expenses for building the fort at Velasco be settled [Haskins Jul-1836], so one might conclude the Texan Fort Velasco was mostly completed by then. One draft to him for $45.00 dated 6-Jul-1836 can be seen in [Bevill 2009 p. 138 Fig. 6.8].

A diagram labeled as "Fort Velasco" and indexed as "Plan of Fort Velasco", which may be a drawing of this battery or fort, is found in the Nacogdoches Archives (see Figure 44), perhaps a design by Harkort. This hypothesis is likely since these archives only extended through 1836, the labeling is in English, and the design is unlike the prior 1832 fort or the subsequent Civil War forts [Nacogdoches 1830s].

The location for this fort/battery is shown on an 1837 plat map of Velasco [Mesier 1837] in Block 61, then on the extreme corner of the Brazos and the Gulf (please see Figure 45), an area now in the open water of the widened harbor channel. Please also note the location of Monument Square, the adjacent Block 13 (with Lots 1-10) and Fort Street between them.

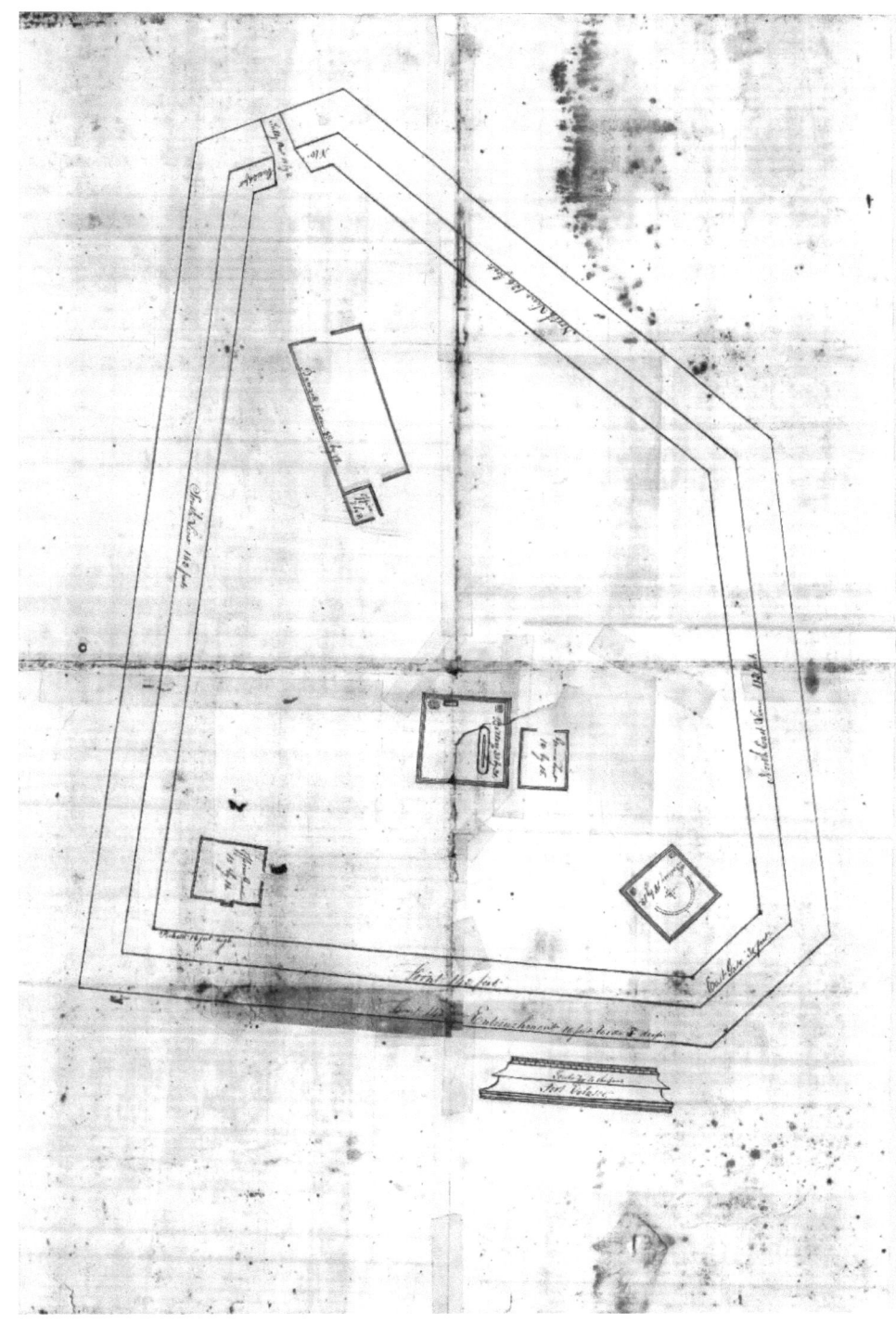

Figure 44: Fort diagram from Nacogdoches Archives, hypothesized to be Republic of Texas battery
Courtesy of Texas State Library and Archives Commission (Map 6312)

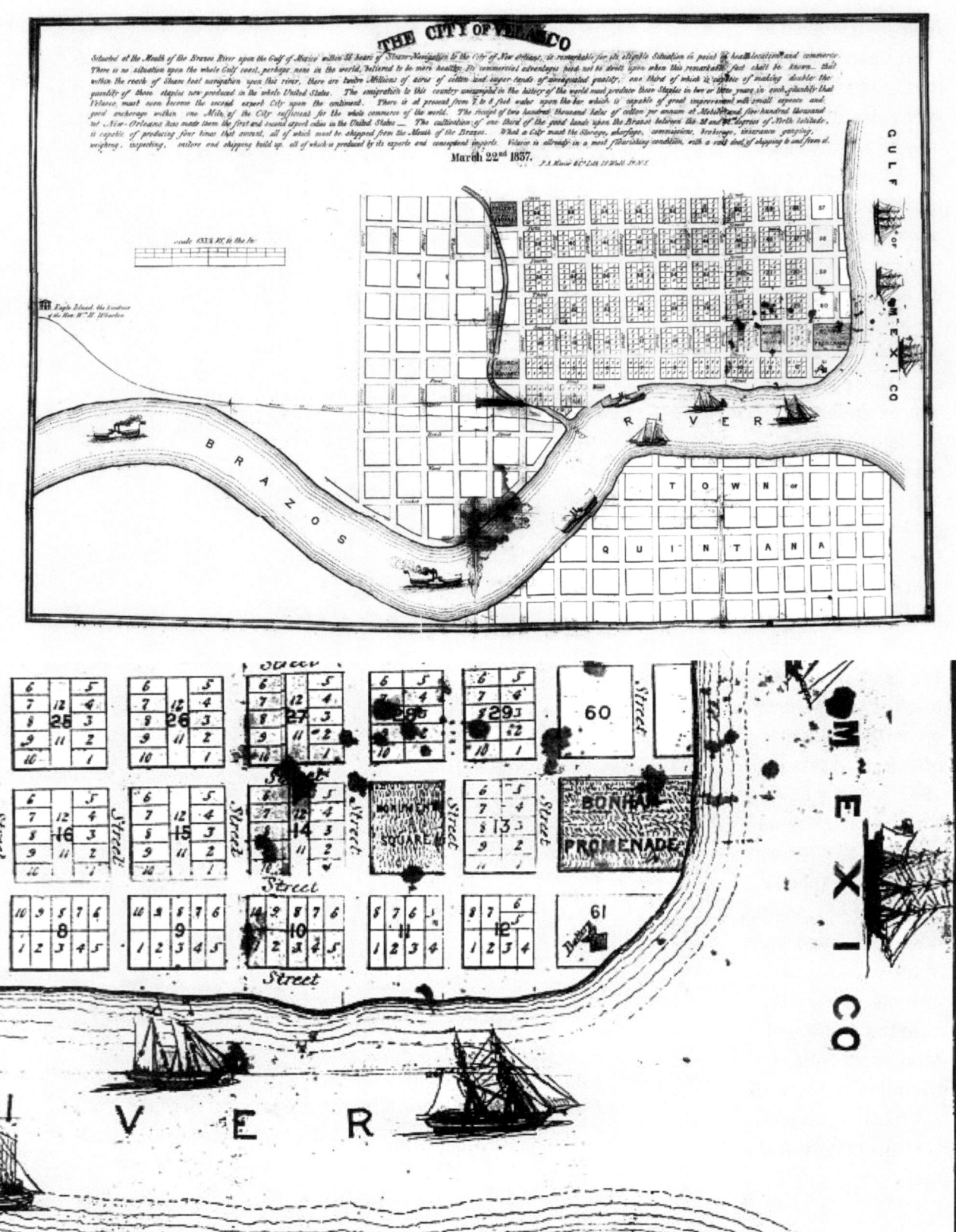

Figure 45: 1837 Plat Map of Velasco (full size + detail) [Mesier 1837]

amended image courtesy of Brazoria County Historical Museum

A similar but less formal map, known as the William H. Hunt map, is thought to have been prepared by this early surveyor of Brazoria County, and was used as a basis for many later deed records. Although the original is thought lost, a later copy is known [Hunt 1838]. This map also shows the same location for the battery and Monument Square, and is reproduced in Figure 46 below.

Figure 46: copy of William H. Hunt Map

Courtesy of Brazoria County Historical Museum

This battery was impermanent, but was known as the best coastal defense work in Texas in May-1836 [Pierce 1969]. Perhaps for this very reason, and the new robust Texas Navy, the full *ad interim* government of the Republic of Texas first convened at Velasco after the Battle Of San Jacinto from May-Oct 1836. One must also remember that many of the towns in Texas had been burned or destroyed in the Texas Revolution or Runaway Scrape, although Velasco escaped such a fate. President David G. Burnet wrote *"The entire want of accommodation at the island, there being no house there, rendered it necessary for the Government to seek some place where the ordinary office business could be transacted, and Velasco was selected."* [Clarke 1969 p. 116-117]. Another wrote "There was an entire lack of accommodations on land, except tents and improvised shelters, many of the residents living temporarily on ships in the harbor." [Hardy & Roberts 1910 p. 302]. Burnet and General Sam Houston, along with Santa Anna and his officers, had been transported on the steamboat *Yellowstone* from Buffalo Bayou to Galveston Island on 5-May-1836. Santa Anna was then placed aboard the *Independence*, and on 8-May-1836 President Burnet and his Cabinet came aboard and made sail for Velasco [Dienst 1909 p. 58, Shearer 1951 pp. 75-79]. As Dienst wrote *"Velasco was the great seaport of the Republic at that time."* A slightly different account was given by Gabriel Nuñez Ortega, whose diary indicates it was on 7-May-1836 when they went to Galveston Island (soon to become Post Galveston), and on 10-May-1836 went to Velasco aboard the steamer *Laura* [Nuñez Ortega 1836]. The wounded Sam Houston was transported in the opposite direction to New Orleans for medical care aboard the schooner *Flora*, accompanied by the war schooner *Liberty*.

The government's records were kept at Velasco for a short period, and the fort was occupied with a small garrison [Winkler 1906, Dorchester & Wilson 1936, Pierce 1969 p.164, Guthrie 1993 p.107, Fox et al 1981 pp. 21-23, Earls et al 1996 p. 49]. Financial warrants, notes and pay certificates were issued by the government from Velasco [Bevill 2009]. Other types of financial documents known as audited drafts can be found in SMU's Rowe-Barr Collection of Texas Currency issued at Velasco. And, it was here that Santa Anna signed the Treaties of Velasco on 14-May-1836. It is known that Santa Anna was held prisoner during this period at Velasco, along with Ramón Martínez Caro (his secretary) and Colonels Juan Nepomuceno Almonte and Gabriel Nuñez Ortega [Henson 1990]. Caro wrote afterwards *"... we were lodged in a small room surrounded by sentinels"* [Caro 1837 p. 135]. It is highly likely that "the government" actually met at existing and modest houses, such as the Brown-Hoskins hotel and tavern (American Hotel) or others. Indeed, "Santa Anna and suite" (Santa Anna and several of his

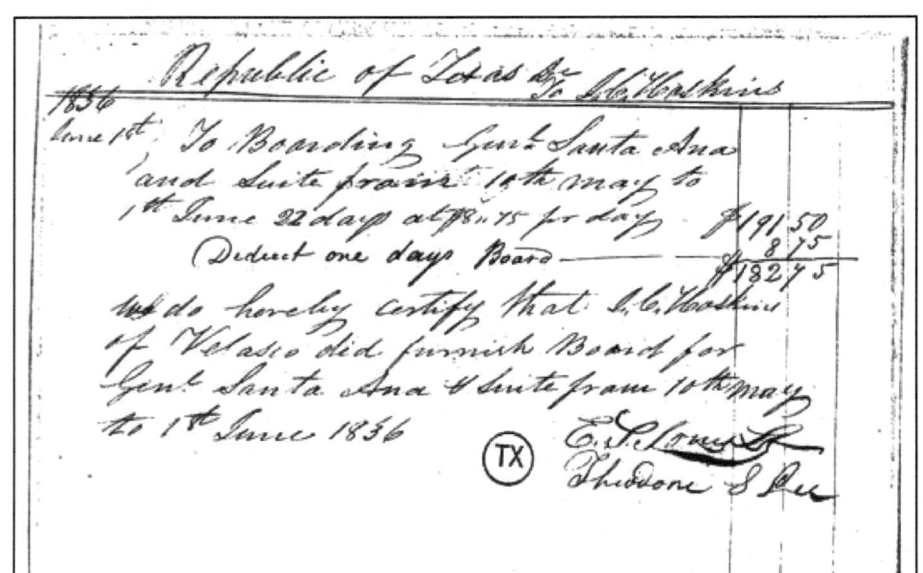

Figure 47: Receipt for board of Santa Anna and officers from 10-May to 1-Jun-1836

officers) were provided board from this establishment (found in Velasco Block 11), as indicated in a receipt sent by the Republic of Texas to Isaac C. Hoskins, in Figure 47 [Hoskins 1836].

Meanwhile, Santa Anna actually stayed in a building owned by Francis J. Haskins, as indicated in another receipt, shown below in Figure 48 [Haskins May-1836].

Gabriel Nuñez Ortega made several entries in his diary during their stay in Velasco [Nuñez Ortega 1836 p. 4]:

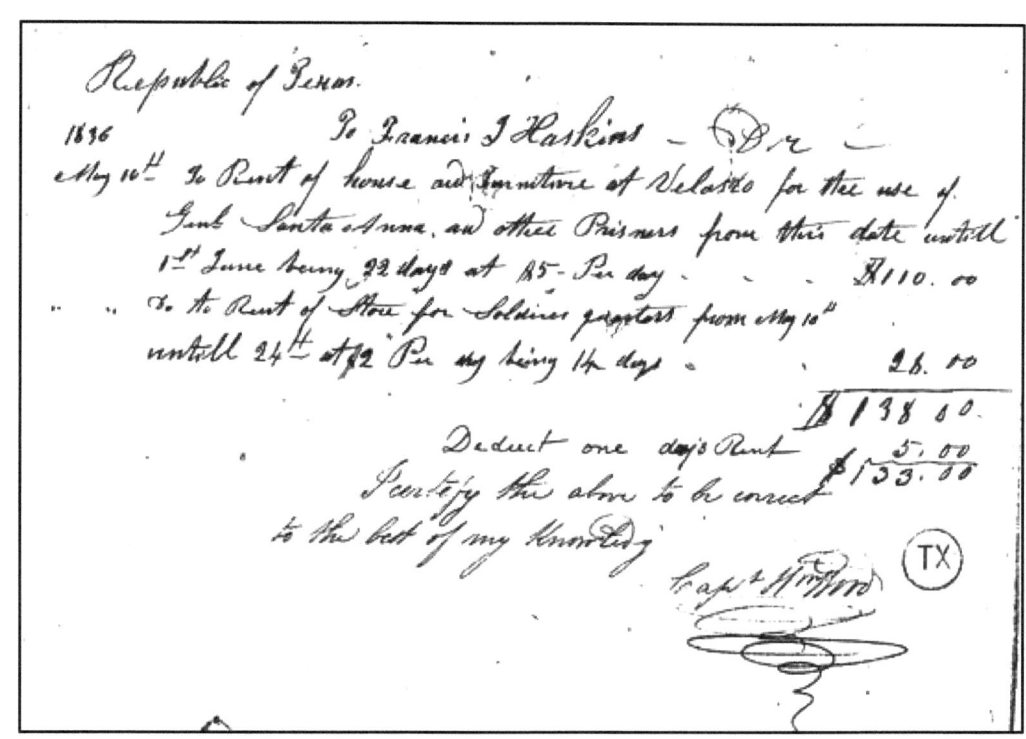

Figure 48: Receipt for rent of house for Santa Anna and officers from 10-May to 1-Jun-1836

May 10 - "*... we were given a small house, very dirty and without hope of means of living. In the evening a hotel sent us a piece of fried fish, coffee and some terrible (ugly) bread*".

May 11 – "*In Velasco we did nothing else but kill and shoo away the many flies that were there.*"

May 12 – "*They talked a bit about the negotiations for the Agreement. Our good friend Wharton arrived with milk, butter and some greens and he went away to bring us back other things.*"

May 13 - "*There were conferences with the Texas Cabinet and almost concerned the Agreement. Colonel Wharton assisted in the discussion. That night our trunk was robbed of $125.00 while we slept.*"

May 14 – "*The Agreement and Public was definitely agreed upon and reached agreement a published, both were put in clean (final) form for signatures with this date, although it must be verified tomorrow Sunday. Present were President Burnet, Hardyman, Collingsworth and Grayson. Mr. Lamar was not present because of occupation elsewhere. Mr. Porter because he was absent.*"

May 15 – "*The agreements were signed in the evening and it was agreed to send them to the Mexican and Texas Generals tomorrow.*"

The capital at Velasco is described briefly in the article "Capitals of the Lone Star" in *National Republic* magazine [Crouch 1932]. In this article, a photograph is shown of a two-story building (reproduced below as Figure 49 which may be the Brown-Hoskins hotel and tavern, but photographed at a much later time (perhaps 1870s). No date or source is given with the photo, and no provenance for it has yet been established.

Figure 49: Former Capitol of Texas at Old Velasco [Crouch 1932]

In compliance with the treaties, Santa Anna was to be returned to Mexico, and indeed was put aboard the ***Invincible*** standing off of Velasco on 1-Jun-1836 for his return to Veracruz. However, hard feelings among the Texans, especially a group of 230 (some references say 130) new volunteers under Gen. Thomas Jefferson Green who had arrived on the steamer ***Ocean*** and other vessels from New Orleans, delayed the departure, wanting to punish Santa Anna [Dienst 1909 p. 58, Binkley 1940, Clarke 1969 pp. 121-131, Pierce 1969 p. 165, Myers & Smith, Francaviglia 1998 p. 126, Crisp 2022 p. 519]. Instead, Santa Anna was brought ashore on the 4th at Quintana for safekeeping, staying a few days hosted by Samuel May Williams and Thomas F. McKinney (from 4- to 9-June according to the Ortega diary), before returning to Velasco, staying at the Brown-Hoskins hotel and tavern until the 15th. In his diary, Herman Ehrenberg (uniquely) described Santa Anna's departure from the ***Invincible***: *"After the longboat carrying the prisoner had laboriously made its way from the small fleet of ships back through the breakers, it had to cut across in front of the harbor of Velasco. All of the townspeople, some travelers, and General Green's whole brigade of volunteers were gathered there. The trembling Mexican president, who happened by chance to be sitting under the fluttering colors of the Republic, took off his hat with a flourish as the boat glided past the darkly murmuring crowd assembled at Velasco. Groveling before his captors and never lifting his eyes as he gazed at the bottom of the boat, he bowed repeatedly to the crowd of spectators on the shore. It was a disgraceful sight. When the boat had gone by the crowd, he collapsed to his seat in the stern of the boat, exhausted and with mortal terror on his face. … This pitiful display said more in favor of the defeated and disgraced president than either Houston or Burnet could have said on his behalf in all their speeches. It served to remind the Texans who had suffered such terrible injuries and losses that Santa Anna was their prisoner now – and the prisoner of a civilized nation. He moved back into rooms he had occupied before in the house where President Burnet was* *living, and under Mister Burnet's generous supervision, Santa Anna resigned himself to his fate.*" [Crisp 2022 pp. 519-520]. The Crisp reference (p. 523n25) is incorrect in devaluing this account by claiming "*the position of Velasco [was] slightly higher up the Brazos River than Quintana*", since the opposite was true at the time (e.g., see Figure 127), so **Invincible**'s longboat would indeed have to pass Velasco to reach Quintana as it traveled up the Brazos River from offshore. The story continues with Ortega's diary entry for the 9th, which says "*There was great excitement for us to go to Velasco in Captain Paton's care .... At 5 in the afternoon ... we were installed in a hotel*" [Nuñez Ortega 1836 p. 7]. Ramón Martínez Caro wrote "*After we were turned over to Captain Patton ... he took us to Velasco and lodged us in the second story of a house whose first floor was a restaurant.*" [Caro 1837 p. 137]. William H. Patton was put in charge of the prisoners, and took them to his family's plantation two miles upriver from Columbia for some weeks (now Varner-Hogg Plantation State Historic Site) on 15-Jun-1836 aboard the steamer **Laura**, until they were again transferred on 30-Jul-1836 to Orozimbo Plantation for several months.

Mary Austin Holley was apparently inspired to write another tune after the Texan victory at San Jacinto (mentioning the Brazos in one of the verses) called "The Texan Song of Liberty" and dedicated it to Sam Houston [Holley 1836b], the first page shown in Figure 50.

Stephen F. Austin returned to Texas from his U. S. trip at the same spot whence he left it - the mouth of the Brazos – on 27-Jun-1836, conferring with the government at the new capital of Velasco for a few days [Barker 1926 p. 432-437, Cantrell 1999 p. 348]. Fearing the war with Mexico was not really over, he hatched a plan to resolve the conflict permanently. During the first few days of Jul-1836, Stephen F. Austin called on Santa Anna several times, to propose that he write to Andrew Jackson, requesting that Jackson mediate a settlement between Texas and Mexico, guaranteeing the security of Texas with U.S. military force if necessary, so that Santa Anna could then go back to Mexico. Austin probably had some sympathy for Santa Anna since, when the roles were reversed a year prior, Santa Anna had been the one to, first, move Austin out

Figure 50: "The Texas Song of Liberty"
by Mary Austin Holley

of prison to house arrest in Mexico City, and then release him altogether. Indeed, Santa Anna wrote two letters (dated 8-Jul-1836 at Velasco) to Andrew Jackson and also General José Urrea, that a political solution was best [Santa Anna 1836]. Austin returned to Velasco on 20-Jul-1836, to rejoin his fellow commissioners to write their report [Archer et al Jul-1836], who had just arrived aboard the *Invincible* from New Orleans [Dienst 1909 p. 47]. At this time, they convinced Austin to run for president of Texas [Barker 1926 p. 437], although he was heavily outvoted by Sam Houston in the elections of Sep-1836. Finally, at the request of the Republic of Texas government, Santa Anna was instead sent to Washington DC, departing Velasco by sea on 6-Dec-1836 [Nuñez Ortega 1836 p. 22]. Austin died three weeks later at the home of George McKinstry near West Columbia, still serving Texas as Secretary of State, since the capital had switched there from Velasco in October [Clarke 1969 pp. 154-159].

Another conflict between the military and civil authorities of the new republic also occurred at Velasco in mid-July, when Lt. Col. Henry Millard of the Texas Revolutionary Army (unhappy about the government's failure to provide for the army) ordered Capt. Amasa Turner to arrest President David G. Burnet, which Turner declined to do [Binkley 1940, Clarke 1969 p. 134-135, Pierce 1969]. So, Turner and his unit must have returned to Velasco after the Battle of San Jacinto.

A hospital was also operated at Velasco, and eight Mexican prisoners (from the Battle of San Jacinto) were requisitioned by Frederick A. Sawyer, acting Secretary of War, for use there from a large group working to build Fort Travis on Galveston Island [Sawyer 1836, Henson 1990].

In late Oct-1836, a visitor to Velasco from New Orleans aboard the schooner *Colonel Fannin* was Francis Richard Lubbock (later governor of Texas in 1861-1863), who wrote of his arrival *"Velasco, on the left bank of the Brazos, at its mouth, was at this time the chief port of the Republic, while Quintana, on the opposite side, was the seat of an extensive foreign trade. American Galveston had not then been established. The main business house here, and perhaps the largest in the whole country, was that of McKinney and Williams."* [Lubbock 1900 pp. 29-30], where he found his brother Thomas S. Lubbock employed. He apparently stayed at a new hotel, stating *"On the very first day a schooner with quite a few passengers and a full cargo was wrecked upon the bar. It was said then that the Velasco bar was a hard sand bar, and when a vessel struck upon it she seldom escaped destruction. … My first night was spent in a hotel kept by J. M. (John Milton) Shreve, a Kentuckian (subsequently he was chief clerk of the House of Representatives of the Republic of Texas and I an assistant). His partner in the hotel proved to be Benjamin F. Grayson, of my native town, Beaufort. He was a brother of Capt. Thos. W. Grayson."* [Lubbock 1900 pp. 33-34]. Afterwards, he traveled to Columbia, experiencing the heady days when the newly elected government moved there, and decided to move to Texas. He returned to New Orleans, convinced his wife to move, and returned to Quintana and Velasco before year's end, describing it as *"Velasco was then the prospective seaport and commercial emporium that was cradled in the rich valley of the Brazos, and now again after half a century she lifts her head with buoyant hope of success."* [Lubbock 1900 pp. 35-43]. The last comment apparently refers to the "boom town" excitement when Velasco was moved upstream in the 1890s.

In Feb-1837, William Fairfax Gray arrived by sea at Velasco aboard the schooner *Texas*, on his second visit to Texas. His diary has excellent depictions of the area, including one of the better descriptions of hazards at the Brazos bar: *"About 4 o'clock (21-Feb-1837) we descried* (caught sight of) *the houses of Velasco and Quintana, and shortly after we were off the mouth of the river. The wind set strongly on shore, the surf ran high, with a great noise, and we now knew that it was these same breakers we had heard at daybreak, having then been off the mouth of the Brazos. The Captain concluded that the pilots could not come out, and determined to run in without one. He mistook the pass, and ran his vessel on the bar, where she thumped awfully. The squaresail sheet parted and the sail fell on deck, the jib sheet also parted, the vessel rolled on the bar, broached to, and several swells dashed over her broadside and was near sweeping the decks before the mainsail could be lowered. It was an awful moment; the Captain himself quailed, and the boldest held his breath for a time, for they thought the vessel would be a wreck, where many others had been before. The wreck of the* **Flora**, *of Middleton, lay a few hundred yards from us, having foundered on the same bar a few months before. By great exertion the mainsail was lowered, she obeyed the flying jib, and again got before the wind, and after a few more shakes which made her crack, she passed over the bar, and we floated under easy sail into the Brazos, passed Velasco, and rounded to at Quintana at sunset …… In the afternoon (22-Feb-1837) went over to Velasco with J. T. Gray, and <u>saw the fort</u>, Mexican prisoners, etc. … Velasco has about one dozen poor houses, looks old and decaying. It is at the mouth of the river, on the east side. Quintana has four dwelling houses and one store; it is on the west side. The river is about 200 yards wide, and very deep; but the bar without the mouth has not more than six feet at its deepest pass. This will always retard the commercial prosperity of the port. There are no trees of any sort within several miles around.*" [Gray 1837 pp. 201-202].

In early Jul-1837, a traveler named Thomas Rexford arrived at Velasco, after a six-week sea voyage aboard the **Belvadier** from New York. They had stopped at the mouth of the Mississippi, to obtain information about "*Mexican cruisers*", and proceeded when the news was favorable. Rexford wrote in his journal that "*The Village (or city as it is called) of Velasco … contains about twenty houses; it has no public buildings unless its Taverns, and Grog-shops 'of which there is a goodly number', can be termed as such … On the west side of the River is a village plot laid out called Quintana with five or six houses. This, however, may be considered a part of Velasco as the harbor is common to both and the River only about three hundred yards broad …… There are large quantities of drift wood about the mouth of the River which serves the inhabitants for fuel and many other purposes: I took notice <u>the Stock-ade fort was made of timber from the beach</u>.*" [Rexford 1837].

A man named Buegel served as a soldier at the fort in the period of 1836-1837, and he said "*I served for sixteen months with the soldiers in Velasco. Our captain's name was Snell. We had to guard the fort since the Mexicans were trying to land. From the fort, which was three hundred paces from the shoreline, we could, during the day, see three ships in the telescope. That was in May 1837.*" [Seele 1979, p. 99]. Snell was apparently Capt. Martin K. Snell of Company E, 1st Regiment of the Army Of The Republic Of Texas (who had first arrived in Texas at Velasco among the New Orleans Greys in Oct-1835). Company E moved to Velasco in Sep-1836. Buegel also describes night-time sentry duty along the beach two miles from the fort, and that he scared off an attempt by three Mexican longboats to come ashore. Buegel also described a sea battle off Velasco, perhaps the incident where the **Independence** was defeated by **Vencedor del Alamo** and **Libertador** on 17-Apr-1837 (sometimes called the Battle of the Brazos River), capturing Capt. George Wheelwright and William H. Wharton who was a passenger, among others. The scene was captured in a painting by Fred Toler (Figure 51 below). The battle has been described in many references [Dienst 1909 pp. 60-65, Douglas 1936 pp. 47-52, Hill 1987 pp. 74-80, Meed 2001 pp. 72-80, Jordan 2006 pp. 83-86, Thompson 2020 pp. 95-97]. This action was part of a broader renewal of war with Mexico, in which Mexico's upgraded naval strength was sent to blockade the Texas coast. Indeed, Sam Houston had ordered his Secretary of the Navy (then S. Rhoads Fisher) to Velasco to observe for such, and devise a defense of the coast [Houston Apr-1837].

Figure 51: Painting of "Capture of the Independence" by Fred Toler
Courtesy of The San Jacinto Museum and Battlefield Association

Capt. Snell was involved in an incident in April 1837, perhaps showing there were additional stresses at the fort. Francis Lubbock apparently saw one angry fight between officers, writing *"A day or two after my arrival in Velasco, while in a billiard room, I witnessed a homicide. Captain Snell, commanding a company of regulars at the post, came in. He accosted Lieutenant Sproul (James T. Sprawl) as to his absence from the post. Hot words ensued, and the lieutenant was shot down by his captain and killed. Snell was exonerated, as Sproul probably attempted to draw his sword."* [Lubbock 1900 p.35]. A newspaper article had a similar story – *"A fatal recontre occurred on the evening of the 26th April, between Capt. Snell, commander of the Fort at Velasco, and his Lieutenant, Sprowl. Captain Snell made the attack upon his officer (said to be for disobedience or orders and was disarmed of his sword by the Lieutenant; he then resorted to his pistols and shot the officer in the forehead. Snell was to be tried at Brazoria by the civil court, on Tuesday, the 30th April. The excitement of the citizens was against him"* [Reed 1837].

Buegel also wrote of Snell, *"He was a Creole, a rich merchant's son from New Orleans. He was too strict on discipline, and his punishments were too severe, just as it now with the regulars. Thus, he came to be hated by the troops, and it was only a matter of time before the troops were ready to mutiny. They were just waiting for an opportunity. Finally, a soldier born in America of Irish parents had a fistfight with a sailor. I have fought with them too. Snell had him arrested, and he was brought to the guardhouse. I immediately went and informed Osthaus. He was our sergeant, a Westphalian born in Cosfeld. He had earlier been a soldier under Napoleon. He got up and said to the others, 'We can't take it any longer, being treated like this. This has got to end!' We were all in agreement, talked it over among ourselves, and then went to the guardhouse with the Poles. We were also joined by some Americans. We had our loaded guns in our hands. Snell came to the fort from the town. Two men were holding the prisoner. Snell hit him the back of the neck. Snell ordered the sergeant 'Put the fellow in chains.' Osthaus replied, 'That I won't do, but you are going to be shot dead.' Snell drew two pistols from his belt and pointed them at Osthaus. But, when he saw us, he took off and ran back to town. Then, on Osthaus' orders, the barracks were set on fire."* [Seele 1979, pp. 101-102].

In this same period, the ***Invincible*** returned to Texas from a lengthy refitting trip to New York, a voyage that captain Jeremiah Brown took against the wishes of president Sam Houston. Upon his return, he was replaced as captain by Henry L. Thompson, but Brown was nominated by Houston as customs collector for the port of the Brazos [Houston May-1837]. Apparently, there was a lively debate between Velasco and Quintana about which side would gain the customs office and warehouse [McKinney 1837]. Jeremiah Brown must have been an advocate for Velasco as he published a list of Velasco tariff duties shown in Figure 52 [Brown 1837], while McKinney favored Quintana.

The new captain Henry Thompson and the Secretary of the Navy (S. Rhoads Fisher) would then take a cruise in summer 1837 to Yucatan with the ***Invincible*** and ***Brutus***, which embittered Sam Houston and eventually resulted in both being removed from their positions. After her return to Texas waters, the ***Invincible*** was involved in a confrontation on 27-Aug-1837 with two Mexican warships (***Iturbide*** and ***Libertador***) much like the ***Independence*** a few months prior, but just outside the mouth of Galveston Bay. Secretary of the Navy Fisher had transferred by boat to the **Brutus** upon their arrival off Galveston the day before, and it had made port that evening [Powers 2006 p. 151]. The next day, the ***Brutus*** tried to come from the safety of Galveston harbor to aid the ***Invincible***, but she grounded on an uncharted sandbar [Thompson 2020 pp. 102-104]. Peter Rindlisbacher has interpreted the scene as the ***Invincible*** attempts to break away and make a run for the safety of Galveston Bay.

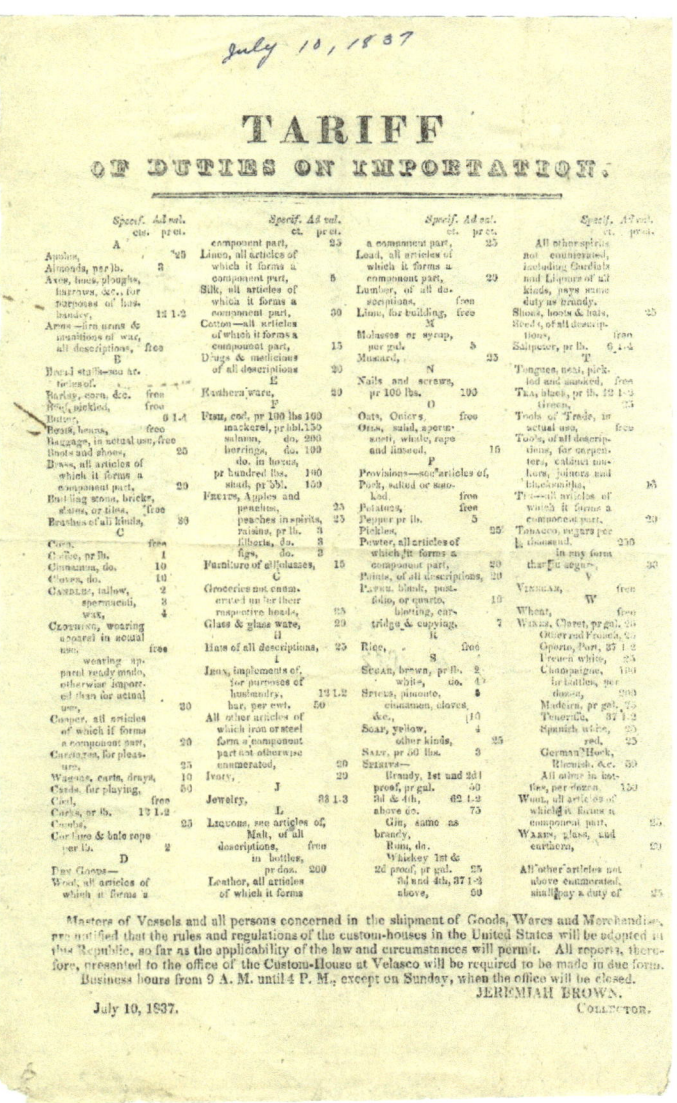

Figure 52: "Tariff of Duties on Importation" at Velasco, by Jeremiah Brown
Courtesy of Dolph Briscoe Center for American History

Figure 53: Painting by Peter Rindlisbacher "Parting Shot; Invincible Off Galveston, 1837"

Figure 54: Painting by Peter Rindlisbacher "Final Minutes; Invincible Aground Off Galveston"

Unfortunately, the *Invincible* misjudged the same shoals and sandbars off the northeastern end of Galveston Island, and also ran aground while entering the pass into the bay and was broken up by a heavy surf (see Figure 54). These shoals have since silted in and compose that end of the island today [Gearhart et al 2020]. S. Rhoads Fisher must have watched in horror from Galveston as his remaining two vessels were lost. The *Brutus*, although stuck, survived for about five weeks, when Racer's Storm destroyed her, the *Thomas Toby* and every vessel in Galveston Harbor save one [Geiser 1944].

Certainly, losing the navy's two remaining vessels just as he returned from his over-extended cruise to Yucatan did not further endear S. Rhoads Fisher and H. L. Thompson to president Sam Houston, and may partially explain his bitter enmity to them and the navy in this period. Fisher was removed as Secretary of the Navy on 28-Nov-1837 after a bitter Senate trial, and William M. Shepherd replaced him as of 5-Dec-1837 for a period of the next year. The *Hannah Elizabeth* controversy, the summer 1837 cruise, and the loss of the *Invincible* and *Brutus* also seems to have started a feud that led to Fisher's mysterious death in 1839 [Compton 2014]. Fisher's replacement Shepherd, a military physician, had written to Sam Houston a long, diplomatic and reasoned explanation, dated 30-Sep-1837 in the wake of the loss of the

"First Texas Navy", for continued support of a Texas navy [Shepherd 1837]. Perhaps not surprisingly, but just prior to Racer's Storm, the government authorized Alexander Thompson to survey the end of Galveston Island for a "navy yard", then occupied by the army's Post Galveston and the first Fort Travis. His report was sent just as the storm was bearing down on Galveston [A. Thompson 1837], in a move that would signify transfer of navy headquarters away from the Brazos. A much larger and better Navy would emerge under the leadership of Mirabeau Lamar, but that story mostly involves Galveston as their homeport, and is told extensively in other books.

Back at the Brazos …. and as stated previously, Mary Austin Holley made another trip up the river in 1838, when she visited the graves from the Battle of Velasco. It must have been on this trip that she also put to music or composed another version of the "Brazos Boat Song" (Figure 21), called "The Brazos Boat Glee" [Holley 1838]. A copy of the first (of three) sheets of music for this tune is shown in Figure 55.

Figure 55: "The Brazos Boat Glee"
by Mary Austin Holley, 1838 [Holley 1838]

The Texan Fort Velasco was apparently still in operation in 1840, when Francis C. Sheridan, a visitor from the British diplomatic service, described that it *"...had an old brass 18-pounder with a touch-hole equivalent to the circumference of the mouth of Mrs. Sharpe (Sharp) – and 3 other small ones whose united ages amount to a greater number, than my arithmetic (which is fair to say was neglected in my youth) will permit me to calculate ..."* [Sheridan 1954 p. 19]. Mrs. Sharp was Sarah Jane Wharton Calvit, the wife of John Sharp, merchant, notary public and the United States consular agent at Velasco, who Sheridan had earlier described (p. 16) as *"...a young lady, with beautiful eyes and an agreeable expression of countenance, but with a mouth of such dimensions, as entitles it to be compared only with the orifice which through which Harlequin jumps in the Pantomimes"*. Sheridan further describes the battery as having a Liberty Pole, *"... which rears high its stately head, crowned with a small beer barrel, intended to represent the Cap of Liberty, which I must take the liberty to represent, it hardly succeeds in doing"*. However, the battery appears to have been discontinued about this time, as the threat from Mexico decreased due to turmoil in that country [Pierce 1969]. However, it appears the site was again needed in early 1843, when Sam Houston telling John Warren of *"... an appropriation of Congress one thousand dollars, have been placed at the disposition of the Executive for the purpose of fortifying the port of Velasco"* [Houston 1843].

At this time, Velasco was described *"... in its infancy containing about 300 inhabitants and daily increasing .... the greatest drawback to this commanding situation is the Bar (sand) stretching directly across the mouth shifting more or less with every heavy gale. The greatest depth was 7 feet at high water .... the land is extremely low and flat presenting nothing more than a long sandy beach."* [Renaud 1840].

Also in 1840, the **Lafitte** was the first steamboat <u>built</u> in Texas, at or near Velasco by John Bradbury Follett (1795-1846) under contract with the firm of McKinney, Williams & Co., for trade between the Brazos and Galveston, as reported by his son, Alexander Glass Follett [Follett 1895, Puryear & Winfield 1976 pp. 52-54]. This ship was used as a coast guard vessel, and used in 1842 to ferry Texas troops [Bollaert 1956 pp. 34-54, Wells 1960 pp. 93-94, Thompson 2020 pp. 211-212].

Additional detailed history can be found about Velasco's use as a new thriving port, which later declined as Galveston developed [Guthrie 1993, Francaviglia 1998]. Eventually, the Brazos Bar proved too hazardous for increasingly larger ships, and with road and railway connections over a causeway, Galveston (and then Houston) began to surpass Velasco as a port city.

The town of Velasco existed afterwards for some decades, through the Civil War and beyond, but was largely abandoned in the late 1800s due to the hazard of hurricanes at its low-lying seaside location, and indeed the town was moved upstream about four miles in about 1891, becoming part of Freeport in 1957.

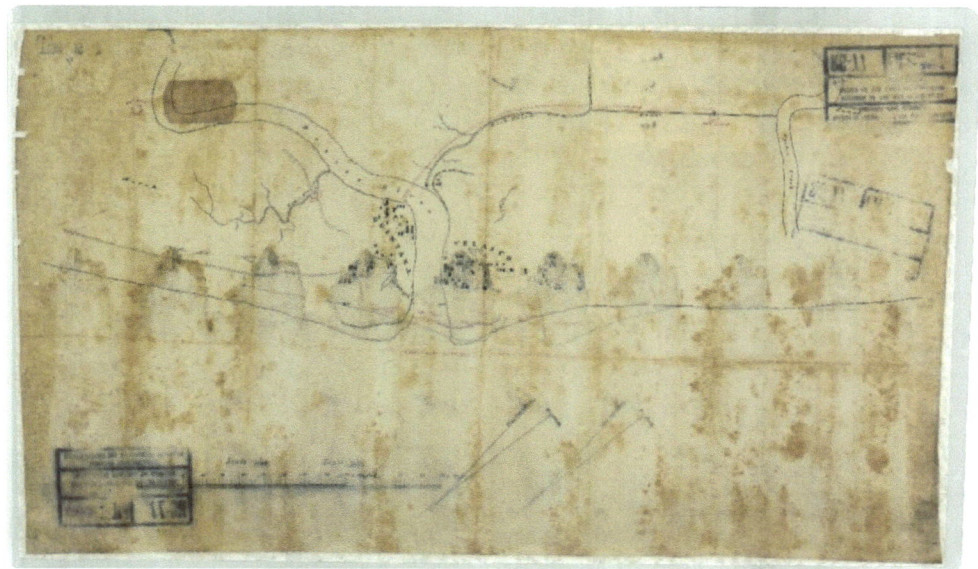

Manuscript map showing Forts Quintana and Velasco at mouth of the Brazos [Unknown 1863]
original source: U. S. National Archives

A map was made of the mouth of the Brazos, printed in 1858 with topographic data measured in 1852 [Bache 1858], shown in Figure 56 below. Please note the lack of buildings in Monument Square, that the Battery is now gone, and that significant growth of the beach has occurred, with a new sandbar forming offshore on the Quintana side.

Figure 56: Upper portion of 1858 Bache Map of the Entrance to Brazos River by Coast Survey Office
digitized by Blueline Print Shop, from an original at Brazosport Museum of Natural Science

During the Civil War, a series of artillery positions were constructed by the Confederate States Army, changed and improved over time, beginning with a simple earthen redoubt of two 18-pound cannons (known as the "Town Redoubt" or "Town Fort"), probably on new beachfront land closer to the Gulf than the position of the former Republic of Texas battery an example is shown in Figure 57 below). In Jan-1862, the Union ships **Midnight**, **Arthur** and **Rachel Seaman** engaged this shore battery, testing its strength and range [Barr 1961 p. 9].

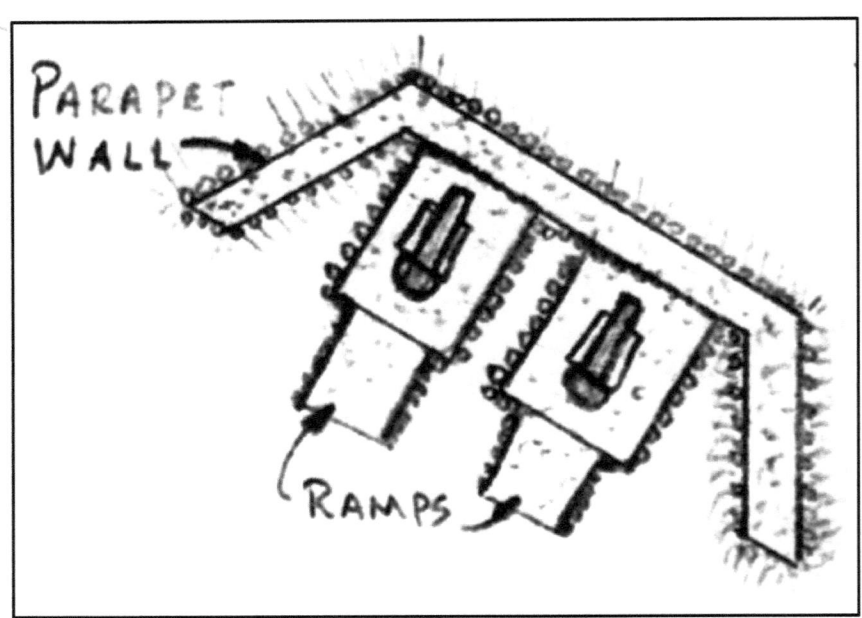

Figure 57: Artillery Redoubt at Velasco circa 1861-1862
Courtesy of Brazoria County Historical Museum

The redoubt was manned by two artillery companies belonging to the Thirteenth Texas Infantry regiment, using at least one eighteen-pound cannon on 11-Aug-1862 to drive off a Union warship [Barr 1961]. This regiment was commanded by Joseph Bates, a local planter appointed as Colonel in the Confederate Army, and for whom Fort Bates (Quintana side) was named. Soldiers posted to this Fort Velasco and nearby camp published their own handwritten weekly newspaper entitled "The Drum Tap", and two issues are known to exist (for 14- and 28-Jun-1862). The surviving issues are two pages each with three columns per page, written in a chatty manner with sarcastic humor, often writing about unit resizing (known as "*razeering*"), elections for officers, and general disdain for quartermasters, sutlers and outside suppliers (especially "*Brazorians*"). Lack of quantity and quality of rations, coffee and uniforms is a frequent topic. A copy of Issue No. 7 (14-Jun-1862) can be found at TSLAC, Call# 2-6/584, where a note says "Original in the U.D.C. Museum". This is assumed to apply to the former Texas Confederate Museum managed by the United Daughters of the Confederacy Museum (Texas Division), formerly housed in a building on the Capital grounds, whose paper records are now housed at the Nita Stewart Haley Memorial Library in Midland TX. The first page of Issue No. 10 (28-Jun-1862), currently owned and shared by Joelle Barnes and Bettie Liebzeit (from the estate of Lyda Lilla Bertrand Bessonette), descendants of Peter Bertrand, is illustrated in Figure 58.

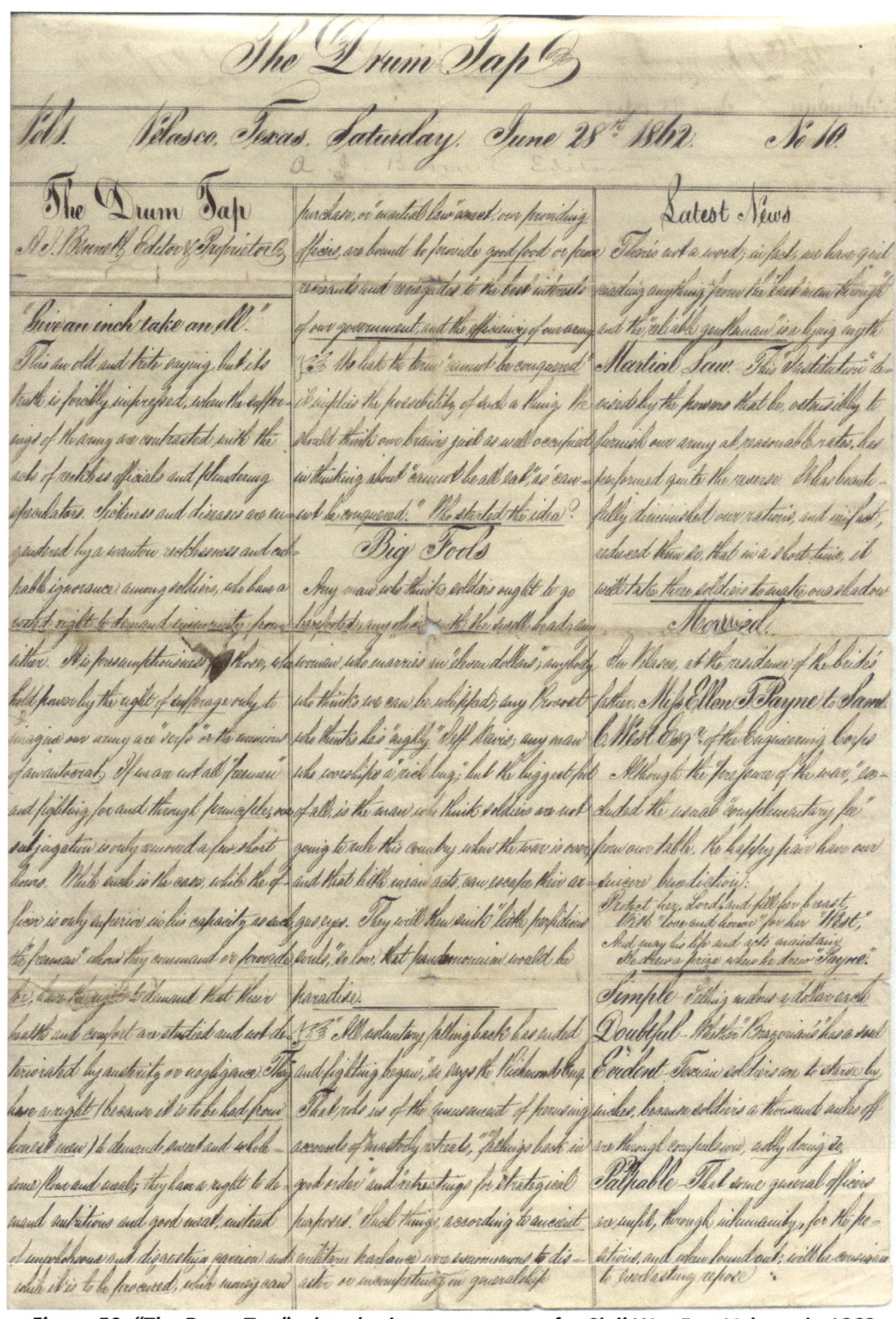

Figure 58: "The Drum Tap" – handwritten newspaper for Civil War Fort Velasco in 1862
From the estate of Lyda Lilla Bertrand Bessonette

The location of this early redoubt is shown in a large hand-drawn map of the central Texas coast by Confederate Army Capt. Tipton Walker from the early Civil War era [Walker 1862, sheet 2 of 3]. A close-up of the Velasco portion is shown in Figure 59 below. The location of Monument Square is marked in this map by a tent-like image, perhaps indicating an encampment used by soldiers in the early part of the war. About five miles upstream, a floating barrier of live-oak logs was also erected across the river, originally guarded by a battery of two 8-inch siege howitzers on the right bank; however, a second battery of two 12-pound siege guns were added on the left bank [Boyd et al 2014 p. 6].

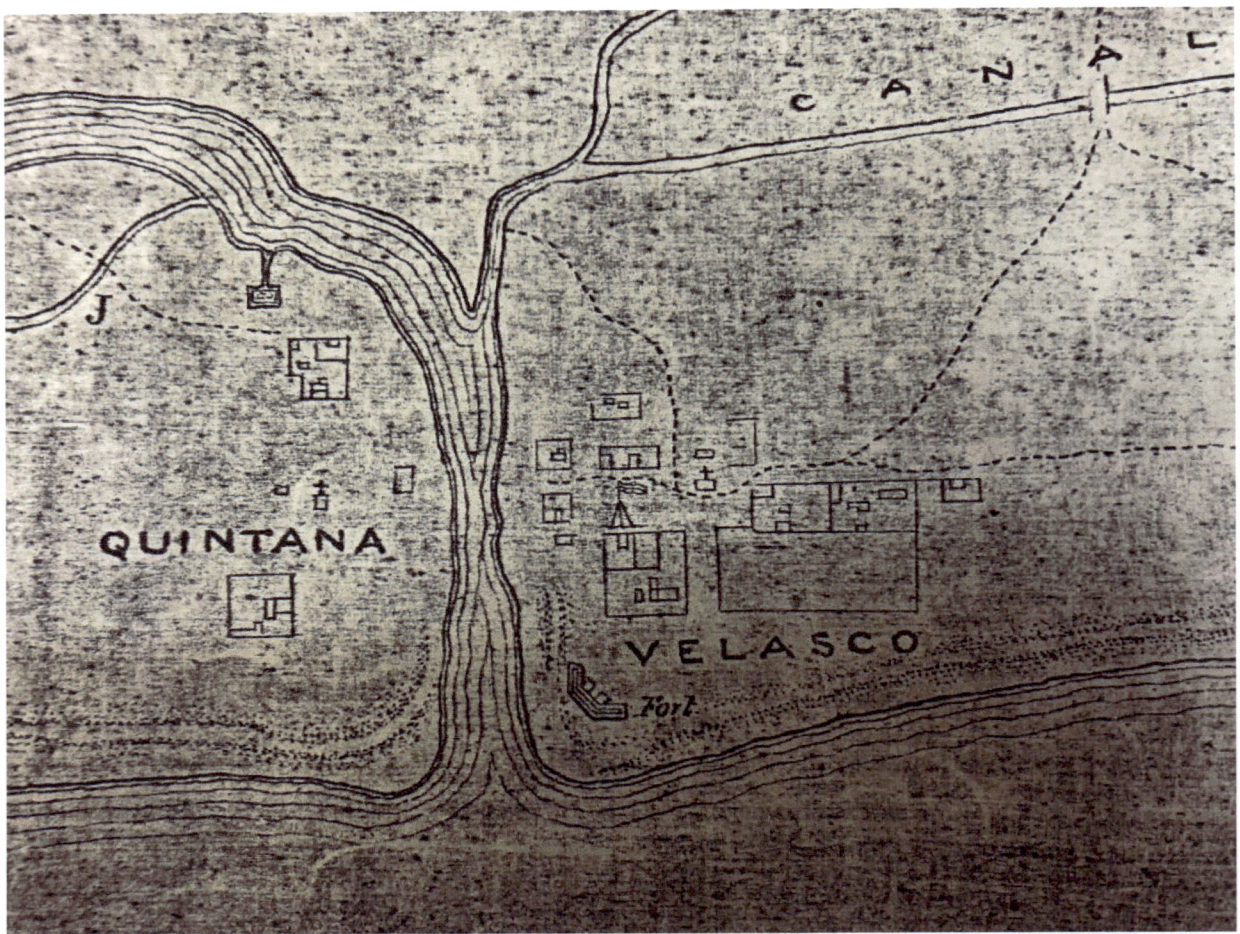

Figure 59: Detail of Tipton Walker map, National Archives Record Group 77, Civil War Map File Z 343
original source: U.S. National Archives

Another map (Figure 60) indicates a row of pilings was also erected across the mouth of the river as a defensive barrier, and that the "Town Redoubt" was also named Fort Velasco [Unknown 1863], with a similar "Fort Quintana" across the river. The British-flagged schooner **Rob Roy** had run the blockade into the Brazos in Sep-1863 looking for a load of cotton, and was commandeered by the Confederates for a few weeks to install the pilings [Wilson 2020 pp. 85-87]. This circa-1863 map also shows a ferry crossing from Quintana over the Brazos to a road along East Union Bayou and canal (labeled as "Covered Way") leading to a structure at the canal crossing northeast of Velasco marked as *Téte de pont*, a term for a military work to protect a bridge. A similar structure is shown on the road over West Union Bayou into Quintana.

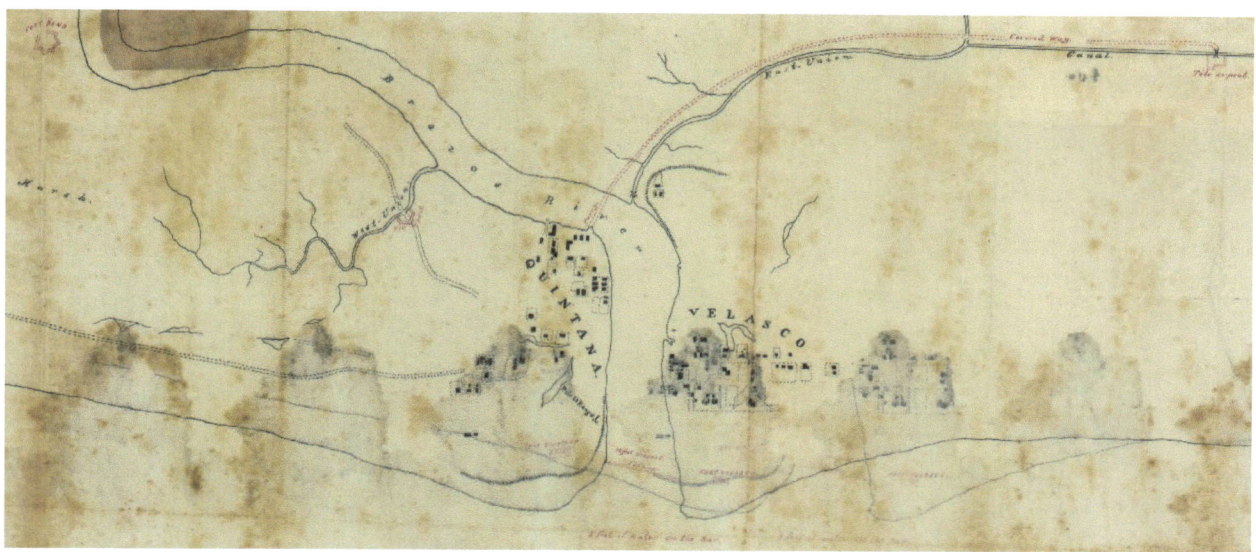

Figure 60: Close-up of Velasco/Quintana portion of National Archives map Z51-9, circa 1863 (the fort on the Velasco side is labeled as Fort Velasco)

The forts shown in Figures 59 and 60 are apparently the ones described by Commodore Henry Haywood Bell aboard the **USS Brooklyn** in his diary entry of 1-Jun-1863 – *"Saw in the river at Velasco one steamer and one schooner. A newly-built fort on the Quintana side, and 100 tents adjacent .... On the Velasco side the battery is not so prominent; situated near the water and to the south of the white house with colonnades, some 40 or 50 men there in the rear of the fort."* [Bell 1863]. The "white house" is presumed to be the Archer-Herndon House [Smith Sep-2014]. In 1932, Mrs. T. A. Humphries wrote *"On a sandy ridge in the neighborhood of the coast guard station, stands a clump of gnarled salt cedars and the crumbling ruins of a huge brick cistern. They are all that remains of the palatial summer home of the Herndons .... this spot was occupied by a stately white mansion, surrounded by wide porches and supported by solid colonial columns. It was the tallest house along the coast and could be seen so far at sea that it became a landmark. It stood on the highest point of land and was used as a lookout by the neighborhood. .... The house was surrounded by salt cedars and oleanders. Hidden among the shrubbery was an icehouse with concrete walls. In the spring of each year, a shipload of ice was brought from the north, carefully packed in sawdust, and stored for their use in the summer. ..... In order that enemy ships should not enter the Brazos, the Confederate soldiers barred the channel with live oak logs driven into the bottom of the stream."* [Humphries 1932]. This original Archer-Herndon house was reported as destroyed in the 1875 hurricane [Smith Sep-2014].

Due to the strategic importance of the Brazos River for blockade runners, work at Velasco eventually resulted in a formal five-gun-platform fortification known as Fort Sulakowski or Fort Velasco, completed in the winter of 1863-1864 adjacent to the town [Freeman 1995], and suspected to have existed at or near the south corner of Surfside-platted Block 568, shown in Figure 61 labeled as Fort Velasco (No. 250) [Unknown 1864a]. Armament comprised one 30-pound Parrot gun, one 32-pounder Navy gun, one 24-pound and one 18-pound Sea coast guns, and one 12-pounder [Cross 1864, Freeman 1995]. So effective was this battery that blockading Union warships estimated in early 1864 that it had six 32-pounders, and never engaged them for any period [Barr 1961 p. 29].

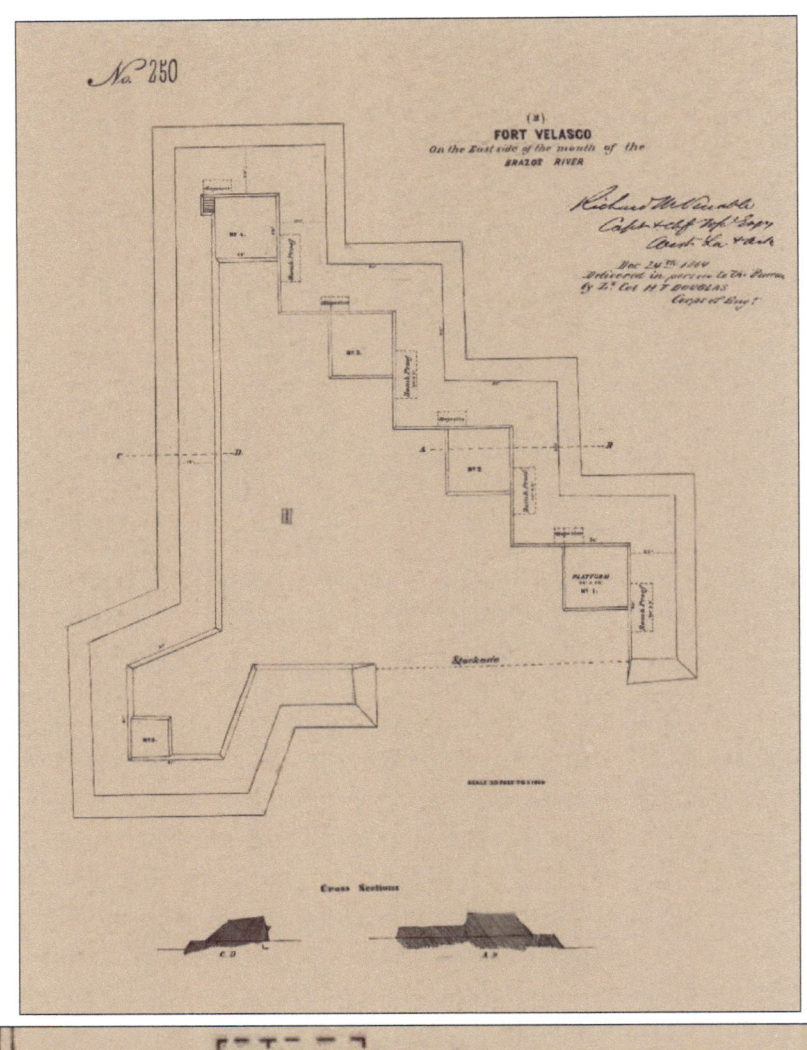

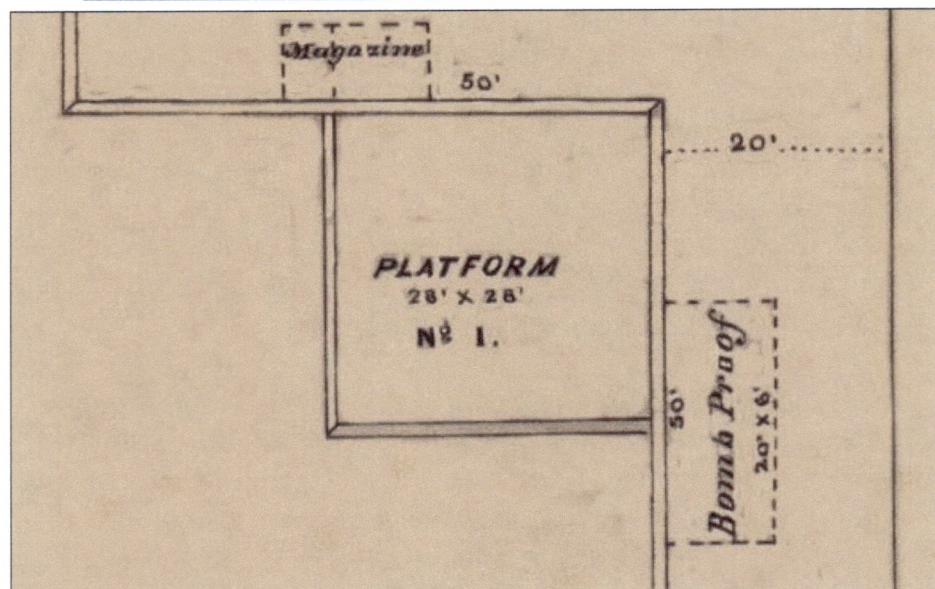

Figure 61: Civil War fort built at Velasco in 1863-1864, labeled as Fort Velasco (original + detail)
from Gilmer Civil War Maps Collection, University of North Carolina at Chapel Hill)
foxed original modified with Photoshop by Christiane Louise Kneupper

The fort was built under the supervision of Lt. Abraham Cross for his commander, Valery Sulakowski (who designed it), then Chief Engineer for the Confederate States Army for the District of Texas, New Mexico and Arizona. The fort was labeled as Fort Sulakowski in one of Cross' reports [Cross 1864] where he reported completion on 11-Jan-1864 – see item 1 in Figure 62 below. The Velasco fort complex was but one of several such forts built at or near the Brazos River mouth in this period, and similar Civil War-era forts existed across the river at Quintana (Fort Bates, also known as Fort Quintana) and about a mile upriver (Fort Terrell, also known as Fort Bend); this last site being thought lost due to riverbank erosion in the 65 years after its founding [Freeman et al 1997, Freeman 1998].

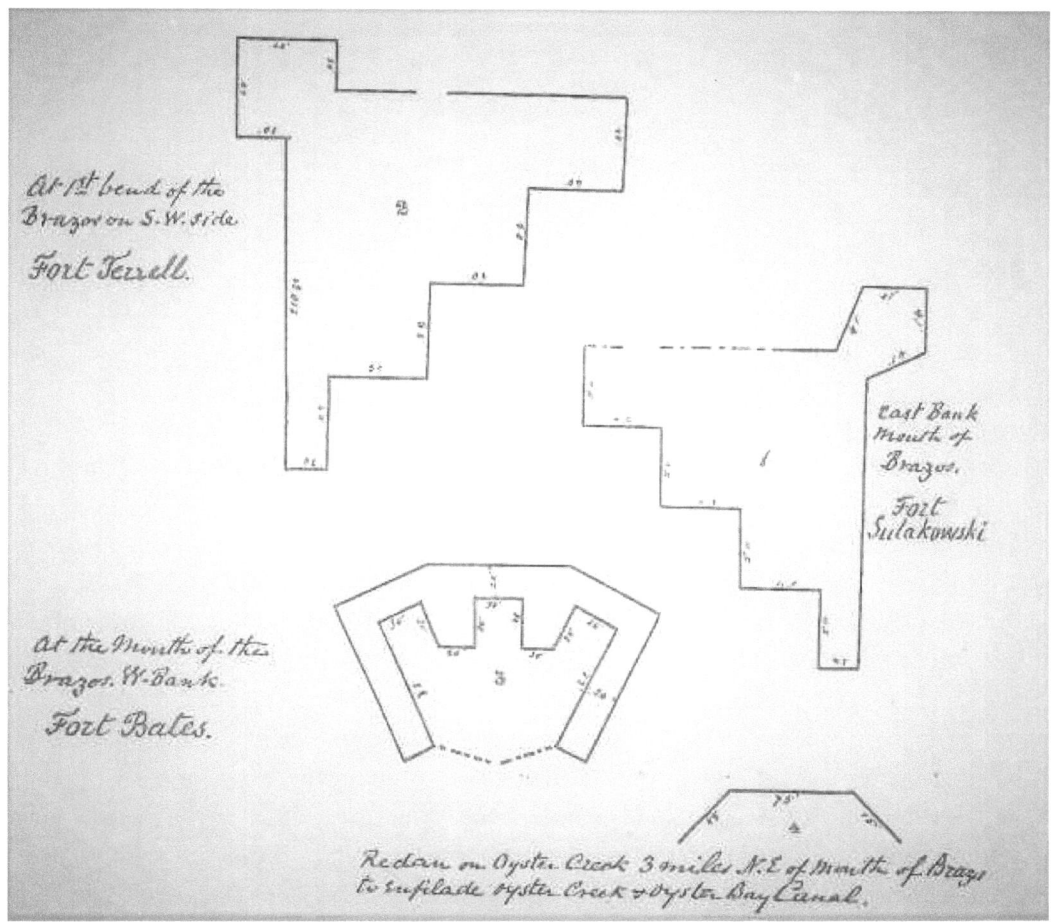

Figure 62: [Cross 1864]; shown in [Freeman 1995, Figure 9]

U. S. National Archives

Detailed diagrams of these other forts can also be found in the Gilmer Civil War Maps Collection, labeled as Redan on Oyster Creek (No. 235), Fort Quintana (No. 251), Fort on Bend of River (No. 252) but also a drawing of Redoubt on Oyster Creek Road (No. 245) not shown in Cross' report. Thus, it appears there were two works that protected the Oyster Creek area, with the redoubt perhaps constructed later. A drawing for the bridge across East Union Bayou is also found there, indicating it was some type of pontoon or barge-type bridge, labeled as Boat Bridge across East Union Canal. There is also an overall map of the entire area, nicely showing the locations of and the roads leading to these works [Unknown 1864b], shown in Figure 63 below.

***Figure 63: Detail from "Map Shewing Locations of Works at the Mouth of the Brazos"
(original from Gilmer Civil War Maps Collection, University of North Carolina at Chapel Hill)***

These forts were thick stacked-earth embankments topped with sod, with the guns *en barbette*, since brick forts (such as Fort Sumter) were by-then considered obsolete [Barr 1961 p. 3]. The Brazos forts resembled Fort Moultrie in coastal South Carolina, an area where Valery Sulakowski had worked earlier in the war (see Figure 64). It was also reported that during this time, the large number of Confederate troops at Velasco scavenged material from the nearby site of the 1832 fort [Looscan 1898].

During the period of construction, Dr. Thomas B. Grayson, a surgeon with the Army, was stationed at Velasco, and he wrote a short passage in a Christmas 1863 letter home "*During the past ten or twelve days quite a number of schooners have run the blockade at this port. A majority of them, so Madam Rumor says, are loaded with gun, ammunition and army stores for 'Old Jeff'. On Wednesday, the Yankees played quite 'a trick' on our pilots. A schooner came in sight and as is usual with the 'blockade running', made a signal for a pilot. Three pilots, not thinking but what it was a vessel desiring to come into our port, jumped in a yawl and went out to them, when to their great surprise they found it was a Yankee boat. They took the pilots on board, carried them out on sea some thirty miles, when they allowed them to take the yawl and make to shore if they could, which they succeeded in doing about 12 o'clock last night. They in future, will I guess, be rather particular before they board another boat.*" He also wrote about a schooner that grounded nearby, which soldiers had to guard from Yankee gunboats, while recovering its cargo of guns and powder [Thomas B. Grayson 1863].

Figure 64: Fort Moultrie by Conrad Wise Chapman

Another painting by Conrad Wise Chapman shows Battery Marshall at Sullivan's Island near Fort Moultrie (Figure 65 below), which may also resemble the Brazos fort.

Figure 65: Battery Marshall at Sullivan's Island by Conrad Wise Chapman

The redoubt on the Brazos-Galveston Canal was remembered by a nearby resident, Susan Adaline "Addie" Hudgins Follett (1876-1977), as being near the Velasco bridge over the canal where her grandfather was the bridge tender and toll collector. She wrote *"Across the bridge, on the north side of the canal, was what was locally called 'Mud Fort'. The inhabitants had built it hastily during the Civil War when the Yankee blockade vessels were patrolling the Gulf of Mexico, trying to keep out shipments of flour, salt, ammunition, and other necessities …. Men with teams (oxen or horses), scrapers, plows and shovels dug a moat about eighteen or twenty feet wide all around the fort area. The material was thrown to the inside, raising the elevation, with part of it being piled higher, forming a breastwork on the side facing the canal. I don't think it was ever used during the war. It was on Grandpa's land."* Later in her document, she wrote *"A few years ago when the canal was widened on the north side, the dredge cut into and destroyed the 'old fort'. Now the spot is taken over by the Surfside Bridge Marina. Thus, end the 'OLD MUD FORT' – UNWEPT, UNHONORED AND UNSUNG, THE MUD FORT'S DEMISE!"* [Follett 1983]. She also mentioned that the canal bridge rotated to allow boats to pass, since it pivoted atop a pedestal on the south bank.

A rough map was published in an article in the New York Herald in 1864 (see Figure 66), which apparently shows the new forts at the mouth of the Brazos [Keim 1864] as estimated from Yankee warships offshore; the article stating *"... north of the river, is situated Velasco ... Here the enemy has constructed his main fort, which mounts three guns, and has also assembled here a sizeable force"*. Please note that the Velasco fort (marked as "Main Fort") is abutting the town and on the river-side of a house labeled as "Story House Porticoed", thought to be the Archer-Herndon House. The map appears to be derivative of the 1858 Bache map, but the illustrator may have chosen an incorrect structure on the map for the "porticoed" house.

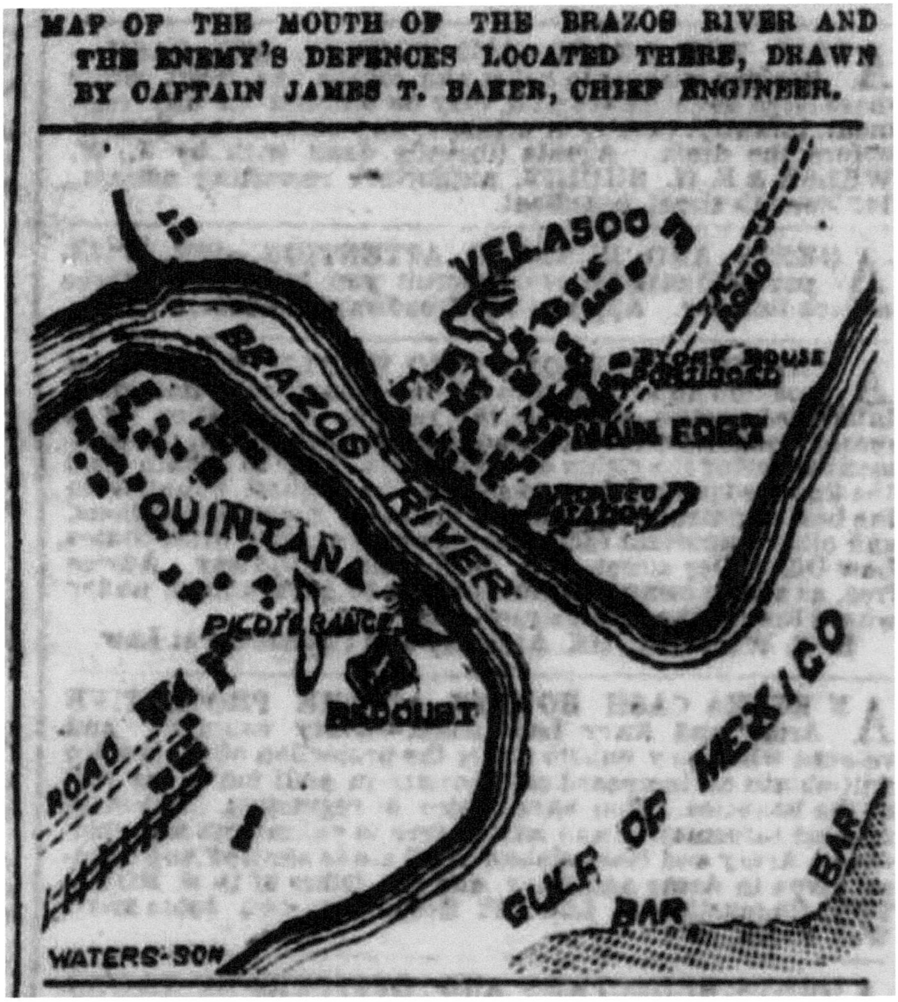

Figure 66: Map found in New York Herald, 9-Jan-1864

A more formal map was prepared by Capt. Tipton Walker in 1864 for the entire coast of Texas showing many of the forts defending the coast. In the original version of the map, a small detail is shown for the mouth of the Brazos (Figure 67 below).

Figure 67: Detail from 1864 Tipton Walker Map

The map was redone and colorized for *The Official Records Union and Confederate Armies* (see Figure 68 below), where the fort details are instead shown in an inset in the upper right corner [Walker et al 1895]. These forts are also featured in newer drawings inspired by this map [Winsor 1978 p. 114].

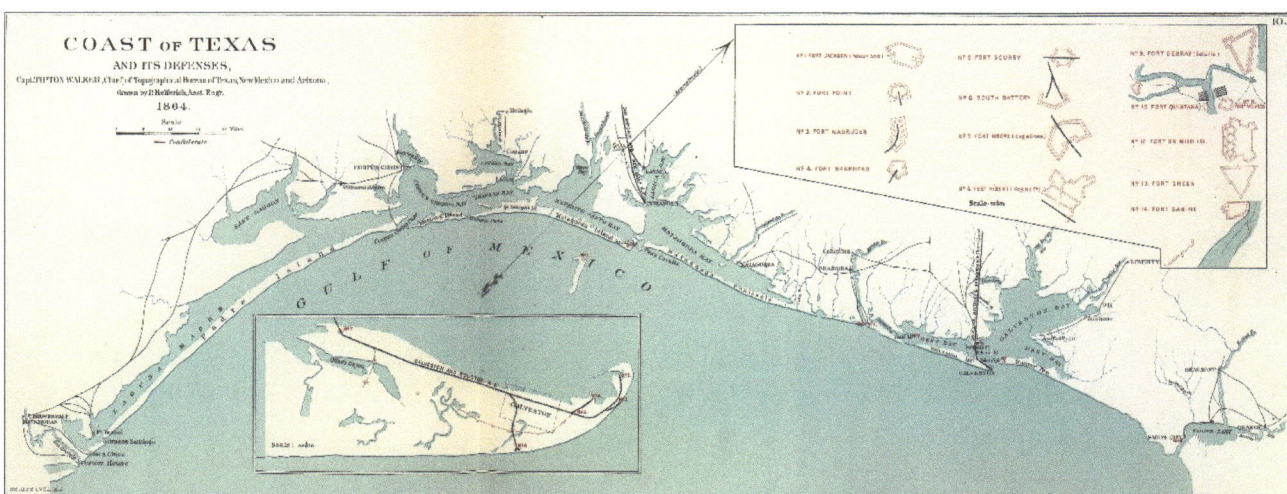

Figure 68: Coast Of Texas and Its Defenses, by Tipton Walker & P. Helferich, 1864 [Walker et al 1895]

In the years following, hurricanes and high tides could be expected to have destroyed or covered any remains of these forts, including one (Racer's Storm) as early as 1837, and others in 1875 and 1886 [Geiser 1944, Glass 2008]. Over time, the exact site of the 1832, Texas Revolution and Civil War forts at Velasco were lost to history.

Post-Civil War Period

"Freeport Sulphur No. 6" tanker sailing up Brazos River past Brazos Lighthouse to Freeport wharves

In 1888, an update of the Bache map was accomplished (Figure 69 below) by the same agency, then known as the U. S. Coast & Geodetic Survey (USCGS), showing that Velasco had many fewer structures (mostly due to damaging hurricanes mentioned previously), with no evidence of the Velasco fortifications, although the site of Fort Terrell was shown on the extreme left edge, marked as "Old Fort".

Also in 1888, a syndicate was formed involving the founding of the Brazos River Channel and Dock Company, the Texas Land and Immigration Co. (principals William M. Lee, George Angle and George Y. Wisner), and the Velasco Terminal Railway. A detailed history of this syndicate is found in a biography of William M. Lee [Schofield 1985, pp. 92-122], discussing the construction of jetties, docks, wharves, ships, hotels and sale of lands. In 1889, as the first actual jetty construction was begun by the syndicate, an attempt was made to finance the project with bonds on the English market, so the British harbor expert Sir John Coode was asked to evaluate the plans [Wisner 1891]. After his son came to Brazoria County to collect data and measurements, they prepared a report including four map drawings. Drawing #1 (227 x 106 cm) was a "General Plan" showing the Brazos River and Oyster Creek areas north to about Chenango, railroads to north of Arcola, and the new double jetties under construction (Figure 70).

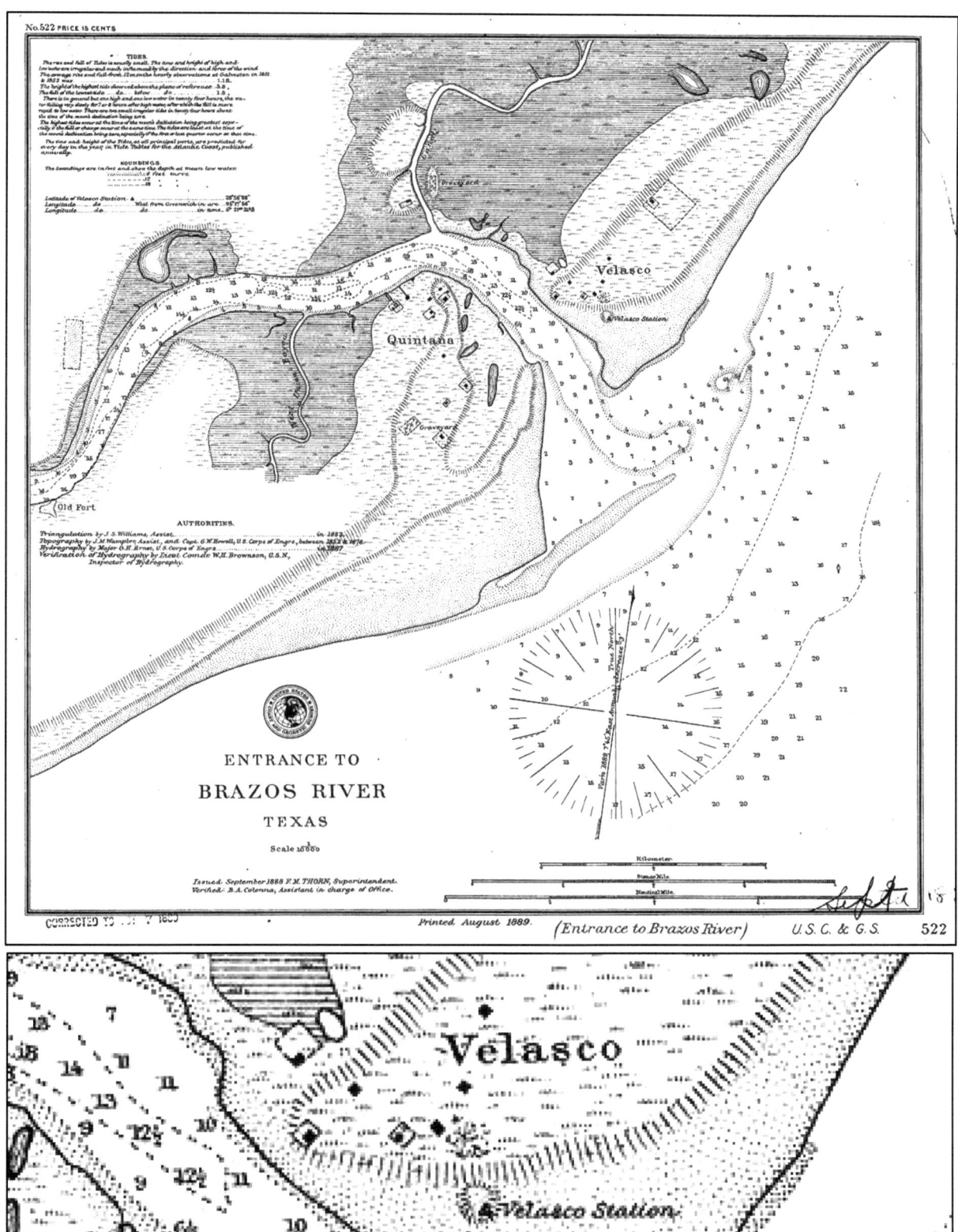

Figure 69: 1888 Map (full size + detail) by United States Coast and Geodetic Survey

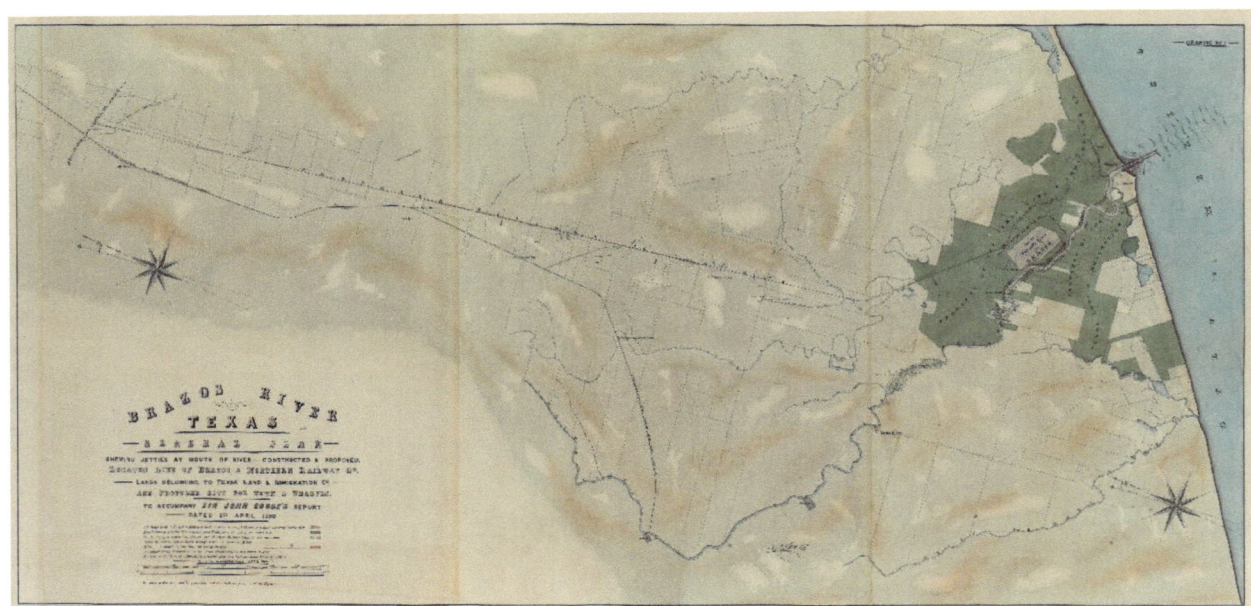

Figure 70: Sir John Coode Drawing #1 of the mouth of the Brazos River in 1890 (227 x 106 cm)
Courtesy of Dolph Briscoe Center for American History

Drawing #2 (370.5 x 111.2 cm) was a "Plan of Brazos River" showing the last few miles of the Brazos River including many fine details and a proposed town of Brazos (soon to be the location of new Velasco), shown in Figure 71 below.

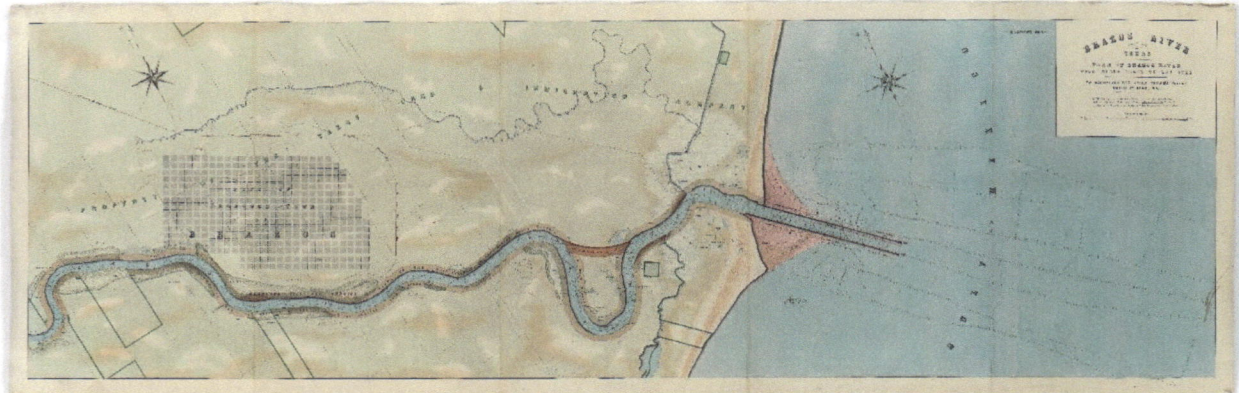

Figure 71: Sir John Coode Drawing #2 of the mouth of the Brazos River in 1890 (370.5 x 111.2 cm)
Courtesy of Dolph Briscoe Center for American History

The author was allowed to make cell phone photos of portions (close-ups) of the originals, and are shown below in Figures 72-74. Drawing #2 also indicates the location of the live-oak-log obstruction from the Civil War near the location of new Velasco (now Riverside Park in Freeport), a detail from Drawing #2 shown in Figure 72. Figure 73 shows the jetties under construction, and Figure 74 shows the Velasco/Quintana area. Interestingly, these drawings indicate the use of "wing dams" at the river's mouth and along the river-side of the jetties, remnants of which were once observed along the muddy bank before the harbor widening of the early 1990s. Drawing #2 also shows the location of an "Old Fort" (Fort Terrell), perhaps derivative of the 1889 USCGC map. Similar to the 1888 USCGS map, it also shows the location of a "Graveyard" along East Bayou near to its mouth on the Brazos River. This cemetery was the burial ground for old Velasco, and has been known in recent years as the "Kramer Cemetery" or "Shannon Family Cemetery", but was lost to history once a new larger and straighter section of the Gulf Intracoastal Waterway (aka Intracoastal Canal) was built

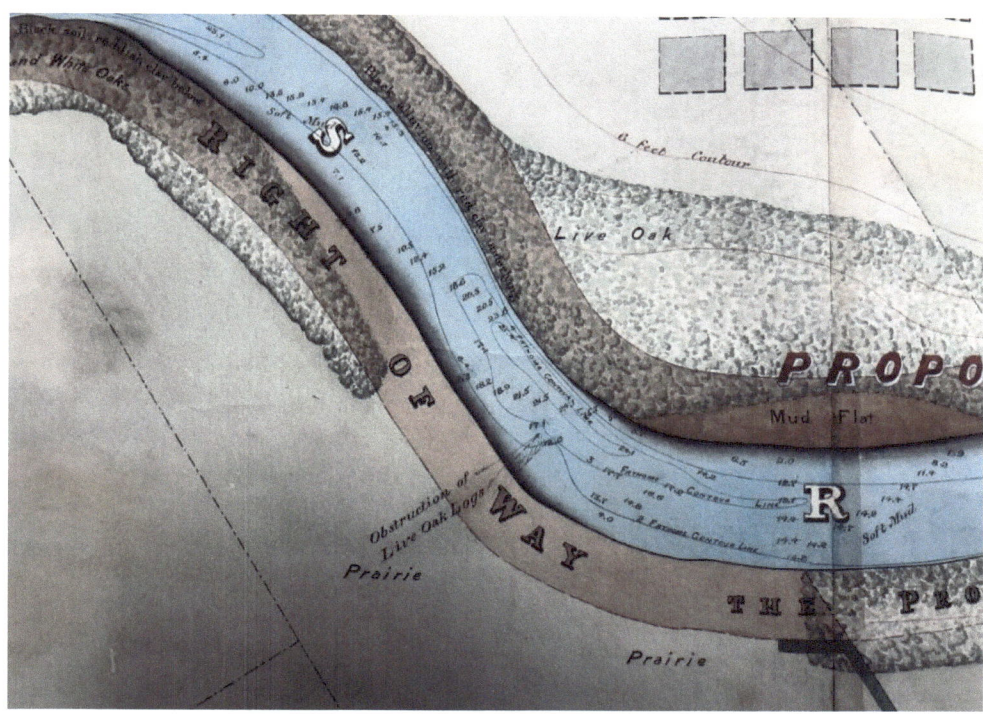

Figure 72: close-up of Coode Drawing #2 focusing on Live Oak Log Obstruction

through the area in the period of 1938-1940, separating its location from old Velasco/Surfside. One of three Shannon graves known from family records to be there was James Thompson Shannon (1818-

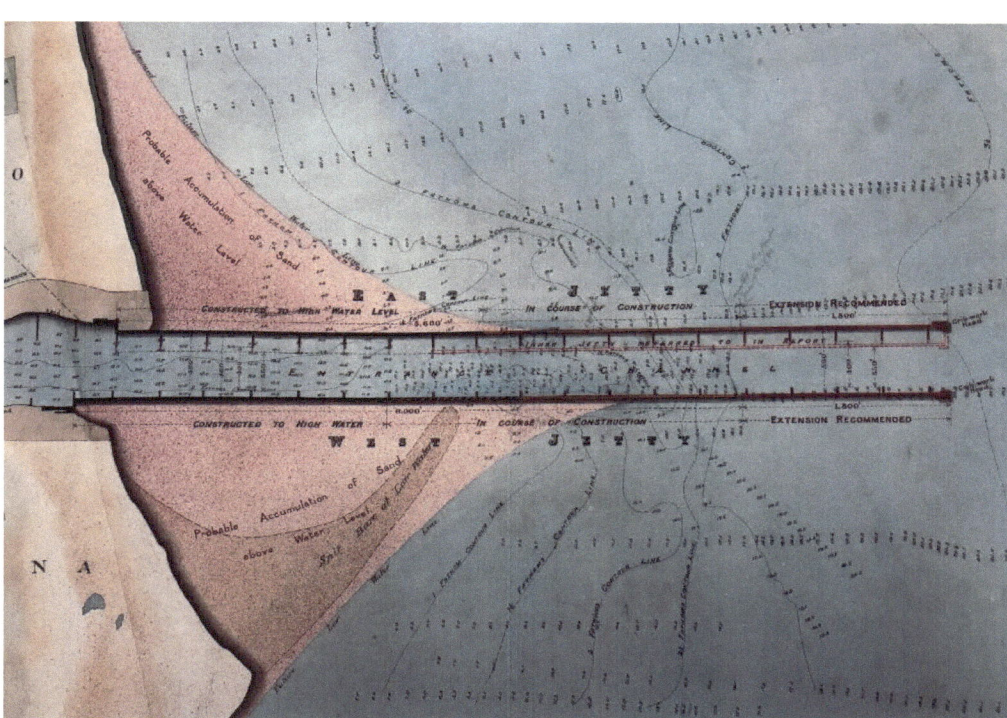

1883). Six identifiable graves of the Kramer family were moved in 1973 to Gulf Prairie Cemetery in Jones Creek, since the area was subsequently dredged away in expansion of the Intracoastal Canal and adjacent port facilities. Graves of other notable persons are listed in Appendix 3.

Figure 73: close-up of Coode Drawing #2 showing jetties under construction

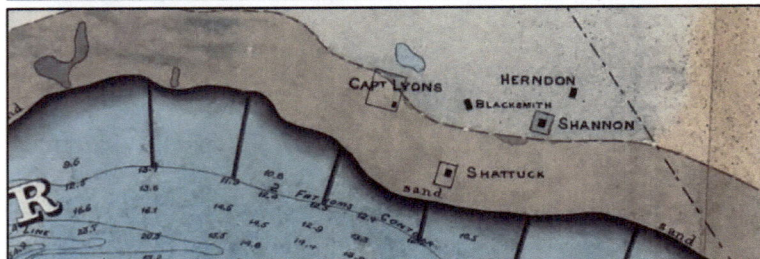

The Coode Drawing #2 is the only known historical map that actually labels individual houses at Velasco and Quintana (critically, the "Shannon" and "Herndon" houses, as seen I Figure 74). It also shows the jetties as construction was completed, thus the date they began in service. This "Herndon house" seems to be an outbuilding or new structure built after the 1875 hurricane, in the west end of that property.

The Coode Drawing #3 (121.3 x 68.5 cm) shows seven figures of the Brazos mouth as it had changed over time, especially showing how land accreted over the years and the beach extended into the Gulf in the period of 1858 to 1889. Please note the accretion over this period of 31 years, in Figure 75 below.

Figure 74: detail of Coode Drawing #2 in Velasco/Quintana

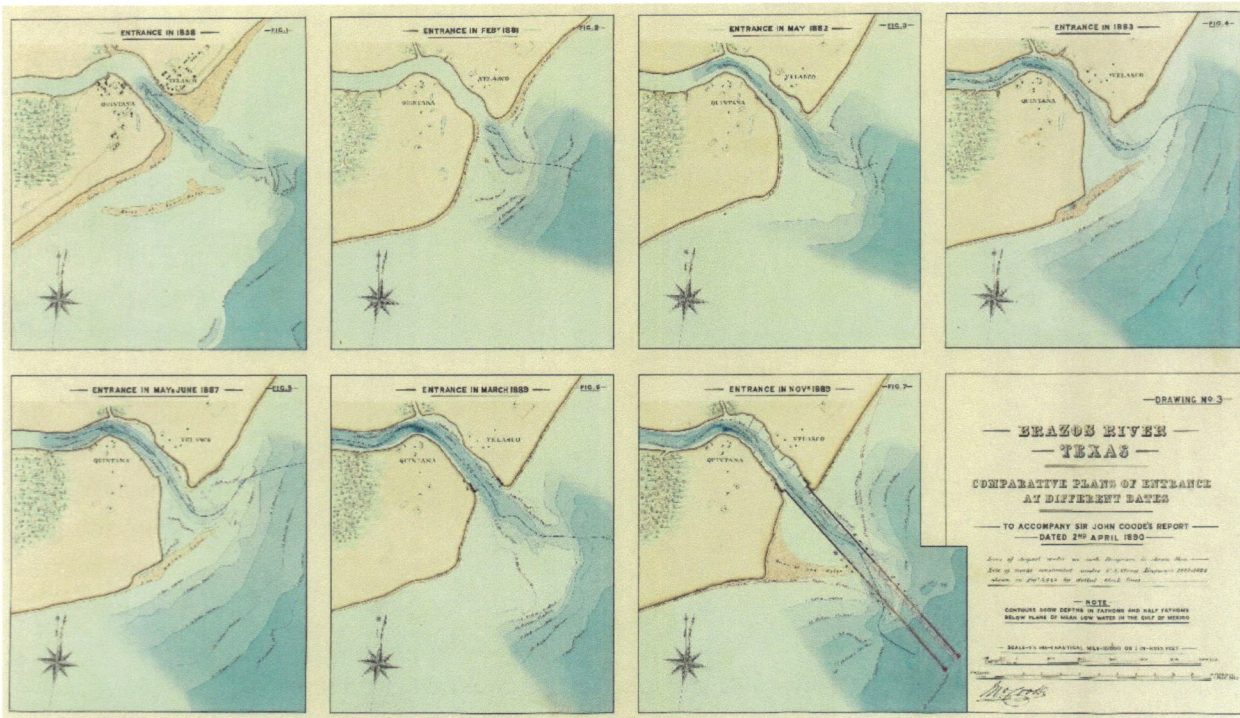

Figure 75: Sir John Coode Drawing #3 of the mouth of the Brazos River in 1890 (121.3 x68.5 cm)
Courtesy of Dolph Briscoe Center for American History

101

There is a fourth drawing (142.2 x 96 cm) showing the lands of the Texas Land and Immigration Company in Brazoria County (Figure 76), not apparently made by Coode but perhaps given to him by the syndicate so these lands could be drawn into his other three drawings. All originals are at the Briscoe Center, mounted on a canvas backing, and stored in a rolled condition [Coode 1890]. A framed and mounted copy of Drawing #3 was later located at BMNS. High-resolution photos of the Briscoe originals were made in Jan-2020 at our request (di_11904 through di_11907).

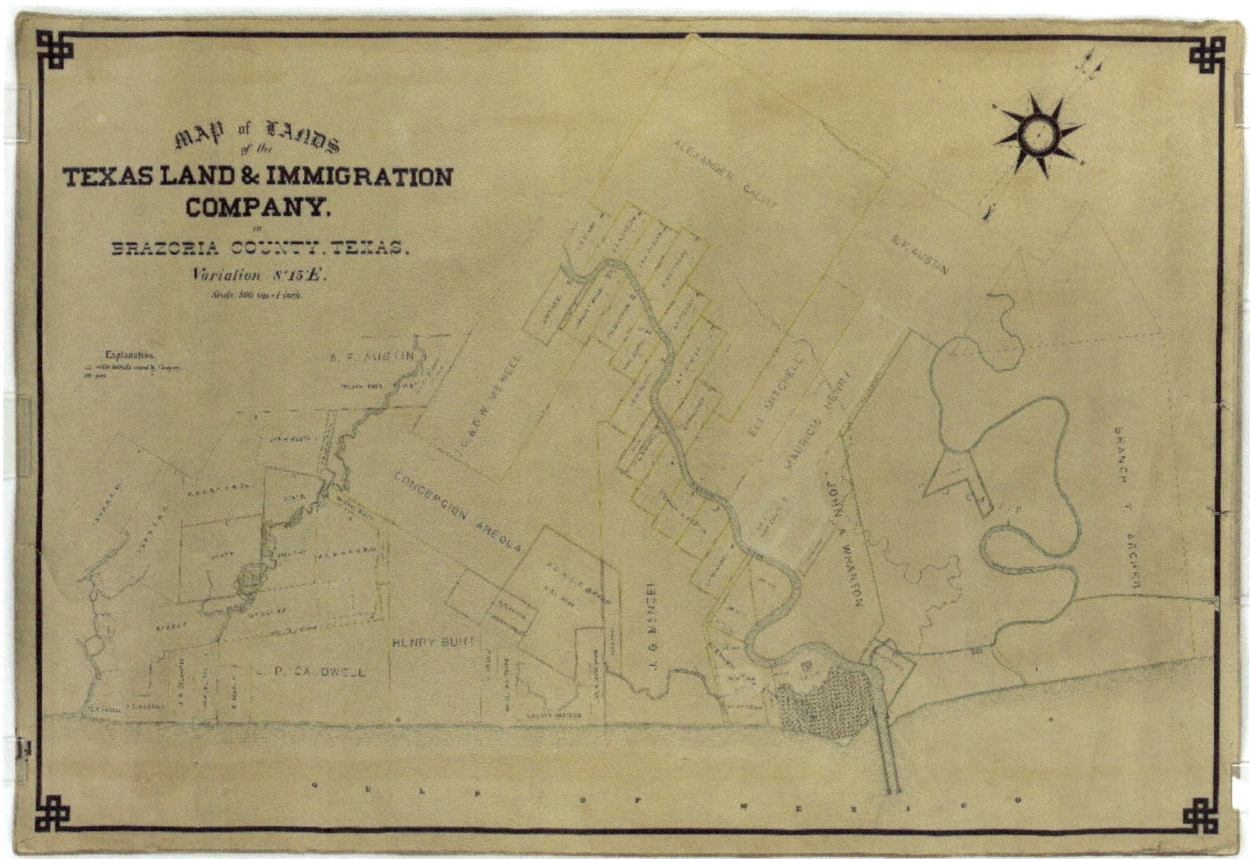

Figure 76: Sir John Coode Drawing #4 of the mouth of the Brazos River in 1890 (142.2 x 96 cm)
Courtesy of Dolph Briscoe Center for American History

These maps apparently were accompanied by a written report on the jetty project, although our efforts to locate a copy of the report since 2019 have been unsuccessful. A small excerpt and some comments about it, though, can be found in [Wisner 1891 pp. 529-530].

In 1891, the new port of Velasco was established, usually called "new Velasco", and another survey of the Brazos was done by the USCGS soon entitled "Map of the Brazos River, Texas", also showing construction of the jetties, and two close-ups of the Velasco area are shown in Figure 77 below. It is notable since it shows some details for houses and a cistern in Velasco Block 13, remnants of which were found in later archaeological excavations. The subsequent updates of the USCGS map in 1904 and 1912 continue to show houses (presumably identified as the Shannon and Herndon houses by comparison to the Coode map), so it is assumed that they survived the 1900 hurricane, although this is unclear since both maps indicate the topography was from 1897.

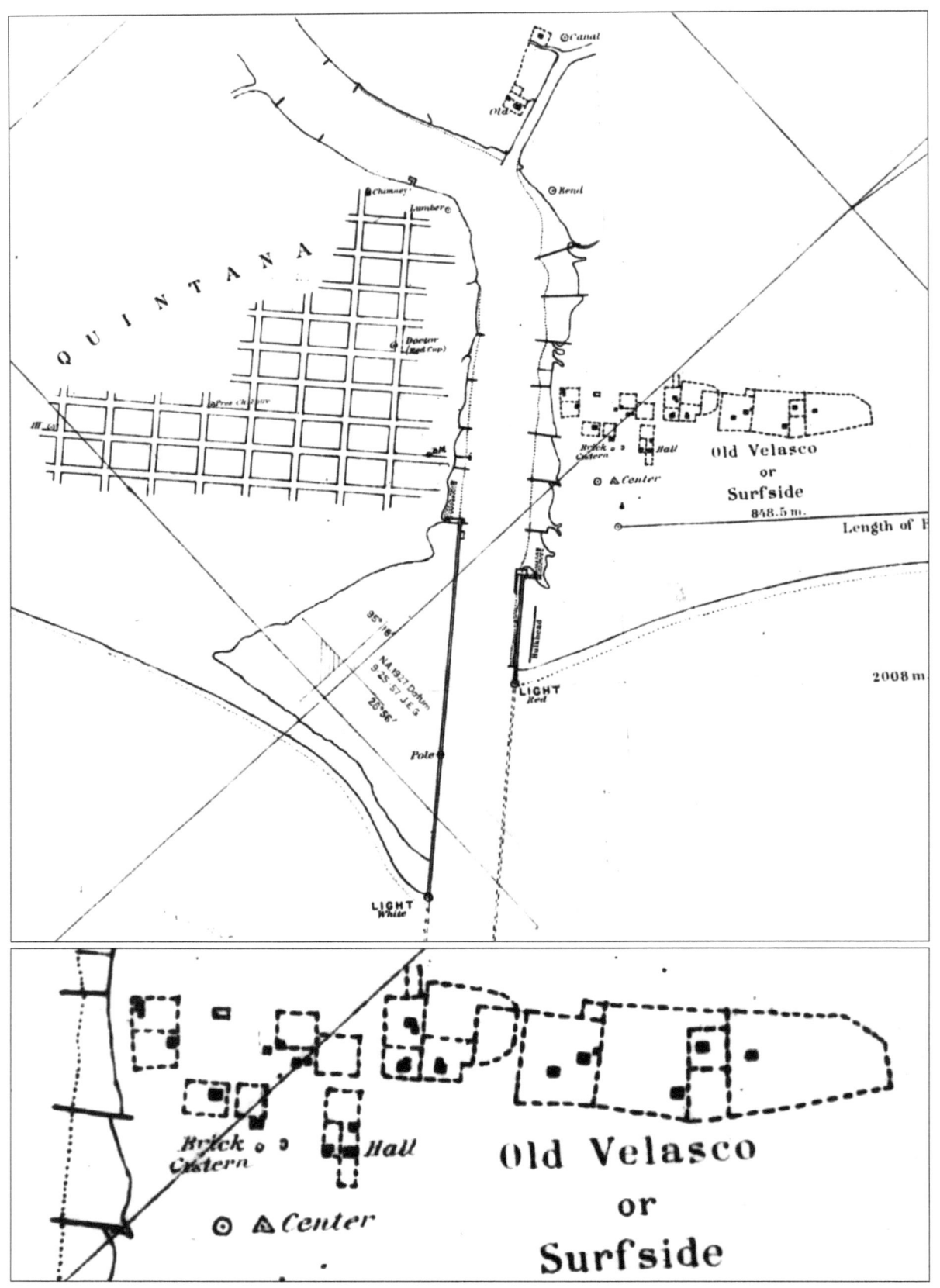

Figure 77: Velasco detail from 1891 USCGS map
Courtesy of Brazoria County Historical Museum (2008.010c.0018)

In this period, there was great hope that the jetty project would allow the Brazos to develop as a major deep-water port, which did not really develop at the time, as Mother Nature continued to make things difficult (major floods in 1899 and 1913, hurricanes in 1900, 1915 and 1932). However, there was a real estate boom in and around the new town in the 1890s. At that time, the site of new Velasco also became a destination for hunting and fishing parties, as seen in one photo from 1891 (Figure 78) at the Capitol Saloon - so named since old Velasco was once capital of the *ad interim* government for the new Republic of Texas, and the Brown-Hoskins hotel served as a capitol building.

Figure 78: Hunting party at the Capitol Saloon in Velasco, circa 1891
photo courtesy of Brazoria County Historical Museum (1986.049p.0005)

A large fold-up brochure (60 x 92 cm, folded into 27 panels), printed on behalf of the Brazos River Channel and Dock Company, was widely circulated. The front side of a pristine copy at the Rosenberg Library is shown below in Figure 79. A slightly worn copy can also be found at BCHM.

The other side had 27 small panels, often with wildly enthusiastic or exaggerated claims, and can be seen in a full view of both sides preserved at the Portal to Texas History. Two of the panels are reproduced in Figure 80 below. Only in more recent decades, has this vision been realized by the Brazos River Harbor Navigation District (now Port Freeport).

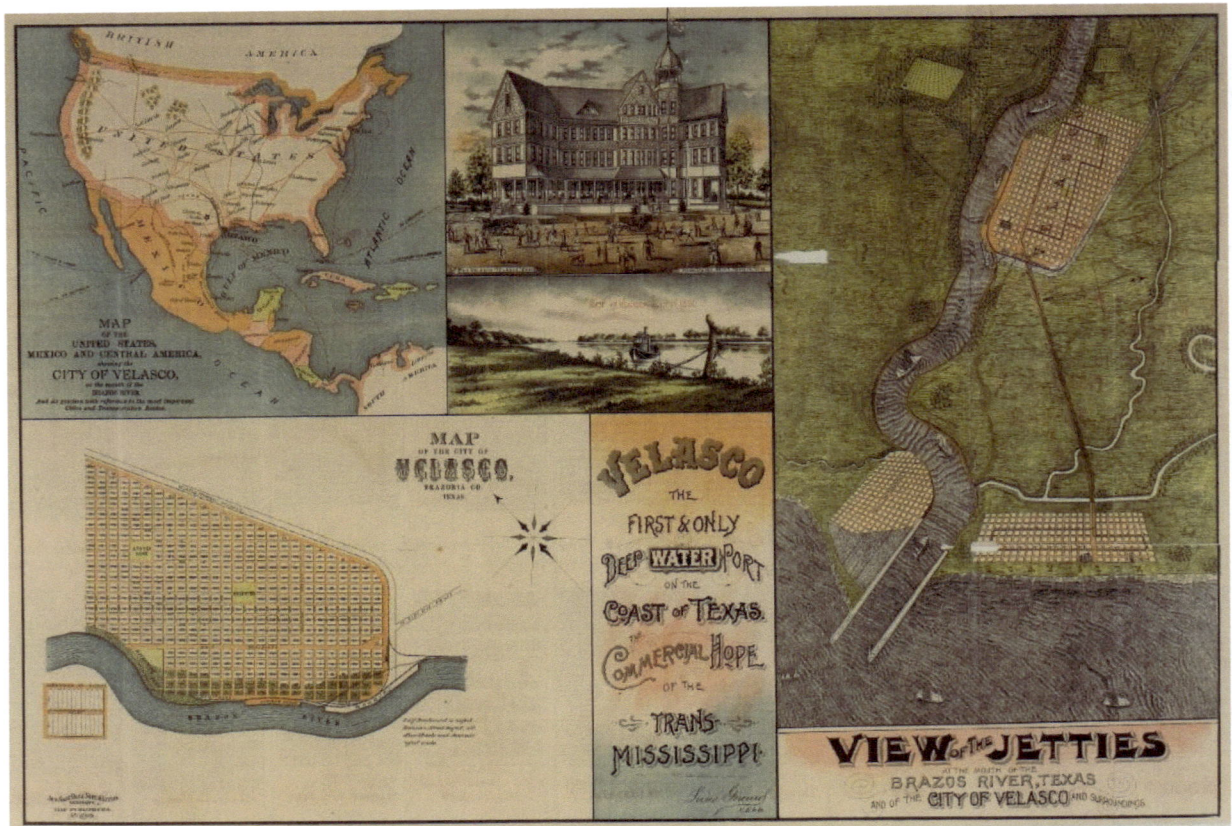

Figure 79: brochure for "The First and Only Deep Water Port on the Texas Coast"

Map 1189A, Galveston & Texas History Center, Rosenberg Library

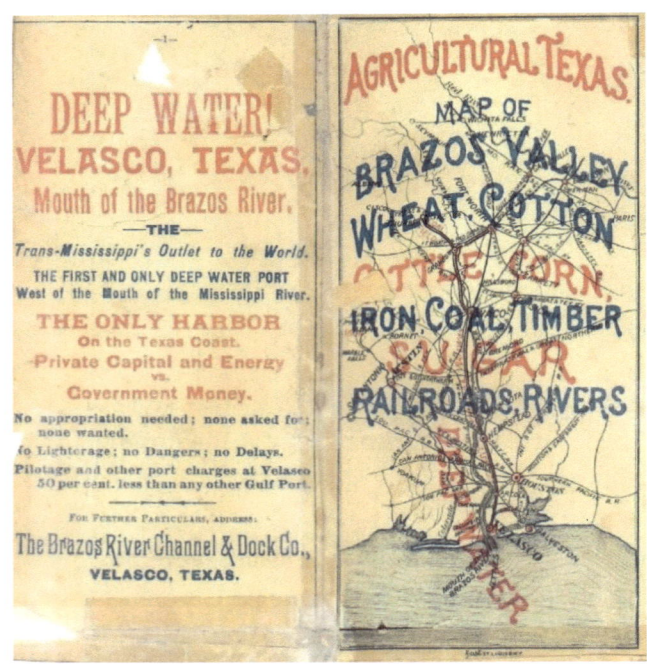

Figure 80: Two panels from back side of brochure

Courtesy of Brazoria County Historical Museum

The hotel shown in the upper central part of Figure 79 appears to be a design drawing, known sometimes simply as "The Velasco", and was built in late 1891 in new Velasco by the Brazos River Channel and Dock Company, as mentioned in a new weekly newspaper, *The Velasco Times* (many issues have been preserved at the Portal to Texas History). This hotel is also mentioned on rear panel 27 of the brochure. Its location was near the intended wharves as seen in the map-like image on the right side of Figure 79 entitled "View of the Jetties". A detail of this area is shown in Figure 81 below. Its grounds occupied an entire city block, today bounded by South Avenue A and B, and Caldwell St. and North Velasco Blvd. (across the street from today's Maria's Kitchen restaurant), with its back near and facing Caldwell St. and its front facing North Velasco Blvd. (southeast direction, to catch prevailing winds?).

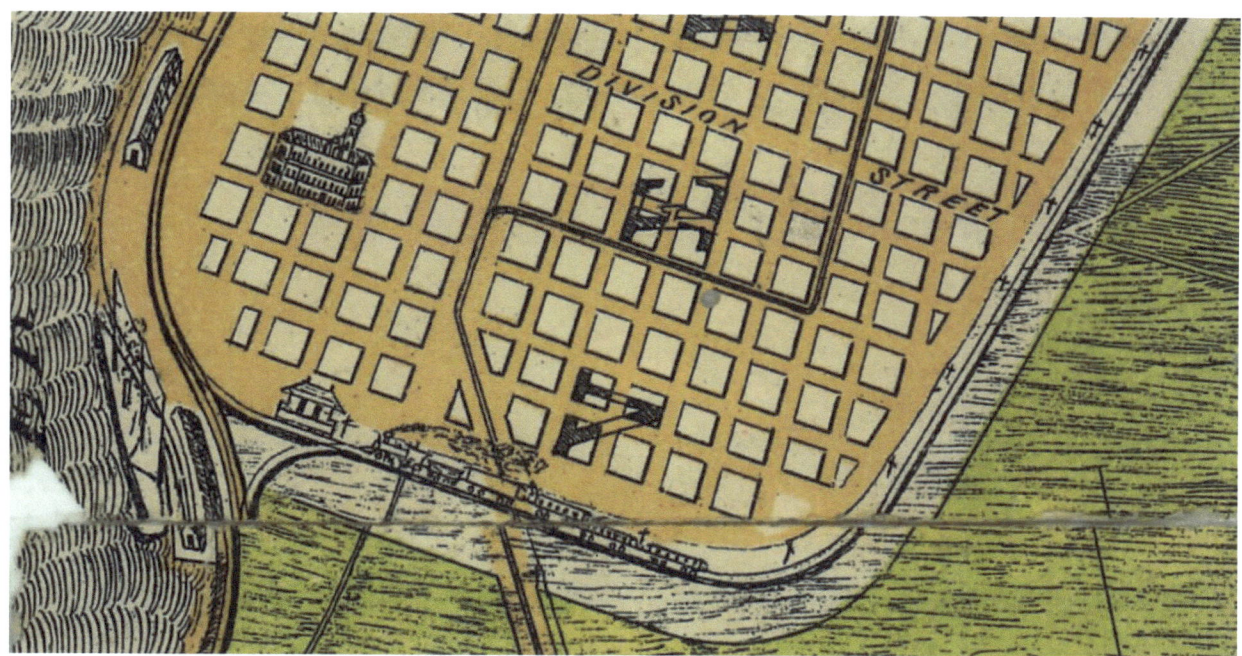

Figure 81: High-resolution detail from "View of the Jetties" – new Velasco portion
Courtesy of Brazoria County Historical Museum

The BCHM has a number of old photographs of the as-built hotel; one is shown in Figure 82 (others are 1983.011p.0019, 1984.011p.0009d & 0016, 1985.040p.0004, 1985.069p.0012 & 1986.049p.0004) and also views from an upper floor (most probably the open gazebo or cupola – 1984.024p.0002, 1985.043p.0002, 1985.116p.0002 & 2000.008p.0075) with some of these showing an inundated Velasco during the 1899 Brazos River flood (1984.011p.0002 & 0008 & 0014, 1985.040p.0001 & 1985.069p.0085), or

after the 1900 hurricane (1984.011p.0007). The Velasco Hotel was "blown down" in the 1900 hurricane [Carlton 1938]. Figure 81 also shows the nearby railroad depot. Figure 82 shows the angled wings of this hotel, distinguishing it from another nearby hotel built by the syndicate.

Figure 82: The Velasco Hotel, built in new Velasco in 1891
Courtesy of Brazoria County Historical Museum (1985.049p.0003)

A similar but separate hotel was built in 1892 near the beach at Surfside, and it can be seen in "View of the Jetties" (Figure 79) near where Gulf Boulevard would meet the beach, today on property owned by the Cradle of Texas Conservancy (CTC) just east of where Hwy-332 ends at the beach. A detail from this area is shown below in Figure 83.

Figure 83: High-resolution detail from "View of the Jetties" – Surfside portion

Courtesy of Brazoria County Historical Museum

An existing Lifesaving Station is also seen in the image near the beach about five blocks east of the Surfside Hotel. A lighthouse is also drawn in "View of the Jetties" (not actually built until 1896), on the outside of the first bend of the Brazos River from the Gulf. These two structures survived the 1900 hurricane. Accounts from Alvin, Lake Jackson and Velasco indicate the "eye" of the hurricane passed over those areas.

The original Surfside Hotel was opened on 16-May-1892 by the Brazos River Channel and Dock Company (as indicated in rear panel 10 of the brochure from Figure 79), and had a similar design to the Velasco Hotel, so the two are often confused. Its original as-built configuration is shown below in Figure 84 from a pre-1900 photograph by Martin Armstrong, which also had a nearby dance pavilion down the beach nearer the river (Figure 85). Another photo at BCHM appears misidentified as the Velasco Hotel, but appears to be a side and rear view of the Surfside Hotel under construction (1985.040p.0003). This hotel was apparently damaged in the 1900 storm but survived and was repaired circa 1903-1904 [Glenn 2019]. It has been reported as burned in 1904 or 1905 [Creighton 1975 p. 316], although we have found no newspaper accounts confirming such dates. In 1906, it was advertised as being new, and photographs of the period by E. F. Roeller show a different (perhaps remodeled, perhaps totally new) structure – 1983.006p.0026 & 0086, 1984.021p.0018 & 1985.069p.0095). Newspaper accounts have been found indicating it burned down to ashes on Sunday, 4-Aug-1907 [Unknown 1907].

Figure 84: The original Surfside Hotel

Photo courtesy of Brazoria County Historical Museum (1984.011p.0011)

Figure 85: Surfside Hotel & Dance Pavilion

Photo courtesy of Brazoria County Historical Museum (1983.006p.0088)

The new newspaper (*The Velasco Times*, later *Velasco Daily Times*), published from 1891 to 1893, was a staunch advocate for new Velasco. On more than one occasion, the paper published one particular image of the new jetties, reproduced below as Figure 86.

Figure 86: Bird-Eye's View of the mouth of the Brazos River, Velasco Times issue of 14-Nov-1891

Still another version was found in a postcard-like image, using a similar catchphrase of "Deep Water – A Fact Not a Promise". This was found in the Digital Collections of Southern Methodist University (SMU) Libraries, Lawrence T. Jones III Texas Photographs, but the contrast was digitally enhanced.

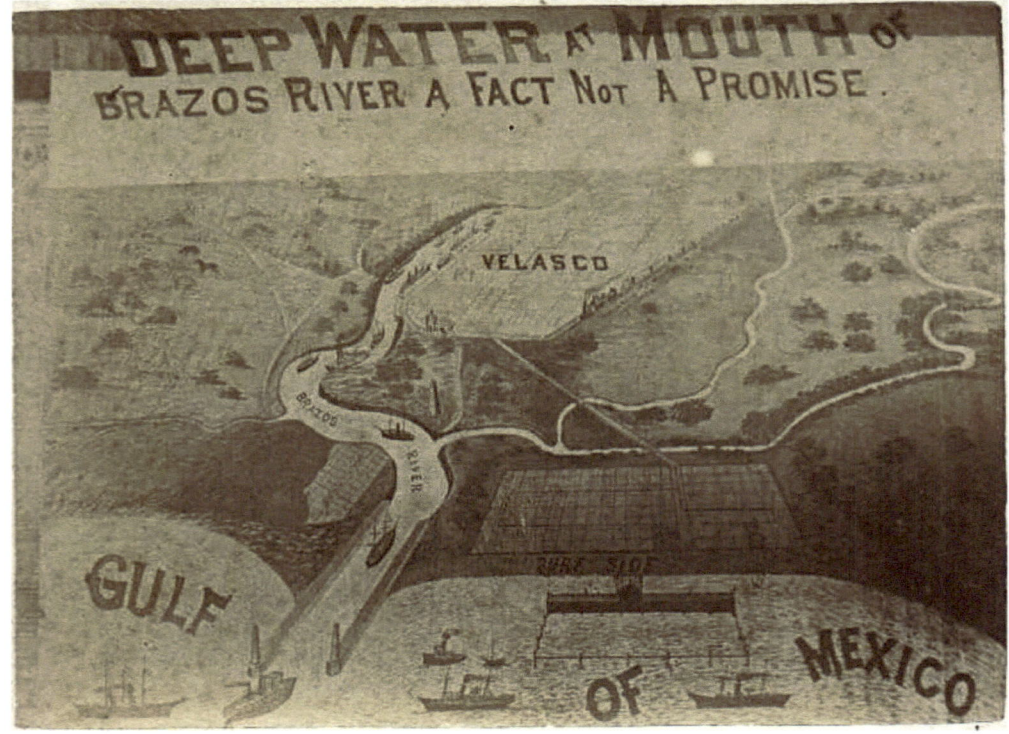

Figure 87: Bird's-Eye view of new Velasco and Surf Side
Courtesy of DeGolyer Library, SMU (Lawrence T. Jones III Texas Photographs, Call# Ag2008.0005)

Also, perhaps just after 1891, an idealized view of "new Velasco" was prepared, obviously derivative of the drawing in the lower left of Figure 79, although with some interesting historical facts added (both the overall image and some details are shown in the Figure below). The location and outline of the Velasco Hotel can be seen in the lower right in Block 19, as can the "Passenger Depot". The image of this map was donated to the Texas General Land Office by George E. Olsen Jr. of Freeport, Texas. The current location of the original (reputed to have been repaired by TGLO and then framed), is unknown.

Figure 88: "Velasco, Brazoria County, Texas" (overall + detail of Block 19 & upper right corner)

Texas General Land Office (Map# 77055)

In the period of 1887-1888, a station had been established at old Velasco by the U. S. Life-saving Service, known as Velasco Station, near the beach one-and-a-half miles northeast of the river. A spare boathouse was reported built in about 1910 on leased land adjacent to the Brazos River. The original Life-saving Station was reported damaged by a Dec-1913 flood (being left on an island), and was destroyed by a 1915 hurricane [BCHM Vertical File-Coast Guard]. An old photo from this period is shown below in Figure 89.

Figure 89: Velasco Life-Saving Station (Pre-1915)
Photo courtesy of Brazoria County Historical Museum (1985.099p.0001)

The exact location of the 1887-1915 station has been a bit of a mystery; however, close examination of the 1914 version of the USCGS chart reveals its location just northeast of the mouth of Oyster Creek (see Figure 90 below, marked with a red arrow), in agreement with that shown in Figure 83. A point there is marked as L.S.S. (elsewhere on the chart, this abbreviation is identified as "life saving station"). It also indicates that the mouth of Oyster Creek, once silted over, has been reestablished and enlarged, presumably by the floodwaters of 1913, endangering the location of the station and also isolating it from Velasco. The station can also be observed in the background in Figure 84 (right side, on horizon just above picket fence). Other documents have also been found that seem to confirm this outlying location of the Life-Saving Station (Portal to Texas History 231403 and BCHM document 1988.070c.0231). The site of the Brazos Lighthouse is also seen in Figure 90, highlighted by a green arrow. This station is also discussed in Appendix II of an archaeological report [Fox et al 1981 pp. 91-92].

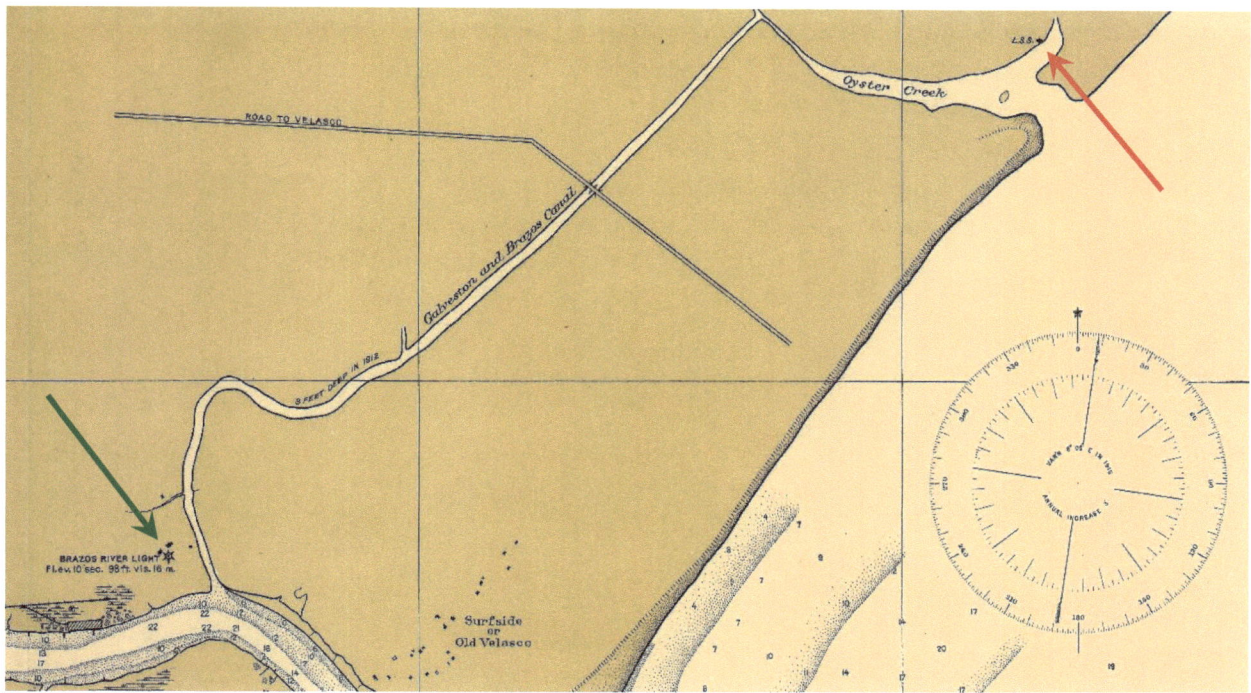

Figure 90: Detail from USCGS chart published Jan-1914

Also, please note that the railroad coming from new Velasco ended at some kind of wharf near to the Brazos Lighthouse and the mouth of East Union Bayou (the bayou was in use as part of the Brazos-Galveston Canal), as seen in the lower left corner of Figure 90.

After the damage from the 1913 flood and the 1915 hurricane, plans were made for a replacement, and the Life-saving Service merged with the Revenue Cutter Service in 1915 to become the U. S. Coast Guard. Thus, in 1916-1917, a new Coast Guard station house and garage were built near the end of Fort Street, by purchasing the leased land (of the spare boathouse).

In 1936, two large granite stones with similar brass plaques about Velasco were installed during the Texas Centennial - one on the lawn on the river side of the Coast Guard station house (now present in front of Surfside city hall) – see Figures 91 and 93, and another was placed in new Velasco (now on the lawn in front of

Figure 91: Velasco-Freeport "Texas Centennial" Celebration and Monument Dedication (14-May-1936) Little Miss Laura Ballinger Randall (of Galveston) and Outstanding Boy Scout Jerry Butler (of Freeport), from article in Freeport Facts, 21-May-1936

Photo courtesy of Brazosport Facts

112

the Velasco Community House in the "Velasco" section of Freeport), the latter additionally entitled "Four Miles Southeast To The Original Site Of Velasco" [Dorchester & Wilson 1936]. Both markers have since been moved from their original locations.

Also, as part of the Texas Centennial celebrations in 1936, many communities developed their own unique postmarks. The (new) Velasco postmark is shown in the Figure below, recollecting the imprisonment of Santa Anna, and his signing of the Treaties of Velasco in 1836.

Figure 92: 1936 Texas Centennial Postmark for Velasco
photo Courtesy of Brazoria County Historical Museum (1991.003c.0069)

A new three-bay boathouse was added to the Coast Guard station in the 1935-1938 period, and the name was changed to Freeport Station. An aerial view of the station (circa 1940) is shown below in Figure 93; the location of the historical marker placed in 1936 is shown with a red arrow. Additional cast-aluminum historical marker/plaques were placed for "Old Velasco, C.S.A" in 1964 and "Velasco" (i.e., Battle of Velasco) in 1965, both were placed on the east margin of Hwy-332 near the beach until 2025. The former was originally located near the Coast Guard station, but was moved in about 1988 to its that location. A separate marker for "Old Velasco" was installed in the wall of the Velasco Elementary School in 1969, to honor the naming of that school, but was moved to its own concrete base along Karankawa Street at a later time, although this is located in the new Velasco area (now Freeport).

The station was surrounded by as many as nine houses for the families of the Guardsmen, as recalled by a visitor in 1941 [Grubbs 1985], and these are easily seen in an undated (probably 1950s) photo below, as Figure 94. The area of Block 568 can be seen in the upper left, just beyond the houses. The road known as Fort Street (later as Ave. C or Coast Guard Rd., now as Monument Dr.) can be seen entering the photo from this same general area.

Figure 93: Aerial View of Coast Guard Station Freeport, pre-WWII (notice location of historical marker)

U.S. COAST GUARD STATION, FREEPORT, TEX.

Figure 94: Coast Guard Station Freeport
photo Courtesy of Brazoria County Historical Museum (2005.036p.0004)

The station house suffered damage from a fire and Hurricane Alicia in 1983, and was eventually demolished. In the period of 1990-1992, a new station was built just upstream of the old one, since the harbor channel was being widened, dredging away the land where the previous station existed. The 1938 boat house was moved and re-purposed as a city hall building for the Village of Surfside Beach. The 1936 granite marker was moved in front of the new city hall.

A separate government agency, the U. S. Lighthouse Board, established the Brazos Lighthouse in 1896 just upstream of Velasco at the first bend of the river, such that the light aligned with the centerline of the river channel as it met the Gulf. The agency was renamed the U. S. Lighthouse Service in 1910, and merged into the Coast Guard in 1939. The Brazos Lighthouse was operated until 1954, but existed until 1967 when it was dismantled, so in its history, it was administered by all these agencies. A photo of the facility is shown below, as Figure 95. The turret or "lens house" from atop the derrick was saved, and today sits on the lawn of the county courthouse in Angleton.

Figure 95: Brazos Lighthouse, as viewed from the southeast (looking northwest)
Photo courtesy of Brazoria County Historical Museum (1985.009p.0002)

The layout of the facility can be seen in another photo (Figure 96 below), seen from above and to the west-southwest. The Dow barge canal (former mouth of East Union Bayou) is seen crossing horizontally across the middle of the image, while the Intracoastal Canal heads northeast in the upper right; the harbor channel (Old Brazos River) is off the edge of the photo to the right.

Brazos River Lighthouse 1964

Figure 96: Brazos River Lighthouse in 1964
Photo courtesy of Brazoria County Historical Museum (2006.014p. 0001)

From the earliest days, access to Velasco was primarily by boat travel; however, a land route was established down the higher ground between East Union Bayou and Oyster Creek, to enter the eastern side of Velasco. Once a Brazos-Galveston Canal was established in the 1850s, the road had to cross over the new canal. Civil War-era maps (as seen in Figures 59, 60 and 63) show such a road, and a spliced image is shown below (western part of Sheet 1 and eastern part of Sheet 2 of the 1862 Tipton Walker maps) as Figure 97. The image also shows how Oyster Creek originally drained directly to the Gulf, and that two segments of canal were used to join Drum Bay to Oyster Creek and then to East Union Bayou and the Brazos River. These canals were originally created in the 1850s by the Galveston and Brazos Navigation Company, although they were originally suggested by Stephen F. Austin as early as 1825 [Smith Jan-2000, Austin 1826]. Indeed, creation of these canals provided an alternate drainage for the flood waters of Oyster Creek, and prevented its freshets from scouring its original channel into the Gulf, eventually causing the original mouth to silt over after the Civil War.

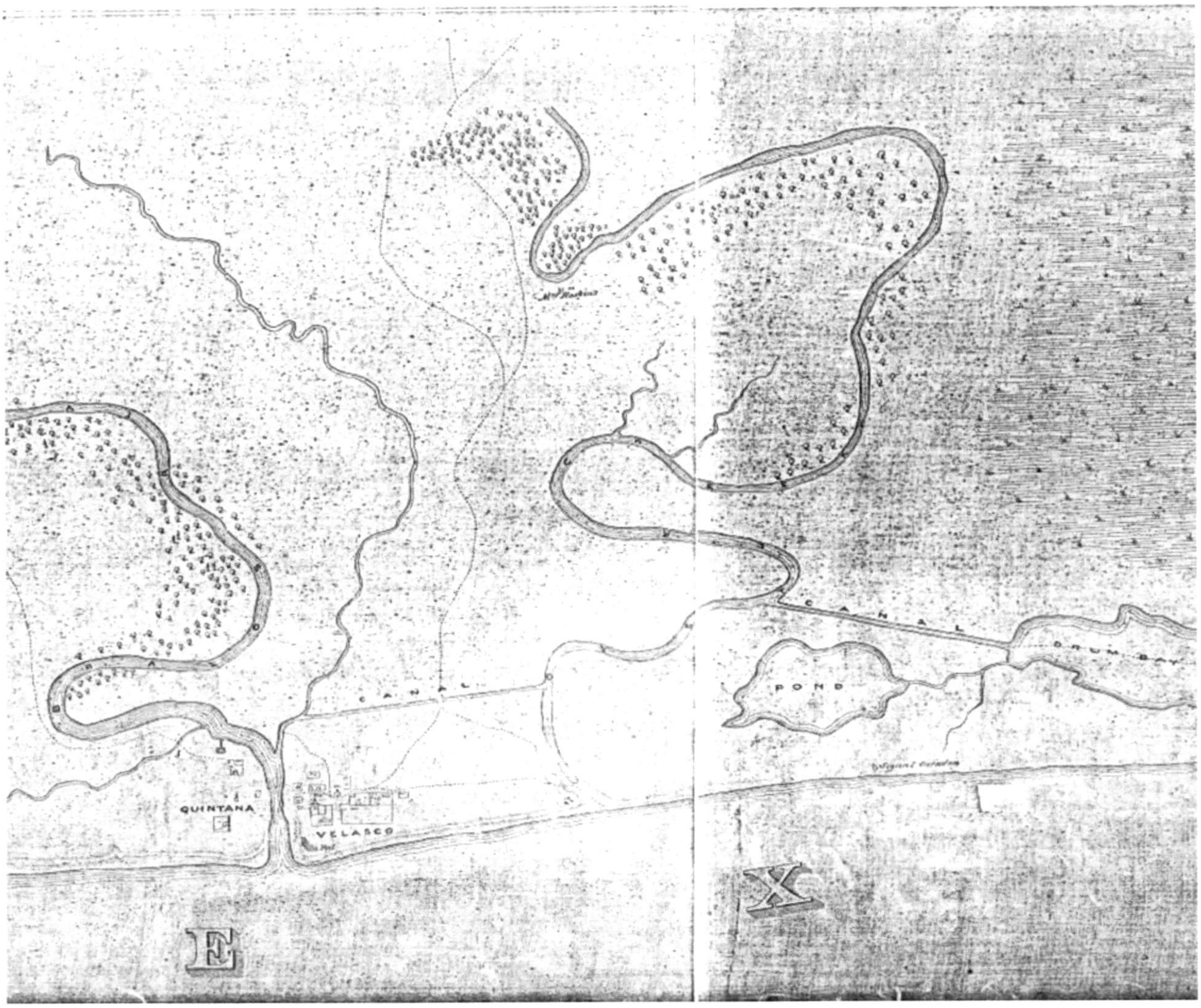

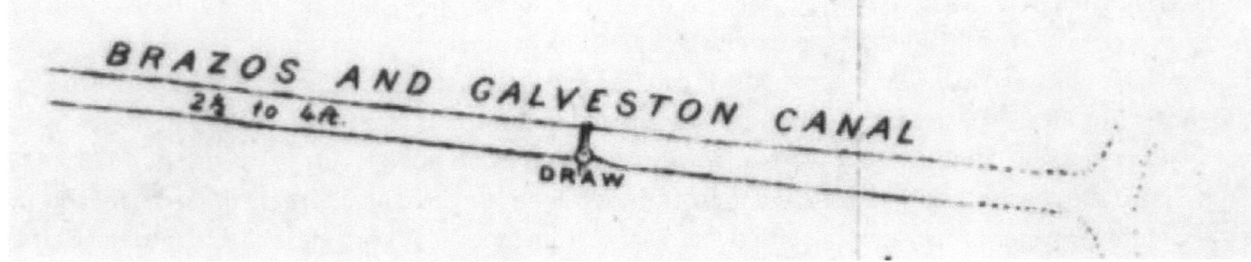

Figure 97: Spliced detail from Tipton Walker maps (circa 1862)

The USCS map of 1891, portions of which are shown in Figure 77, also has a feature on the far right showing the Brazos and Galveston Canal, and an apparent drawbridge to cross that canal, here featured as a cropped image in Figure 98.

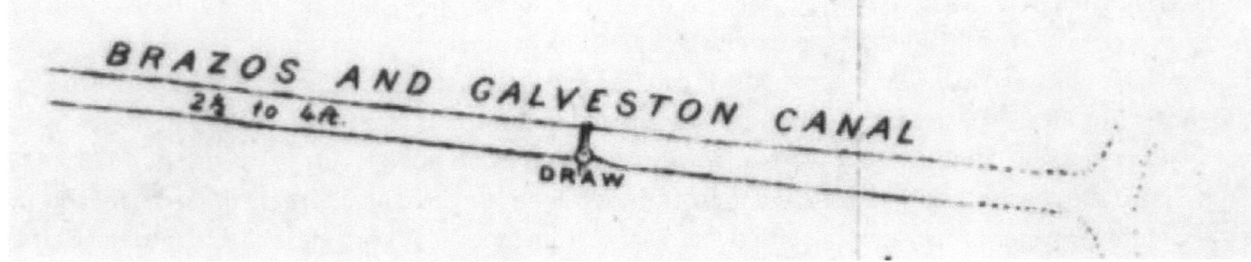

Figure 98: Detail from 1891 USCGS map

This canal crossing northeast of Velasco was operated by the John Longest Hudgins family for many years, and a photo of the swing bridge used is shown below in Figure 99, also showing their residence and blacksmith shop. For many years, the bridge was a pivot swing bridge, atop a column on the south bank, as indicated in Figure 98. The bridge is labeled as "Drawbridge" on Coode Drawing #2, showing a fenced area (residence?) on the southeast bank (Figure 71).

Figure 98: First bridge into Velasco – center-pivot swing type – and John L. Hudgins dwelling and blacksmith buildings - circa 1885
Photo courtesy of Brazoria County Historical Museum (1985.074p0001)

At some point after 1912 and before 1930, perhaps to service the new Coast Guard station, a new route was established directly from new Velasco, crossing East Union Bayou near the Brazos River and the Brazos Lighthouse, to enter the west side of Velasco. Addie Hudgins Follett described it as the "Boulevard" [Follett 1983]. Indeed, one of the plan-type documents for new Velasco show this road as an extension of Gulf Boulevard in new Velasco (Portal to Texas History 50380 & 231403). The original "Oyster Creek Road" was apparently abandoned, although a 1930 aerial photo shows that a new straight pathway (pipeline, electrical lines, unimproved road?) of some type had been built from new Velasco crossing East Union Bayou connecting with the old Hudgins canal crossing. This pathway at the canal crossing is indicated with a blue arrow, and the new crossing into west Velasco is indicated with a red arrow, in Figure 100 below. The Brazos Lighthouse location is shown with a green arrow, and the Coast Guard Station with a yellow arrow.

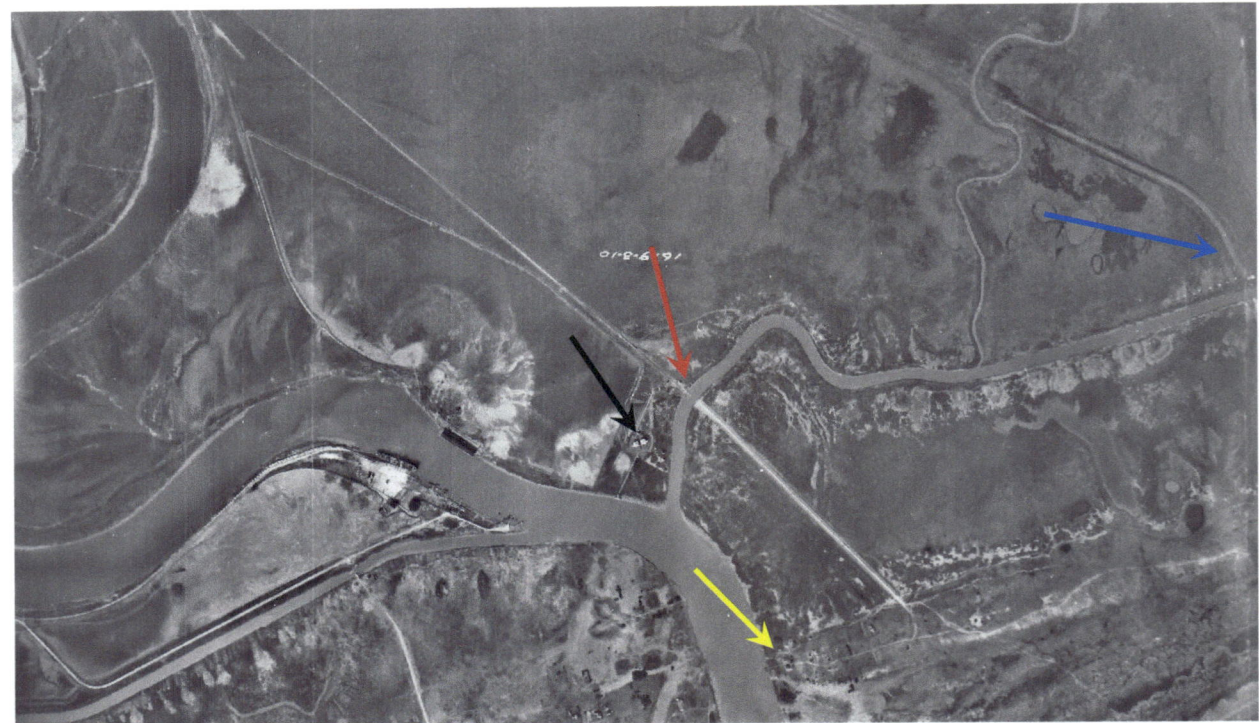

Figure 100: Detail from Tobin Surveys Inc. Photo 1619-3-10 (28-Nov-1930)

Close examination of the west crossing (red arrow) indicates no bridge at this time, but a small ferry was apparently used, revealed in a 1931 photo, obtained from the Dan Kessner collection [Kessner 2007], and shown in Figure 101. This lack of easy access to Surfside is probably one reason that Surfside remained a bit of a ghost town.

Figure 101: Cable Ferry across early version of Intracoastal Canal, circa 1931

Indeed, earlier records exist telling of the crossing as the end of the Velasco Terminal Railway, another part of the syndicate from 1891, and that rail passengers had to disembark, cross the ferry, and then take a wagon to travel further into Surfside. Joy Grubbs described it in 1941 *"As we approached the canal, we had to drive out on a small ferry supported by oil drums and run by a motor. I was so afraid the car might roll off into the canal, but we made it safely across to the island."* [Grubbs 1985]. Later, a two-way pontoon swing bridge replaced a one-way pontoon ferry [Creighton 1975 p. 374]; a print from BCHM (also found in the Dan Kessner collection) is shown in Figure 102. A newspaper article indicates the ferry was replaced with the swing bridge in 1941 [Soefje 1988]. It was not until after World War II that Surfside began to develop as a resort town.

Another important aspect is revealed in the entire 1930 series of Tobin aerial photographs – please note the great number of spoil mounds along the widened canals, and also even-larger mounds along the Brazos River (including one at Velasco – just off the tip of the yellow arrow, at the bottom edge of Figure 100). Apparently, in the period before 1930 (and probably afterwards as well) the practice was to place dredge spoil up on the banks. This will become important in later considerations of archaeology at the site.

Figure 102: Pontoon swing bridge over Intracoastal Canal, circa 1941-1954

The 1888 and 1891 USCGS maps (Figures 71 and 77) were updated again in 1892, beginning a series of charts identified as Chart# 525 published by the U. S. Dept. of Commerce/NOAA. The original Chart #525 was published in Oct-1892 (topography and hydrography from 1891), with updates in Mar-1899 (1897), Sep-1904 (1897, 1904), Jun-1909 (1897, 1907), 1914 (1897, 1912), May-1934 (1933) and Oct-1935. A portion of the 1914 chart is shown above in Figure 90. Some outlying details are shown on these charts, for example the dome of the Velasco Hotel (illustrated in Figures 79, 81 and 82) is marked in the new Velasco area in the 1891, 1892, 1899, 1904 and 1909 versions, although the hotel was believed destroyed in the 1900 storm. The site of Fort Terrell is marked as "Old Fort" on all versions from 1888 to 1914. The Brazos Lighthouse is shown on the USCGS charts of 1899 on. The Oyster Creek Road is shown on the 1914 chart, and both it and the new roads are shown on the 1934 and 1935 versions, indicating that the original road remained in service until at least 1935.

As the entire series of USCGS charts and other maps in this report reveal, beach accretion at Velasco occurred due to storms and delta formation both before and after creation of the jetties, accumulating about 1725 feet of total land to the seaward of the original beach in front of the 1832 fort. Although several early attempts failed to improve access for ships over the Brazos Bar by creation of jetties, the first permanent construction did not occur until 1889 [Brazos 1890, Wisner 1891, Kramig]. Further accretion mostly stopped and even reversed some after 1929, when the Brazos River was diverted seven miles to the southwest through a purposefully excavated 'Diversion Channel", since river silt no longer nourished any further "delta" deposits. Thus, the original 1832 fort location is now inland from the beach by about 2150 feet and considered less-than-optimal for recreational use, and indeed any remaining remnants of these original forts or graves might be disturbed by replica reconstruction. A Coast Guard radar tower has also recently been built to seaward, hindering any unobstructed view towards the beach, sea and river mouth.

The earliest topographic map of the modern era is found with the 1943 USGS Quad for Freeport (Figure 103 below). No wooded areas are seen near the Brazos mouth and, indeed only a few are found along the course of lower Oyster Creek, in the area of the original Oyster Creek Road. By this point, the modern Intracoastal Canal had been created (in 1938-1940), and lower East Union Bayou was channelized around the new Dow Chemical Plant-A complex to create a barge and seawater canal to Dow's Plant-B. The Oyster Creek Road into east Velasco is not seen, so its use must have discontinued prior to 1943. The former Velasco Terminal Railroad line has been converted for use at Plant-A, and the new road has been re-routed (following the new barge canal), which was done in 1941. The new road is also seen to cross both canals, and was marked as County Road 229 on a 1948 Brazoria County road map. In 1949, the new route was designated as FM-1460, but this route was discontinued when a new "high-bridge" was built in 1954 over the Intracoastal Canal near the original Hudgins canal crossing. This "high-bridge" was eventually replaced in about 1998 with a new version right beside it, and the 1954 version was demolished. Parts of these two former paths into west Velasco are today known as Dow Canal Rd. (S. Avenue D when leaving Freeport) and Old Surfside Rd./CR-229 (Gulf Boulevard when leaving Freeport). Beginning in the 1970s, the spit of land between the two canal crossings was dredged away to expand the Intracoastal Canal and create additional harbor areas. The path of the former road into west Velasco (shown in the 1943 map as a segment to "Brazosport" on the Gulf side of the canal) is known today as Thunder Rd.

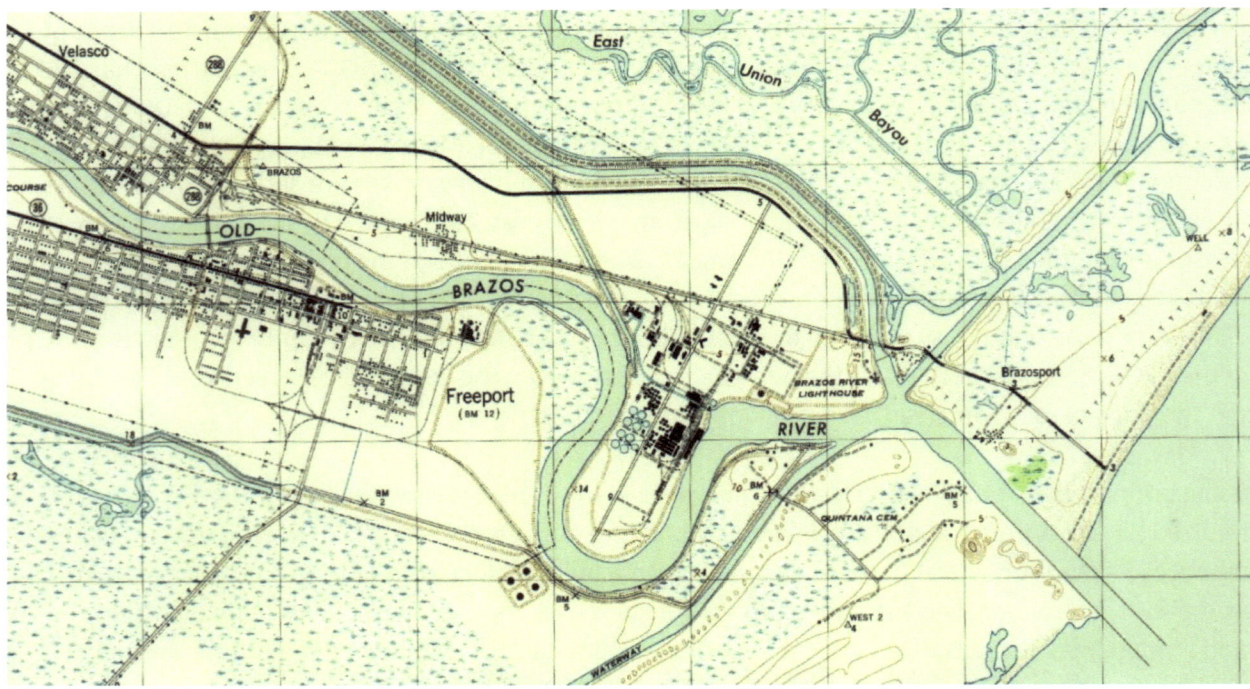

Figure 103: Detail from 1943 USGS 1:24000 "Freeport" Quad Map

The articles by Mrs. T. A. Humphries mention that the 1913 flood caused erosion in the salt marsh, revealing a narrow mile-long brick-paved road to the "Old Steamboat Landing" on East Union Bayou

[Humphries 1932], which may be the road shown in the 1862 Tipton Walker map (as seen in Figures 59 and 97, leading to East Union Bayou near the Brazos), and which had a bridge installed over the bayou later in the Civil War to facilitate movement of troops and equipment (as seen in Figures 60 and 63). Thus, such a brick-paved road (at least in Surfside) may have been created during the Civil War or before. This segment may have been re-purposed after 1913 to become the "new road" segment at Surfside, today lying buried under the road base and asphalt of Thunder Road. As seen in the 1943 USGS map, an unimproved road can be seen with a hairpin shape at Surfside (labeled then as Brazosport); the length nearest the beach is the former path of Fort Street, and future path of Monument Drive. The length on the landward side is today found as an undeveloped right-of-way – an extension of modern Militia Drive. The former dune ridge of the 1830s appears to be marked by a series of T shapes, and along this line is seen a mound near the river (Civil War fort?). Finally, this map reveals how little development had occurred even up through 1943 at Surfside.

No fortifications are known to have been placed during World War I or II on the Velasco side, although troops from Company A of the 3rd Texas Militia were stationed in 1917 at nearby Bryan Mound to protect the Freeport Sulphur Company's works [Creighton p. 329]. This activity resulted in the founding of Freeport in 1912, across the Brazos River from new Velasco. Sulfur was mined at Bryan Mound from 1912 to 1935, and also at the nearby Hoskins Mound beginning in 1922, transported by rail to wharves just upstream of old Velasco. The rail lines were operated by the Houston and Brazos Valley Railroad Company, a descendant of the Velasco Terminal Railway and the Velasco, Brazos and Northern Railway Company. The quantity mined there was about five million tons, and added greatly to the nation's sulfur industry. The port itself was administered by the Brazos River Harbor Navigation District since 1925, with a name change to Port Freeport in 2007.

During World War II, a pair of gun mounds were placed on the Quintana side, each mounting a single rotating 155-mm coastal artillery piece, installed in late 1942 using the Panama Mount, but withdrawn in Feb-1944 [Germany & Bailey 2007].

Updates of the USGS maps were made in 1964, 1974, 1984, 2010, 2013, 2016 and 2019. Google Earth has historical images (archived aerial photos) for 1974, 1982, 1985, 1995, 2004 and many later images. BCHM has aerial photos from Tobin in 1930 (as in Figure 100) and 1956-1957, Kargl in 1940 and Williams-Stackhouse in 1976. All these are not shown here, but which can be viewed to show the continuing development of the area, if you will, the rebirth of old Velasco as the new Surfside.

Then I saw a magic city, the metropolis of the west,
On the Brazos bank reclining, like a rose upon the breast,
Of a maiden fair, while suitors from every nation came,
To do homage to her beauty, and her splendor leaped to fame;
For the major part of commerce of every Western state,
Found egress to the ocean through her deep and narrow gate;
And art and science flourished in that balmy, healthful air,
And her men were brave and noble and her women pure and fair.

- *poem by Charles Diggs Hudgins, son of John Longest Hudgins, about Velasco*
(from "Maid of San Jacinto", a book of poetry [Hudgins 1900])

Carving on 1940 Brazoria County Courthouse above east-side (now employee) entrance

Before beginning, it may be useful to review the fact that the Velasco-platted blocks (e.g., shown in Figures 45 and 46) and those created later for Surfside are not the same. The angle of the streets was slightly different, as were the block size and shape. But in some cases, modern attempts to overlay the Surfside block margins with those platted in 1837 for Velasco, revealed some overlap (see Figure 115 below). For example, Velasco Block 13 and Surfside Block 568 are largely congruent, although not exactly. The same goes for the Velasco block labeled as Monument Square and modern Surfside Block 569. One important alignment is that the modern Monument Dr. (previously known as Ave. C or Coast Guard Road) sits largely atop the old Velasco road known as Fort Street, especially so on the southwest end, near the river. A chart of the modern Surfside blocks is shown in Figure 104 below, colorized by the author for the current owners in the area of property owned by the Cradle of Texas Conservancy (CTC), shown in yellow, and showing the right-of-way for the new jetty line installed in the early 1990s. The CTC owns Lots 5-8 in Block 560, Lots 1-5, 10, 12 and 14 in Block 568, and some undivided interest in several lots of Block 561. The city hall for Surfside Beach sits on Lots 2-4 of Block 560, and the Brazos River Harbor Navigation District (now Port Freeport) owns lots along the current jetty right-of-way.

Figure 104: Chart showing Surfside blocks and lots (colorized for current owners) in area of CTC property

In 1961, just upstream of old Velasco, a 9-pound cannonball was discovered at Dow's Plant-A property, and revived interest in the 1832 fort and battle [Dow 1961]. Featured in the article was a drawing by Zella May McDaniel (1929-2018), reproduced in Figure 105 below, the first of several artist's renditions of Fort Velasco, this one from a perspective high above the Gulf and during the Battle of Velasco.

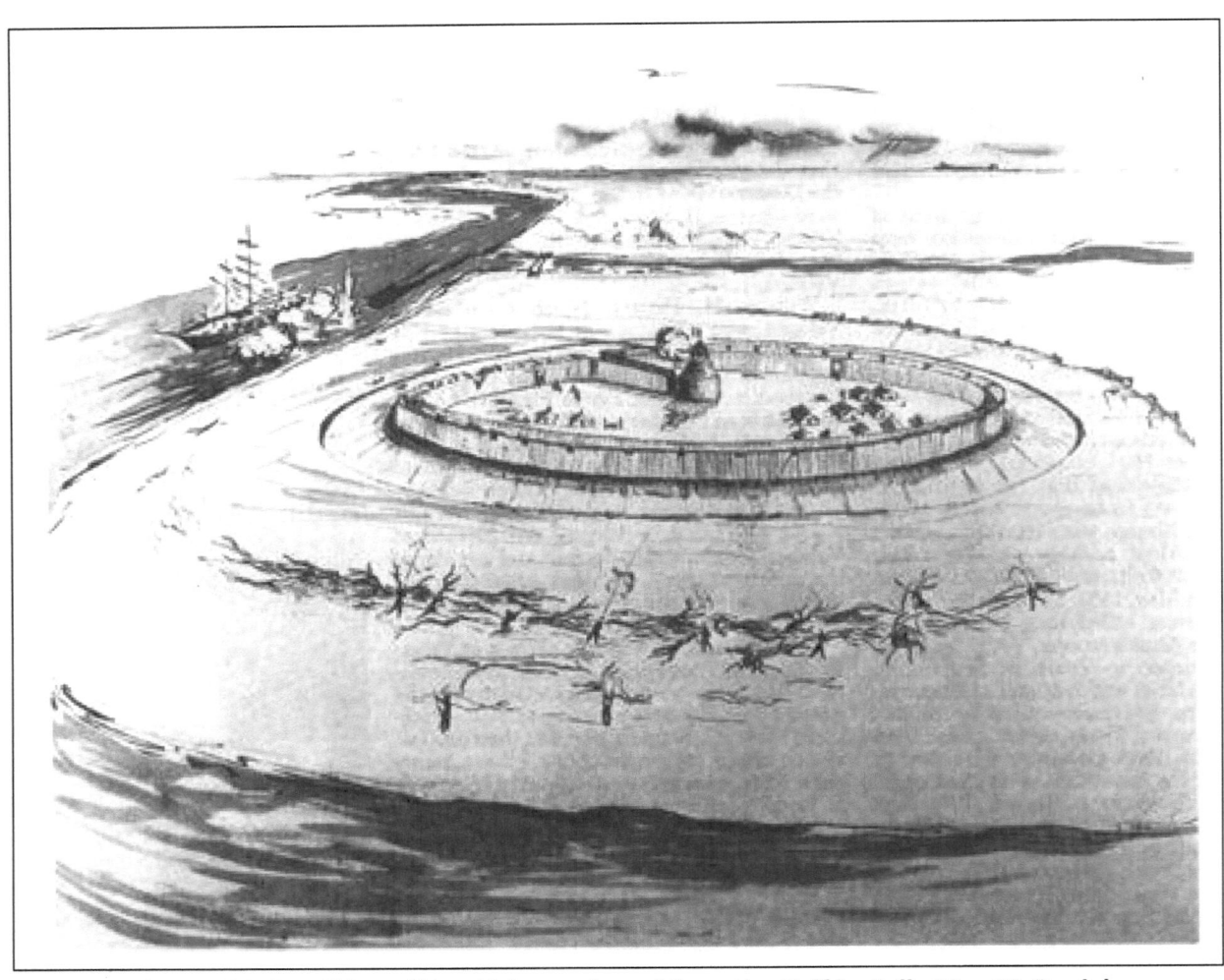

Figure 105: Rendition of Fort Velasco viewed from the Gulf by Zella May McDaniel
Photo courtesy of Brazoria County Historical Museum (1989.007p.0006)

Shortly thereafter, many members of the local Gulf Coast chapter of the Texas Society of Professional Engineers (TSPE) became interested in researching, finding and reconstructing this fort (see Kramig papers). By the late 1960s, property was bought piecemeal and privately in Surfside Blocks 560 and 568 by TSPE members and donated to the effort, ultimately resulting in an organization called the Texas Gulf Coast Parks and Historical Restoration Association, later changed to the Fort Velasco Restoration Association (FVRA), led by the late Messrs. Harold Singleton (1922-1978), Dale Sandlin (1913-2010), George Kramig (1919-2011) and Howard B. Fearn (1923-2012), among others. Inspections and excavations were accomplished in 1970-1971 by TSPE members, finding a cistern and several brick foundations in Surfside Block 568. This period also saw the use of informal excavations by Boy Scouts under the direction of Lagett Cleaver, Dale Sandlin and Howard B. Fearn to excavate the cistern, and also in Block 568 by a local avocational archaeologist (Raymond Walley) in 1972-1973 [Fox et al 1981 p. 4]. Some of the artifacts from this work are archived at the Brazoria County Historical Museum (BCHM), some being termed the Dale Sandlin Collection. For example:

Metal military button (1.5" diameter) of 11th Permanent Battalion of the Mexican Army, a unit that had some portions of it stationed at the 1830-1832 forts such as Anahuac and Barranco Colorado:

Staffordshire "transfer ware" shards:

Other artifacts from this period are stored at the Brazosport Museum of Natural Science (BMNS), although some items apparently were kept for private collections. <u>At the time, their belief was that this was direct evidence of the 1832 Mexican fort</u>.

The Brazoria County Historical Survey Committee and Adele Perry (Mrs. John S.) Caldwell (1895-1974) provided personal knowledge and research on the subject, and then the Brazosport Chamber of Commerce created a tourist brochure about the Battle of Velasco in about 1970; several versions were published over the next few years [Brazosport 1970]. One of the drawings included in these brochures is shown in Figure 106 below, illustrating the schooner **Brazoria** at the moonlit battle.

Figure 106: Drawing by Dan Parkinson; featured in Chamber of Commerce brochure
Courtesy of Brazoria County Historical Museum (2019.005.c0022)

The Chamber of Commerce brochure also mentions the fort was 300 feet in diameter, and another drawing was included showing a two-dimensional plot diagram and layout for such a fort (Figure 107 below). Examination of the McDaniel drawing (Figure 105) reveals an uncanny resemblance to the aforementioned 1822 diagram found in the Stephen F. Austin Map Collection (Figure 22) which showed a fort-like structure of 120 varas (about 330 feet) diameter. Although the origin of the McDaniel drawing remains unknown to this author, it almost seems that her three-dimensional rendition (prior to 1961?), and also the FVRA conclusions circa 1970 about a fort of 300-foot diameter, had their origins with this Austin diagram. A 1959 film also mentioned the 1822 diagram as a design for the 1832 fort, so it was known locally by this time [Boddie & Colegrove 1959, at 7:11-7:43 in the film]. As stated above, the Austin 1822 diagram was apparently known to the FVRA and Anne Fox in 1980 [Fox 1991].

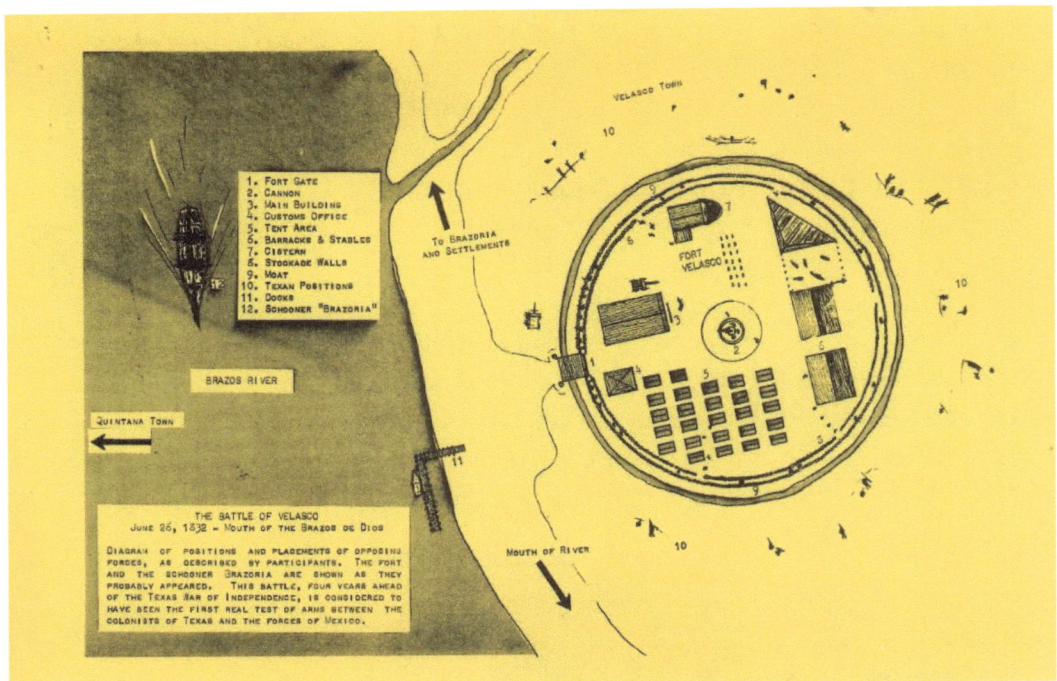

Figure 107: Drawing featured in Brazosport Chamber of Commerce brochure
Courtesy of Brazoria County Historical Museum (2019.005.c0022)

Ultimately, plans were drawn up for a circular fort replica of 300-feet diameter (see Figure 108 below), incorporating the structural features found in the TSPE and other excavations of the time [Fearn 1971].

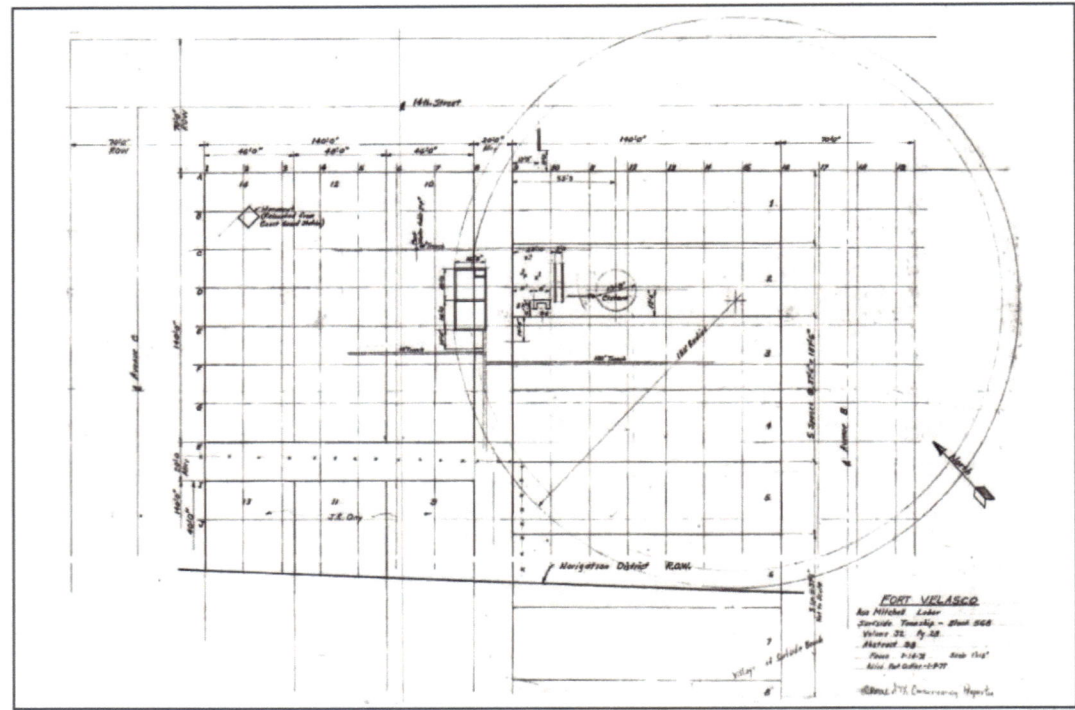

Figure 108: Digitized copy of 1970s FVRA design drawing
Courtesy: Blueline Print Shop, Freeport TX

However, in this drawing is information found nowhere else in print concerning the archaeological efforts in the 1970s, including the size and location of the cistern (19' 9"), details on the brick structures (width of chimney base of 8'), and the location of certain trenches. This area of the drawing is shown in greater detail below in Figure 109.

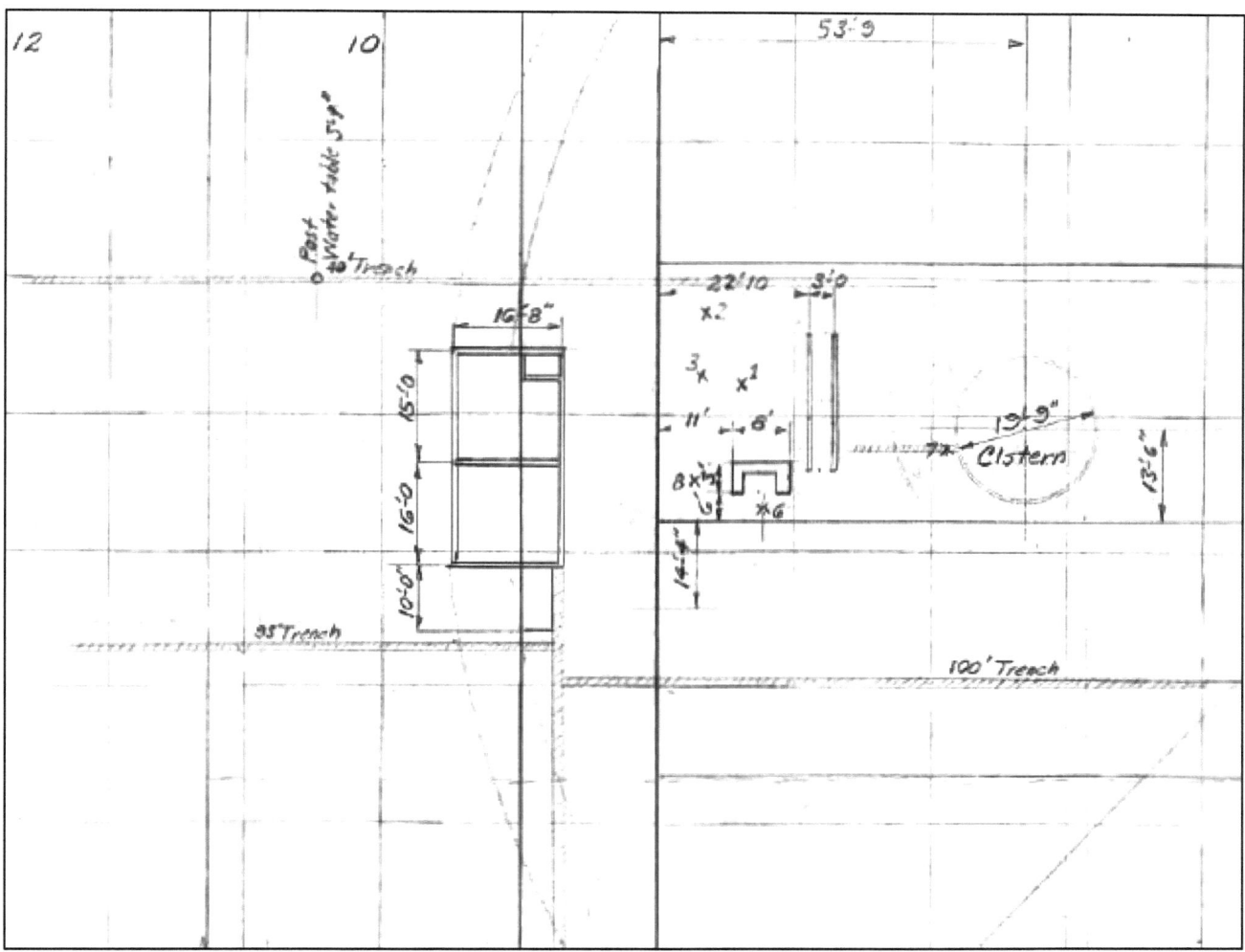

Figure 109: Detail from FVRA blueprint

Another drawing was found in the Map Case at the BCHM, which appears to be a CAD-type blueprint of a more-detailed "reconstruction concept", although unlabeled as to source, author or creation date (Figure 110). It was originally found in about 1995 in the Map Case Drawer 8 among many other unlabeled oversize drawings and maps, and then cataloged as BCHM Ref# 96.98.01 in 1996, although its stated radius of 150' suggest it belongs to the earlier FVRA efforts.

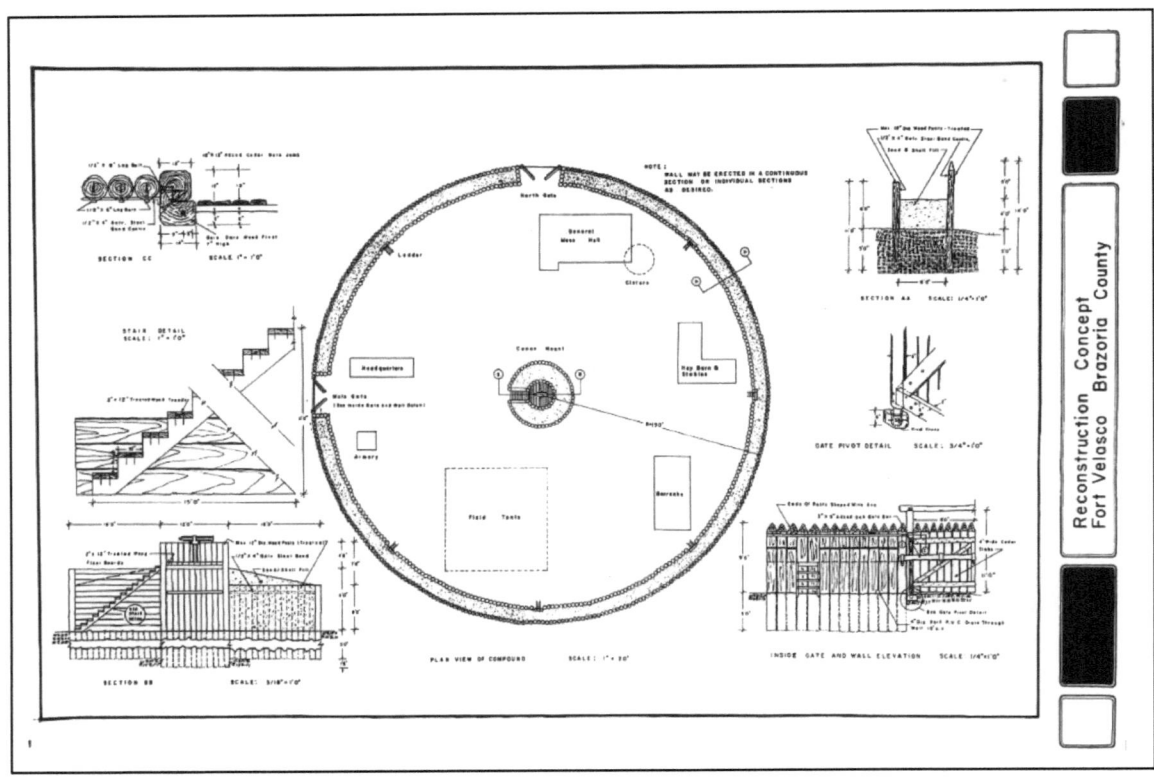

Figure 110: "Reconstruction Concept – Fort Velasco Brazoria County" Drawing
Courtesy of Brazoria County Historical Museum (96.008c.0001)

Although much public outreach was done through the 1970s, in the form of a traveling exhibit (with character posters, script and music), including a diorama (see Figure 111 below) and many presentations to public groups, the lands and funds for such a large project did not materialize.

Figure 111: George Kramig showing diorama (traveling exhibit); no longer in existence
Photo courtesy of Brazoria County Historical Museum (2003.005p.0268)

The character posters were drawn by Anna Brightwell in 1975, and copies of the dozen characters are shown together in Figure 112 below, provided by courtesy of BCHM.

Figure 112: Character Posters by Anna Brightwell, circa 1975 (© BCHM)
Henry Brown, Domingo Ugartechea, Britt Bailey, William Russell, Juan Davis Bradburn, Uncle Bubba
Thomas Bell, John Austin, Strap Buckner, Ben Brigham, unnamed Texian, Ed Robinson
Courtesy of Brazoria County Historical Museum (2003.006c.1-12)

At one point, a historical play entitled "Birth Of A Giant" was to be written by the late Kermit Hunter (1910-2001), a playwright and dean at SMU [Brazosport 1975], with the goal of the play for advertising and fundraising [Frantz 1974]. However, no script has ever been found, including in the Kermit Hunter Papers at the University of North Carolina at Chapel Hill, so the project must never have been completed. The plans also included creation of a large amphitheater in Freeport [Freeport 1975], although only a more-modest outdoor stage was built in about 1985 extending over the water at the extreme upper end of the Freeport harbor channel (known as "The Landing") as part of Freeport Municipal Park, and it is still in existence.

An excellent history of Brazoria County was published in this period [Creighton 1975], which included a passage about the 1832 fort and battle, and published again the rendition of Fort Velasco by Zella May McDaniel, previously shown in Figure 105.

During this period, the U.S. Army Corps of Engineers hired the Anthropology Lab at Texas A&M University to accomplish a reconnaissance survey around the harbor area in late 1975. It focused on prehistoric sites but more or less seconded the FVRA conclusion that the 1832 fort was in Surfside Block 568, and also resulted in the formal registration of the presumed site of the 1832 fort as archaeological site 41BO125 at the Texas Archeological Research Laboratory (TARL) in Austin [Baxter & Ippolito 1975, Ippolito & Baxter 1976].

One outcome of the FVRA group was the occasional newspaper article, sometimes including artwork showing an interpretive drawing of Fort Velasco, for example see Figure 113 below.

Another outcome of the FVRA group was the formal publication of a small book entitled "Thunder On The Brazos" by one of the members, Mary Delaney Boddie, which is an excellent summary of the precursors, order of battle and especially the political aftermath of the Battle of Velasco [Boddie 1978]. In the same time period, the Brazosport Chamber of Commerce and its president (from 1967 to 1988) Dan Parkinson continued to contribute artwork about the 1832 Fort Velasco (for example, see Figure 114 below).

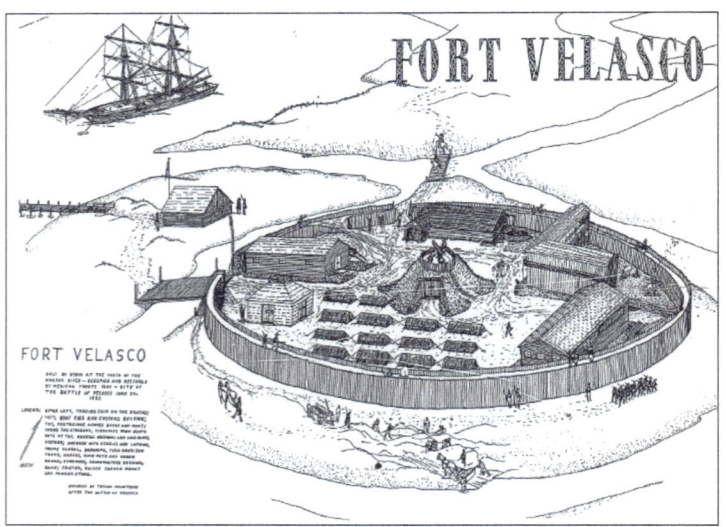

Figure 113: Drawing by B. Hackney of Fort Velasco in 13-Jun-1976 Brazosport Facts article
Photo courtesy of Brazosport Facts

A visiting David Hicks found the Chamber Of Commerce brochures, and with Mr. Parkinson developed it into a historical novel about the Anahuac Disturbances and the Battle of Velasco, entitled "The Texians" [Hicks & Parkinson 1980].

In anticipation of the Freeport harbor widening, the Center for Archaeological Research (CAR) at the University of Texas at San Antonio (UTSA) was contracted to do a cultural resource survey around the harbor channel, including further minor excavations in Blocks 568 and 569 in the period of Oct-Nov 1980 [Fox et al 1981]. The artifacts collected have been archived at TARL in Austin. In this report, one key diagram is their Figure 7 (page 39), repeated here as Figure 115 below. The interesting part is the overlay of new Surfside streets and blocks over the old Velasco blocks, indicating that modern Ave. C/Coast Guard Rd./Monument Dr. lies at an odd angle from other streets, and approximates the path of Velasco's Fort Street. This was probably due, as we will see in subsequent pages, to the fact that Fort Street was one of the few streets to remain in service after Velasco was moved upstream in 1891. In Figure 115, please also note that 14th St./Parkview Rd. intersects at an angle such that its imaginary extension to the northwest would pass into the area of the old Monument Square block. In a departure from previous thinking, the location of the 1832 fort was hypothesized to be within Monument Square, and a small dashed circle is proposed as the probable location, just west of this intersection.

Figure 114: Drawing by Dan Parkinson; featured in 8-Feb-1980 Brazosport Facts
Courtesy of Brazoria County Historical Museum

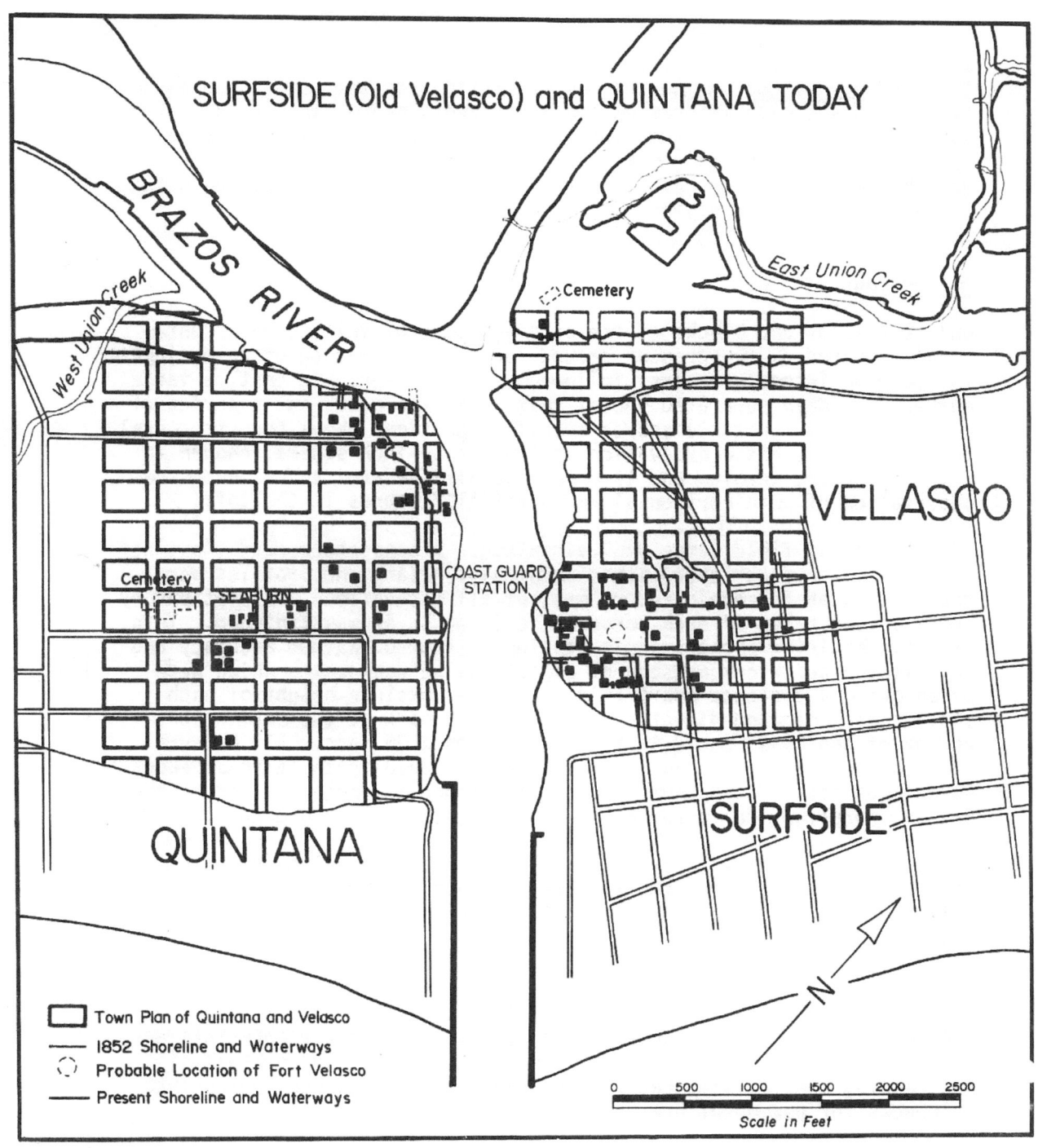

SURFSIDE (Old Velasco) and QUINTANA TODAY

BRAZOS RIVER

West Union Creek

East Union Creek

Cemetery

VELASCO

COAST GUARD
STATION

Cemetery

SEABURN

QUINTANA

SURFSIDE

N

☐ Town Plan of Quintana and Velasco
— 1852 Shoreline and Waterways
◌ Probable Location of Fort Velasco
— Present Shoreline and Waterways

0   500   1000   1500   2000   2500

Scale in Feet

Figure 115: copy of Figure 7 (page 39) in [Fox et al 1981]
Courtesy of Center for Archaeological Research, UTSA

In the same report, another diagram (Figure 8, p. 41) shows the locations of their excavations, but also reveals further details, such as their conclusion for the "Most likely area for fort remains" in the corner formed by intersection of Ave. C/Coast Guard Rd. and the jetty line (Surfside Block 569), and also the FVRA investigations in Block 568. It is reproduced below as Figure 116 of this report.

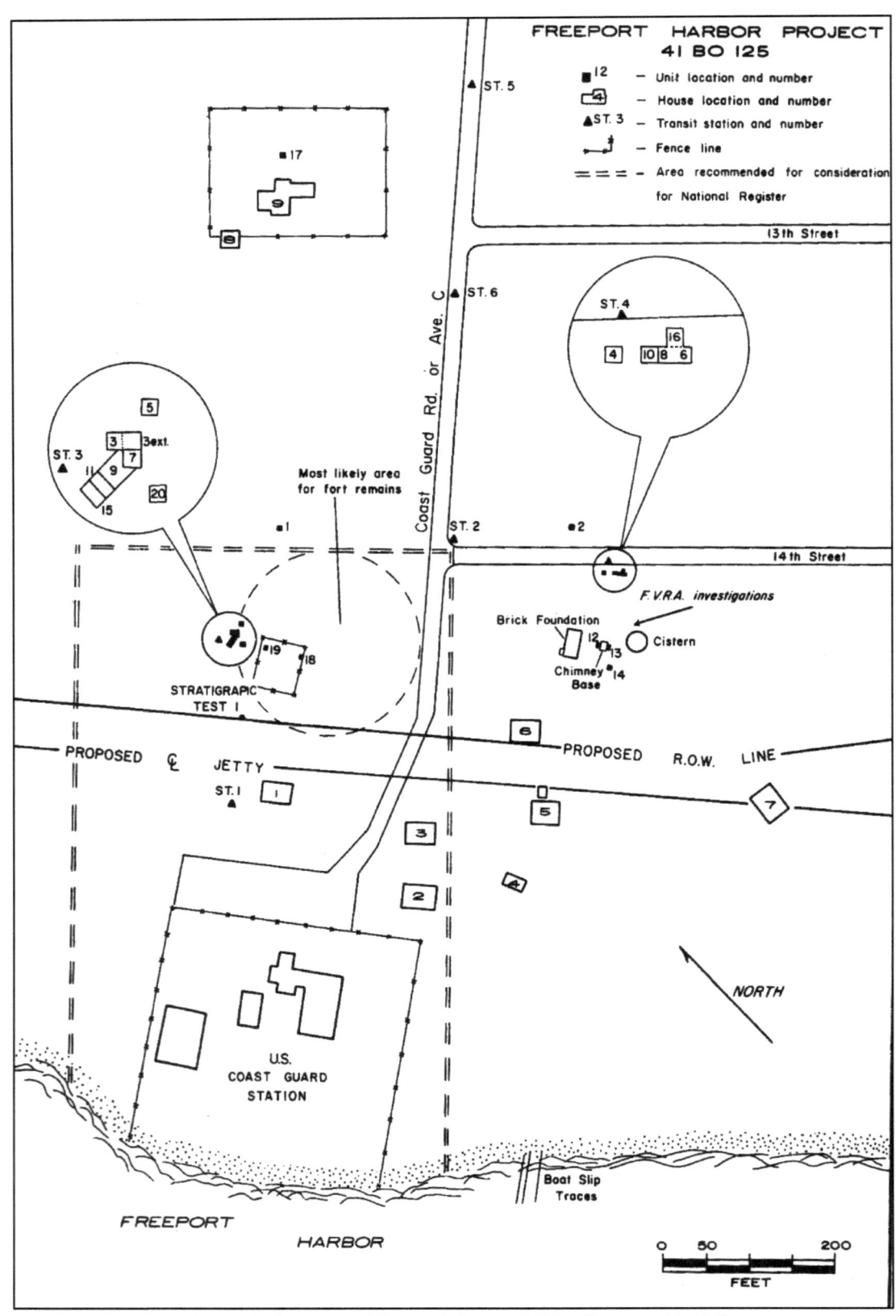

Figure 116: copy of Figure 8 (page 41) in [Fox et al 1981]

Courtesy of Center for Archaeological Research, UTSA

At about the same time, an underwater survey of the harbor channel was conducted based on magnetic anomalies detected in earlier studies, although no historically significant artifacts were found [Bond 1980].

The appearance of the 1822 Austin diagram in 1982 seemed to confirm the earlier FVRA design for a fort replica of 300-foot diameter. Ultimately, the property in Block 568 was transferred officially from the Texas Gulf Coast Parks and Historical Restoration Association (Dale Sandlin, President) to the CTC via a Warranty Deed on 30-Jul-1985. George Kramig became one of the CTC directors until a few years before his death in 2011. Since transferring the land, the CTC fully adopted the FVRA's goal of a replica Fort Velasco, although several subsequent approaches to build a replica have also not been successful.

During the actual Freeport Harbor widening in the early 1990s, a dense collection of artifacts (a "trash pit") was observed in the ground where the old Coast Guard station and its fenced-in area had stood for many years, and then excavated by emergency salvage techniques (as the dredge began its work), collected and studied by members of the Brazosport Archaeological Society (BAS), an affiliate group of the BMNS. The location of this excavation was approximately where the concrete pad is shown in the center of the photo image (Figure 117) below, which is a northwest-facing (upstream) view of the Coast Guard station in 1991 just before its removal for the harbor widening operations.

Figure 117: Panoramic view from multiple photos of Coast Guard Station in 1991

Courtesy of James L. Smith

The cleaned artifacts from this salvage operation, often called the "Velasco Collection", are archived at the BMNS [Pollan et al 1996]. One interesting find among the debris was an unfused but fired 20-pound Parrott shell, and later research revealed such rounds had been fired at Velasco by the *USS Midnight* in 1862 [Smith 1992] and by others in 1864-1865 [Freeman 1995 p. 44]. The shell was restored, and is shown in the photos of Figure 118 below.

VELASCO – 20 POUND PARROTT SHELL

Initial Condition

Initial Electrolysis

Final Electrolysis

Final Preservation

Figure 118: 20-pound Parrott shell found among trash pile in early 1990s

The BAS communicated the findings to the Army Corps of Engineers (COE) and also the Texas Historical Commission, even prevailing upon James Bruseth (while visiting a site over on Galveston Island) to come to Velasco. An interesting anecdote is that a member of BAS, Johnney Pollan, while examining the cut bank, pulled an item from the eroding edge, handing it to Dr. Bruseth, explaining it was a bayonet from a Brown Bess musket. Dr. Bruseth then calmly but wryly asked the Corps representative, if they might have a contractor who could excavate the area. Based on these discoveries and artifacts revealed in the exposed "cut bank", the COE halted further dredging temporarily and hired a professional excavation of the area by Prewitt & Associates of Austin [Earls et al 1992, Earls et al 1996], and these artifacts are housed at TARL. In their final report, one key diagram is their Figure 134 (p. 294), reproduced below as Figure 119. Please notice their excavation locations were mostly associated with former Velasco Block 11, and they essentially concurred with the overlay in [Fox et al 1981], also overlaying the structures observed in the 1858 Bache map. In their Block 13, the structure just to the left of the numeral 13 is thought to be the original Shannon house [Smith Dec-2014], and the structures alongside and underneath the line representing 14th St. are the Archer-Herndon property [Smith Sep-2014].

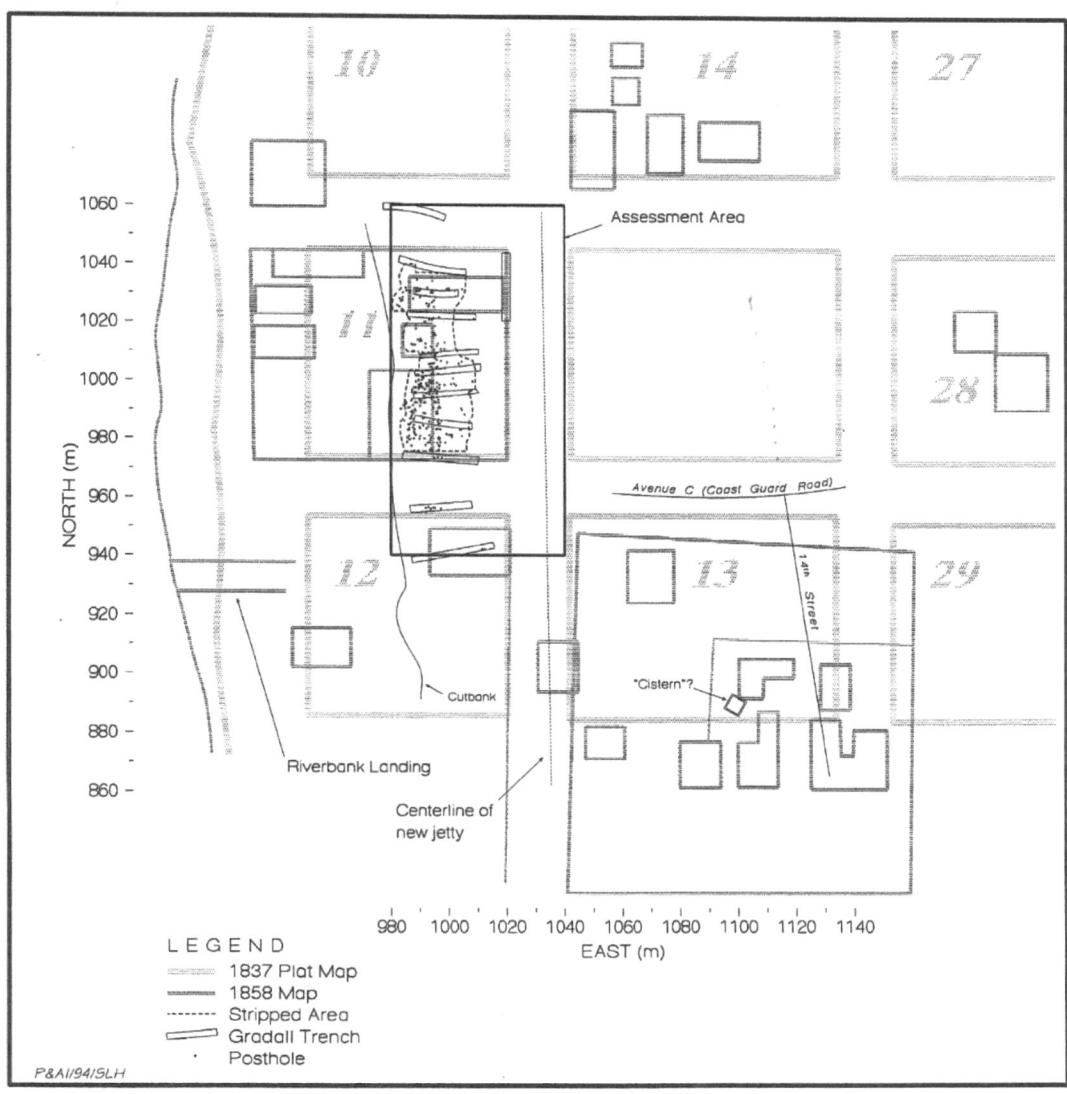

Figure 119: copy of Figure 194 (p. 294) in [Earls et al 1996]

Courtesy of Prewitt & Associates

During this period, one early construction activity of the harbor widening project in this area had been the excavation of a 40'-wide trench by a mechanized "track hoe" for placement of large granite boulders from the old jetty) as a landward extension of the new jetty line, circa 1990. At the time, no dredging had yet started, so there remained a substantial band of "land" between this row of granite boulders and the open water of the harbor channel. Most of this area was subsequently dredged away, and that remaining has since eroded and sloughed-in such that the boulders now act in their intended role as a bulwark against further erosion. Afterwards, we learned that the operator of this machine had uncovered 27 cannonballs, some mortar rounds and wooden structures in the approximate location where Treaty Avenue intersects the new jetty line (see Figure 104 for location of this street). At a later time, BAS-member James L. Smith was able to interview the machine operator, and rendered the operator's recollections into a drawing, which he added to the TARL file for 41BO125 (Figure 120). This diagram and other information were also shared with the U.S. Army Corps of Engineers [Pollan 1990], after which it is believed they came out and dug some trenches, too shallow to reach the depth of the structures drawn in Figure 120, and with no known written report. Please note the multiple structural elements found, but especially their great depth. This may explain why multiple CRM surveys failed to find anything previously. Perhaps these elements were originally built by excavating underground and/or were covered in later years by dredge spoil (as shown in Figure 100, since one large spoil mound is seen atop this very spot).

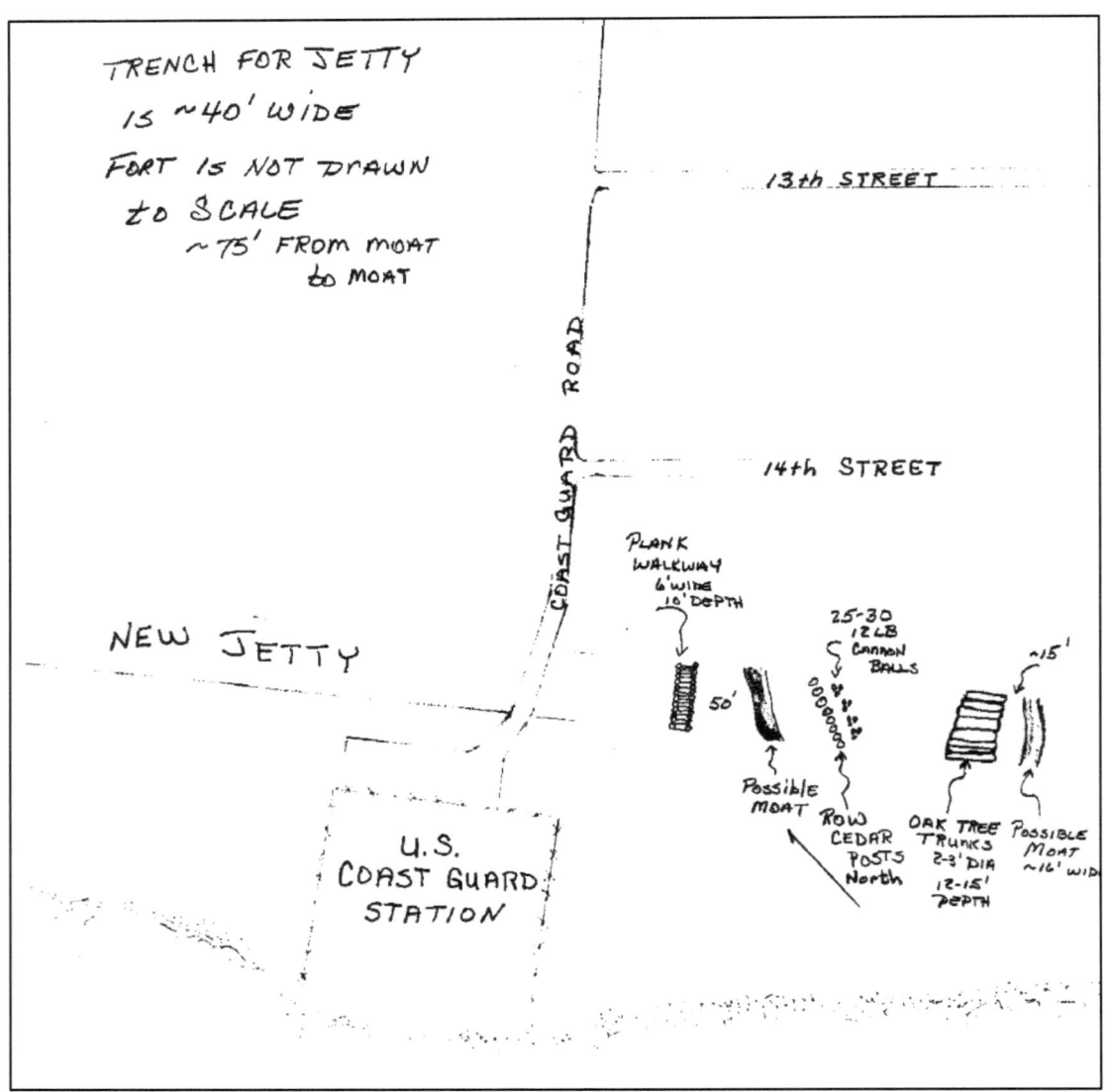

Figure 120: Drawing made by James L. Smith based on recollections of "track hoe" operator, ~1990

We were also able to secure a photo of two of the cannonballs at a later time, (and estimated they were 12-pounders) after a fire at the machine operator's residence in Surfside, shown below in Figure 121. We have concluded that these were likely from the Civil War Fort Sulakowski, perhaps one "Magazine" as seen in Figure 61.

Figure 121: Two (of 27) 12# cannonballs found when jetty line was built in early 1990s

Photo courtesy of James L. Smith

Also in this period, a private collector found two other examples of 11th Battalion buttons on the "beach" along the water's edge below the eroding cut-bank along the harbor channel adjacent to 41BO125. They were smaller (19mm diameter), shown in Figures 122 and 123 below). The numerals resemble, and had been previously identified, as JJ but are now thought to show an "antique cursive" 11 and be that of the 11th Battalion. So, it might appear that "soldados" from this unit were stationed as well at the 1832 Fort Velasco.

Figure 122 – Front and Back views of 11th Battalion button found at site of Fort Velasco

Photos courtesy of Bobby McKinney

Unlike forts such as Anahuac and Barranco Colorado, which submitted detailed monthly reports (including muster lists) of their complement (involving both the 11th and 12th Permanent Battalions), Ugartechea does not seem to have had time to do that, but in one letter he did mention that he had deserters from both of these Battalions [Ugartechea 7-Jun-1832b].

Other artifact types were found as well, including brass shot about the caliber of the 4-oz. "swivel gun" reportedly used at the 1832 Battle of Velasco, as well as occasional coins or other hardware (see Figure 124 below). The BAS excavations of the early 1990s had also found similar items, and the brass shot was initially identified as Mexican canister shot, although it is now believed it to be the solid shot of the "swivel gun".

Figure 123: Another 11th Battalion button found at site of Fort Velasco

Photo courtesy of Bobby McKinney

Figure 124: Other artifacts collected at water's edge at site of 1832 Fort Velasco

Photos courtesy of Bobby McKinney

In the period after construction of the onshore "jetty line" with granite boulders from the older north jetty, a dredge was used to remove most of the remaining land between the jetty line and the open water of the harbor channel. During this period (circa 1991), additional cannonballs and other artifacts were found. Some of the photos are shown below as a montage (collectively, as Figure 125), nicely showing the dredge which was in operation at the time. Round lead shot and the cannonballs (6, 12 and fused 24-pound balls) were found as concretions. One of the larger (24#) balls still had an intact fuse. Some of the shot looks to be about 1.25" diameter, which may have come from the 1832 fort's swivel gun, or perhaps were Civil War-era canister shot. As stated in the text of this report above Figure 61, the 1863 Fort Velasco was armed with heavy cannon (32, 24, 18 and 12-pounders), so these balls are probably related to these.

Figure 125: Photo montage of artifacts found during dredging of Freeport Harbor Channel, circa 1991

Photos courtesy of Joe Owen

Also beginning about 1990, an assemblage of artifacts (mostly ceramics) had been collected gradually over several years by BAS members on the eroding beach of the harbor channel on the Quintana side (since excavations on land were requested but not allowed), often referred to as the "Quintana Collection" [Blake & Freeman 1998], and are housed at BMNS. One interesting discovery from there was a military coat-size button for the Republic of Texas Marine Corps [Kneupper 1996]. Similar collections on the Velasco-side eroding "cut bank" and its "beach" over the following years were added to the "Velasco Collection".

Some exterior portions of the brick foundations in Surfside Block 568 were excavated more fully by BAS in the period of 1996-2003; with artifacts archived at BMNS. One key finding was that the cistern and brick foundation were really of Anglo-American origin, and most likely from the early days of old Velasco (1835-1860s), since very few Mexican or military artifacts were uncovered in this excavation (or in the previous excavations of the same area). Indeed, as mentioned above, it is believed that the brick foundations represent outbuildings or a later structure associated with the Archer-Herndon property (Lots 4, 5, 6 and 7 of Velasco Block 13) [Smith Sep-2014], and that the James T. Shannon (Lots 8 and 9) and Jeremiah Brown (Lot 10) houses were nearby [Smith Dec-2014] - for key of Velasco-platted lots, please see Figures 45 or 46.

In 1995, a fictional children's novel (*Race to Velasco*) was published, describing the exploits of two boys traveling to the Battle of Velasco, to seek one's older brother (Leander Woods) who died in the battle [Spellman 1995].

In about 1999, a Master Plan was developed for the entire left bank of the old Brazos River at Surfside by Duke Landscape Architecture and Planning of Galveston, financed jointly by the Brazoria County Parks Commission, the Village of Surfside Beach and the CTC. It contained, again, the proposed fort replica of 300-feet diameter (largely in CTC-owned Block 568), advocated by the FVRA and then the CTC. The full Master Plan was illustrated by creating five adjacent drawings or "panels", and the fort's detail in Panel 4 is shown below in Figure 126. The full series of panels is shown in Appendix 4.

Figure 126: Detail in Panel 4 of the Duke 1999 Master Plan
Courtesy of Bob Duke

At about the same time, a journal by Eduard Harkort was found with descendants in Germany, translated and published [Brister 1999], which included a scale drawing of Velasco in Spring 1836, showing a circular fort (in red) of just less than 100-feet diameter, now believed to be the only extant document to show or even mention the actual SIZE of the as-built 1832 fort [Harkort 1836a], shown In Figure 127 below.

Figure 127: Spliced drawings 3 and 4 from Harkort journal
Stiftung Westfälisches Wirtschaftsarchiv, Dortmund

It is unclear exactly when this drawing was made, but Harkort's journal indicates he arrived in Velasco about 8-Feb-1836, staying in the Brazoria area until leaving for San Felipe on 21-Feb-1836. The drawing is found in the journal between the entries of 12- and 15-Mar-1836, when the text reveals he was at Washington-on-the-Brazos, so perhaps he copied it into his journal then from observations made as he came through Velasco some weeks earlier. Harkort was ordered back to the coast (from Beeson's Ford) by Sam Houston on 27-Mar-1836, when the journal stops for six weeks. Sam Houston wrote to Thomas Rusk saying *"I sent Colonel Harcourt, as principal engineer of the army, down to the coast, to erect fortifications at the most eligible point of defence."* [Brister 1999 p. 361]. As stated above, in the Bell letter of 31-Mar-1836, the "coast" was Velasco and Galveston Island, so it would seem likely that Harkort was directly involved in any fort construction at Velasco circa Apr-1836. His name seems to appear in a document previously cited [Morgan 1836], when the "Twin Sisters", Robert Potter and others were transported on the schooner *Flash* from Velasco to New Washington in early Apr-1836, with the entry reading as *"Col. Harricourt ... passage from Velasco"*.

On this 1836 drawing, the distance to the beach is about 500 feet from the fort's seaward wall, and about 200 feet to the river from the fort's riverside wall. A close-up of the Velasco portion is shown below in Figure 128. At the time, the parties to the Duke Master Plan were unaware of the Harkort journal published that same year. The Master Plan also included a RV park (*never built, instead the county built a parking lot and restroom building*) and a boat ramp (*since built by Surfside*).

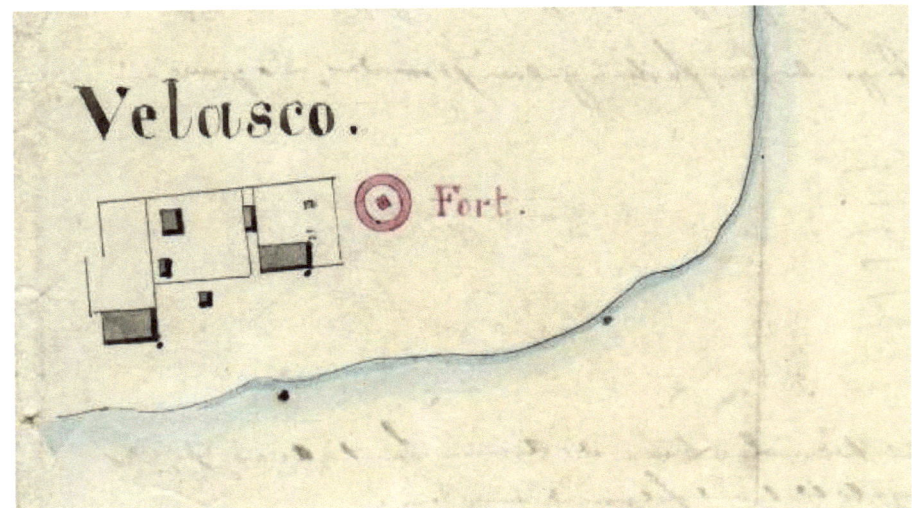

Figure 128: Close-up Detail of Velasco from scale drawing [Harkort 1836a].
Stiftung Westfälisches Wirtschaftsarchiv, Dortmund

This pair of drawings were not the only ones included in Harkort's journal. In total, ten drawings were found in the journal for various areas of southeast Texas, and high-resolution photo duplicates were generously made in 2020 by the Dortmund archive for each from the original journal at our request. One other has relevance for Velasco, as it shows a large-scale drawing of the lower Brazos River, and an excerpt for the mouth of the Brazos is shown in Figure 129 below (in this drawing, the direction of southeast is at the top of the map). Please note the dark writing for "Little Fort" and the faint writing for "Batterie", perhaps showing it just northeast of the town of Velasco.

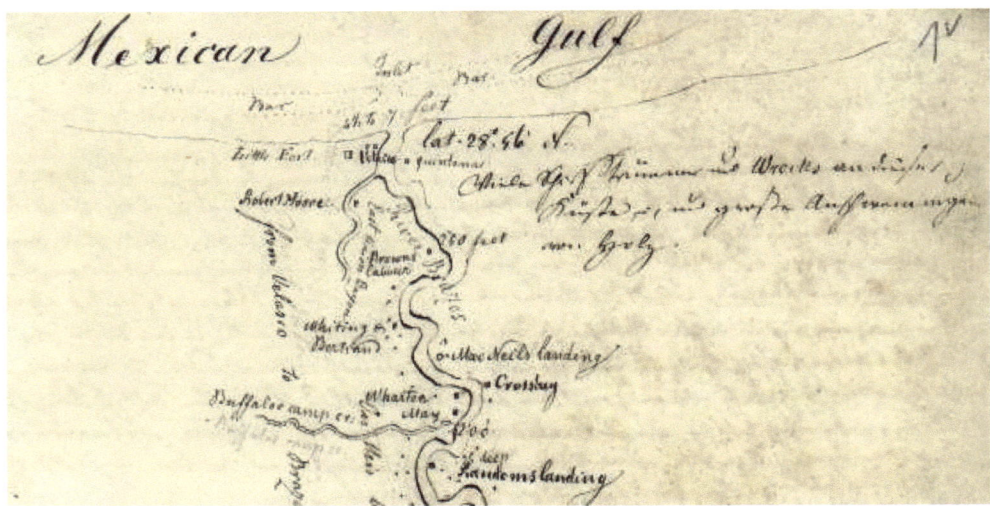

Figure 129: Detail of mouth of Brazos from Harkort Drawing No. 6
Stiftung Westfälisches Wirtschaftsarchiv, Dortmund

In 2002, the Village of Surfside Beach became interested in purchasing land around the City Hall for future community parks. The portion of Block 569 not involved in the jetty line (Lots 1-4, 10, 12 and 14) was donated by private owners to the Village in 2002 (Brazoria County Deed #2002019805, 27-Mar-2002). Plans for the boat ramp in the 1999 Duke Master Plan were amended to branch off the new harbor servicing the new Coast Guard Station. Starting in about 2005, and due to the appearance and accepted use of modern non-invasive techniques (such as ground-penetrating radar or GPR), discussions occurred between the Village of Surfside Beach and the CTC to potentially examine Block 569 with such techniques to see if any definitive evidence could be found for the 1832 fort. The activity was called the "Fort Velasco Discovery Project", but nothing became of these early efforts. In 2006, plans to build the boat ramp resulted in a contract with Prewitt & Associates to survey and test the impacted area for historical remains. Their report indicates the area involved the former Velasco Block 14 but was heavily disturbed, and intact remnants of old Velasco were no longer present [McWilliams & Boyd 2007].

In 2008, some additional excavations (by trenching) were done by a firm (PBS&J, Austin TX) to test remaining areas between the harbor channel and the jetty line, before the area was lost to erosion [Stahman 2008]. In this report, one Figure shows not only the PBS&J trenches but also the USACE trenches, circa 1990 – the only known published record of this latter trenching. Although some evidence of old Velasco was found, the authors concluded there was low potential for further investigations. Earlier, the same firm had done an underwater survey, finding no significant anomalies would be disturbed [Borgens et al 2006], although this report is not publicly available.

Among the artifacts collected in all these various excavations, only a small portion are of display quality, but may have a role in future displays (for example, color photographs for any on-site displays) or in other local museums such as the one maintained in Surfside City Hall.

In the period of 2014-2016, Surfside Block 569 was considered for reconstruction of a replica by the Village of Surfside Beach and the CTC, and a first-generation document was published informally [Llewellyn & Kneupper 2014]. It involved a general concept plan for a fort of 100-foot diameter, but also included an "executive summary" of the history of the site and more-recent archaeological investigations in that immediate area. As seen in this document, two published archaeological reports mention the hypothesis about the location of the 1832 fort [Fox et al 1981, Earls et al 1996], basically in Block 569, which borders the current Freeport Harbor channel, and is currently owned by the Brazos River Harbor Navigation District (part) and Village of Surfside Beach (part), as seen in Figure 104. This conclusion was largely based on the reasonable assumption that Monument Square marked the location of the 1832 fort. The CTC owns the adjacent portion of Block 568 not involved with the jetty line (and four lots in Block 560), which as stated previously has been held in trust for a fort reconstruction since the 1960s, and which has been found to contain historical remnants of the old town of Velasco and (perhaps portions of) the Civil War Fort Velasco.

However, as these discussions for a replica became more serious, it was thought best to first attempt to look for any evidence of the 1832 fort prior to any construction using non-invasive techniques to cover the widest possible area. Bid requests were issued in Feb-2015 to four cultural resource management (CRM) firms, to request proposals for a remote-sensing geophysical survey, in a joint effort between CTC and the Village of Surfside Beach. Moore Archaeological Consulting (Houston) was selected, who proposed using GPR and Magnetometry to conduct the survey. The fieldwork was accomplished over the course of two visits in Sep-2015, under Texas Antiquities Permit No. 7350, and their final report was produced in 2017 [Hadley & Mangum 2017]. Several low- and medium-priority anomalies were identified, but no definitive evidence of the 1832 fort or any other identifiable features were depicted in the resultant geophysical maps.

Following the 2015 survey, no ground-truthing excavations were conducted to investigate and verify any of the geophysical anomalies identified. Also, the Village of Surfside Beach spread several feet of dredge spoil (from boat ramp channel dredging, previously inventoried in large piles on the NW end of Block 569) over the surface of Block 569 and also atop the asphalt surface of Monument Dr. west of Parkview Rd., in furtherance of their plans to build an extensive connecting trail system funded through a Texas Parks & Wildlife Department (TPWD) grant. The Village of Surfside Beach then built a circular fence-like structure of 100' diameter starting in 2017 at the approximate location in Block 569 presumed (since 1981) to be the historic location of the 1832 fort. Since that time, however, efforts have largely ceased to build a replica at this location, and the structure is now called the Timeline Circle.

In the late spring of 2017, the Village of Surfside Beach leased the surface area of Block 568 from the CTC to place connecting trails according to the previously obtained TPWD grant. Although the lease agreement prohibited excavations or soil disturbance, proper instructions were not given to a bulldozer operator hired to clear the area of brush and weeds, and several inches of soil were bladed up into three piles of dirt and rubble. The well-known and exposed cistern cavity was filled in with a portion of the bladed soil. Some weeks later, the owners (CTC) discovered this, and observed historical artifacts crushed and scattered across the block. During the following weeks, surface collections were attempted by CTC members to recover exposed artifacts [Callahan 2017]. The one surviving datum marker from the BAS excavations of 1996-2003 (two others had been previously destroyed by drainage earthwork) was apparently swept away as it could not be located.

Considering the fact that Monument Square may have instead commemorated the graves of the Texian dead from the Battle of Velasco (perhaps where John Austin's division took many casualties), the exact location of the 1832 fort might be just adjacent (south) of this area. It is well to remember that the graves of Texan dead are buried on the bluff at LaGrange (called Monument Hill), and in Goliad it is the Fannin Memorial Monument, both created in the same era. Again, Ellen Shannon claimed her 1887 residence (in Lots 8 and 9 of Velasco Block 13, fronting on the southeast side of Fort Street) as the sight of the Mexican fort, which was agreed with by Mr. Alexander Glass Follett, Sr. [Looscan 1898]. Since both were long-time Velasco residents when remnants of the 1832 fort remained visible, their accounts should be accorded substantial authority. Also, the 1845 MacGreal-O'Connor deed mentions that the Archer-Herndon property was near the "Old Fort" [Brazoria 1845]. The assumption that Monument Square was the location of the 1832 fort does not share similar first-hand accounts. In 1931, Mrs. T. A. Humphries described the location as "*For many years, a cedar post marked the site of the old Mexican fort captured by the Texans in the Battle of Velasco in 1832. It was finally washed away and the location forgotten.*" [Humphries 1931]. This area today is thought to exist in the west corner of Surfside Block 568, very close to the current jetty right-of-way. The 1887 Shannon house is the one apparently shown in the 1888 map (Figure 69), 1890 Coode Drawing #2 (Figure 74) and 1891 map (Figure 77) surrounded by a fence, and (in Figure 77) along Fort Street (which is approximated today by Monument Dr.). This last map even shows the cistern found in various archaeological examinations of the area. Thus, it seems the 1832 fort should lie beach-ward from the current Monument Dr., not northward of this street.

Based on this hypothesis, another attempt was made for a geophysical survey in the 2019-2020 period, but instead focusing on Block 568 and the surrounding rights-of-way, funded by the CTC. Bids were solicited in late 2019, and Cultural Resources Analysts Inc. was selected in Feb-2020. Fieldwork was done in Jun-2020 involving ground-penetrating radar, magnetic gradiometry and electric resistance, followed by analysis and minor ground-truthing (selective excavations) through Jan-2021. The final report [Pye 2021] was published on 23-Aug-2021, and a copy has been uploaded for public access at the Index of Texas Archaeology (ITA): **https://scholarworks.sfasu.edu/ita/vol2021/iss1/23/**. The report also contains significant archival research done in the period since August-2019, revealing new details about the 1832 Fort Velasco location, the townsite of (old) Velasco, a Republic of Texas battery, and two Civil War-era forts – *an early excerpt of the preceding discussion in this document*. Based on the geophysical results, the data show strong evidence for the presence of the rear bastion of the 1863 (Civil War era) Fort Velasco, as well as almost the entire 1832 Fort Velasco – located in the approximate area of the Shannon house in current Block 568. The GPR anomalies for these items were found at some depth (2.5 to 3.5 meters), suggesting again that they may be remnants of the original trenches built around the 1832 fort dug deep into the then-existing soil and/or covered later by dredge spoil. No definitive geophysical evidence was found to suggest that graves, associated with casualties in the 1832 Battle of Velasco, were present in the surveyed area. However, as stated above, the Texian graves probably exist in the Block 569 area.

Various artists' renditions of the 1832 fort have also been done over the years as dioramas (shown in Figure 111 above, and another one by museum volunteer Elmer Kerls in Figure 130 below), that were once used at the Brazoria County Historical Museum (BCHM) in Angleton, now no longer in existence. Most historical descriptions of the fort describe two concentric sharpened wood-pole palisades, with sand filling the annular space in between (for an elevated walkway), and a sand mound in the center where a single long eight or nine-pounder (naval) cannon was mounted on a pivot surrounded by a parapet, to engage ships in the harbor channel or nearby Gulf waters. The smaller swivel gun was apparently mounted on the north wall, intended mostly for anti-personnel use.

Figure 130: Image of diorama by built Elmer Kerls formerly at BCHM
Photo courtesy of Brazoria County Historical Museum (2006.009p.0001)

Still another diorama has been built and is on display at the Freeport Historical Museum (see Figure 131 below), and there is a similar diorama at the Surfside Museum (upper floor of city hall) shown in Figure 132 below:

Figure 131: Diorama on display at Freeport Historical Museum

Figure 132: Diorama on display at the Surfside Museum

As can be seen, and due to lack of specific details in the historical record, some *"artistic license"* has been used in these interpretations of the fort. Later dioramas seem to adhere to a smaller size for the fort, probably based on the 1999 appearance of the Harkort drawing.

Research has revealed that a popular coastal fortification in Europe of the era was known as a Martello tower [George Nelson personal communication], typically equipped with a single naval cannon on a standard wooden carriage, but atop a rotating frame secured to a central pole or pivot (at the rear of the frame) to aim in any direction (for example, see Figure 133 below).

Figure 133: pivot-mounted cannon on a Martello tower

Other photos can be found on-line, by using search terms such as *Martello*, *tower*, *cannon* and *mount*. Indeed, if the 1822 Austin drawing is scrutinized closely, there is a detail that looks very similar to this arrangement (see Figure 134). Thus, it would seem that the concept of a Martello tower was known to professionally trained soldiers of the Mexican army in this period, and likely that a crude but working version of a pivot-mounted cannon was constructed at Fort Velasco.

Another version, more like a horizontal wheel mount, was suggested by the type used on ships of the First Texas Navy, an example from a wooden model of the ***Invincible*** found at the Houston Maritime Museum is shown in

Figure 134: Detail of gun tower from 1822 Austin drawing

Figure 135 below. Such a design for a rotating cannon mount seems to have come directly from those developed for use on the "Jeffersonian gunboats" of the U.S. Navy in the period of 1801-1812, and subsequently used to arm "Baltimore Clipper" schooners built in 1820-1821 [Chapelle 1949].

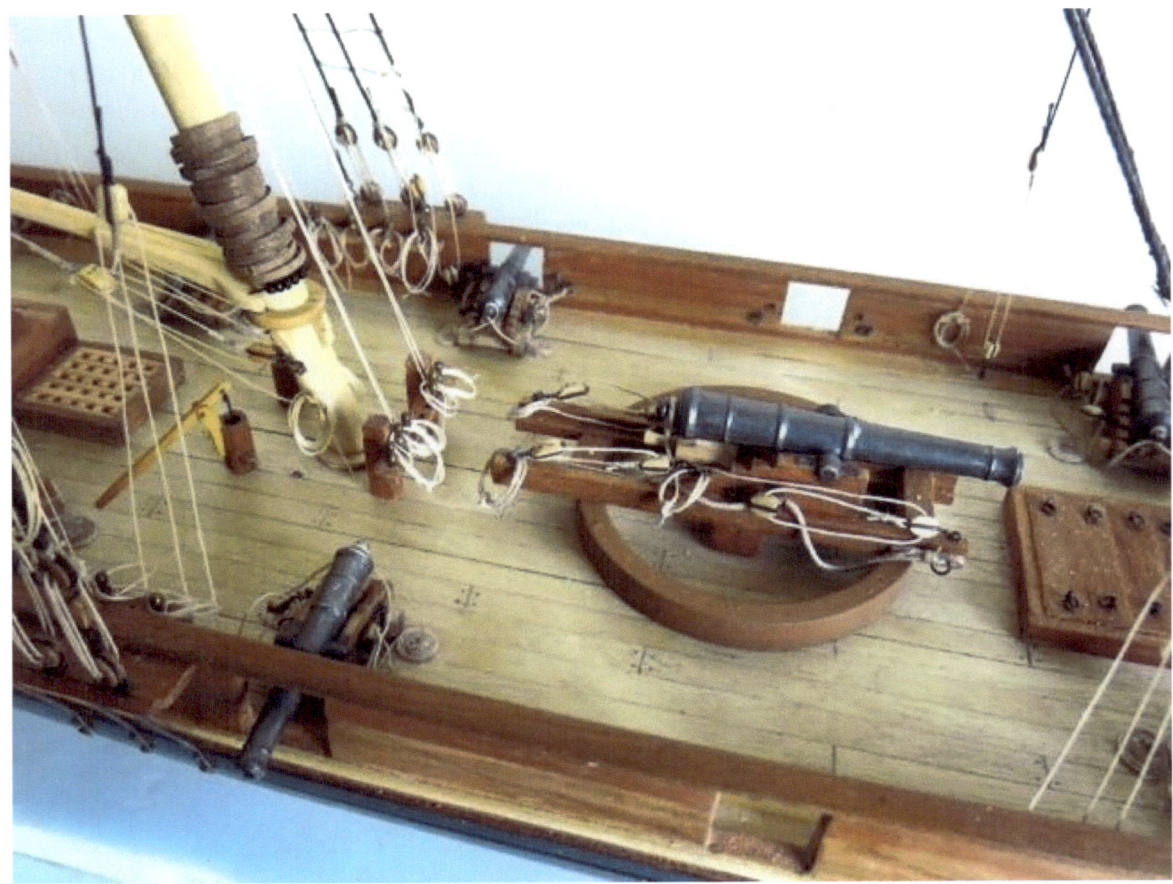

Figure 135: Pivot gun & rotating carriage, on Charles Cozwith's wooden model of the Invincible
Photo courtesy of Peter Rindlisbacher

Still another type of pivot mount was used for the cannon type known as a carronade in this era, where the pivot was at the front. Please see the Wikipedia page for Carronade (at the bottom) for an image of this mount: https://en.wikipedia.org/wiki/Carronade

The specific size of the bastion's cannon that was at Fort Velasco is not perfectly clear, since several sizes were mentioned in various references, including 6-, 8-, 9- and long 9-pounder cannon. However, among the first-hand accounts, only two sizes are mentioned - a "Cannon of 8" (in Ugartechea's letters [Ugartechea 26-Mar-1832, 1-Jul-1832] or 8-pound cannon (in John Austin's inventory of arms returned to Mexía [Cotten 1832, Holley 1883], and a long 9-pounder (in [Smith [1836] and [Russell 1872]). The "long 9" is a term for a smallish piece of naval artillery, typically having a bore of 4.2" and using a ball of 4.1" diameter. The French-designed 8-livre cannon had a ball that weighed 8.633 English pounds, so these may all refer to the same or similar cannon. Indeed, the French Gribeauval artillery system used from 1765 to 1829 involved a lightweight series of three cannon sizes (4, 8 and 12 livre) for field artillery, which were phased out in the period of 1803-1829 (see Figure 136).

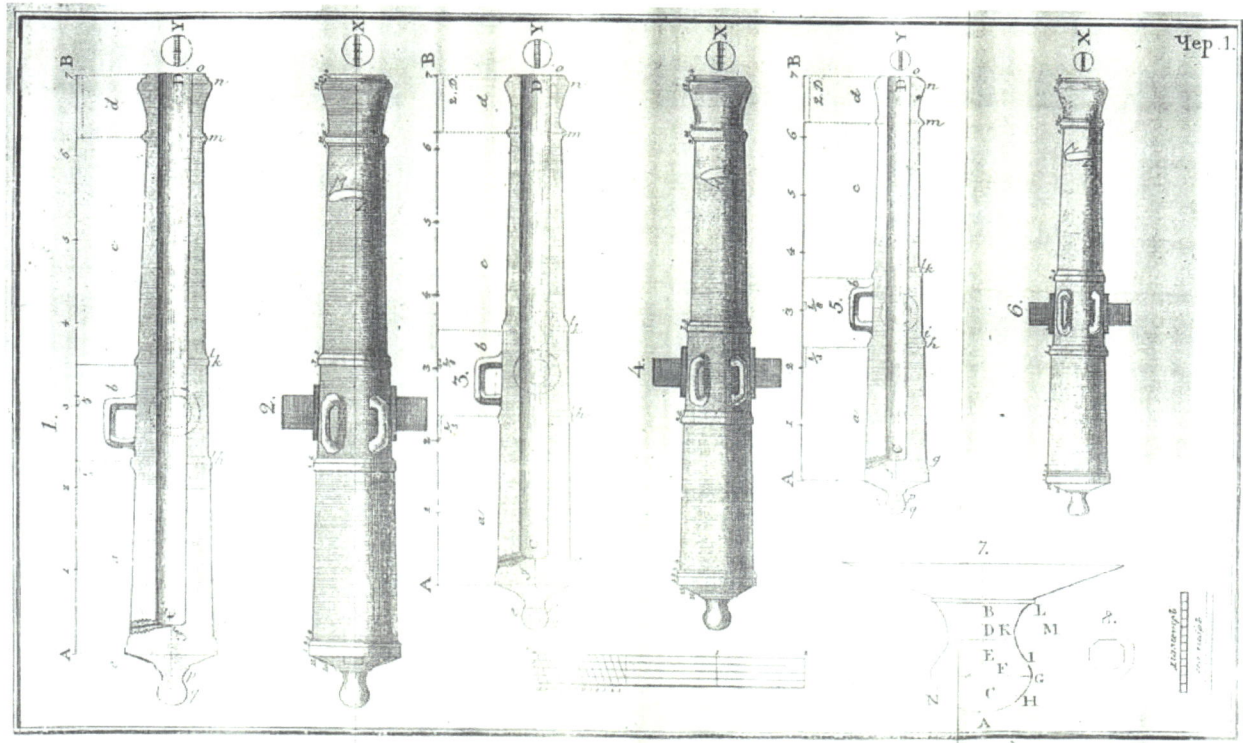

Figure 136: Cannons of the Gribeauval field artillery system (12, 8 and 4-livre)

The obsolete and retired Gribeauval 8 cannons (Figure 137) were among those sold to Mexico, and this type was used by Mexican forces at the Battle of Palo Alto in 1846 [National 2009]. The Gribeauval 8 is also displayed in the trail-side Battery Six at the Chalmette Battlefield near New Orleans, even though it seems to have originated as a trophy in the same Mexican-American War.

Figure 137 - Gribeauval 8's on field artillery carriages at Musée de l'Artillerie in Draguignan, France

It may be important to note that Ugartechea NEVER used the word "pound" or "long" in any of his descriptions. Additional secondary Texas references repeat the cannon size as 9- or long-9 pounds. The mention of a "cannon of 6" is found in an early letter of Ugartechea while still preparing at Anahuac

[Ugartechea 13-Mar-1832], and is interpreted as "six-pound cannon" in [Henson 1982]; however, this may not have been the cannon he eventually took to Velasco, since he left Anahuac about a month later, and this description can be discounted in favor of the many and contemporaneous mentions of 8 to 9 pounds. So, it seems like the Gribeauval 8 may be the best model if a replica cannon is ever required at a replica Fort Velasco, and (since it was reported as made of brass) it should be made to have an antique *verdigris* color.

In contrast, the swivel gun's size is only mentioned as 4-ounces among first-hand accounts, where Ugartechea mentions it (twice) in his after-report [Ugartechea 1-Jul-1832]. Henry Smith in his account a few years later mentioned a "four pounder" [Smith 1836], and this seems to be the source of later references mentioning a 4-pound cannon. However, a 4-pound cannon has a 3" diameter bore, and was probably too heavy for such a use. The authors of "The Texians" used instead a description of a two-inch ball for the swivel gun. The U. S. Army 1862 Ordnance Manual defines a 4-ounce cast-iron shot as being 1.231 inches diameter, and calculations confirm this size of cast-iron shot does indeed weigh right at 4 ounces. We conclude that the weapon was probably an iron-barreled muzzle-loading weapon (similar to a "wall gun") but the size that Ugartechea mentioned, something like that shown in Figure 138 below, but we are uncertain of the exact configuration.

Figure 138: Various images of Swivel Guns of 1 to 1.5" bore

Other images: http://www.vikingsword.com/vb/showthread.php?t=24913

Swivel gun info at: https://en.wikipedia.org/wiki/Swivel_gun or
https://en.wikipedia.org/wiki/Breech-loading_swivel_gun
National Park Service Manual: https://www.nps.gov/stri/upload/Swivel-gun-manual-revised.pdf

Another attempt was made in 2019 by Robert Bradley to map the area of old Velasco, overlaying the old Velasco blocks (dotted lines) and modern Surfside block/lot boundaries (solid lines) atop an aerial photo map. Mr. Bradley involved the surveying firm of Doyle & Wachstetter Inc., who used Quintana survey information and that of the Fox report [Fox et al 1981] to produce this overlay, one version of which is shown in Figure 139 below. Importantly, this attempt confirmed that the current Monument Dr. lies nearly atop the old Fort Street, Velasco Block 13 is mostly congruent with Surfside Block 568, and also concurs with the Fox report's estimate of location for Monument Square (as well as re-drawing their hypothesis that the 1832 Fort Velasco was in Monument Square).

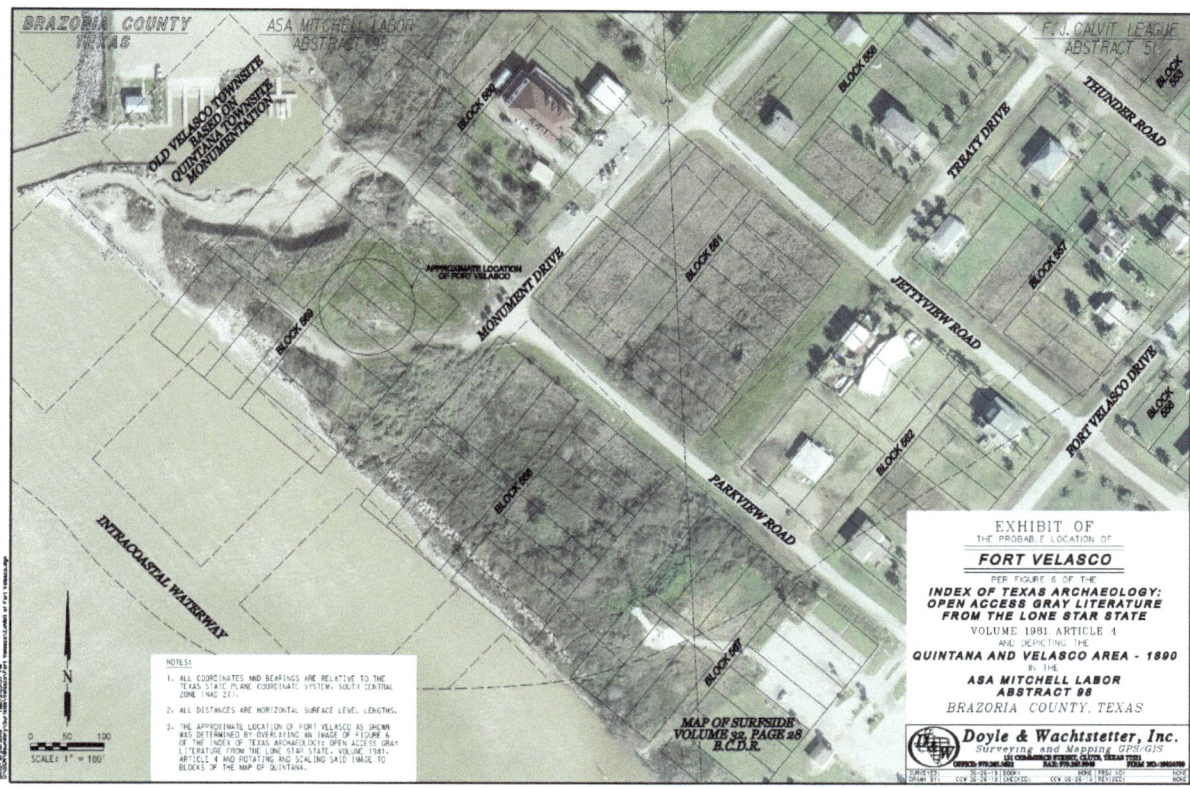

Figure 139: Overlay diagram of Old Velasco area by Doyle & Wachstetter

In the period of 2019-2020, a potential relic from Velasco was re-discovered in the area of Brownsville, Texas. Descendants of William Jarvis Russell in that area have handed down a flag reported by them to have been flown from the schooner ***Brazoria*** during the Battle of Velasco in 1832, and recovered by Russell after the ship was damaged. It was restored by the Brownsville Historical Association at Jessica Hack Textile Restoration in New Orleans with funds from a Historic Preservation Grant from the Daughters of the American Revolution [American Spirit 2020]. The restored flag is currently on display at the Brownsville Heritage Museum: **https://www.brownsvillehistory.org/assets/bha-banner-newsletter_april-2019.pdf**. Historians disagree whether this flag is actually from the 1832 battle, since no flag is mentioned in contemporaneous accounts, although a similar red/white/blue flag was used to represent the firm of McKinney, Williams and Company [James Glover, personal communication] which was founded in 1834, and this design was ultimately adopted as the ensign of the Republic of Texas Navy. Such a design was known as early as 1834, since a Bill Of Lading for the schooner ***Brazoria*** has a printed image of a steamboat flying such a flag [Maberry 2001 p. 29]. Perhaps the Russell flag was used or recovered in the years afterwards, as he was involved in the Texas Revolution. The program for the Velasco-Freeport Centennial Celebration on 14-May-1936 at the Velasco Coast Guard Station stated, *"At 9:45 A. M., a replica of the flag flown on the Schooner Brazoria during the Battle of Velasco, June 26, 1832 … will be hoisted to the breeze."*; however, the subsequent paragraph continues *"The flag that was nailed to the mast of the Schooner Brazoria … was the Mexican flag with the word 'Constitution' in the center"*. In 1958, Texas governor Price Daniel reestablished the Texas Navy as a ceremonial

Figure 140: Ceremonial flag of the Texas Navy Association

organization to publicize the marine interests of Texas, and this mostly social group was (and informally still is) referred to as the "Third Texas Navy", re-designated as the Texas Navy Association in 1972. This group uses a flag design essentially similar to the Russell flag (see Figure 140).

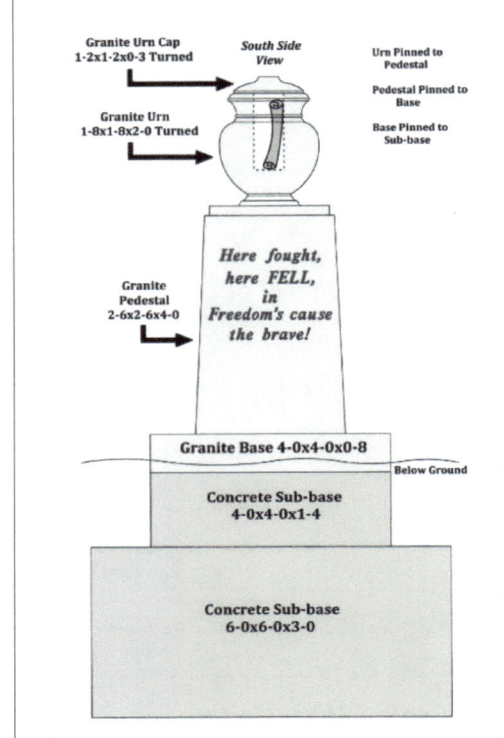

Since discovery of the 1833 **Arkansas Advocate** article [Bertrand 1833], creation of a replica for the monument suggested for the graves of Texian dead from the Battle of Velasco has been discussed, and a design was prepared in 2022 by Leslie Bryson of Bryson Memorials (see Figure 141).

Such a monument was built in early 2023, and installed in Jun-2023, being unveiled on the 191st anniversary of the Battle of Velasco. In early 2025, a plaza with antique-brick walkway, two flagpoles and two re-located historical markers was constructed (see Figure 142 below), known collectively as the "Battle of Velasco Memorial".

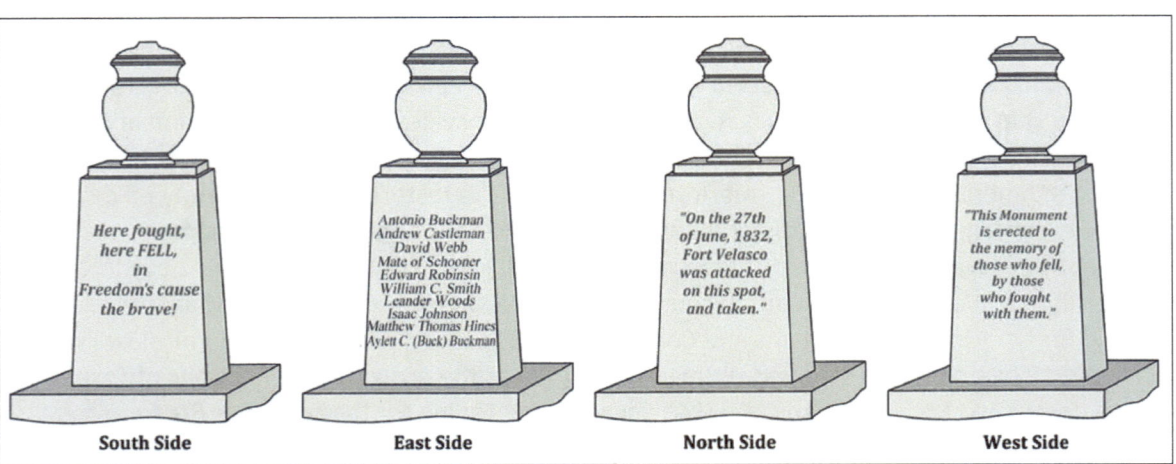

Figure 141: Drawing of potential re-creation of 1833 Monument, by Leslie Bryson

Figure 142: Photo of refurbished Battle of Velasco Memorial, soon after its unveiling in Apr-2025

As seen flying on the left flagpole under the U.S. flag, a new tri-color flag was custom produced through the Eagle Mountain Flag and Flagpole company (Wimberley, Texas), with the design for the Brazoria militia company, which was commanded by John Austin during the 1832 Battle of Velasco. To date, we have found no reference that such a flag was actually used at the battle, nor a surviving example, but the design was inspired by its written description in an 1828 law [Cotten 1828 p. 4, Jenkins 1969], seen in Figure 143, and the corresponding flag image for the Nacogdoches company (of 4x5 aspect ratio) shown in the book "Texas Flags" [Maberry 2001 pp. 9-10]. Few other Texas flags of the 1832 period are known, but this design is one of the few unique to this site and time.

> ART. 86. Each battalion of this militia shall have a flag whose staff shall be eleven quarters of a bar long with a ferrule and spear; the staff to be covered with red cloth; the flag shall be of silk, five-quarters square, in three verticle stripes, green at the staff, white in the centre, and red at the extremity. In the white shall be stamped an Eagle in the attitude of flying, and around it, in letters of gold, the words, "RELIGION, INDEPENDENCIA, UNION." In the upper part of the white stripe shall be placed the name of the State; under the Eagle, "FEDERACION MEXICANA;" and below this the name of the town and the number of the battalion, should there be more than one. The decorations shall also be of the same three colors.

Figure 143: Militia Law, Article 86 – description of militia flag

COAHUILA Y TEJAS
FEDERATIÓN MEXICANA

UNION, RELIGION, INDEPENDENCIA,

BRAZORIA MILITIA
AUSTIN'S BATTALION
COMPANY 3

Figure 144: Recently created flag image for the militia company of the Brazoria municpalidad (district)

The flag design was digitally re-created by Michael Bailey, and is shown in Figure 144. This was used to create outdoor-rated nylon flags with a printed central image during the year 2024 in both 36x45" and 48x60" sizes, for use at events held at the Battle of Velasco Memorial and others. To our knowledge, this is the only attempt to create a flag of the Brazoria militia company, although a similar design was created by the Refugio company about ten years or more years ago.

The local Cradle of Texas chapter of the Daughters of the Republic of Texas (DRT) awarded the site their historic medallion as a "Historic Site of the Republic of Texas", based on the story of the San Felipe Incident and the Treaties of Velasco. This topic was thought especially fitting for the DRT, since these two events are like bookends for the Texas Revolution, occurring very near each other at old Velasco. A matching pedestal of antique brick was constructed at the same time as the surrounding plaza, and it was dedicated in Jun-2025. This can be seen on the far side of the plaza in Figure 142, and a close-up is shown in Figure 145.

At an earlier point, during the early months of 2024, a series of six interpretive signs were installed along the jetty-side trail (the example for the First Republic of Texas Navy is shown in Figure 146), and all six signs have been documented in the on-line Historical Marker Database:

Figure 145: Daughters of the Republic of Texas "Historic Site of the Republic of Texas"

Figure 146: Jetty-side Historical Trail Sign for First Republic of Texas Navy, 1835-1837

Other points of interest, might be considered for new markers, perhaps even modest ones sponsored by the county or village. For example, since the location of the U.S. Lifesaving Station has been clarified to be near the old mouth of Oyster Creek, it may be appropriate to place a marker near this spot, perhaps adjacent to the Blue Water Highway. Others might be placed for the Republic of Texas fort, Civil War forts, or the Surfside Hotel.

Plans for a replica of the 1832 Fort Velasco have met with various difficulties over the years, most recently the issue of cost. So, a revised plan is being considered as of 2025, to focus on historic interpretation at the site instead of a full replica.

EPILOGUE

I hope this book will be educational, aiding future research, archaeology and historical interpretation efforts in the Brazosport area. Any proceeds from publication of this book will be directed to historical interpretation projects in the area.

In summary, it can be said that a number of important conclusions have been reached or clarified:

1. Especially in the early years of Austin's Colony, the mouth of the Brazos was the foremost port of entry for that colony, beginning in late 1821 up to and through the Texas Revolution. Those 15 years helped form the most successful colonization of Texas to date, and would ultimately reshape the fate of the entire province. Although the Brazos port was not ideal, the rustic state of development at the time, together with the smaller ships of the era, caused it to be the best choice. This situation would change in the years between the Texas Revolution and the end of the American Civil War.

2. The "puerto de Galvezton" was officially established in 1825, but chiefly operated out of the mouth of the Brazos until late 1831, when its administration was transferred to Anahuac. The city known today as Galveston, though, did not exist until after the Texas Revolution, although ships used its excellent anchorage in prior years.

3. Premature and unsuccessful efforts by George Fisher were made as early as the summer of 1830 to establish a customs post at the mouth of the Brazos, including many plans and the seizure of at least one schooner for smuggling tobacco. However, actual creation of the first customs post was delayed until early 1831, built by Mexican soldiers under the command of Juan Davis Bradburn, using Anahuac as a base of operations.

4. Although some sort of customs house or post existed for about a year prior, the construction of the palisaded "first" Fort Velasco occurred over a rather short period of about four weeks in Apr-May 1832, under the direction of Lt. Col. Domingo de Ugartechea. The Battle of Velasco occurred only a month later, so the occupation period by the Mexican garrison of the fort was very short.

5. The 1832 fort built by Mexican soldiers is now thought to have been about 100' in diameter, and some if not most buildings such as customs house, barracks, stables, offices and warehouses were probably built outside such a small fort, some of which were burnt down just prior to the Battle of Velasco. Strategically important items such as a cistern or well, as well as armory, magazines or powder room were probably inside the fort walls.

6. Recent research, as described in this report, reveals that graves from the Battle of Velasco exist in the immediate vicinity of the 1832 fort. The presence of graves, suspected to exist in Block 569, provides an additional but important reason to continue archaeological efforts.

7. The 1832 fort's precise location has also now been confirmed, in the current Block 568, an area once occupied by the Shannon house in Velasco Block 13. The size of the circular images found in the 2020 geophysical survey may indicate the dry ditch surrounding the circular fort, and also support a fort diameter of approximately 100', as shown in the Harkort drawing. The significant depth of the GPR anomalies, along with a similar depth for the features found by the "track hoe" operator about 1990 (suspected to be from the Civil War fort), may explain why previous efforts have failed to find direct evidence of these forts.

8. The abandonment by the Mexican military of Fort Velasco after the Battle of Velasco (and similar garrisons at Anahuac and Nacogdoches) in the late summer of 1832 left a vacuum, that was filled by ever-increasing immigration from the United States, thus creating an important antecedent for the Texas Revolution of 1835-1836.

9. In this period, Brazoria County seems to have been a center of early and growing dissent among the Texian colonists leading to the Texas Revolution, catalyzed by the Law of 6-Apr-1830 and its zealous implementation by the likes of George Fisher, Juan Davis Bradburn, Thomas M. Thompson and later Santa Anna. Mexican leaders such as José Antonio Mexía, Domingo de Ugartechea, Lorenzo de Zavala and perhaps even Manuel de Mier y Terán were more liberal and diplomatic with the Texians and, if their policies had prevailed, the Texas Revolution might have taken a much-different course.

10. Velasco had an important role in the beginning and end of the Texas Revolution of 1835-1836. The San Felipe Incident seems to have been the true opening shot of the Revolution, and it actually caused witness Stephen F. Austin to side with the cause. After the Battle of San Jacinto settled the issue by force of arms, the Treaties of Velasco were the formal end of the Revolution, ushering in the new Republic of Texas. These two events, happening just yards apart at old Velasco, can be said to be "bookends" of the Revolution.

11. During the same period of 1835-1836, the mouth of the Brazos also had a key part in creation and maintenance of the First Texas Navy, with Quintana merchants Thomas McKinney and Samuel May Williams acting quickly to obtain and arm suitable vessels. In this way, this small fleet protected the southern flank of the land forces, even to the point of allowing Sam Houston's victory at San Jacinto.

12. The *ad interim* government of the new Republic met at Velasco for about five months after the Battle of San Jacinto, in and around the Brown-Hoskins tavern and hotel. Thus, the town of Velasco can be considered an early capital of the Republic, and the hotel can be considered its first capitol building.

13. Other forts were built after the 1832 fort, also called Fort Velasco, during the Texas Revolution and the American Civil War, amounting to FOUR forts by that name. The Republic of Texas battery and the original Civil War fort known as the "Town Fort" existed in areas now lost to modern harbor widening. However, near the current jetty line may be remains of the rear bastion of the Civil War fort known also as Fort Sulakowski. The redoubt on the Brazos-Galveston Canal was also lost, to widening of the Intracoastal Canal, and was approximately where the new high bridge crosses it today. Only the location of the redan on Oyster Creek appears to still be intact.

14. Old Velasco played a more significant role in early Texas history than is generally recognized today, and efforts should be made to redress the situation by historical interpretation of the area to promote heritage tourism. As mentioned by author James Llewellyn Allhands - *"To a close observer there is wealth of information about the early days of Texas; stored in the immediate vicinity of Brazoria. The story of its settlement is interesting, for the county, which name it bears, was truly the cradle of Texas liberty and virtually Texas at one time, yet not a monument has been erected, nor a marker placed, nor a spot in this immediate territory set aside as a memorial."* [Allhands 1931 p. 217].

15. New Velasco and then Freeport, just a few miles inland from the mouth, became the center of port activity (mostly for cotton and sulfur) after jetties were completed in 1891, and have gradually diversified since that time. Today, Port Freeport has become an important hub for imports as varied as bananas, container cargo and cars, export of petrochemicals and Liquified Natural Gas (LNG) --- maybe Stephen F. Austin's dreams for the Brazos have finally come true!

A people which takes no pride in the noble achievements of remote ancestors will never achieve anything worthy to be remembered with pride by their descendants.
- *Thomas Babington Macaulay-*

REFERENCES

*Stamp used on letters from Horatio Chriesman in 1832, while Alcalde and President
of the Ayuntamiento of San Felipe de Austin (Béxar Archives 150:47, 50 & 53)*

Collections (in alphabetical order by abbreviations - used afterwards in references)

AGMC - Archivo General de Mexico Collection, Dolph Briscoe Center for American History, The University of Texas at Austin, Austin, Texas

AJHC - Andrew Jackson Houston Collection, Texas State Library and Archives (Austin, Texas)

AP - Barker, Eugene C. (editor), The Austin Papers, Vol. I (2 parts, Annual Report of the American Historical Association For The Year 1919, United States Government Printing Office, Washington DC, 1924), Part 1 (1789-1824) and Part 2 (1825-1827); *confusingly, the spine and title page of the original volumes label it as Vol. II, Parts 1 or 2, although there does not seem to have been a separate published Volume I;* Vol. II, 1828-1834, (Annual Report of the American Historical Association for the Year 1922, United States Government Printing Office, Washington DC, 1928); Vol. III (Oct, 1834-Jan, 1837), The University of Texas Press, Austin, Texas, 1926

BA - Béxar Archives, Dolph Briscoe Center for American History, The University of Texas at Austin, Austin, Texas

BCB - Broadside Collection, Dolph Briscoe Center for American History, The University of Texas at Austin, Austin, Texas

DCRT - Diplomatic Correspondence of the Republic of Texas (Annual Report of the American Historical Association for the Year 1907, Government Printing Office, Washington DC)

ECBP, Eugene Campbell Barker Papers, Dolph Briscoe Center for American History, The University of Texas at Austin, Austin, Texas

EJP - Edward Johns Papers, Call# CAH-MS JOHNS, Edward, Dolph Briscoe Center for American History, The University of Texas at Austin, Austin, Texas

GFC - George Fisher Collection, Archives and Information Services Division, Texas State Library and Archives Commission (Lorenzo de Zavala State Archives and Library Building), Austin, Texas

GFP - George Fisher Papers, 1830-1948, Dolph Briscoe Center for American History, The University of Texas at Austin, Austin, Texas

HRWC - Henry R. Wagner Texas And Middle West Collection, S-339, Beinecke Rare Book And Manuscript Library, Yale University, New Haven, Connecticut

J&SPP - James F. and Stephen S. Perry Papers 1785-1942, Dolph Briscoe Center for American History, The University of Texas, Austin, Texas

JFGP - Jeremy Francis Gilmer Papers, Southern Historical Collection, Wilson Library, University of North Carolina at Chapel Hill

JGTP – John G. Tod Papers, Collection 74-0018, Galveston & Texas History Center, Rosenberg Library, Galveston,

Texas)

JLBP - Jean Louis Berlandier Papers, WA MSS S-300, Beinecke Rare Book And Manuscript Library, Yale University, New Haven, Connecticut

JMP - James Morgan Papers, Galveston & Texas History Center, Rosenberg Library, Galveston, Texas

LOT – The Laws of Texas, 1822-1897, compiled & arranged by H. P. N. Gammel, 1898

LP - Gulick Jr., C. A.; Allen, W.; Elliott, K.; Smither, H., *The Papers of Mirabeau Buonaparte Lamar, Edited from the original papers in the Texas State Archives* (6 Volumes, The Pemberton Press, 1968)

M&SFAP - Moses and Stephen F. Austin Papers, Dolph Briscoe Center for American History, The University of Texas, Austin, Texas

MSHP - Margaret Swett Henson Papers, Galveston & Texas History Center, Rosenberg Library, Galveston, Texas)

OCTR - *Official Correspondence of the Texan Revolution, 1835-1836,* edited by William C. Binkley, 2 volumes, Appleton-Century Co., 1936

PTR - The Papers of the Texas Revolution, (John H. Jenkins III, general editor, 10 volumes, Presidial Press, Austin TX, 1973)

PTTH – The Portal to Texas History, The University of North Texas Libraries

RBBRC – Robert Bruce Blake Research Collection, compiled in the Eugene C. Barker Texas History Center Archives Collection, 1958-1959 (*full set available at Clayton Library, Houston, Texas*)

SHPB - Sam Houston Papers, 1814-1857, and undated, Dolph Briscoe Center for American History, The University of Texas at Austin, Austin, Texas

SHPC - Sam Houston Papers 1818-1967, Catholic Archives of Texas, Texas Catholic Conference of Bishops (Austin diocese chancery), Austin, Texas

SHPR - Sam Houston Papers, 1821-1863, Woodson Research Center, Fondren Library, Rice University

SMWC - Samuel May Williams Collection, Galveston & Texas History Center, Rosenberg Library, Galveston Texas

SWHQ - *The Southwestern Historical Quarterly* (journal of The Texas State Historical Association), 1912-present; including previous version *The Quarterly of the Texas State Historical Association*, 1897-1912

TGLO – Texas General Land Office, Spanish Archives (Austin, Texas)

TJGP - Thomas Jefferson Green Papers, Southern Historical Collection, University of North Carolina Library, Chapel Hill, North Carolina

TNP - Texas Adjutant General's Department Navy Papers, Texas State Library and Archives Commission (Lorenzo de Zavala State Archives and Library Building), Austin, Texas

TNP-R – Texas Navy Papers, Collection 72-0001, Galveston & Texas History Center, Rosenberg Library, Galveston, Texas

TSC – Thomas W. Streeter History of Texas Collection, as found in *Bibliography of Texas 1795-1845*, 2nd Edition (Harvard University Press, Cambridge MA, 1955), and associated Microfilm

TWSC-Y - Thomas W. Streeter Collection of Texas Manuscripts, Yale Collection of Western Americana, Beinecke Rare Book and Manuscript Library, Yale University, New Haven, Connecticut

WSH - The Writings of Sam Houston 1813-1863, 8 volumes, edited by Amelia W. Williams and Eugene Barker, University of Texas Press, Austin, Texas, 1938

Other abbreviations:

BAS – Brazosport Archaeological Society

BCHM – Brazoria County Historical Museum

BMNS – Brazosport Museum of Natural Science

TSLAC – Texas State Library & Archives Commission

Ahumada, Mateo,

1-Feb-1826   Letter to Stephen F. Austin, **BA**, Microfilm Roll 89, frames 76-78; see also Ahumada to Rojo & Ahumada to Austin, 10-Apr-1826, Roll 91, frames 470-473 & 474-479

Allen, Augustus C.,
17-Oct-1835   Letter to President of Consultation, **PTR**, Document #884, Vol. 2, pp. 141-142

Allen, John M.,
31-Mar-1836   Letter to Sam Houston, **PTR**, Document# 2489, Vol. 5, p. 245

Allhands, J. L.,
1931   *Gringo Builder*s, privately published book (The Clio Press, Iowa City, Iowa); an excerpt about Brazoria County (pp. 223-232 in the book) was published in The Corpus Christi Caller-Times (newspaper) on 28-May-1939

Almonte, Juan,
2005   *Almonte's Texas – Juan N. Almonte's 1834, Inspection, Secret Report & Role in the 1836 Campaign*, Jack Jackson (editor), John Wheat (translator), Texas State Historical Association

American Spirit (magazine of the Daughters of the American Revolution),
Jan-Feb 2020   page 7

Anthony, D. W. (editor),
5-Sep-1832   The Constitutional Advocate and Texas Public Advertiser (Brazoria, Texas), newspaper, Vol. 1, Ed. 1; available on-line at **PTTH**: https://texashistory.unt.edu/ark:/67531/metapth235664/, accessed 18-Mar-2022; crediting The Dolph Briscoe Center for American History

Arévalo, Mariano (publisher),
1829   *Colección de Ordenes y Decretos de la Soberana Junta Provisional Gubernativa, y Sobernas Congresos Generales de la Nación Mexicana*, (Mexico City, 1829), Vol. IV, p.6

Archer, Branch T., William H. Wharton, Stephen F. Austin
10-Jan-1836   Letter to Henry Smith, **DCRT**, Vol. II, Part I, p. 55
21-Jul-1836   Letter to David G. Burnet, **DCRT**, Vol. II, Part I, pp. 111-112

Arteaga, Aniceto
28-Jun-1832   Letter to Antonio Elosúa, **BA**, Microfilm Roll 151, frames 100-108
1-Jul-1832   Letter to Antonio Elosúa, **BA**, Microfilm Roll 151, frames 226-227
9-Jul-1832   Letter to Antonio Elosúa, **BA**, Microfilm Roll 151, frames 475-476
10-Jul-1832   Letter to Antonio Elosúa, **BA**, Microfilm Roll 151, frames 518-519; includes enclosure of note from Domingo de Ugartechea to Arteaga of 8-Jul-1832

Austin, John,
24-Nov-1830   Letter to Thomas Barnett, copy sent to Samuel May Williams on 29-Nov-1830, **SMWC**, Manuscript 23-0482
18-Dec-1832   "To The Public", **TSC**, Document# 24, Broadside printed by D. W. Anthony with John Austin's reply to accusations by William H. Wharton; see also **TSC** Documents 30 (Beinecke Library, Call# BrSides Zc52 832sm), 31 & 34

Austin, Stephen F.,

1822	"untitled diagram of circular fort, circa 1822", Stephen F. Austin Map Collection, Call Number SA 121822 (stored in 2.325/OD20), Dolph Briscoe Center for American History, The University Of Texas at Austin, high-resolution photos available as [identifier number: di_11854, di_11863]
27-May-1823	Letter to Felipe de la Garza, transcript in **AP**, Vol. I, pp. 651-653; *at Digital Austin papers:* http://digitalaustinpapers.org/document?id=APB0597
1-Oct-1824	Letters to Supreme Executive Power of the Mexican Republic, 1-Oct-1824 and 6-Nov- 1824, ... State Congress, 6-Nov-1824, ... Governor of Coahuila and Texas, 4-Feb-1825, ... Governor Rafael Gonzales, 4-Apr-1825, transcripts in **AP**, Vol. I, pp. 912-913, 935-936, 936, 1034-1035, 1065-1067; *latter two are in English and found at Digital Austin Papers*: http://digitalaustinpapers.org/document?id=APB1035 and http://digitalaustinpapers.org/document?id=APB1071
12-Dec-1825	Letter to Emily M. Perry, transcript in **AP**, Vol. I, pp. 1238-1239
18-Mar-1826a	Letters to José Antonio Saucedo & Erasmo Seguin, transcripts in **AP**, Vol. I, pp. 1281-1283 and 1288-1290 (original of letter to Saucedo is in **TGLO**, Document# 730, Box 126/3, p. 19); see also letters of Austin to Emily Perry, 28-Jan-1826 (**AP** I:1260-1262) and Austin to Saucedo, 27-Mar-1826 (**AP** I:1299).
18-Mar-1826b	Letters to Rafael Manchola & Mateo Ahumada; also see Ahumada to Austin, 24-Jul-1825, transcripts in **AP**, Vol. I, pp. 1285, 1285-1288 and 1155-1156
1829	Introduction. To the Settlers in what is called Austin's Colony", in Texas, preface to summary of applicable laws in Austin's Colony in [White 1839], circa 1829, pp. 559-583
24-Dec-1829	Letter to José Antonio Navarro, transcript in **AP**, Vol. II, pp. 302-303; at Digital Austin Papers: http://digitalaustinpapers.org/document?id=APB1816
13-Mar-1830	*Notice and editorial published in Texas Gazette issues of 13- and 27-Mar-1830,* transcript of latter in **AP**, Vol. II, p. 351; at Digital Austin Papers: http://digitalaustinpapers.org/document?id=APB1884
29-Mar-1830	Letter to Ramón Músquiz, Spanish transcript in **AP**, Vol. II, p. 354-355
19-May-1830	Three Letters to Thomas Barnett, Militia (as a circular), and George Fisher, Spanish transcripts in **AP**, Vol. II, pp. 392-394
4-Jul-1830	Letter to James F. Perry, transcript in **AP**, Vol. II, p. 440; *at Digital Austin Papers: http://digitalaustinpapers.org/document?id=APB1978*
13-Jul-1830	Letter to Manuel de Mier y Terán, transcript in **AP**, Vol. II, pp. 461-462 (this letter is identified in Austin Papers with a date of "about 1-Aug-1830, Terán's letter of 15-Aug-1830 identifies the date as 13-Jul-1830)
17-Sep-1830	Letter to Manuel de Mier y Terán, 17-Sep-1830, transcript in **AP**, Vol. II, pp. 483-486
18-Oct-1830	Letter to Lucas Alamán, transcript in **AP**, Vol. II, pp. 512-515
13-Jan-1831	Letter to Samuel May Williams, transcript in **AP**, Vol. II, p. 584-586, original in **SMWC**, Manuscript 23-0543
19-Feb-1831	Letter to Samuel May Williams, transcript in **AP**, Vol. II, pp. 599-604; original in **SMWC**, Manuscript 23-0582; *at Digital Austin Papers: http://digitalaustinpapers.org/document?id=APB4154*
12-Mar-1831	Letter to Samuel May Williams, transcript in **AP**, Vol. II, pp. 611-613, original in **SMWC**, Manuscript 23-0595
2-Apr-1831	Letter to Samuel May Williams, transcript in **AP**, Vol. II, pp. 636-639, original in **SMWC**, Manuscript 23-0627
30-Dec-1831	Letter to John Davis Bradburn, transcript in **AP**, Vol. II, pp. 731-732; original in **HRWC**; *at Digital Austin Papers: http://digitalaustinpapers.org/document?id=APB4304*
8-Jan-1832	Letter to Manuel de Mier y Terán, transcript in **AP**, Vol. II, pp. 733-735; original in **HRWC**
5-Feb-1832	Letter to Manuel de Mier y Terán, transcript in **AP**, Vol. II, pp. 747-748
21-Mar-1832	Letter to Samuel May Williams and Asa Mitchell, transcript in **AP**, Vol. II, pp. 758-761, original in

SMWC, Manuscript 23-0907; *at Digital Austin Papers:*
http://digitalaustinpapers.org/document?id=APB4335

19-Jun-1832	Letter to Horatio Chriesman, transcript in **AP**, Vol. II, pp. 782-787, transcript of original in **SMWC**, Manuscript 23-0958; *at Digital Austin Papers:* https://digitalaustinpapers.org/document?id=APB4354.xml
20-Jun-1832	Letter to Samuel May Williams, transcript in **AP**, Vol. II, pp. 791-792, original in **SMWC**, Manuscript 23-0907; *at Digital Austin Papers:* https://digitalaustinpapers.org/document?id=APB4358.xml
29-Jun-1832	Letter to Domingo de Ugartechea, Spanish transcript in **AP**, Vol. II, pp. 804-805
1-Jul-1832	Letter to Samuel May Williams, transcript in **AP**, Vol. II, pp. 807-809; original and typescript transcription in **SMWC**, Manuscript 23-0966; *at Digital Austin Papers:* *http://digitalaustinpapers.org/document?id=APB4371*
9-Jul-1832	Letter to José Antonio Mexía, transcript in **AP**, Vol. II, p. 813; transcript also in **RBBRC**, Vol. XIII, p. 29; see also Letter to José Mariano Guerra, 10-Jul-1832, transcript in **AP**, Vol. II, pp. 815-817; transcript in **RBBRC**, Vol. XIII, pp. 31-35; *at Digital Austin Papers:* https://digitalaustinpapers.org/document?id=APB4378.xml https://digitalaustinpapers.org/document?id=APB4380.xml
22-Jul-1832	Letter to Samuel May Williams, transcript in **AP**, Vol. II, pp. 823-824; original and typescript transcription in **SMWC**, Manuscript 23-0975; *at Digital Austin Papers:* *http://digitalaustinpapers.org/document?id=APB4388*
28-Jul-1832	Letter to Ramón Músquiz, English transcript in AP, Vol. II, pp. 825-828; transcript also in **RBBRC**, Vol. XIII, pp. 57-62; *at Digital Austin Papers:* https://digitalaustinpapers.org/document?id=APB4393.xml
30-May-1833	Letter to Capt. Wily Martin, transcript in **AP**, Vol. II, pp. 977-981; *at Digital Austin Papers:* *http://digitalaustinpapers.org/document?id=APB4574*; also see Letters to Ayuntamiento of Nacogdoches (pp. 975-977) and Ayuntamiento of Brazoria (found in [Brown 1887] pp. 19-23) dated 30-May-1833, John Austin (pp. 981-982) and Oliver Jones et al (p. 982) dated 31-May-1833. Copies by George Fisher also found in **LP** #1664 (Appendices) at TSLAC.
21-Aug-1835	Letter to Mary Austin Holley (from New Orleans), transcript in **AP**, Vol. III, pp. 101-103; *at Digital Austin Papers:* https://digitalaustinpapers.org/document?id=APB4851
22-Dec-1835	Letters to F. W. Johnson et al (from Quintana) & to Provisional Government (from Velasco), transcripts in **AP**, Vol. III, pp. 289-290 & 290-292; available on-line *at:* https://texashistory.unt.edu/ark:/67531/metapth225496/m1/325/ https://digitalaustinpapers.org/document?id=APB5087
25-Dec-1835	Letters to R. R. Royall & James F. Perry (from Quintana), transcripts in **AP**, Vol. III, pp. 292-294 & 294-295; *at Digital Austin Papers:* https://digitalaustinpapers.org/document?id=APB5090 https://digitalaustinpapers.org/document?id=APB5091
7-Jan-1836	Letters to Sam Houston, R. R. Royall & S. Rhoads Fisher, and to Mary Austin Holley (from New Orleans), transcripts in **AP**, Vol. III, pp. 298-299, 299-300 & 300-301; *at Digital Austin Papers:* https://digitalaustinpapers.org/document?id=APB5094 https://digitalaustinpapers.org/document?id=APB5095 https://digitalaustinpapers.org/document?id=APB5096

Ayish, People of,

5-Jul-1832	Letter to Citizens of Coahuila and Texas, transcript in **RBBRC**, Vol. XIII, pp. 16-18

Bacarisse, Charles A.,

Oct-1952	"The Texas Gazette, 1829-1831", *SWHQ*, Vol. LVI (56), No. 2 (Oct 1952), pp. 239-253

Bache, Alexander D.; William, J. S.; Wampler, J. M.; DeHaven, J. D.; Duer, J. K.,

1858   *Preliminary Chart Of Entrance To Brazos River, Texas*, From a Trigonometrical Survey under the direction of A. D. Bache Superintendent of the Survey Of The Coast of The United States

Bailey, James B.,

27-Jun-1832   Letter to David Shelby, **BA**, enclosure in Microfilm Roll 151, frames 341-344; English translation in **RBBRC**, Supplemental Volume IX, pp. 266-267; the Bailey letter at BA is a copy by Aniceto Arteaga on 2-Jul-1832 of a Spanish translation by Jose M. J. Carbajal on 29-Jul-1832 of the original English letter, and then enclosed in a letter from Aniceto Arteaga to Antonio Elosúa on 4-Jul-1832. The Spanish-language Carbajal translation is found in the Nacogdoches Archives, Vol. 62, pp.194-195 (and its translation back into English is also in the **RBBRC**, Vol. XII, pp. 369-370).

Bancroft, Hubert H.,

1889   *The Works of Hubert Howe Bancroft, Volume XVI: History of the Mexican States and Texas, Vol. II, 1801-1889* (The History Company, San Francisco), especially pages 110-129

Barber, Alan,

Mar-2009   " 'Schooner Flash, Captain Falwell...', The Short Wartime Life of a Texian Sailing Vessel, 1835-1837", *East Texas Historical Journal*, Vol. 47, Issue 1 (Mar-2009), pp. 18-28; on-line at https://scholarworks.sfasu.edu/cgi/viewcontent.cgi?article=2561&context=ethj

Barker, Eugene C.,

Jan-1901   "Difficulties of a Mexican Revenue Officer", *SWHQ*, Vol. IV (4), No. 3, pp. 190-202

1901   "The Organization of the Texas Revolution", paper published at Washington DC

Apr-1904   "Journal of the Permanent Council (October 11-27, 1835)", *SWHQ*, Vol. VII (7), No. 4, pp. 249-278; available on-line at:
https://www.jstor.org/stable/27784973?seq=1

1905   "The First Clash in the Texas Revolution – The Taking of Anahuac by Travis –Documents, 1835", *Publications of the Southern History Association*, Vol. IX (9), No. 2 (Mar 1905) and No. 4 (Jul 1905), pp. 87-98 and 226-233; references for [Barker Jan-1901]

Jan-1918   "The Government of Austin's Colony, 1821-1831", *SWHQ*, Vol. XXI (21), No. 3 (Jan 1918), pp. 223-252

Jun-1918   "Stephen F. Austin", *The Mississippi Valley Historical Review*, Vol. 5, No. 1, pp. 20-36

Jul-1919   "Minutes of the Ayuntamiento of San Felipe de Austin, 1828-1832, VII", *SWHQ*, Vol. XXIII (23), No. 1, pp. 69-77

1926   *The Life of Stephen F. Austin, Founder of Texas, 1793-1836, A Chapter in the Westward Movement of the Anglo-American People* (Cokesbury Press, 1926; University of Texas Press, Austin and London, 1969; AMS Press, New York, 1970); *copy available at the Brazosport College library (2nd Ed. Paperback) and the Angleton branch of Brazoria County Library & BCHM (AMS, 1970, different paging, e.g. p. 380 in this edition is 327 in original and paperback)*

Barnett, Jim,

20-Oct-1982   "Mexican colonel's papers may be plan for Fort Velasco", *Brazosport Facts (newspaper)*, pages 1A and 16A

Barnett, Thomas,

18-May-1830   Letter to Stephen F. Austin (as a Circular), Spanish transcript in **AP**, Vol. II, pp. 392

Barnett, Thomas and George Fisher,

Jun-1830   Statements about *Cañon* embargo, 18- and 19-Jun-1830, **SMWC**, Manuscript 23-0465, Rosenberg Library (Galveston, Texas)

Barr, Alwyn,
Jul-1961   "Texas Coastal Defense, 1861-1865", *SWHQ*, Vol. LXV (65), No. 1, pp. 1-31

Barrett, Don Carlos,
17-Dec-1835   Report, Proceedings of the General Council, found in **LOT**, Vol. 1, pp. 672-674; available on-line at: https://texashistory.unt.edu/ark:/67531/metapth5872/m1/680/

Baxter, Edward P., Ippolito, John E.,
1975   *An Archaeological Survey of Freeport Harbor Modifications to 36-Foot Project, Brazoria County, Texas*, Report No. 20, Anthropology Laboratory, Texas A&M University

Bell, H. H.,
1-Jun-1863   Diary entry found in *Official Records of the Union and Confederate Naies in the War of the Rebellion*, 1-Jun-1863, Vol. 20, p. 758

Berlandier, Jean Louis,
1829a   Map entitled *"Bahia de San Bernardo ou Bahia de Matagorda"*, **JLBP**, Box 8; available on-line as 5th image at https://collections.library.yale.edu/catalog/16155703; accessed 6-Aug-2025
1829b, circa Map entitled *"La costa desde Matagorda hasta la boca del Rio Bravo del Norte"*, **JLBP**, Box 18, Folder 4; available on-line: https://collections.library.yale.edu/catalog/2028634; accessed 6-Aug-2025
1980   *Journey to Mexico During the Years 1826 to 1834*, (two volumes, translated by Sheila Ohlendorf, Josette M. Bigelow and Mary M. Standifer, introduction by C. H. Muller), Texas State Historical Association

Bertrand, Charles Pierre (editor),
6-Feb-1833   "Monument – (to be erected at the mouth of the Brazos River)", *The Arkansas Advocate newspaper (Little Rock AR)*, 6-Feb-1833, page 2, columns 1-2

Bevill, James P.,
2009   *The Paper Republic – The Struggle for Money, Credit and Independence in the Republic of Texas* (Bright Sky Press, Houston Texas), especially pp. 133-143

Binkley, William C.,
Aug-1940   "The Activities of the Texas Revolutionary Army After San Jacinto", *Journal of Southern History*, Vol. VI (6), No. 3, pp. 331-346
1952   *The Texas Revolution* (Louisiana State University Press; reprint by Texas State Historical Association, 1979)

Blake, Marie E.; Freeman, Martha D.,
Dec-1998   *Nineteenth-Century Transfer-printed Ceramics from the Texas Coast: The Quintana Collection*, Prewitt & Associates

Boddie, Mary D.,

Aug-1978   *Thunder on the Brazos, The Outbreak of the Texas Revolution at Fort Velasco, June 26, 1832* (Taylor Publishing Company)

Boddie, William W., William D. Colegrove,
Apr-1959   *Watermarks of History – An informal Memoir of Brazoria County*, a film of approximately 23.5 minutes, presented by the Dow Chemical Company at the Brazoria County Fair, 6-10 Apr 1959; available on-line at https://texasarchive.org/2011_02277; accessed 21-Jul-2023

Bollaert, William, (W. Eugene Hollom, editor),
1956   *William Bollaert's Texas* (First Paperback Printing, University of Oklahoma Press, Norman and London, 1989)

Bond, Clell L.,
Nov-1980   *A Cultural Resources Assessment of Selected Magnetic Anomalies, Freeport Harbor, Texas, 45-Foot Project*, Report submitted to Corps of Engineers, Galveston District, Texas A&M University Cultural Resources Laboratory, College Station, Texas

Borgens, Amy,
May-2004   *Analysis of the Pass Cavallo Shipwreck Assemblage, Matagorda Bay, Texas*, MA Thesis, Texas A&M University

Borgens, Amy, R. L. Gearhart II, S. Hoskins,
Aug-2006   *Marine Close-Order Remote-Sensing Survey for the Freeport Ship Channel Widening, Brazoria County, Texas*, Document prepared for the Brazos River Harbor Navigation District, Document No. 060097, PBS&J, Austin, Texas

Boyd, Douglas K.; Frederick, Charles D,; Freeman, Martha D.; Griffith, Timothy B.; Kibler, Karl W.,
Jan-2014   *Cultural Resources Survey of Two Proposed Dredged Material Placement Areas for the Freeport Harbor Channel Improvement Project, Brazoria County, Texas*, Prewitt & Associates Inc., Technical Report No. 95, Jan 2014

Bradburn, Juan D.,
4-Nov-1830   Letter to Col. Antonio Elosúa, **BA**, Microfilm Roll 135, frame 980
20-Aug-1831   Two lists of ships entering Brazos River and Galveston Bay, **SMWC**, Manuscript 23-0784; apparent cover letter and explanation found with same date, **BA**, Microfilm Roll 143, frames 904-905
1-Sep-1831   Military census report – Detachment of Anahuac, Digital Image di_04538, original in **BA**, Box 2S276 (also Microfilm Roll 144, frames 189-190)
4-Apr-1832   Letter to Antonio Elosúa, **BA**, Microfilm Roll 149, frames 119-121
12-Apr-1832   Letter to Antonio Elosúa, **BA**, Microfilm Roll 149, frames 358-359
1832   Account prepared for Vicente Filisola, English translation published as "**Bradburn Memorial**" as Appendix 1 in [Henson 1982 pp. 129-144]; original Spanish draft document and two previous translations located in **HRWC**, Box 3, Folder 91

Brazoria County Deed Records,
11-May-1845   Vol. B, page 493, *sale of Archer House and four lots by Peter and Mary Caroline MacGreal to Peter James O'Connor*, sold 9-Jan-1845, recorded 11-May-1845

Brazos River Channel and Dock Company, The;

Mar-1890   Board of Directors Report, featuring progress reports by Elmer L. Corthell (Chief Engineer) and George Y. Wisner (Resident Engineer), 32 pages

Brazosport Chamber of Commerce,

1970   Various brochures and handouts about Battle of Velasco, circa 1970s

Brazosport Facts (newspaper),

1975   "Dramatic story of first clash", editorial 4-May-1975, p. 26, photo with caption 9-Jun-1975; "Drama wakens history pages", editorial 23-Aug-1975

Breedlove, A. W.,

12-Jul-1832   Official Return of Effects Left in Fort Velasco, **LP** #155, Vol. I, p. 141 (original at Archives and Information Services Division, TSLAC, Austin, Texas)

Breedlove, James W.,

25-May-1830   Certificates issued to schooner **Cañon** and Edward L. Petitt, handwritten copies by George Fisher on 26-Apr-1831 at Matamoros, **SMWC**, Manuscripts 23-0368 and 23-0681

Brister, Louis Edwin,

Jan-1999   "The Journal of Eduard Harkort, Captain of Engineers, Texas Army, February 8-July 17, 1836", *SWHQ*, Vol. CII (102), No. 3, pp. 344-379, especially diagram on page 358

Brown, Gary,

1999   *Volunteers in the Texas Revolution: The New Orleans Greys* (Republic of Texas Press)

Brown, Jeremiah,

10-Jul-1837   Tariff of Duties on Importation (at Velasco), Broadside, 1 page, **BCB**, Call# BC DB 1837, digital copy BC_0201_pub, from papers of Stephen F. Austin; also **TSC**, Document #202 https://collections.briscoecenter.org/repositories/2/archival_objects/823365

Brown, John H.,

1887   *Life and Times of Henry Smith, The First American Governor of Texas*, A. D. Aldridge & Co., Dallas, Texas (reprinted by The Steck Company, Austin, Texas in 1935)

1892   *History of Texas from 1685 To 1892, Volume I* (Becktold & Co., St. Louis); reprinted by Jenkins Publishing Co., 1970), especially pp. 178-183 (his father Henry S. Brown was a participant at the Battle of Velasco)

Brown, N. S. (confirmed by David G. Burnet),

19-Jun-1836   Republic Claims, Audited Claim 826, Reel 47, Images 323-324 (digital file ID 29515, TSLAC, Austin, Texas)

Bryan, Moses Austin,

1897   "Personal Recollections of Stephen F. Austin", *The Texas Illustrated Monthly Magazine*, Sep-1897 (pp. 101-109), Nov-1897 (pp. 161-173)

Bryant, William Cullen (editor),

7-Jun-1832   "The Schooner Topaz", *New-York Evening Post*, page 2, column 5

Bugbee, Lester G.,
Oct-1899   "What Became of the Lively?", ***SWHQ***, Vol. III (3), No.2, p. 141-148

***Bulletin, The* (newspaper at Angleton, Texas, founded about 1993)**,
29-Jul-1999   "The Window Pane" column – "Research of Fort Velasco Continues", pp. 3-4

Burnet, David G.,
21-Apr-1836   Decree Establishing a Naval Depot at Galveston, **PTR**, Vol. 6, pp. 5-6, Document# 2814;
also reprinted in [Unknown 1869, p. 57] including a follow-up order to Secretary of the Navy

Callahan, Erin,
23-Aug-2017   *Feud at the Fort*, article in the *Brazosport Facts* (newspaper), p. 1A and 8A

Cantrell, Gregg,
1999   *Stephen F. Austin, Empresario of Texas* (Yale University Press, New Haven and London)

Carlton, Benjamin Hardy,
1938   The Autobiography of Benjamin Hardy Carlton, MD, White Co., AR, circa 1938 at Freeport TX, on-line at: http://files.usgwarchives.net/ar/white/bios/carlton.txt, accessed 29-Mar-2021

Caro, Ramón Martínez,
1837   *A True Account of the First Texas Campaign and the Events Subsequent to the Battle of San Jacinto*, English translation in *The Mexican Side of the Texan Revolution – 1836*, translated by Carlos E. Castañeda (Graphic Ideas Inc., Austin, Texas, 1970)

Chapelle, Howard I.,
1949   *The History of the American Sailing Navy - The Ships and Their Development* (Bonanza Books, New York, NY), especially pp. 179-241 and 324-334

Castañeda, Francisco,
10-Jul-1832   Letter to Antonio Elosúa, **BA**, Microfilm Roll 151, frame 521

Chriesman, Horatio,
Mar-1832   Letters to Ramón Músquiz, Nacogdoches Archives, Vol. 61, p. 141 (31-Mar-1832) and Vol. 62, pp. 2-3 (26-Apr-1832); and their translation into English in the **RBBRC**, Vol. XII, pp. 307, 314
16-May-1832   Letter to Ramón Músquiz, **BA**, Microfilm Roll 150, frames 47-49
13-Oct-1832   Letter to Ramón Músquiz, **TGLO**, Document# 816, Box 126:14, p. 153

Citizen Newspaper,
1951   "'Port of Houston' newspaper supplement.", Rice University: https://hdl.handle.net/1911/37645; accessed 29-Sep-2021

Clarke, Mary Whatley,
1969   *David G. Burnet* (Pemberton Press, Austin & New York)
Clay, Comer,

Apr-1949   "The Colorado River Raft", *SWHQ*, Vol. LII (52), No. 4 (Apr 1949), pp. 410-426

Coastal Testing Laboratories Inc.,
12-Sep-2019   *Report – Soils Investigation Unit – Proposed Residence at 101 Parkview Road, Surfside Beach TX*, Report No. 1909/1253

Coleman, Ann Raney Thomas,
1971   *Victorian Lady on the Texas Frontier, The Journal of Ann Raney Coleman*, edited by C. Richard King (University of Oklahoma Press, Norman, Oklahoma)

Compton, Diana F.,
Fall-2014   "Once Upon a Time in Matagorda: The Death of Samuel Rhoads Fisher", East Texas Historical Journal, Vol. 52, Issue 2, Article 10, pp. 79-117

Coode, Sir John,
1890   *Four drawings or maps, circa 1890, backed with canvas and stored in a rolled condition,* USGS Map Collection, Call Number G 4032 B73 1890 C (No. 1, 2, 3 and 4), Dolph Briscoe Center for American History, The University Of Texas, Austin, Texas

Cos, Martín Perfecto de,
15-Oct-1835   Spanish typescript transcript in **AGMC**, Box 2Q223, Volume 563, p. 32

Cosío, Mariano,
30-May-1832   Letter to Antonio Elosúa, **BA**, Microfilm Roll 150, frames 307-308
3-Jul-1832   Letter to Antonio Elosúa, **BA**, Microfilm Roll 151, frames 287-290

Cotten, Godwin B. M. (printer),
23-Jun-1828   *Laws, Passed by the Legislature of the State of Coahuila and Texas*, especially Militia Law, Ch. VI, Article 86, p. 4

Cotten, Godwin B. M. (editor and publisher),
1830   *Texas Gazette*, Vol. 1 issues of 8-May-1830 (No. 22, p. 2, col. 3), 22-May (No. 24, p.3, cols. 2 & 3), 5-Jun (No. 26, p. 3, col. 2), 12-Jun (No. 27, p. 3, col. 1 and p. 4, col.2), 19-Jun (No. 28, p. 3, col. 3, p. 4, col. 2), 26-Jun (No. 29, p. 4, cols. 2 & 3), 3-Jul (No. 30, p. 4, cols. 2 & 3), 23-Oct (No. 45, p. 2, cols. 1-3 and p. 3, col. 1) and 21-Nov-1830 (No. 49, p. 2, col. 1); Photostat copies found in Archives section at TSLAC, Call# 2-2/28; also found as copies of typescript transcripts and notes in bound untitled 3-volume set donated to BCHM in memory of James A. Creighton; *indexed as Texas Gazette, San Felipe de Austin, Volumes 1, 2, 3 - REF 079.764 TEX at BCHM research library*
23-Jul-1832   *Texas Gazette And Brazoria Commercial Advertiser newspaper*, EXTRA issue, copy of original and also transcription courtesy of BCHM

Cotton, Stella (presumed author),
1968   *"Valasco and The Battle of Valasco" (11-page undated typescript), Stella Cotton Collection, Box 2-23/827 (Archives Division, TSLAC, Austin, Texas)*

Creighton, James A.,
1975   *A Narrative History of Brazoria County* (Texian Press, Waco, Texas)

Crisp, James E. (editor), Brister, Louis E. (co-editor & translator),
2022   *Inside the Texas Revolution – The Enigmatic Memoir of Herman Ehrenberg* (Texas State Historical Association, Austin, Texas)

Cross, Lt. Abraham,
11-Jan-1864   Sketch of the plans and dimensions of the works at and near the mouth of the Brazos river, National Archives, Record Group 109, Consolidated Service Record 12: A. Cross

Crouch, Carrie J.,
Sep-1832   "Capitals of the Lone Star", *National Republic (magazine)*, Vol. XX (20), No. 5, pp. 6-7, 23, 32

Cushing, S. W.,
1857   *Adventures in the Texas Navy and at the Battle of San Jacinto* (W. M. Morrison Books, Austin, Texas, 1985), excerpt from *Wild Oats Sowings* (New York, New York)

Daniell, L. E.,
1892   *Personnel of the Texas State Government with Sketches of the Representative Men of Texas* (Maverick Printing House, San Antonio, Texas), sketch of John H. Wood pp. 629-641, especially pp. 631-636; available on-line at https://archive.org/details/personneloftexas00indani/page/ n1065/mode/2up?ref=ol&view=theater, accessed 21-Dec-2022

De las Piedras, José,
7-May-1832   Letter to Antonio Elosúa, **BA**, Microfilm Roll 149, frames 873-874
16-Jul-1832   Letter to Domingo de Ugartechea, **SMWC**, Manuscript 23-0971

De Mora, Ignacio,
21-Jul-1832   Letter to Antonio Elosúa, **BA**, Microfilm Roll 151, frames 772-777

DeMorse, Charles,
14-Dec-1870   Republic Claims, Pension Claim, Reel 212, Images 73 to 89 (TSLAC, Austin, Texas)

Dienst, Alex,
1909   *The Navy of the Republic of Texas, 1835-1845*, self-published book (Temple, Texas); same material published in four installments in **SWHQ**, Vol. XII (12), No.3, p. 165 (Jan-1909), 12(4) p. 249 (Apr-1909), 13(1) p. 1 (Jul-1909), 13(2) p. 85 (Oct-1909)

Dinsmore, Silas & John G. McNeel,
1-Nov-1835   *Sea Letter* for **San Felipe**, **TNP-R**, Folder 8, Document #53

Dorchester, Ernest D., Louis J. Wilson,
14-May-1836   *Velasco in Texas History*, pamphlet published by Brazoria County Centennial Club for Texas Centennial Day

Douglas, C. L.,
1936   *Thunder on the Gulf or The Story of the Texas Navy* (Turner Company, Dallas, Texas), especially Ch. 6, pp. 47-59

Dow Texan, The (company newsletter),

4-Apr-1961   "Discovery of Cannonball Revives Battle of Velasco", pp. 2-3

Duclor, Francisco,
2-Jun-1832   Letter to Samuel May Williams, **SMWC**, Manuscript 23-0949
17-Jul-1832   Letter to Samuel May Williams, and response Letter (plus typescript transcription of both), **SMWC**, Manuscript 23-0972
27-Sep-1832   Letter to Ayuntamiento of San Felipe, Spanish transcript in **AP**, Vol. II, pp. 867-868); another copy can be found as Spanish typescript transcript in **AGMC**, Box 2Q172, Volume 330, p. 26
13-Nov-1832   Letter to Antonio López de Santa Anna, Spanish typescript transcript in **AGMC**, Box 2Q172, Volume 330, p. 27-28

Dunlap, W. D.,
Jul-1830   Letter to George Fisher, copy by Fisher on 27-Jul-1830 of two letters (on 21- and 24-Jul-1830), **SMWC**, Manuscript 23-0391

Duval, John Crittenden,
1892   *Early Times in Texas*, H. P. N. Gammel & Co., Publishers (Austin, Texas), printed and bound by Eugene Von Boeckmann (Austin, Texas). Available on-line at https://www.google.com/books/edition/Early_Times_in_Texas/YPU0AAAAMAAJ?hl=en&gbpv=1&printsec=frontcover

Earls, Amy C.: Myers, Terri L.; Hannum, Sandra L.,
Nov-1992   *Preliminary Report on Testing in the Core Area East of the Cutbank at Old Velasco (41BO125), Brazoria County, Texas;* Prewitt & Associates

Earls, Amy C., Myers, Terri L.; Shaffer, Brian S.; Kibler, Karl W.; Gardner, Karen M.; Zimmerman, Laurie S.; Prewitt, Elton R.; Hannum, Sandra L.,
May 1996   *Testing and Data Recovery at the Townsite of Old Velasco (41BO125), Brazoria County, Texas;* Prewitt & Associates, Reports of Investigations, Number 94, esp. pp. 292-294

Ellis, Richard (President), H. S. Kimble (Secretary),
1838   *The General Convention at Washington, March 1-17 1836*, 84 pages, published at Houston; on-line at https://landgrantpatent.org/law-texas/law01018.pdf, accessed 29-Sep-2025

Elosúa, Antonio,
5-Jun-1832   Letter to Commanders at Goliad (Mariano Cosío) and Guadalupe (Aniceto Arteaga), **BA**, Microfilm Roll 150, frame 595
18-Jun-1832a   Letter to Domingo de Ugartechea, English translation in **RBBRC**, Supplemental Vol. IX, pp. 256-257; original at **BA**, Microfilm Roll 150, frames 897-898
18-Jun-1832b   Letters to Ramón Músquiz, José de las Piedras, Juan Davis Bradburn and Domingo de Ugartechea, **BA**, Microfilm Roll 150, frames 884, 892, 893-894 and 895-896
20-Jun-1832   Letters to José de las Piedras, Juan Davis Bradburn and Domingo de Ugartechea, **BA**, Microfilm Roll 150, frames 955-959 (especially 957-959; English translation of Piedras letter (frame 957) can be found in **RBBRC**, Supplemental Vol. IX, p. 262; see also Músquiz to Béxar Revenue Administrator, BA, Roll 150 frames 932-933
7-Jul-1832   Letter to Domingo de Ugartechea, **BA**, Microfilm Roll 151, frames 451-452; also, see Elosúa letter on 17-Jul-1832, Roll 151, frames 675-676
13-Jul-1832   Letters to Aniceto Arteaga, **BA**, Microfilm Roll 151, frames 602-604

17-Jul-1832   Letter to Domingo de Ugartechea and separate Letter to Ramón Músquiz, **BA**, Microfilm Roll 151, frames 678-679 and 686-687

Epperson, Jean L.,

Aug-1986   "Early Custom Houses In Galveston", *Houston Archeological Society Journal*, No. 85, pp. 1, 8-11; also found as chapter in *Historical Vignettes of Galveston Bay*, Dogwood Press, Woodville, Texas, 1995, pp. 117-126

1991   "Captain Thomas M. (Mexican) Thompson", in *Still more studies In Brownsville History*, edited by Milo Kearney, UTRGV & TSC Regional History Series, UTRGV Digital Library, The University of Texas – Rio Grande Valley, 1991; also found (with slight additions) as chapter in *Historical Vignettes of Galveston Bay*, Dogwood Press, Woodville, Texas, 1995, pp. 102-116

1995   "Mutiny of the Topaz", found as chapter in *Historical Vignettes Of Galveston Bay*, Dogwood Press, Woodville, Texas, pp. 25-28

Erath, Lucy A.,

Jan-1923   Erath, George Bernard, "Memoirs of Major George Bernard Erath", *SWHQ*, Vol. XXVI (26), No. 3, pp. 207-233

Falvel, Luke A.,

14-Dec-1870   Republic Claims, Pension Claim, "Oath of Identity", Reel 214, Images 508 to 510 (TSLAC, Austin, Texas)

Fannin, James W.,

11-Dec-1835   Letter to Henry Smith & General Council, transcript inclusion in [S.R. Fisher 1836]

25-Dec-1835   Letter to William Ward et al (from Velasco), **PTR**, Vol. 3, Document #1614; another copy (with some added paragraphs) is in [Foote 1841], II, pp. 189-192. Available on-line at: https://www.sonsofdewittcolony.org/goliadofficial.htm#fanninward25dec

21-Jan-1836   Letter to James W. Robinson (from Velasco), **PTR**, Vol. 3, Document #1872, pp. 103-106; also published in a Circular published at San Felipe by Baker and Bordens (*Telegraph and Texas Register*), 2 pages, **BCB**, Box BC DB 1836, digital copy BC_1052a and b.

Farrar, Roy Montgomery,

1926   "The Story of Buffalo Bayou and the Houston Ship Channel." (Houston Chamber of Commerce), page 8; available on-line: https://hdl.handle.net/1911/61522, accessed 6-Aug-2025

Fearn, Howard B.,

14-Jan-1971   Fort Velasco, hand-drawn blueprint of archaeological remains in Surfside Block 568, with revisions (dated 9-Jan-1978) to show outline of potential replica fort of 300' diameter, Brazosport Archaeological Society collection, BMNS

Filisola, Vicente,

1848   *Memorias para la historia de la guerra de Tejas,* Mexico City, 2 volumes; English translation available as *Memoirs for the History of the War in Texas*, translated by Wallace Woolsey (2 volumes, Eakin Press, Austin, Texas, 1985), especially Vol. I, pp. 62-89

Fisher, George,

10-Feb-1830a   Letter to Anastasio Zerecero, Spanish typescript transcript in **AGMC**, Box 2Q223, Volume 562, pp. 23-25

10-Feb-1830b   Letter to Lorenzo de Zavala, Spanish transcript in **AP**, Vol. II, pp. 330-331

18-May-1830a	Letter to Stephen F. Austin, Spanish transcript in **AP**, Vol. II, pp. 391
18-May-1830b	Letter to Civil Militia Commander (Stephen F. Austin), Spanish transcripts in **AP**, Vol. II, pp. 391-392
2-Jun-1830	Letter to Antonio Elosúa, 2-Jun-1830, **SMWC**, Manuscript 23-0372
5-Jun-1830	Separate letters to Samuel May Williams (5-Jun-1830) and Thomas Barnett (7-Jun-1830), and their replies (10-Jun-1830), found as photostat of handwritten copy by George Fisher on 6-Nov-1830, in **GFP** as "Port of Galveston report", Box 2.325/V36, Dolph Briscoe Center for American History; same "original" document is found in **SMWC**, Manuscript 23-0466, but last page in latter is the same as first page of former. Also, another copy of Williams' reply of 10-Jun-1830 (and a copy of his enclosed Decree No. 28) can be found in **SMWC** as the first two sections in Manuscript 23-0368.
6-Jul-1830	Letter to Samuel May Williams, **SMWC**, Manuscript 23-0382
21-Jul-1830a	Letter to Andres Mauricio Voss, 21-Jul-1830a, English typescript transcript in **AGMC**, Box 2Q223, Volume 563, pp. 15-22
21-Jul-1830b	Letter to Fred. (Federico) Holdsworth, English typescript transcript in **AGMC**, Box 2Q223, Volume 563, pp. 8-14
27-Jul-1830	Letter to Manuel de Mier y Terán, Spanish typescript transcript in **AGMC**, Box 2Q171, Volume 327, pp. 144-149
22-Sep-1830	Letter to Asa Mitchell, **SMWC**, Manuscripts 23-0432 (Seguin copy) and 23-0433 (Guerra copy); supporting documents includes Manuscript 23-0423 (a translation of a notice in the New Orleans Mercantile Advertiser newspaper that the schooner *True Blue* was sailing for Brazoria and Bell's Landing in early September) and 23-0442 and 23-0443 (Asa Mitchell's response – his account of the foundering at the Brazos bar)
16-Oct-1830	Letter to Manuel de Mier y Terán, copy within Letter from Terán to Secretary of Relations, 10-Nov-1830; including attachment of translation of a notice in the New Orleans Mercantile Advertiser newspaper that the schooner *True Blue* was sailing for Brazoria and Bell's Landing in early September, Spanish typescript transcripts in **AGMC**, Box 2Q223, Volume 563, pp. 29-31
29-Nov-1830	Letter to Godwin Brown Cotten, under heading of "Maritime Custom-House of Galvezton No. 5", transcript in **LP** #99, Vol. I, pp. 86-87; also found in a typescript broadside which re-published an article in 10-Feb-1831 issue of "The Advertiser of the Port of Matamoros" with cover letter by Fisher dated 9-Feb-1831 (itself in **LP**, Vol. I, Document #106), copy of broadside available in **TSC**, Document# 769
14-Feb-1831	Letter to Governor of Coahuila and Texas (José Maria Letona), Spanish typescript transcript in **AGMC**, Box 2Q223, Volume 563, pp. 25-28; an excerpt dated 19-Feb-1831 apparently sent on to Stephen F. Austin, found as transcript in **AP**, Vol. II, pp. 598-599
26-Apr-1831	Letter to Manuel Mier y Terán, **SMWC**, Manuscript 23-0667
6-Oct-1831	Typescript broadside published at Matamoros under heading of "Maritime Custom-House of Galvezton" primarily featuring a copy of a letter from Manuel Mier y Terán to Stephen F. Austin; copy available in **TSC**, Document #771 (Spanish) and Document #771A (English)
20-Mar-1832	Letter to William P. Harris, Papers 1832-1833, Box 2D157, Benjamin Cromwell Franklin Papers 1805-1915, Dolph Briscoe Center for American History, The University of Texas, Austin, Texas
16-Apr-1833	Letter to Stephen F. Austin, English/Spanish transcript in **AP**, Vol. II, pp. 947-950
1830s	"Biographical Sketch of George Fisher", circa late 1830s (about events in 1833-1835), in **LP**, Vol. V, Document #1664, pp. 386-390

Fisher, S. Rhoads,

17-Dec-1835	Letter to Provisional Government of Texas, **PTR**, Document #1508, Vol. 3, pp. 218-221
12-Jan-1836	To the People of Texas, Broadside, **TSC**, Document# 121; Fisher portion and partial extract in Letter to Mirabeau Lamar, 10-Dec-1836, available on-line at:

https://www.sonsofdewittcolony.org/fishersm3.htm. Supplemental documents on same topic are in **LP**, Documents 278 & 502, also **PTR** #1679 3:387-388 (10-Dec-1836)

Fiske, M. (attributed),

1836   *A Visit to Texas in 1831, Being the Journal of a Traveller Through Those Parts Most Interesting to American Settlers, With Descriptions of Scenery, Habits, &c. &c*, 2nd Edition, (Van Nostrand and Dwight, New York); an updated and colorized copy of William Hooker's "Map of the State of Coahuila and Texas" (folded) was included; *copy available at Texas State Library (Austin, Texas); 3rd Edition at BCHM. First edition (1834) is on-line at: https://archive.org/details/avisittotexasbe00fiskgoog/mode/2up ... although paging appears different in all 3 editions.*

Follett, Addie Hudgins,

1983   *Retrospect*, published in portions in the Quarterly of the Brazosport Genealogical Society

Follett, Alexander G.,

7-Oct-1895   *A. G. Follett, Sr.*, The Galveston Daily News (newspaper), page 4, column 3

Foote, Henry S.,

1841   *Texas and The Texans: or, Advance of The Anglo-Americans to The Southwest* (two volumes, Thomas, Cowperthwait & Co., Philadelphia, Pennsylvania), especially pp. 20-26 in Volume II

Fox, Anne A.; Ivey, James E., J. Carroll Markey,

1981   *Cultural Resource Survey – Freeport Harbor, Texas (45-Foot) Navigation Improvement Project, Brazoria County, Texas*, Center for Archaeological Research (UTSA, San Antonio), Archaeological Survey Report No. 107

Fox, Anne A.,

4-Nov-1991   Letter to Margaret Swett Henson, **MSHP**, Box 48, File 7

Francaviglia, Richard V.,

1998   *From Sail To Steam, Four Centuries of Texas Maritime History, 1500-1900*, (University of Texas Press, Austin, Texas)

Frantz, Joe B. (editor),

Apr-1974   "Clippings" section – 4th paragraph, *SWHQ*, Vol. LXXVII (77), No. 4, pp. 501-502

Freeman, Martha D.,

Apr-1995   *A History of Civil War Military Activities at Velasco and Quintana, Brazoria County, and at Virginia Point, Galveston County, Texas*, Prewitt & Associates, Reports of Investigations, Number 103

Dec-1998   *A History of Quintana, A Nineteenth-Century Coastal Port In Brazoria County, Texas*, Prewitt & Associates, Reports of Investigations, Number 117

Freeman, Martha D.; Blake, Marie E.; Prewitt, Elton R.,

Oct-1997   *Archival and Archeological Investigations at Quintana Townsite and Fort Terrell*, Prewitt & Associates, Reports of Investigations, Number 118

Freeport Historical Museum,

11-Jul-1971   *Fort Velasco 1830-1836*, informally published pamphlet, unknown date, text from *Brazosport Facts* Heritage Edition

Freeport, The City Of; The Old Brazos Drama Association,
Feb-1975   *Outdoor Drama on the Old Brazos – An Outdoor Theatre for a Historical Drama, Freeport Municipal Park*, informal publication detailing concept for a new theater

Fry, William (editor),
3-Aug-1832   "(From a New Orleans paper.) – Texas.", *The National Gazette and Literary Register (daily newspaper)*, Philadelphia, Pennsylvania, page 2

Gambrell, Herbert,
1948   *Anson Jones, The Last President of Texas* (Doubleday & Co., Garden City, New York)

Gearhart, Robert, Andy Hall, Tom Oertling, Mark Everett,
Feb-2020   *Search for the Invincible, Remote-Sensing Survey, Galveston County, Texas*, Report by BOB Hydrographics LLC, BOB Project 2018-05

Geiser, S. W.,
1944   *Racer's Storm (1837), with Notes on Other Texas Hurricanes in the Period 1818-1886* (Field and Laboratory, Southern Methodist University Press), Vol. 12, No. 2, pp. 59-67

Germany, Garvin; Michael J. Bailey,
May-2007   *Guns of Quintana*, informal publication, BCHM.

Glass, James L.,
1986   *A Replica Chart of the Galveston-Houston Area Circa 1836 – The History of the Houston-Bay Country Region from the Foot of Main Street to the Galveston Bar*, Kelvin Press
Summer 2008   "Racer's Storm – The Benchmark Hurricane of 1837", Houston History, Vol. 5, No. 3, pp. 20-27

Glenn, Lon,
Mar-2019   *The Grand Surfside Hotel, 1891-1907*, Image (magazine), Volume 19, No.1, pp. 20-23

Gray, Franklin C. (editor),
Texas Republican newspaper (Brazoria, Texas), usually 4 pages
27-Jun-1835; available on-line at
https://texashistory.unt.edu/ark:/67531/metapth80264/?q=brazoria%20texas%20republican
8-Aug-1835; available on-line at
https://texashistory.unt.edu/ark:/67531/metapth80268/?q=brazoria%20texas%20republican
19-Sep-1835; available on-line at
https://texashistory.unt.edu/ark:/67531/metapth80271/?q=brazoria%20texas%20republican
26-Sep-1835; available on-line at
https://texashistory.unt.edu/ark:/67531/metapth80272/?q=brazoria%20texas%20republican
3-Oct-1835; available on-line at
https://texashistory.unt.edu/ark:/67531/metapth80273/?q=brazoria%20texas%20republican
10-Oct-1835; available on-line at
https://texashistory.unt.edu/ark:/67531/metapth80274/?q=brazoria%20texas%20republican
17-Oct-1835; available on-line at
https://texashistory.unt.edu/ark:/67531/metapth80275/?q=brazoria%20texas%20republican

17-Oct-1835; available on-line at
https://texashistory.unt.edu/ark:/67531/metapth80276/?q=brazoria%20texas%20republican
24-Oct-1835; available on-line at
https://texashistory.unt.edu/ark:/67531/metapth80276/?q=brazoria%20texas%20republican

Gray, Franklin C.,
7-Nov-1835 Letter (unaddressed), **PTR**, Vol. 2, p. 348-349, Document# 1118

Gray, William Fairfax,
1997 "The Diary of William Fairfax Gray, From Virginia to Texas, 1835-1837", Edited from the original manuscript, with an Introduction and notes, by Paul Lack, De Golyer Library & William P. Clements Center for Southwest Studies - Southern Methodist University, Dallas, Texas

Grayson, Thomas B.,
1863 *What Great-Grandpa Said to Great-Grandma – Copies of letters written by Dr. Thomas B. Grayson, a surgeon during the Civil War, to his wife, Carrie, during the years 1863, 1864, and 1865*, typescript manuscript, BCHM

Grubbs, Joy (Evelyn Joye nee Hamberlin, Mrs. William Edward Grubbs),
30-Jan-1985 "Early memories of Freeport Coast Guard Station told", The (Freeport) Light (newspaper), BCHM Vertical File-Coast Guard

Guerra, José Mariano,
20-Jun-1832 Letters to Antonio Elosúa and Mariano Cosío, **BA**, Microfilm Roll 150, frames 927-930 and 931; see also Guerra to Elosúa (27-Jun-1832) Roll 151, frames 73-74 and 77
7-Jul-1832a Letter to Antonio Elosúa, **BA**, Microfilm Roll 151, frames 426-427
7-Jul-1832b Letter to Stephen F. Austin, transcript in **RBBRC**, Vol. XIII, p. 26

Guthrie, Keith,
1993 *Texas Forgotten Ports, Vol. II* (Eakin Press), especially chapter on Velasco (pp. 101-113)

Hadley, Bryan; Mangum, Douglas G.,
Jul-2017 *Cultural Resources Geophysical Remote-Sensing of the Proposed Fort Velasco Reconstruction Area in Brazoria County, Texas*, Moore Archaeological Consulting Inc., Report of Investigations No. 657

Hardy, Dermot H., Ingham S. Roberts (editors)
1910 Historical Review of South-East Texas and the Founders, Leaders and Representative Men of its Commerce, Industry and Civic Affairs, Vol. 1 of 2 (Lewis Publishing Co., Chicago, Illinois)

Hall, William,
23-Nov-1835 Letter to Stephen F. Austin, **PTR**, Vol. 2, pp. 493-494, Document# 1275

Hancock, John L.,
Dec-2020 "Federalism, Constitutionalism, and the Texas Revolt" (Thesis, Master of Arts in History, Liberty University, Dec-2020); copy available at BCHM

Harkort, Eduard,
1836a Tagebuch Eduard Harkorts (Fragment), 1836a, Stiftung Westfälisches Wirtschaftsarchiv, Dortmund, N 7/47 Nr. 2

3-Apr-1836b   Letter to Sam Houston, **SHPC**, Box 7, Folder 22

Haskins, Francis J.,
14-Mar-1836   Republic Claims, Audited Claim 1189, Reel 42, Image 475 (digital file ID 27059, TSLAC)
10-May-1836   Republic Claims, Audited Claim 542, Reel 42, Image 458 (digital file ID 27040, TSLAC)
13-Jul-1836   Letter to James Morgan, **JMP**, Manuscript 31-0249 (on microfilm only)

Haugh, George F. (editor),
1960   "History of the Texas Navy", **SWHQ**, Vol. LXIII (63), No. 4 (Apr 1960), pp. 572-579, "The Texas Navy at New York", Vol. LXIV (64), No. 3 (Jan 1961), pp. 377-383; first item originally published as "History of the Texan Navy" in *Texas Almanac for 1860* (Galveston, 1860), pp. 162-166.

Hayes, Charles W.,
1879   *Galveston: History of the Island and the City*, 2 volumes, Jenkins Garrett Press, 1974; reprint of the 1879 manuscript entitled *Island and City of Galveston*

Helm, Mrs. Mary Sherwood Wightman,
1884   *Scraps of Early Texas History, 1828-1843* (B. R. Warner & Co., Austin, Texas)

Henson, Margaret S.,
1982   *Juan Davis Bradburn: A Reappraisal of the Mexican Commander of Anahuac* (Texas A&M University Press)
Oct-1990   "Politics and the Treatment of Mexican Prisoners after the Battle of San Jacinto", **SWHQ**, Vol. XCIV (94), No. 2 (Oct 1990), pp. 189-230

Hicks, David L.; Parkinson, Dan,
1980   *The Texians* (The Larksdale Press, Houston, Texas)

Hill, Jim Dan,
1937   *The Texas Navy – In Forgotten Battles and Shirtsleeve Diplomacy* (State House Press, 1987 reprint of 1937 original)

Holley, Mary Austin,
1831   *Brazos Boat Song* (music sheets for), circa 1831, Dolph Briscoe Center for American History, TXC-ZZ Collection; -Q- M 1629.7 T35 H655
1833   *Texas. Observations, Historical, Graphical, and Descriptive, In a Series of Letters; Written During a Visit to Austin's Colony with a View to Permanent Settlement in That Country in the Autumn of 1831* (Armstrong & Plaskitt, Baltimore MD, reprinted by Arno Press, New York, 1973); a copy of the William Hooker's 1833 "Map of the State of Coahuila and Texas" (folded) was included
1836a   *Texas* (J. Clarke & Co., Lexington, Kentucky); reprinted by Texas State Historical Association, 1990); an updated and colorized copy of William Hooker's "Map of the State of Coahuila and Texas" (folded) was included.
1836b   *The Texan Song of Liberty* (music sheets for), circa 1836; available on-line at https://jscholarship.library.jhu.edu/items/45a96f4e-8fba-49a1-8dec-318896a1cfb0/full and https://levysheetmusic.mse.jhu.edu/collection/016/058 and tune at: https://www.youtube.com/watch?v=a04BhE_IZN4; once available in **TSC**, Document #1208
1838   *Brazos Boat Glee* (music sheets for), **TSC**, Document# 1314; also available on-line at: https://books.google.com/books?id=3-OPCwQ8Sy8C&q=

1965   *The Texas Diary, 1835-1838* (edited by J. P. Bryan, University of Texas Press)

Hooton, Charles,
1847   *St. Louis' Isle, Or Texiana, &c. & c., with Additional Observations Made in the United States and Canada*, Simmonds and Ward, London, 1847; book is on-line at: https://catalog.hathitrust.org/Record/008650385

Hoskins, Isaac C.,
1-Jun-1836   Republic Claims, Audited Claim 546, Reel 47, Image 289 (digital file ID 29457, TSLAC)
11-Jul-1836   Republic Claims, Audited Claim 826, Reel 47, Image 362; also 316 (digital file ID 29512, TSLAC)

House, Boyce,
Jul-1960 "An Incident at Velasco, 1832", **SWHQ**, Vol. LXIV (64), No. 1, pp. 92-95

Houston, Sam,
29-Mar-1836   Letter to Thomas J. Rusk, **WSH**, Vol. 1, pp. 384-386
5-Apr-1837   Letter to S. Rhoads Fisher (typed transcript of), **SHPB**, Box 2R49, 1837-1841, Vol. II; original appears to be in **SHPR**, Box 1, Folder 2, Item 7; also found in **WSH**, IV:28-29
19-May-1837   Letter to Senate (typed transcript of), **SHPB**, Box 2R45, Jan-1837 to Jul-1838, Vol. IV, pp. 1-2
18-Jan-1843   Letter to Col. John Warren, **SHPB**, Box 2E250, Presidential Letters

Howren, Alleine,
Apr-1913   "Causes and Origin of the Decree of April 6, 1830", **SWHQ**, Vol. XVI (16), No. 4, pp. 378-422

Hudgins, Charles Diggs,
1900   "Maid of San Jacinto, the Maid of the Orient, and other poems", J. S Ogilvie Publishing Co., New York, New York, circa 1900

Humphries, Mrs. Thomas Andrew (Flora Lillian Steele),
9-Jul-1931   "Velasco and Quintana Were Important Ports in Early Days; Load of Cotton Shipped to Mexico in 1861 at 62½c lb.", *Freeport Facts (newspaper)*
1-Jan-1932   "Deserted Old Velasco Once Busy Place", *Houston Chronicle (newspaper)*, 1-Jan-1932; also re-printed as "Old Velasco at Mouth of Brazos, Now Deserted, Once Busy Place; Figured in Early Texas History", *Freeport Facts (newspaper)*, 19-Jan-1933 and again as "Velasco, Texas' First Seaport Plays Important Role in History", *Freeport Facts*, 23-Nov-1950, pp. 1-2

Hunt, Richard S., Jesse F. Randel,
1839   *Guide to the Republic of Texas: Consisting of a Brief Outline of Its Settlement ... Accompanied by a New and Correct Map* (J. H. Colton, New York, NY); a copy of their 1839 *"Map of Texas compiled from surveys on record in the General Land Office of the Republic"* (folded) was included.

Hunt, William H.,
1838   *Hand-drawn copy of a plat map of Velasco*, found in Brazoria County Deed Records, Vol. 32, pp. 8-9; original is lost but assumed to be circa 1838. *Mention is found in Brazoria County Deed Records, Vol. B, page 30 (1841), among others.*

Huson, Hobart,
1953   *Refugio, A Comprehensive History of Refugio County from Aboriginal Times to 1953*, 2 Volumes

(Guardsman Publishing, Houston, Texas)

Huston, Almanzon,

8-Apr-1836   Letter to Daniel Pittman, **PTR**, Vol. 5, p. 381, Document# 2646

Ingram, Ira, Richard Ellis, Sam Houston,

9-Dec-1836   *An Act Relinquishing One League and One League of Land to Michael B. Menard and others, on the east end of Galveston Island,* found in **LOT**, Vol. 1, pp. 1130-1132; available on-line at: https://texashistory.unt.edu/ark:/67531/metapth5872/m1/1138/

Ippolito, John E.; Baxter, Edward P.,

Jan-1976   *An Archaeological Survey of the Freeport Harbor 45-Foot Navigation Project, Brazoria County, Texas,* Report No, 21, Anthropology Laboratory, Texas A&M University

Jackson, Jack,

2005   *Indian Agent, Peter Ellis Bean in Mexican Texas* (Texas A&M University Press, College Station, Texas)

Jenkins III, John H. (editor),

1969   "Regulations for the National Militia of the State of Coahuila y Texas", Texas Military History (a quarterly publication of the National Guard Association of Texas), Vol. VII, pp. 195-220

Johns, Edward,

1841   "Journal of the Texas Schooner of War *San Antonio,* William Seeger, Lieutenant Commanding (November 13, 1841, through December 25, 1841)", Call# CAH-MS Johns, Edward, original in **EJP**

Johnson, Frank W., (author), Eugene C. Barker, Ernest William Winkler (editors),

1914   *A History of Texas and Texans,* 5 volumes, pages numbered consecutively (The American Historical Society, Chicago & New York); *available on-line at Portal to Texas History:* https://texashistory.unt.edu/ark:/67531/metapth760581/?q=velasco

Johnson, Malcom Lee,

2015   *Texas Tales and Tall Ships, Vol. I (2015) & Vol. II (2016),* 1st Edition (Tate Publishing & Enterprises, Mustang, Oklahoma)

Jones, Anson,

1859   *Memoranda and Official Correspondence Relating to the Republic of Texas, Its History and Annexation, Including a Brief Autobiography of The Author* (D. Appleton & Co., New York, NY)

Jordan, Jonathan W.,

2006   *Lone Star Navy – Texas, The Fight for the Gulf of Mexico, And the Shaping of the American West* (Potomac Books Inc., Washington DC)

Keim, De Benneville Randolph,

9-Jan-1864   Dispatch of 20-Dec-1863 from Matagorda Island Texas, apparently conveyed aboard the *Yazoo,* published in *New York Herald* (9-Jan-1864 issue, page 1, column 5), along with rough map by James T. Baker (Chief Engineer) – *appears somewhat derivative of the 1858 Bache map*

Kennedy, William,

1841   *Texas: The Rise, Progress, And Prospects of the Republic of Texas. In One Volume,* Reprint of 1841

Edition (The Molyneaux Craftsmen Inc., Fort Worth, Texas, 1925), especially pp. 368-374

Kessner, Dan,
2007   *Remembering Brazosport's Past*, privately published pamphlet of historic photos
undated   *Pictures from the Martin Armstrong Photo & Art Gallery of Velasco, Texas 1891-1900*

Kneupper, Chris,
Oct-1996   *T. M. C. Button – How Research Found Its Identity*, La Tierra – Journal of the Southern Texas
              Archaeological Association, Vol. 23, No. 4 (Oct 1996)

Kramig, George,
undated   *The Freeport/Velasco Harbor, A History of Frustration by Local Entities to Develop a Deepwater
              Port, 1821-1947*, undated and unpublished typescript manuscript, 6 pages

Lamar, Mirabeau B.,
1832   Militia Journal, 22-Jun-1832, **LP**, Vol. I, Document# 1618, p. 116 (transcript of original at BCHM)
1836   Handwritten notes on "The Taking of the Martha, Anahuac, etc.", circa 1836 (about events in
              1831-1835), original Lamar Papers, 16 pages, Folder 1618, Box 1909/001-18, TSLAC, Archives
              Division (Austin, Texas); transcript found in **LP**, Vol. V, Document# 1618, pp. 351-356

League, Hosea H.,
27-Jul-1830 Letter to Ramón Músquiz, and reply, **BA**, Microfilm Roll 132, frames 880-881

League, Hosea H., James C. Ludlow, Elias Wightman, Richard Matson
2-Aug-1826 Letter to Stephen F. Austin. transcript in **AP**, Vol. I, pp. 1395-1397; *at Digital Austin Papers:
              https://digitalaustinpapers.org/document?id=APB1227*

Letona, José María,
25-Feb-1832 Letter to Ramón Músquiz, English translation in **RBBRC**, Supplement Vol. XII, pp. 303-304; original
              in Nacogdoches Archives, Vol. 61, pp. 138-139

Letts, Bessie Lucille,
Aug-1928   "George Fisher" (M.A. Thesis, University of Texas); exceedingly rare document, original at Dolph
              Briscoe Center for American History, TXC-Z Collection, TZ 976.4 F533BL; an almost-complete copy
              exists in **MSHP**, Box 53, Files 31-32 and Box 54, File 1

Lewis, Ira R.,
5-Dec-1835 Letter to Council of Texas, **PTR**, Vol. 3, p. 98, Document# 1389

Lewis, W. S.,
1899   "The Adventures of the 'Lively' Immigrants", **SWHQ**, Vol. III (3), No. 1 (Jul 1899), pp. 1-32 and No.
              2 (Oct 1899), p. 81-107

Linn, John J.,
1986   *Reminiscences of Fifty Years in Texas* (State House Press, copy of 1883 original edition)

Llewellyn, Peggy; Chris Kneupper,
Dec-2014   *A Plan for the Fort Velasco Historic Park, Surfside Beach, Texas*, informal first-generation

document for fort replica in Block 569

Looscan, Adele B.,

Apr-1898   "The Old Mexican Fort at Velasco", *SWHQ*, Vol. I (1), No. 4, pp. 282–284

Lubbock, Francis Richard,

1900   *Six Decades in Texas or Memoirs of Francis Richard Lubbock, Governor of Texas in Wartime, 1861-1863, A Personal Experience in Business, War, and Politics*, edited by C. W. Raines (Ben C. Jones & Co. Printers, Austin Texas); available on-line as:
            https://babel.hathitrust.org/cgi/pt?id=loc.ark:/13960/t25b0d333&view=1up&seq=9&skin=2021

Maberry Jr., Robert,

2001   *Texas Flags* (Texas A&M University Press, College Station, Texas)

Manchola, Rafael,

29-Jul-1826 Letter to Antonio Elosúa, **BA**, Microfilm Roll 95, frames 478-481; also see Ahumada to Austin (3-Aug-1826) & reply (25-Aug-1826), **AP**, Vol. I, pp. 1398 & 1439

Martin, Robert S.,

Apr-1982   "Maps of an Empresario: Austin's Contribution to the Cartography of Texas", *SWHQ*, Vol. LXXXV (85), No. 4, pp. 371-400

Martinez, Francisco Pizarro,

22-Mar-1832 Letter to Secretary of Relations (enclosing copy of Letter from Bradburn dated 29-Feb-1832 and his own reply to Bradburn dated 19-Mar-1832), Spanish typescript transcript in **AGMC**, Box 2Q224, Volume 566, pp. 97-99

24-Nov-1834 Letters to Secretaries of State and Relations, Spanish typescript transcripts in **AGMC**,
& 18-Feb-1835 Box 2Q223, Volume 565, pp. 138, 140-141

Matagorda, Citizens of,

2-Jul-1832   Public meeting and resolution, transcript in **RBBRC**, Vol. XIII, pp. 3-4

Mauermann, Gus B.,

1950   *Mitchell Ranch, Bexar County, Texas, An Anthology*, typescript manuscript with photos, 23 pages, circa 1950, unknown publisher; *available at Dolph Briscoe Center for American History, The University of Texas at Austin, Austin TX (929.2 M692M)*

McKinley, Lela Ethel,

Aug-1934   "Life of James F. Perry" (M. A. Thesis, University of Texas), especially pp. 97-98

McKinney, Thomas F.,

24-Oct-1835 Letter to Gail Borden and R. R. Royall, **PTR**, Vol.2, p. 211-212, Document# 967 and Letter

26-Oct-1835 Letter to Gail Borden and R. R. Royall, transcript in **AP**, Vol. III, p. 211; *at Digital Austin Papers: http://digitalaustinpapers.org/document?id=APB4987*

29-Oct-1835 from McKinney & Williams to R. R. Royall, Vol. 2, p. 260, Document# 1023

5-Sep-1837   Letter to Sam Houston, **AJHC**, Box 2-22/164, Document# 1313

1870   *Facts to Which Thomas F. McKinney Begs Leave to call the Attention of the Committee on Public Debt*, Broadside (digital image of original), BCHM digital files, 2013.039c.0001, logged there as from 1870, includes affidavit from Edwin Waller, John M. Swisher, William J. Russell, John Adriance & F. W. Johnson; Available on-line at:

https://bchm.pastperfectonline.com/archive/03E127D7-B58B-4ACC-AE20-543949025743

McKinstry, George B.,

21-Jul-1830	Letter to George Fisher, copy on 27-Jul-1830 by Fisher, **SMWC**, Manuscript 23-0391
2-Aug-1830	Letter to George Fisher (copies made by Guerra and Seguin), **SMWC**, Manuscripts 23-0397 and 23-0398
1832	Notes on Troubles Leading to Texan Revolution, ~1832, **LP**, Vol. III, Document #1621, pp. 242-243

McQueen, Thomas,

17-Aug-1832	Receipt to Samuel May Williams, **SMWC**, Manuscript 23-0980

McWilliams, Jennifer K.; Boyd, Douglas K.,

Jan-2007	*Archeological Survey of a Portion of Old Velasco (41BO125), Proposed Boat Ramp Facility, Brazoria County Texas*, Prewitt & Associates, Reports of Investigations, No. 150

Meed, Douglas V.,

2001	*The Fighting Texas Navy, 1832-1843* (Republic of Texas Press, Plano, Texas)

Mesier, Peter A., & Co. (lithographers),

22-Mar-1837	*The City Of Velasco*, plat map (62 x 42 cm), New York, copy on microfilm in **TSC** (Reel 26, No. 1283); also known as Map #7573, TSLAC (Austin, Texas) (https://www.tsl.texas.gov/apps/arc/maps/maplookup/07573); from an original at the Beinecke Library, Yale University, Call# 796 V541 1837; on-line at https://brbl-dl.library.yale.edu/vufind/Record/4208863

Mexía, José Antonio,

6-Jul-1832	Agreement between Colonels Don José Mariano Guerra, principal commander of Matamoros and of the Tejas expedition, and Don José Antonio Mexía, commander of the Tampico forces in possession of the town of Matamoros, **M&SFP**, Series IV, 1831-1834; Spanish transcription available at The Portal to Texas History: https://texashistory.unt.edu/ark:/67531/metapth217547/; accessed 13-Jul-2023 English translation also found in **RBBRC**, Vol. XIII, pp. 19-22
8-Jul-1832	Letter to Stephen F. Austin, transcript in **RBBRC**, Vol. XIII, p. 27
23-Jul-1832	Letter to Francisco Duclor, Spanish typescript transcript in **AGMC**, Box 2Q172, Volume 330, p. 29

Mitchell, Asa,

18-Jun-1826	Letter to Stephen F. Austin, transcript in **AP**, Vol. I, Part 2, p. 1362; at Digital Austin Papers: https://texashistory.unt.edu/ark:/67531/metapth121739/m1/356/

Mooney, Kevin E.,

Fall 2008	*Centennial Songs: Forging a Texas Tradition*, South Central Music Bulletin, Vol. VII, No. 1, pp. 6-19; available on-line at https://www.scmb.us/SCMB_VII_1.pdf

Morehouse, Edwin,

1836	Account of Military Movements in March & April, 1836, **LP** #1646, Vol. III, pp. 272-274

Morgan, James,

9-Apr-1836	Republic Claims, Audited Claim Unnumbered 01, Reel 75, Image 22 (digital file ID 57000, TSLAC

Morse, Henry,

5-Aug-1832	Letter to James F. Perry, transcript in **AP**, Vol. II, p. 831-832; *at Digital Austin Papers:*

http://digitalaustinpapers.org/document?id=APB4396

Morton, Ohland,

1944-1945   "Life of General Don Manuel de Mier y Terán, as it affected Texas-Mexican Relations, Chapter IV – The Law of April 6, 1830 and Chapter V --- Affairs in Texas, 1831-1832", *SWHQ,* Vol. XLVIII (48), No. 1 (Jul 1944) pp. 51-66, No. 2 (Oct 1944) pp. 193-218 and No. 4 (Apr 1945) pp. 499-546; these chapters (and the others) published in book form as *Terán and Texas* (Texas State Historical Association, Austin, Texas, 1948)

Muir, Andrew Forest (editor),

1958   *Texas in 1837 – An Anonymous, Contemporary Narrative*, University of Texas Press, Austin, Texas, 1958 (3rd printing, 1988)

Músquiz, Ramón,

20-Jun-1830   Letter to José Maria Viesca, **BA**, Microfilm Roll 131, frames 809-812 (especially 809-810); also see Múzquiz to Alcalde of San Felipe, 24-Jun-1830, frames 956-959 (especially 959)

31-Jul-1831   Letter to José María Letona, **BA**, Microfilm Roll 143, frames 365-370 (especially 365-366); also see Letona to Músquiz, 17-Aug-1831, frames 802-805 (especially 804-805, Músquiz to Letona, 7-Nov-1831, Roll 145, frames 822-826 (especially 824-825), Letona to Músquiz, 23-Dec-1831, Roll 146, frames 834-844, & Músquiz to Flores, 10-Jan-1832, Roll 147, frames 263-267

24-Apr-1832   Letter to Horatio Chriesman, **BA**, Microfilm Roll 149, frames 589-590

26-Jun-1832   Letter to Antonio Elosúa, English translation in **RBBRC**, Supplement Vol. XII, pp. 371-372

30-Jun-1832 &   Letters to Aniceto Arteaga, English translation in **RBBRC**, Supplement Vol. XII, pp. 384-
2-Jul-1832a   385 and 400-401; 30-Jun-1832 original found in **BA**, Microfilm Roll 151, frame 202

2-Jul-1832b   Letter to Domingo de Ugartechea, English translation in **RBBRC**, Supplement Vol. XIII, pp. 1-2

7-Jul-1832   Letter to the People of Austin's Colony, transcript in **RBBRC**, Supplement Vol. XIII, p. 23

Myers, Terri L., Smith, James L.,

undated   informal research compilation involving excerpt of Ch.3 – Historical Background from [Earls et al 1996] with added material by secondary author

Nacogdoches Archives,

1830s   "Plan of Fort Velasco" diagram, Map #6312 (Archives and Information Services Division, TSLAC), circa 1830s, original appears to be composed of four sections taped together (now 80 x 55 cm), and archived in a large clear Mylar sleeve in the Map Drawer of the Nacogdoches Archives. A low-quality copy of the quarter sections can be found on 4 frames on Microfilm Roll 25 (which does not have frame or page numbers). A hand-drawn copy (not to scale) can be found in the vertical files at BCHM. Several large and small copies (with transcriptions of words) can be found in **MSHP**, Box 48, File 7

National Park Service,

2009   "Palo Alto Battlefield: A Thunder of Cannon, Chapter 4". U.S. National Park Service; especially the "Mexican Artillery" section; available on-line at: https://www.nps.gov/parkhistory/online_books/paal/thunder-cannon/chap4.htm

Newell, Chester,

1838   *History of the Revolution in Texas, particularly of the War of 1835 & '36: Together with the Latest Geographical, Topographical, and Statistical Accounts of the Country, from the Most Authentic Sources* (Wiley & Putnam, New York). Available on-line at: https://books.google.com/books/about/History_of_the_Revolution_in_Texas_Parti.html?id=CH4FAAAAQAAJ. A 2015 re-publication by Copano Bay Press is available, but uses larger print per page, so page spacing is different.

Nuñez Ortega, Gabriel,

1836   *Diario de un Prisionero de la Guerra de Texas*, (begins 19-Feb-1836), original in *Boletín del Archivo General de la Nación,* IV, No. 6 (1933), pp. 833-879; English translation by Monica Kolaya, copy at BCHM, Adriance Research Library

Ocampo, Carlos,

21-Sep-1835   Declaration, **PTR**, Vol. 1, Document #653 pp. 473-476

Oliphant, Ashley and Beth Yarbrough,

2021   *Jean Laffite Revealed: Unraveling One of America's Longest Running Mysteries* (University of Louisiana at Lafayette)

Parker, Amos A.,

1836   *Trip to the West and Texas, Comprising a Journey of Eight Thousand Miles, Through New-York, Michigan, Illinois, Missouri, Louisiana and Texas, in the Autumn and Winter of 1834-5, Interspersed with Anecdotes, Incidents and Observations, With a Brief Sketch of the Texian War,* 2nd Edition (William White, Concord, New Hampshire and Benjamin B. Mussey, Boston, Massachusetts)

Parker, Nancy Boothe (editor),

1981   "Mirabeau B. Lamar's Texas Journal", **SWHQ**, Vol. LXXXIV (84), No. 2 (Oct-1980), pp. 197-220 & No. 3 (Jan-1981), pp. 309-330

Parmenter, Mary Fisher; Fisher, Walter Russell; Mallette, Lawrence Edward,

1959   *The Life of George Fisher (1795-1873), The History of the Fisher Family in Mississippi* (The H. & W. B. Drew Co., Jacksonville, Florida)

Pavón, José Ignacio,

1832   Three Letters to George Fisher, 24-Dec-1832 and 4-Mar-1833, #'s 4706 (1) and 4711 (2), Spanish originals in **GFC**, Box 2-23/677, TSLAC; two similar but later Pavón letters to Fisher are found in [Perez y Calleja 1834], enclosures #13 and 14.

Peareson, P. E.,

Jul-1900   "Reminiscences of Judge Edwin Waller", **SWHQ**, Vol. IV (4), No. 1, pp. 33-53, reprint of a pamphlet entitled "Sketch of the Life of Judge Edwin Waller" published at the *Galveston News* office in 1874, and apparently also copied into the *Biographical Encyclopedia of Texas* (Southern Publishing Co., New York, 1880), pp. 60-69

Pedraza, Manuel Gómez,

17-Oct-1825   Circular announcing authorization of the port of Galveston, and translation into English, **SMWC**, Manuscript 23-0022

Perez y Calleja, José M.,

1834   Collection of 19 letters concerning (and apparently from the archives of) George Fisher in period of 25-Sep-1831 to 9-Jul-1834, assembled 28-Aug-1834 for Commissioner of Tamaulipas, Spanish typescript transcripts in **AGMC**, Box 2Q223, Volume 563, pp. 34-43

Perry, James F.,
6-Sep-1832   Letter to the firm of Ferguson, Jones and Campbell of Philadelphia, in transcript volumes of **J&SPP**, Series A, Vol. III, Document 30
1836   Letters to wife Emily, 15-Apr-1836 and 26-Apr-1836, in transcript volumes of **J&SPP**, Series A, Vol. IV, Documents 78 and 79

Pierce, Gerald S.,
1969   *Texas Under Arms – The Camps, Forts & Military Towns of the Republic of Texas, 1836-1846* (Encino Press, Austin, Texas), especially section on Velasco, pp. 163-167

Poe, George W.,
3-Mar-1836   Letter to Henry Smith, **OCTR**, Vol. I, p. 479

Pollan Jr., Johnney T.,
7-Aug-1990   Letter to Gail Celmer (U.S. Army Corps of Engineers), Fort Velasco vertical file, BCHM

Pollan, Sandra D.; Gross, W. S.; Earls, Amy C.; Pollan, Johnney T.; Smith, James L.,
Jun-1996   *Nineteenth-Century Transfer-printed Ceramics from the Townsite of Old Velasco (41BO125), Brazoria County, Texas: An Illustrated Catalogue*, published by Prewitt and Associates

Potter, Reuben M.; F. F. Wells,
6-Mar-1836   Proceedings of a meeting at Velasco, **TJGP**

Potter, Robert,
31-Mar-1836   Letter to Thomas B. Bell, **OCTR**, Vol. II, PP. 566-567, and response Letter from Thomas B. Bell to Robert Potter, 12-Apr-1836, Vol. II, pp. 633-634

Powers, John,
2006   *The First Texas Navy*, Woodmont Books (Austin, Texas)
undated   *The Texas Navy and San Jacinto*, undated and unpublished article in collection of Bill Turner, on-line from link at: https://texasnavy.com/Articles

Prichard, Richard (editor),
Jul-1937   "George Graham's Mission to Galveston in 1818: Two Important Documents Bearing Upon Louisiana History", The Louisiana Historical Quarterly, Vol. 20, No. 3, pp. 619-650; on-line at: https://archive.org/details/per_louisiana-historical-quarterly_the-louisiana-historical-quarterly_1937-07_20_3/page/618/mode/2up

Primera Secreteria de Estado,
1824   *Constitución federal de los Estados Unidos Mexicanos sancionada por el Congreso General Constituyente, el 4. de octubre de 1824, Imprenta del Supremo Gobierno de los Estados Unidos Mexicanos, en Palacio*, Stanford University Rare Book Collection: KGF2914 1824 .A2 1824

Puryear, Pamela Ashworth, Nath Winfield Jr.,
1976   *Sandbars and Sternwheelers – Steam Navigation on the Brazos*, Texas A&M University Press, College Station, Texas)

Pye, Jeremy W., Chris Kneupper,
23-Aug-2021   *A Geophysical Investigation of an Approximately 1.95 Acre Portion of the Old Velasco Site (41BO125), Village of Surfside Beach, Brazoria County, Texas – Texas Antiquities Permit No. 9419,* Contract Publication Series 20-210, Cultural Resource Analysts Inc.; available on-line at ITA: https://scholarworks.sfasu.edu/ita/vol2021/iss1/23/

Raine, Frances Rebecca Bouldin Spragins Brown,
1903   *Reminiscences 1816-1903 - Personal Recollections of Frances Rebecca Bouldin Spragins,* Manuscript Mss5:1 R1346:1, Call number 21487, Virginia Museum of History & Culture, Richmond, Virginia

Reed, John (editor),
1837   Arkansas Times and Advocate newspaper, article "Latest From Texas", issue of 1-May-1837, p. 1

Reinhartz, Dennis,
Winter-2015   "Maps of Stephen F. Austin: An Illustrated Essay of the Early Cartography of Texas", *The Occasional Papers,* Series No. 8 (Winter 2015), a Philip Lee Phillips Map Society Publication, Library of Congress – Geography and Maps Division

Renaud, A.,
Mar-1840   Remarks on Velasco and Galveston, **TWSC-Y**, WAA MS S-500, Box 1, folder 9

Rexford, Thomas,
1837   "Thomas Rexford Journal", unpublished typescript manuscript provided by a Rexford descendant to BCHM, Vertical Files

Riggan, Marshall, Gordon Blocker,
2019   *Forsaken Patriot – the Strange Life and Times of Samuel May Williams of Texas* (Blocker Publishing, Plano, Texas)

Robinson, James W., E. M. Pease, Henry Smith,
25-Nov-1835   *An Ordinance and Decree establishing a Navy,* found in **LOT**, Vol. 1, pp. 931-932; available on-line at: https://texashistory.unt.edu/ark:/67531/metapth5872/m1/939/

Robles, Vito A.,
1945-1946   *Coahuila y Texas – desde la consumación de la Independencia hasta el tratado de paz de Guadalupe Hidalgo,* (1945–1946) [Coahuila and Texas from the consummation of Independence until the peace treaty of Guadalupe Hidalgo (1945–1946)], Volumes I and II, 542 pages

Roller, John E.,
Jan-1906   "Capt. John Sowers Brooks", *SWHQ,* Vol. IX (9), No. 3, pp. 157-209

Roper, Chris O'Shea, Linton, Tom, illustrations by Joseph A. Hoover,
2019   *Legacy of the Early Gulf Coast Cowboys,* privately published

Rowe, Edna,
Apr-1903   "The Disturbances at Anahuac in 1832", *SWHQ,* Vol. VI (6), No. 4, pp. 265-299

Rowland, John G., John B. Tinker, Daniel W. Betts, Richard Grousbeck,

29-Jun-1832   Schooner Brazoria Protest, Document No. 30, pp. 34-35, Docket for the Precinct of Victoria
Municipality of Austin, for the year 1832, A. Brigham, Comisario, Brazoria County District Court
Records, housed at BCHM; plus p. 227 of Vol. 14 of Register of Debates In Congress (published by
Gales & Seaton 1837)

Russell, William J. (presumed author),

1872   "Battle of Velasco in 1832 – Full Particulars. By A Participant", found in 1872 section of *The Texas
Almanac 1857-1873, A Compendium of Texas History* (compiled by James M. Day, Texian Press,
Waco, Texas, 1967), pp. 670-674; also found in *Texas Scrap-Book – Made up of the History,
Biography, and Miscellany of Texas and its People* (compiled by D. W. C. Baker, A. S. Barnes &
Company, 1875), pp. 30-34; also printed in *Frontier Times*, Vol. 11, No. 1 (Oct 1933). pp. 531-535

San Felipe, Ayuntamiento of,

7-Jul-1832   Declaration of allegiance to Mexican constitution, and letter to Ramón Músquiz, 8-Jul-
1832, transcripts in **RBBRC**, Vol. XIII, pp. 24-25 & 28

San Martin, Juan de,

1772   *Reglamento e instrucción para los presidios que se han de formar en la linea de frontera
de la Nueva España.* (Spanish), 1772 (reaffirmed 1826), paperback reprint from 2012,
Sabin Americana

Santa Anna, Antonio López de,

8-Jun-1836   Letters to Andrew Jackson & José Urrea, **DCRT**, Vol. II, Part I, pp. 106-108

Sawyer, Frederick A.,

10-Sep-1836   Letter to James Morgan, **JMP**, Manuscript 31-0319

Schofield, Donald F.,

1985   *Indians, Cattle, Ships and Oil - The Story of W. M. D. Lee*, (University of Texas Press, Austin, Texas)

Seele, Hermann,

1979   *The Cypress and other Writings of a German Pioneer in Texas* (The University of Texas Press), pp.
99-103, English translation of 1936 German-language version

Seguin, Erasmo,

9-Dec-1830   Letter to Samuel May Williams, including an excerpt from a Letter from Terán of 11-Nov-1830,
SMWC, Manuscript 23-0489

Sharp, Jay W.,

Jan-1961   "The Maps of the Stephen F. Austin Collection in the Eugene C. Barker Texas History Center",
SWHQ, Vol. LXIV (64), No. 3, pp. 388-397

Shearer, Ernest C.,

1951   *Robert Potter, Remarkable North Carolinian and Texan* (University of Houston Press, Houston)

Shepherd, William M.,

30-Sep-1837   Letter to Sam Houston, **TNP**, Box 401-1195, Folder 12, Texas Adjutant General's Department Navy Papers, Archives and Information Services Division, TSLAC

Sheridan, Francis C.,

1954   *Galveston Island - Or, A Few Months Off the Coast of Texas - The Journal of Francis C. Sheridan, 1839-1840* (edited by Willis W. Pratt, reprint of the original, University of Texas Press)

Shook, Robert W.,

2007   *Caminos y Entradas – Spanish Legacy of Victoria County and the Coastal Bend, 1689-1890*, Victoria County Heritage Department

Smith, Henry,

15-Nov-1835   Letter to the President and members of the Legislative Council of Texas, original at TSLAC, Records of the Provisional Government, 1835-1836; on-line at https://www.tsl.texas.gov/exhibits/navy/hen_smith_nov16_1835_1.html

16-Dec-1835   Letter to the President and members of the Legislative Council of Texas, **PTR**, Document #1505, Vol. 3, pp. 215-216

1836   "Reminiscences of Henry Smith", written in Brazoria on 18-Nov-1836 for Mirabeau Lamar, **SWHQ**, Vol. XIV (14), No. 1 (Jul 1910), pp.24-73, especially pages 38-44

Smith, James L.,

Aug-1992   *Velasco Reclamation Work – Parrott Shell*, Brazosport Archaeological Society newsletter

30-Jan-2000   *Transportation Enterprises for the Brazos River Valley, 1836-1861*, informal research compilation, Brazosport Archaeological Society

Sep-2014   *Velasco, Archer House-Herndon Beach Home, ca. 1838, Block 13, Lots 4, 5, 6 and 7*, informal research compilation, Brazosport Archaeological Society

Dec-2014   *Velasco, Captain Jeremiah Brown Residence, ca. 1838, Block 13, Lot 10*, informal research compilation (also includes section on Shannon property), Brazosport Archaeological Society

Sep-2016   *John Sharp, Merchant of Velasco*, informal research compilation, Brazosport Archaeological Society

Smith, Ruby Cumby,

1919   "James W. Fannin, Jr., in the Texas Revolution", **SWHQ**, Vol. XXIII (23), No. 2 (Oct 1919), pp. 79-90; No. 3 (Jan 1920), pp. 171-203; No. 4 (Apr 1920), pp. 271-284

Soefje, Tim,

28-Aug-1988   "First permanent bridge at Surfside opens in 1941", Brazosport Facts, page 6CC

Soler, Miguel Cayetano,

28-Sep-1805   Letter transmitting King's authorization for free trade at Bahia de San Bernardo, **BA**, original in Box 2S81; microfilm copy on Roll 33, frames 652-653; CAH translation in Box 2C6, Series II, General Manuscripts, Vol. VIII, p. 420; microfilm of translation on Reel 20

Spellman, Paul N.,

1995   *Race to Velasco*, (Hendrick-Long Publishing Co., Dallas, Texas)

Stahman, Andrea,

Dec-2008   *Cultural Resource Survey at Old Velasco Townsite, 41BO125, Brazoria County, Texas*, Document No. 080231, PBS&J Job No. 0441591, Austin, Texas; only a redacted version of this report is publicly available

Streeter, Thomas W.,

1955   *Bibliography of Texas 1795-1845*, 2nd Edition (Harvard University Press, Cambridge MA), especially Document 119 (p. 71)

Supremo Gobierno de los Estados Unidos Mexicanos,

1825   *Coleccion De Los Derectos Y Ordenes Del Soberano Congreso Mexicano, Desde su instalación en 24. de Febrero de 1822, hasta 30. de Octubre de 1823. en que cesó* (Mexico City), pp. 196-197

Sweet, Alex E., J. Armoy Knox,

1883   "On a Mexican Mustang Through Texas, From the Gulf to the Rio Grande" (Franklin Press, Boston Massachusetts); on-line at:
https://archive.org/details/onmexicanmustang00swee/page/n47/mode/2up
1905 edition (Chatto & Windus, London, 1905); on-line at:
https://archive.org/details/onmexicanmustangb002swee/page/40/mode/2up

Terán, Manuel de Mier y,

24-May-1830   Letter to George Fisher, Spanish transcript of a copy by Guerra on 23-Jun-1830, **AP**, Vol. II, pp. 394-395; another copy was forwarded from Erasmo Seguin to Samuel May Williams on 24-Jun-1830, **SMWC**, Manuscript 23-0374; an English excerpt can be found in the *Texas Gazette* issue of 23-Oct-1830, p.2, col. 1; see [Cotten 1830]

15-Aug-1830   Letter to Sec'y of Interior & Exterior Relations, Spanish typescript transcript in **AGMC**, Box 2Q223, Volume 562, pp. 20-21; including excerpt from letter from Stephen F. Austin of 13-Jul-1830

22-Oct-1830   Letter to Samuel May Williams, English translation (presumably by Williams, then sent to G. B. Cotten) published in the *Texas Gazette* issue of 21-Nov-1830, p. 2, col. 1; *see [Cotton 1830]*; refers to Terán's earlier letter of 21-Aug-1830 which is found in **SMWC**, Maunuscript 23-0417

16-Feb-1831   Letter to Secretary of Interior & Exterior Relations, Spanish typescript transcript in **AGMC**, Box 2Q223, Volume 563, pp. 23-24; including enclosure of letter to Governor of Coahuila y Tejas (José Maria Letona) on same date

26-Mar-1831   Letter to Ramón Músquiz, **TGLO**, Document# 1284, Box 129:13, p. 137

3-May-1831   "Certificate" about George Fisher, Spanish original, **GFC**, Document #4703, Box 2-23/677; subsequent transcripts/copies are found as broadside in "Guia del Pueblo, Alcance Al Num. 37." on 14-Jul-1831 in Ciudad Victoria (Tamaulipas); copy available in **TSC**, Document #770 and in [Rowe 1903 p. 273]; a translation can be found in **M&SFAP**; on-line at **PTTH** at
https://texashistory.unt.edu/ark:/67531/metapth216733/ and
https://texashistory.unt.edu/ark:/67531/metapth216727/

27-Sep-1831   Letter to George Fisher, Spanish typescript transcript in **AGMC**, Box 2Q223, Volume 563, p. 33

3-Oct-1831   Letter to Stephen F. Austin, **SMWC**, Manuscript 23-0810; see also Terán to Seguin (3-Oct-1831), **BA**, Microfilm Roll 145, frames 35-36; Erasmo Seguin also copied message to Samuel May Williams in **SMWC**, Manuscript 23-0820 on 28-Oct-1831; also copy in both Spanish and English found in [Fisher Oct-1831]

19-Nov-1831   Letter to George Fisher, Spanish original (INV 5735, #4704) in **GFC**, Box 2-23/677

20-Nov-1831   Letter to Stephen F. Austin, Spanish transcript in **AP**, Vol. II, pp.708-709; handwritten English translation can be found in **ECBP**, Box 2B116, Folder "Research Material: Transcriptions and notes, Texas, Mexico relations, ca. 1829-1833"

22-Nov-1831	Letter to George Fisher, Spanish original (#4705) in GFC, Box 2-23/677
27-Jan-1832	Letter to Stephen F. Austin, transcript in **AP**, Vol. II, pp. 742-744
14-Apr-1832	Letter to Stephen F. Austin, **TWSC-Y**, original and typed translation, Box 3, folder 187, WAA MS S-498, Personal Files 1787-1882, Manuel de Mier y Teran, **TWSC-Y**
29-Jun-1832	Orders to Domingo de Ugartechea, transcript in **AP**, Vol. II, pp. 805-806
2000	*Texas by Terán – The Diary Kept by General Manuel Mier y Terán on his 1828 Inspection of Texas* (English translation, edited by Jack Jackson, University of Texas Press)

Texas State Historical Survey Committee,

| **1969** | "Old Velasco", Historical Marker 9604, established 1969, Freeport, Texas; description at on-line Historical Marker Database: https://www.hmdb.org/m.asp?m=167498, last accessed 5-Feb-2023 |

Thompson, Alexander,

| **5-Oct-1837** | Letter to Navy Dept., **TNP**, Box 401-1309, Folder 15 |

Thompson II, S. A. (Sherman Allen),

| **2020** | *Notes on The Republic of Texas Navy, Marine Corps, Coast Guards, And Their Vessels (1836-1846), and Other Vessels Involved in the War for Texas's Independence And its Maritime Defense* (Page Publishing Inc., Conneaut Lake, Pennsylvania) |

Thompson, Thomas M.,

26-Jul-1835	Broadside entitled "T. M. Thompson's Proclamation to the Citizens of Anahuac, &c.", **BCB**, Box BC OB 1830-1835, digital copy BC_0268; also listed in **TSC**, Document 107; transcript also in [Brown 1887 pp. 62-64]; also found in Texas Republican issue of 19-Sep-1835, and **PTR**, Document# 533, I:278-279
18-May-1838	Letter to John G. Tod, **JGTP**, Box 8, File 28; includes copies of Letters of George Wheelwright to Thompson (2-Feb-1838) and William M. Shepherd to Thompson (28-Feb-1838).
26-May-1838	Navy of the Republic Service Records, Call# 401-25, Texas Adjutant General's Department, Archives and Information Services Division, TSLAC; on-line at: https://www.tsl.texas.gov/apps/arc/service/viewdetails/21318

Thrall, Homer S.,

| **1883** | *A Pictorial History of Texas – From the Earliest Visits of European Adventurers, to A. D. 1883.* (N.D. Thompson & Co., St. Louis, Missouri), especially pp. 178-186 and footnote on pp. 519-521 |

Turner, F. H.,

| **Jul-1903** | *The Mejía Expedition*, **SWHQ**, Vol VII (7), No. 1, pp. 1-28 |

Ugartechea, Domingo de,

13-Mar-1832	Letter to Col. Antonio Elosúa, English translation in **RBBRC**, Supplemental Vol. IX, p. 253; original at **BA**, Microfilm Roll 148, frames 602-603
26-Mar-1832	Letter to Col. José de las Piedras, original has apparently not survived, but a copy is found in Letter from Piedras to Elosúa, 9-Apr-1832, **BA**, Microfilm Roll 149, frames 302-312 (especially 302-305)
15-May-1832a	Letter to Antonio Elosúa, **BA**, Microfilm Roll 150, frames 29-30
15-May-1832b	Letter to Antonio Elosúa, **BA**, Microfilm Roll 151, frame 524
7-Jun-1832a	Letter to Commander at Goliad, copy made by Mariano Cosío, **BA**, Microfilm Roll 150, frame 621
7-Jun-1832b	Letter to Antonio Elosúa, **BA**, Microfilm Roll 150, frames 622-623
7-Jun-1832c	Letter to Antonio Elosúa, **BA**, Microfilm Roll 150, frames 624-625. This letter was also copied by

Elosúa into a letter dated 18-Jun-1832 to Ramón Músquiz, found in the Nacogdoches Archives (English translation in **RBBRC**, Vol. XII, pp. 332-333)

29-Jun-1832	Capitulation Agreement, **BA**, Microfilm Roll 151, frame 137; probably an original enclosure with **BA** 151:220-225
1-Jul-1832	Letter to Antonio Elosúa (aboard the schooner *Brazoria* at the mouth of the Brazos River), Spanish transcription and English translation by Dora Guerra of UTSA in Apr 1981; original at **BA**, Microfilm Roll 151, frames 220-225, Dolph Briscoe Center for American History, Austin TX. A separate presumably older English transcript can be found in **LP** I:132-136, Document No. 148. Another original is found in **HRWC**, Box 3, Folder 87
8-Jul-1832	Letter to Aniceto Arteaga, original has apparently not survived, but a copy is found in Letter from Arteaga to Antonio Elosúa, 10-Jul-1832, **BA**, Microfilm Roll 151, frames 518-519
10-Jul-1832	Letter to Antonio Elosúa, **BA**, Microfilm Roll 151, frame 522
23-Feb-1835	Letter to Martín Perfecto de Cos, **TGLO**, Document# 641, Box 125:13, pp. 173-175

Underwood, Ammon,

Nov-1827	"Journal Kept by Ammon Underwood, 1834-1838, Being an Account of His Journey From Near Lowell, Massachusetts, by Ship from Boston to Marion, now East Columbia, Texas, and of His Later Experiences in Texas", typescript copy made in the office of J. H. Winterbotham (Galveston, Texas), Nov 1927, copy available at BCHM; also published by James K. Greer in *SWHQ*, Vol. XXXII (32), No. 2 (Oct 1928), pp. 124-151

Unknown,

1832	Report without signature or direction, 3-7-Jul-1832, transcript in **RBBRC**, Vol. XIII, pp. 5-10

Unknown,

1863	*A manuscript map showing Forts Quintana and Velasco at mouth of the Brazos, the piling across the mouth of the river and ferry and inland fortification at Quintana*, circa 1863, National Archives 1.130 Local Coastal Defenses, Record Group 77: Z 51-9

Unknown,

24-Dec-1864a	*Fort Velasco on the east side of the Brazos River*, hand-drawn diagram in **JFGP** #276; on-line at https://dc.lib.unc.edu/cdm/singleitem/collection/gilmer/id/171/rec/4; accessed 1-Mar-2021
24-Dec-1864b	*Fort Map Shewing Locations of Works at the Mouth of the Brazos River*, hand-drawn diagram in **JFGP** #276; on-line at https://dc.lib.unc.edu/cdm/singleitem/collection/gilmer/id/169/rec/3; accessed 1-Mar-2021

Unknown,

1869	*The Texas Almanac for 1869, and Emigrant's Guide to Texas*; available on-line at **PTTH**: https://texashistory.unt.edu/ark:/67531/metapth123774/m1/1/

Unknown,

1907	Newspaper articles: *Palestine Daily Herald* (Palestine TX), 5-Aug-1907, p.1; *The Texas Mesquiter* (Mesquite, Texas), 16-Aug-1907, p.2; *The Sunday Gazetteer* (Denison, Texas), 11-Aug-1907 p.1

Walker, Tipton,

1862	*A large-scale map of the coast from (NE end of East) Matagorda Bay to (SW end of) Galveston Island showing the signal locations and forts, signed by Captain Tipton Walker (in 3 sheets, each approximately 17" x 42")*, circa 1862, National Archives Record Group 77, Civil War Map File Z 343

Walker, Tipton; Helferich P.,

1895   *Coast of Texas and Its Defenses*, published colorized map found as part of Plate LXV in *Atlas to Accompany the Official Records of The Union and Confederate Armies*, published under the direction of the Hons. Redfield Proctor, Stephen B. Elkins and Daniel S. Lamont, secretaries of war, by Maj. George B. Davis, U.S. Army, Mr. Leslie J. Perry, civilian expert, Mr. Joseph W. Kirkley, civilian expert, Board of Publication. Compiled by Capt. Calvin D. Cowles, 23d U.S. Infantry. Washington: Government Printing Office, 1891-1895. Original plain map published in 1864, one such copy is found at National Archives Record Group 77, Civil War Map File Z 298. Another copy is found in **JFGP**; on-line at https://dc.lib.unc.edu/cdm/singleitem/collection/gilmer/id/37/rec/1, accessed 1-Mar-2021

Ward, Forrest E.,

Oct-1960   "Pre-Revolutionary Activity in Brazoria County", ***SWHQ***, Vol. LXIV (64), No. 2, pp. 212-231

Jan-1962   "The Lower Brazos Region of Texas, 1820-1845" (Ph.D. dissertation, University of Texas, TX, Jan-1962); *full copy available at BCHM research library*

Weems, John Edward & Jane,

1971   *Dream of Empire, A Human History of the Republic of Texas, 1836-1846* (Simon and Schuster, New York, New York)

Weir, Merle,

1976   Handbook of Texas Online, "Velasco, TX", 1976; available at https://www.tshaonline.org/handbook/entries/velasco-tx; last accessed on 5-Feb-1996

Wells, Tom Henderson,

1960   *Commodore Moore & the Texas Navy*, ©1960 (Second Paperback Printing, University of Texas Press, Austin, TX, 1988)

Wells II, William R.,

Autumn-1998 "'Every Protection That Was Asked For' - The United States Revenue Cutter *Ingham*, Texas Independence, and New Orleans, 1835", Louisiana History: The Journal of the Louisiana Historical Association, Vol. 39, No. 4, pp. 457-479; on-line at: https://www.jstor.org/stable/4233538?seq=1#metadata_info_tab_contents

Wharton, John A.,

26-Jan-1836 Letter to Henry Smith, **OCTR**, Vol. I, p. 341

Wharton, William H., William Brown, Asa Mitchell,

4-Jul-1832   Letter to the Committee at Brazoria, transcript in **LP** #153, Vol. I, p. 139; original at TSLAC; available on-line at https://www.tsl.texas.gov/exhibits/navy/wm_wharton_july4_1832_1.html

White, Joseph M.,

1839   *A New Collection of Laws, Charters and Local Ordinances of The Governments of Great Britain, France and Spain, Relating to the Concessions Of Land In Their Respective Colonies; Together with the Laws Of Mexico And Texas On The Same Subject* (T. & J. W. Johnson, Philadelphia, Pennsylvania), especially Vol. I, Book V, pp. 421-622

Williams, Samuel May,

12-Jul-1830	Letter to Comisario Subalterno of Béxar (Erasmo Seguin), **BA**, Microfilm Roll 132, frames 531-532
27-Jul-1830	Letter to Comisario Subalterno of Béxar (Erasmo Seguin), (quoting a letter from George Fisher of 15-Jul-1830), **BA**, Microfilm Roll 132, frames 884-886
10-Mar-1831	Two Letters to W. D. Dunlap, transcripts in **AP**, Vol. II, p. 609-610
30-Jun-1831	Letter to Governor, **BA**, Microfilm Roll 142, frames 397-398; additional copies are found in **SMWC**, Manuscript 23-1532 and **AP**, Vol. II, pp. 671-672
7-Feb-1832	Letter to Gaspar Flores, **BA**, Microfilm Roll 147, frames 916-917
1-Jul-1832	Letter to Bartlett Samuel Sims, transcript in **LP** #147, Vol. I; p. 131, original at TSLAC
29-Jul-1832	Letter to James Kerr, **SMWC**, Manuscript 23-0980
31-Mar-1835	Letter to Stephen F. Austin, transcript in **AP**, Vol. III, pp. 56-58; at Digital Austin Papers: http://digitalaustinpapers.org/document?id=APB4752.xml

Willich Jr., George,

6-Sep-1834	Letter from Anahuac to Doris Willich in Germany, German transcript and English translation of letter from Albert of Livingstone Manor, New York, by Language Professors of Lamar University (Beaumont, Texas), Sam Houston Regional Library and Archives, Liberty, Texas; especially p. 11 of English translation; another copy is found in William Ransom Hogan Papers, University of Texas at Arlington, Special Collections Library, Box GA21, Folder 14; another previous translation by Theodore Willich about 1933 (from the original in an archive at Leipzig) was published in *Texas Highways* magazine, Sep-1993, pp. 2-4.

Willson, Marcius,

1847	*American History, Part III (History of Texas)*, Chapter II (Mark H. Newman & Co., New York), especially pp. 635-643

Wilson, Walter E.,

2020	*Civil War Scoundrels and the Texas Cotton Trade* (McFarland & Co., Jefferson, North Carolina)

Winkler, Ernest William,

Oct-1906	"The Seat of Government of Texas, I. Temporary Location of the Seat of Government", *SWHQ*, Vol. X (10), No. 2, pp. 140-171, especially section 6 on page 156
Jul-1917	"The 'Twin Sisters' Cannon", *SWHQ*, Vol. XXI (21), No. 1, pp. 61-68

Winthrop, John,

1835	*Report of the Trial of Thomas M. Thompson, For A Piratical Attack Upon the American Schooner San Felipe; Before the United States Court for the Eastern District of Louisiana* (E. Johns & Co., New Orleans), 44 pages

Winsor, Bill,

1978	*Texas in the Confederacy – Military Installations, Economy and People* (Hill College Press)

Wisner, George Y.,

Nov-1891	"The Brazos River Harbor Improvement", *Transactions of the American Society of Civil Engineers*, Vol. XXV, Part 2, pp. 519-562

Wooten, Dudley Goodall (editor),

1898	*A Comprehensive History of Texas, 1685 to 1897*, 2 volumes (William G. Scarff, Dallas, Texas), reprint by Texas State Historical Association, 1986

Wortham, Louis J.,

1924   *A History of Texas – From Wilderness to Commonwealth*, 5 volumes (Wortham-Molyneaux Co., Fort Worth Texas)

Yates, A. J.; Moreland, I. N.; Allen, A. C.,

29-Aug-1835   Sworn statement published in a broadside entitled "T. M. Thompson's Proclamation to the Citizens of Anahuac, &c.", 29-Aug-1835, **BCB**, Box BC OB 1830-1835, digital copy BC_0268; also found in **TSC**, Document 107; statement also published in *The Texas Republican*, 19-Sep-1835 and in [Barker 1905]; transcript also in [Brown 1887 pp. 64-68] and **PTR**, Document# 560, I:376-378

Yoakum, Henderson K.,

1855   *History of Texas, From Its First Settlement in 1685 to its Annexation to The United States in 1846* (two volumes, Redfield, New York, NY)

Ongoing research will be posted at **https://velascohistoryarchaeology.weebly.com/**

Stamp used on letters from José María Viesca, Governor of Coahuila y Tejas from 1827 to 1831 (e.g., TGLO Spanish Archives #568, Box 125/9 p.97

Appendix 1 – Details on 1822 Austin diagram

Words found on 1822 fort diagram in Stephen F. Austin Map Collection, Call# SA121822
Briscoe Center for American History (Austin, Texas)

High-resolution photocopies of each side were purchased in Sep-2019 from the Briscoe Center, as TIF files. Each image is about 236 MB in size, allowing fine details to be observed
The preferred citation: Stephen F. Austin Map Collection, Call Number SA 121822 (stored in 2.325/OD20), high-resolution photos available as [identifier number: di_11854, di_11863], The Dolph Briscoe Center for American History, The University of Texas at Austin

<u>Front side:</u>
  Center:

Varas quadradas	square varas
Area 11296	area 11296 (*equivalent to 60 varas radius*)
aumentado el radio a 100 varas	increasing the radius to 100 varas
se dan 31,380 Varas quadradas	gives 31,380 square varas
y 120 dan 45187 V.^{s} quad. Espacio suficiente	and 120 gives 45187 square varas space
p.^{a} (para) contener 25,000 cabezas de ganado	sufficient to contain 25,000 head of cattle

lower center, left of fence (faintly, in English script): …… trouble
about 110° from vertical   ….. to prevent cattle falling

upper left square: 120 varas	120 varas
14400 varas quadradas	14400 square varas
(*repeated for square in lower right square*)	
above the square (faintly): tala --|-	felling, (*for abattis*)
????	
___lueta p.^{a} tropa	_____ for troops
___l foso	_____ moat
buildings: Torre	Tower
vigas	beams
barricade?: Mantelete	Mantlet or mantelet[*]
gate?: x x hucas (tuercos?)	???? (*nuts?*)
p p laes (pernos?)	???? (*bolts?*)
y llave p.^{a} (para) x x	and wrench for x x
roof?: g gozne	hinge

<u>Back side:</u>
  Top:

Escala de varas castellanos	scale of Castilian rods

(Note: a Castilian rod or vara = 2.74247 feet = 0.914157 yards, so 60 varas = 164.5 feet, thus a radius of

60 varas = 329.1 feet diameter)

Upper center (to right of tower and above the profile):
at etcalade & with the Skins fine shade (*very faint, in English script?, and unsure of letters*)

Left side:
a a a a Superficie ó nivel de la tierra
o o foso profundo de 3 pies
x x tierra sacada del foso y amontonada en forma de glacis siguiendo la linea de tiro D̲ x̲ x̲
D x x linea de tiro superior
D o o id id _ inferior_
f f f f foso si se cree necesario
E estacada _ estando cada estaca á la distancia de 2 pies de la otra se necesitarán
564 estacas _ dando 22 pulgadas a cada soldado 615 guarnecerán el foso
en una fila y 1230 en dos filas – pero como regulam.^te no habrá banqueta
los soldados subirán lo mejor que puedan sobre las estacas y de allá
tirarán _ La Torre necesitará p.ª su guarnacion de 6 a 8 hombres _

a a a a Surface or ground level
o o 3-foot deep moat
x x earth pulled out of the moat and piled in glacis[**] shape along the firing line
D x x line of top fire
D o o line of lower fire
f f f f moat if thought necessary
E stockade _ each stake being at the distance of 2 feet[***] from the other, 564 stakes will be needed.
Giving 22 inches[***] to each soldier, 615 will garrison the moat
in one row, and 1230 in two rows – but as there will regularly not be a bench,
the soldiers will climb as best they can over the stakes and shoot from there.
The Tower will need for its garrison 6 to 8 men.

Lower right:
Horizontal: A Map (*in black ink, crossed out in pencil*)
        Drawing of fort by S F Austin (?) (*in pencil*)
        1822

Vertical: Stephen Fuller Austin of the Province
        of Texas Stephen Fuller Austin
        Stephen Fuller Austin of the
        Province of Texas (? S J Sunuary ?).
        Mexico – 1822.

[*]*mantlet - a large shield or portable shelter used for stopping projectiles in medieval and later warfare. For more info and images see: https://en.wikipedia.org/wiki/Mantlet*
[**]*glacis - a gently sloping bank, in particular one that slopes down from a fort, exposing attackers to the defenders' missiles.*
[***]*these are Castilian measurements, with a foot and inch being about 0.92 of the English equivalent.*

Transcribed and translated by Chris Kneupper and James E. "Jake" Ivey, 2-Oct-2019

Appendix 2 – Reference Details about 1832 fort construction

Any specific mention of details about the 1832 fort are quoted below.

Note: first-hand and/or contemporaneous accounts are **larger & emboldened text**.

[Ugartechea 13-Mar-1832]

"... getting myself ready for marching, within eight days, **with one cannon of 6 (un cañón á 6.) and 100 infantrymen**, carrying at the same time aboard, all of the utensils for fortifying myself at the mouth of the Brazos River, carrying with me the receiver named by the government for that point, Don Francisco Duclor ...".

[Ugartechea 26-Mar-1862]

He was still at Anahuac on 26-Mar-1832, when he wrote another letter from there to José de las Piedras, commander at Nacogdoches, twice mentioning his "**cañón de á 8**" and "**cañón de á ocho**". Further, he wrote he had **no gunpowder cartridges for his "cannon of eight", but he will make 100 cartridges from Anahuac's supply** and asks Piedras to replace it.

[Ugartechea 1-Jul-1832] – Guerra translation to English (unless noted otherwise)

p. 2: "... (Jun) 24th, around eleven, a force of about 150 men on horseback was observed coming toward the fort, and while still a long distance away, they maneuvered their horses to and fro. I chose not to fire cannon; because **I could not afford to waste the powder. It was in such short supply.**"

"... My cannon never failed to return their fire; and I had foreseen, I had the rifle and carbine men on the barbette so that is some way they could cover the artillerymen.

p.3: " ... the schooner moored on the river at **about two hundred paces from the fort.**"

p. 4 of original: "... *y en un lado del fuerte tenia un cañonsito de 4 onzas* que casualmente estava colocado al frente del parapeto de los decidentes.

Translation: "... **and on one side of the fort, I had a little cannon of four ounces** which incidentally was located in the front of the parapet of the dissidents."

p. 6 of the original: "... ningun tiro tenia para **el pedrero** pero de la misma polbora quedo probisto con 40 asi mande alavez a mi tropa con dezirles que haun unas utiliwzeran las ballonetas en el fuerte pues que ya los habiamos hecho corer."

Translation: "... we had no shot for the **swivel gun**, but from the same powder it resulted in providing for 40 so I commanded at the same time to my troops by saying to them perhaps some can use the bayonets in the fort now that we have made them run."

p. 6 of the original: "En este permanecimos y despues de haver comido la tropa que estava bastante fatigada por haver sostenido un largo y vivo fuego en el que se tiraron por una pequena fuerza 4,600 tiros de fucil, 96 con **el cañon de a ocho**, y setenta y seis con **el pedrero de cuatro onzas**, se dispuso para sufrir un neubo golpe al tiempo que con el anteojo se bio que una columna come de 150 hombres de caballa se avansava asia al fuerte, pero a distancia de media milla echaron pie a tierra; ..."

Translation: In this state we found ourselves and after having eaten, the troops which were plenty fatigued for having sustained a large and lively fire which were shot by a small force 4,600 musket shots, 96 with the **cannon of eight**, and seventy-six with **the swivel gun of four ounces**, disposed themselves to suffer a new attack at the time which could be seen with binoculars that a single column of 150 men on horseback was advancing toward the fort, but at a distance of half a mile, they dismounted ..."

p.7 ... after the battle, he mentions "I ordered that my wounded be taken out from the fort, and placed in one of the two houses that I had left unburned." – **thus indicating that buildings were mostly OUTSIDE of the small fort.**

Note: certain parts of the original Spanish handwritten text appear to have been incorrectly and only partially translated in both previous translations, complicated by the confusing syntax used by Ugartechea. The term he used for the swivel gun was **"cañonsito de 4 onzas"** *and* **"pedrero de cuatro onzas"** *(meaning 4 ounces). At another point, he writes* **"cañon de a ocho" (meaning "cannon of eight"),** *a term not found in either original translation. So, it appears the swivel gun was not a hefty swivel-mounted cannon but more like a large smoothbore flintlock weapon. The "cannon of eight" then agrees with John Austin's identification of the main cannon (see next section). The Guerra translation did correctly translate the term for* <u>ounces</u>, *but this has been marked out in local copies and replaced with* <u>pounds</u> *– probably a misinterpretation that has been promulgated into later secondary references. The Ordnance Manual of the U. S. Army for 1862 lists that 4-ounce cast-iron shot has a diameter of 1.231 inches, so it seems most likely that Ugartechea had a small swivel-pin-mounted muzzle loader (i.e., a "wall gun") of this size.*

[Fisher 1832]

"In few day a vessel goes from here to the mouth of the river Brazos with **100 men and a 8 pounder**, under command of Leut. Colonel Domingo Ugartechea, with all the necessaries for a fortification at the entrance of said River, accompanied by two other officers and two customhouse officers; in consequence of these preparations, it is necessary that you should with possible despach place said **buildings and the ferry boat**, also sufficient lumber to make the **sheds to the warehouse**, and in case of need, to put some repairs to Mitchells house. The officers of the *Constante* accompany the expedition, on board the *Topaz*."

[Cotten 1832, Holley 1833]

Return of arms and ammunition taken at Fort Velasco, 26th June, 1832.
1 Brass cannon, 8 pounder, 1 Small Iron Swivle;
30 Cartridges for the cannon 45 do For the swivel
2000 do For muskets 40 Cartouch boxes
2 Brass blunder-busses

8th. **The Cannon of 8, and the Swivel Gun**, shall remain on Fort Velasco, with all the public stores, superaumerary guns and ammunition. *Note: this provision has been copied into [Rowe 1903 p. 291].*

[Breedlove 1832]
Another version of the effects returned to Fort Velasco and Mexía:
1 Brass long nine Pounder (mounted on carriage) 1 Small iron Swivel (mounted on Block)
A Small Quantity cartridges Grape Shot and Balls for ea(ch) 1 Broken Rifle
1 Lott old Bayonets and Scabbards, 1 do Cartruch Boxes, etc.

[Wharton 1832]
"We have kept about 80 rounds of powder for the **9 pounder & all the shot & slugs**."

[Fry 1832]
" … The Fort of Velasco was attacked by the American colonists under the command of Captain John Austin, with a force of 120 men …. **The Fort, mounting one long brass nine pounder** and 90 men … '

[Russell 1872]
"… The plan and structure of the fort were well understood, of **circular form, of logs and sand, with strong stakes, sharpened, and placed close together, all around the embankment. In the center, stood a bastion, in height considerably above the outer wall, on top of which was mounted a long nine-pounder, worked on a pivot, and around which, on top of the bastion, was a parapet made of wood, about two feet in height**."
"… It was well known by that attacking party (Capt. John Austin's party) that there was **mounted on the wall of the fort a small piece of artillery facing the point of their approach**, but it was believed that the wooden breastwork was of sufficient thickness to protect those behind them. This proved quite a mistake. Very much damage was done by this small gun, the balls often passing through the planks, inflicting death or wounds. The man Robinson, who gave the alarm, was the first man killed."
"… the distance being only **one hundred and sixty-nine yards from the schooner to the bastion gun** in the fort …"
"… The only serious damage done on board the (Brazoria) vessel by the post was, that during the night a **nine-pound shot** passed through her side, striking the mate (who, as per agreement, had retired, as was supposed, to a place of safety) just between his shoulders, passing entirely through him. His death was instantaneous."

[Linn 1986 p. 18]
The fort of Velasco was **constructed in circular form, covering about one half acre**. It was situated on the east bank of the Brazos River, and near its mouth. *Note: half acre circle equals about 166.5 feet diameter.*

[Peareson 1901]: *quoting Edwin Waller from 1873 to 1874*
… fort of circular form, having in the center a mound or raised platform of earth, whereon the artillery was placed *en barbette*, so as to fire over the outer wall, and command a range on every side. This outer wall was surrounded by a *fosse* or ditch, and perhaps something intended for *chevaux de frize*

or *abattis*.

[Smith 1836]

p. 38: "… It will be recollected that there was a strong fortress at the mouth of the river Brazos [Velasco] garrisoned by about one hundred and fifty men, well armed and provisioned with **one long brass nine mounted on a carriage and one iron four pounder on a pivot**."

p. 39: "… During the time our vessel [*Brazoria*] was getting in readiness, we had prepared a kind of breastwork for the land forces which was made **of cypress plank ten or twelve feet in length nailed on battons to the widths of about four feet** which were to be set up with props".

p. 40: "… we must suffer severely from the effects of their **nine-pounder** …"

p. 41: "… they let off their **nine-pounder** and threw a double headed shot through her [*Brazoria's*] rigging …"https://tshaonline.org/handbook/online/articles/qtb01

p. 41-42: "**The fort was a complete circle enclosing but a small area so that it was full and completely manned. The nine-pounder was planted on an elevation in the center of [or] perhaps ten feet above the musquetry**. As soon as our company opened on the fort, it seemed to ignite instantaneously and flame like a volcano. And from that time until the battle ended, the fort seemed to emit one continued blaze of fire. **They had burned all the houses but two, one was used as a custom house, and the other a small office**.

p. 42: "We … learned one thing, and that was in some measure to escape the shot of the **nine-pounder**."
"… **planted the palisades within thirty paces of the fort so that their nine-pounder could not be depressed enough to bear upon us, but [we] were compelled to stand the four pounder and the musquetry**."

[Brown 1970]: *original edition is from 1893*

"… The fort at Velasco stood about **a hundred and fifty yards both from the river and the Gulf shore** which formed a right angle. It consisted of **parallel rows of posts six feet apart, filled between with sand, earth and shells, for the outer walls**. Inside of the walls was an embankment on which musketeers could stand and shoot over without exposing anything but their heads. **In the center was an elevation of the same material, inclosed by higher posts**, on which the artillery was planted and protected by bulwarks.

[Looscan 1898]:

quoting Guy M. Bryan: "**… logs were used, but in the manner of stockade … The fort was circular in shape and composed of sound drift logs set perpendicularly in two circular rows, the space of several feet between them being filled in with sand. A mound of sand in the center, raised above the pickets, was surrounded by wood to prevent the sand being blown off. On this mound was mounted a nine-pound cannon, which was on a swivel so as to make a complete circuit guarding the mouth of the river**; it could not, however, be depressed so as to protect the immediate vicinity, hence on the night of the attack by John Austin, it could not play upon the Texians close to the fort, but was used against the schooner *Brazoria*, commanded by Capt. Wm. J. Russell."

"Mrs. Ellen A. Shannon …. gives a reliable account of the site of the old fort, which, she says **is now marked by her own residence**. …. Her husband had often called her attention to one of the posts or upright logs of the old fort, with muskets stuck in it. During the Civil War the Confederate soldiers used all of the fences, posts, etc. of every kind for firewood, and probably every piece of iron that pertained to the accoutrements of an army."

Quoting Mr. A. G. Follett: "… in 1875 the severe storm revealed evidence of the location of the old fort … it washed up a number of small Mexican coins of the value of twenty-five cents and a **small copper cannon ball** on its site." *(Mexican soldiers used brass canister shot, one such ball was also recovered in the salvage excavations of the early 1990s.)*

[Seele 1979 p. 99]

Buegel states "…. **From the fort, which was three hundred paces from the shoreline**, we could, during the day, see three ships in the telescope."

[Rowe 1903]
p.277: "…As soon as Colonel Ugartechea reached Anahuac with the troops furnished him by Terán to reinforce that place, he was sent by Bradburn **on April 2, 1832 with one hundred and ten men and an eight-pounder, to establish a fort at the mouth of the Brazos.**"

[Filisola 1848]
p. 81 (of English translation): "… Lieutenant Colonel Ugartechea … arrived in Anahuac … Davis ordered on the following April 2 that he **go with one hundred ten men and one piece of eight caliber artillery (*Spanish p. 192: una pieza de á ocho*)** to set up a fort at the mouth of the Brazos."

[Dow 1961]
"The new momento is a **cast-iron cannonball, weighing a trifle less than 9 pounds**. In a remarkable state of preservation, it was unearthed in some excavation work at the Chlorine-5 plant at Plant A. The weight of the cannonball, and the place where it was dug up, have led local historical researchers to conclude that it was fired by the Mexicans at the Texans during the battle of Velasco, June 25-26, 1832. **A long brass cannon, throwing a ball of nine pounds was the main defensive armament of the Mexican fort at Velasco during the battle.**"

[Creighton 1975]
p. 62: "When they (*John Austin and others*) passed by Velasco at the mouth of the Brazos, **Colonel Ugartechea, who had been sent there early in April (*1832*) with one hundred and ten men and an eight pounder to establish a fort …..**"
p. 65: "The fort at Velasco was not then strong. **It was built in circular form of drift logs standing perpendicularly in two rows. The intervening space was filled with sand. In the middle of the fort, raised on a bastion of sand somewhat higher than the outer walls, a nine-pound swivel gun covered all approaches. The main defect in this deployment was a two-foot parapet atop the bastion, which protected the gunners but prevented the gun from being deflected low enough to fire on attackers approaching the fort.**"

[Lamar 1836, Henson 1982, Bulletin 1999]

As mentioned previously, references indicate that men and material were transferred to Anahuac and then Velasco over a period time. Lamar says "The Vessel reached Anahuac in safety, landed the soldiers; and then **<u>filling her with pickets to build a fort at Velasco</u>**, she sailed with Col. Ugartechea aboard to the mouth of the Brazos, where she was wrecked and lost."

[Henson 1982 p. 88]

"… By the third week in March (1832), Ugartechea, accompanied by Francisco Duclor, the customs collector, had reached his destination on the eastern bank of the Brazos with 100 troops, **one six-pound cannon**, and all the materials needed to build the fort, to be named Velasco. Fisher had already ordered repairs to the old building that was being used as a customs house, and had also contracted for a new office, a ferryboat, and a warehouse. By May the little fort was complete, and **the mounted cannon commanded not only vessels crossing the bar but also all of the private buildings on the point of land near the entrance to the river**.

Note: the mention of a 6-pound cannon is obviously derivative of Ugartechea's letter of 13-May-1832 mentioning a cannon of 6-calibre; however, he departed later for the Brazos, and subsequently mentioned instead a "cañon of 8" several times.

[Boddie 1978] p. 8, columns 2-3

"… In the center was a higher structure on which was a **9-pound cannon mounted on a swivel**. The fort also had a **4-pound cannon**."

[Hicks & Parkinson 1980]

pp. 173-174: " … **Three hundred yards from the seashore and a hundred yards from the river's edge**, the big stockade dominated the gateway to Texas' main water highway. The **fort was a circle, three hundred feet in diameter, the outer wall a double wall of large upright stakes, sharpened at the top. Six feet inside the first row was a second row of logs, with the space filled in with sand to about four feet from the top**. The resulting barricade was nearly impregnable to small cannon fire, and the final rise of the outer fence gave protection to the defenders at the wall.

   In the center of the compound was a high mound of earth, taller than the facing walls. Hollowed into the side of this was a powder magazine, and on top was a **pivot-mounted nine-pound cannon**, surrounded by a wood parapet. Elsewhere in the compound, their roofs showing above the stockade, were various buildings. A wide, waist-deep moat surrounded the entire fort at a distance of fifty yards, fed from a small bayou that entered the river here."

pp. 217-218: "There was one weapon the Texians did not know about. It was a **small swivel gun** that could be mounted at any of the several points on the perimeter wall. **Smaller than a cannon**, it could nevertheless **fire a two-inch ball** at great velocity and with deadly accuracy. Both the Texians and the Mexicans, most of them, were unaware of this weapon, but it might just make the difference. He was very sure they would try to get under the range of the big cannon. It was here, at close range, that the swivel gun would come into play."

p.220: "Ugartechea called a lieutenant to him and directed the **swivel gun to be mounted on the north wall**. Within minutes it was there, and the gunners opened fire. … The swivel gun was almost directly above him, and the gunner saw his flash and brought it around and down. He fired, and the ball found the bulwark, ripped through the planking and took Buckner high in the chest. He gasped and grabbed Britt Bailey's arm, his hand crushing down on his friend's bicep, then relaxing. Even a giant was no match for a **two-inch ball**."

p. 226: "... we are low on ammunition for both our cannon and our muskets. We have **forty-five cannon balls, seventy-eight for the swivel gun and about six hundred musket rounds**."

Appendix 3 – Burial Locations of Persons with Connection to old Velasco

Allhands, James Llewellyn (1879-1978)
https://www.findagrave.com/memorial/204247294/james-llewellyn-allhands

Archer, Branch Tanner (1790-1856)
https://www.findagrave.com/memorial/6064464/branch-tanner-archer

Austin, Moses (1761-1821)
https://www.findagrave.com/memorial/5267453/moses-austin
Austin, Stephen Fuller (1793-1836)
https://www.findagrave.com/memorial/6464/stephen-fuller-austin
https://www.findagrave.com/memorial/45/stephen-fuller-austin
Austin, Henry (1782-1852)
https://www.findagrave.com/memorial/7778932/henry-austin

Bache, Alexander Dallas (1806-1867)
https://www.findagrave.com/memorial/6450164/alexander-dallas-bache

Barker, Eugene Campbell (1874-1956)
https://www.findagrave.com/memorial/56889391/eugene-campbell-barker

Barnett, Thomas (1798-1843)
https://www.findagrave.com/memorial/235368292/thomas-barnett

Bates, Joseph (1805-1888)
https://www.findagrave.com/memorial/7779204/joseph-bates

Bell, Josiah Hughes (1791-1838)
https://www.findagrave.com/memorial/9447082/josiah-hughes-bell

Binkley, William Campbell (1889-1970)
https://www.findagrave.com/memorial/6699390/william-campbell-binkley

Brown, Henry Stevenson (1783-1834)
https://www.findagrave.com/memorial/9443055/henry-stevenson-brown
Brown, John Henry (1820-1895)
https://www.findagrave.com/memorial/9803/john-henry-brown

Brown, Jeremiah (-1839)
https://www.findagrave.com/memorial/213852706/jeremiah-brown
Raine, Frances Rebecca *Spragins* Brown (1816-1907)
https://www.findagrave.com/memorial/197331293/frances-rebecca-raine

Bryan, Moses Austin (1817-1895)
https://www.findagrave.com/memorial/27927401/moses_austin-bryan

Burnet, David Gouverneur (1788-1870)
https://www.findagrave.com/memorial/6475360/david-gouverneur-burnet

Carson, Samuel Price (1798-1838)
https://www.findagrave.com/memorial/7121026/samuel-price-carson

Chriesman, Horatio (1792-1878)
https://www.findagrave.com/memorial/16066259/horatio-chriesman

Coode, Sir John (1816-1892)
https://www.findagrave.com/memorial/71379354/john-coode

Cross, Abraham "Abram" (1837-1905)
https://www.findagrave.com/memorial/153209654/abraham-cross

De Zavala, Lorenzo (1788-1836)
https://www.findagrave.com/memorial/8063114/manuel-lorenzo_justiniano-de_zavala

Fearn, Howard B. (1923-2012)
https://www.findagrave.com/memorial/122255128/howard-b-fearn

Fisher, Samuel Rhoads (1794-1839)
https://www.findagrave.com/memorial/8078169/samuel-rhoads-fisher

Follett, Alexander Glass (1822-1906)
https://www.findagrave.com/memorial/60130951/alexander-glass-follett
Follett, Susan Adaline "Addie" Hudgins (1876-1977)
https://www.findagrave.com/memorial/41584680/susan-adaline-follett

Gray, William Fairfax (1787-1841)
https://www.findagrave.com/memorial/15123170/william-fairfax-gray

Grayson, Peter Wagener (1788-1838)
https://www.findagrave.com/memorial/91107671/peter-wagener-grayson
Grayson, Thomas Wigg (1808-1873)
https://www.findagrave.com/memorial/16233346/thomas-wigg-grayson

Green, Thomas Jefferson (1802-1863)
https://www.findagrave.com/memorial/8057227/thomas-jefferson-green

Hall, Warren DeWitt Clinton (1794-1867)
https://www.findagrave.com/memorial/33011284/warren-dewitt_clinton-hall

Hamilton, Robert (1781-1845)
https://www.findagrave.com/memorial/140986927/robert-hamilton

Hardeman, Bailey (1795-1836)

https://www.findagrave.com/memorial/18047/bailey-hardeman

Harris, William Plunkett (1707-1843)
https://www.findagrave.com/memorial/177399146/william-plunkett-harris

Hawkins, Charles Edward (1802-1837)
https://www.findagrave.com/memorial/148124854/charles-edward-hawkins

Herndon, John Hunter (1813-1878)
https://www.findagrave.com/memorial/55665368/john-hunter-herndon

Holley, Mary Austin Phelps (1784-1846)
https://www.findagrave.com/memorial/29348131/mary-phelps-holley#

Hoskins, Isaac C. (1797-1859)
https://www.findagrave.com/memorial/193877292/isaac-c.-hoskins
Hoskins, Nancy Ann Spragins (1803-1873)
https://www.findagrave.com/memorial/60049680/nancy-ann-hoskins

Houston, Sam (1793-1863)
https://www.findagrave.com/memorial/510/sam-houston

Hudgins, John Longest (1822-1909)
https://www.findagrave.com/memorial/102247137/john-longest-hudgins
Hudgins, Charles D. (1857-1924)
https://www.findagrave.com/memorial/102251132/charles-d-hudgins

Hunter, Kermit Houston (1910-2001)
https://www.findagrave.com/memorial/40621971/kermit-houston-hunter

Jack, Spencer Houston (1811-1840)
https://www.findagrave.com/memorial/7730963/spencer-houston-jack

Johnson, Francis White (1799-1884)
https://www.findagrave.com/memorial/10707955/francis-white-johnson

Kramig, George Jr. (1919-2011)
https://www.findagrave.com/memorial/150228141/george-kramig

Lamar, Mirabeau Buonaparte (1798-1859)
https://www.findagrave.com/memorial/6548954/mirabeau-buonaparte-lamar

Lee, William McDole (1841-1925}
https://www.findagrave.com/memorial/127388320/william-md-lee

Letts, Bessie Lucille (Mrs. Clark Wright, 1901-1996)
https://www.findagrave.com/memorial/1347566/bessie-wright

Looscan, Adele Lubbock Briscoe (1848-1935)
https://www.findagrave.com/memorial/28689477/adele-lubbock-looscan

Lubbock, Francis Richard (1815-1905)
https://www.findagrave.com/memorial/8062038/francis-richard-lubbock

Manning, William Ray (1871-1942)
https://www.findagrave.com/memorial/179025954/william-ray-manning

McKinley, Lela Ethel (1905-1978)
https://www.findagrave.com/memorial/107751395/lela-ethel-mckinley

McKinney, Thomas Freeman (1801-1873)
https://www.findagrave.com/memorial/32784985/thomas-freeman-mckinney

Mitchell, Asa (1795-1865)
https://www.findagrave.com/memorial/173267663/asa-mitchell
Mitchell, Charlotte *Woodmancy* (1800-1830)
https://www.findagrave.com/memorial/213476181/charlotte-mitchell
Mitchell, Emily *Brisbane* (1816-1863)
https://www.findagrave.com/memorial/213476429/emily-mitchell

Morgan, James (1787-1866)
https://www.findagrave.com/memorial/8813220/james-morgan

Neill, Andrew John
https://www.findagrave.com/memorial/16360017/andrew-john-neill

Nunn, Alleine Spivey *Howren* (1881-1952)
https://www.findagrave.com/memorial/286704010/alleine-spivey-nunn

Perry, James Franklin (1790-1853)
https://www.findagrave.com/memorial/14005072/james-franklin-perry
Perry, Emily Austin Bryan (1795-1851)
https://www.findagrave.com/memorial/14005093/emily_margaret-bryan_perry

Potter, Robert (1800-1842)
https://www.findagrave.com/memorial/6638581/robert-potter

Russell, William Jarvis (1802-1881)
https://www.findagrave.com/memorial/16292035/william-jarvis-russell

Sandlin, Dale (1913-2010)
https://www.findagrave.com/memorial/50096683/dale-strait-sandlin

Santa Anna, Antonio López de (1795-1876)

https://www.findagrave.com/memorial/11566057/antonio-l%C3%B3pez_de_santa_anna

Shannon, James Thompson (1818-1883)
https://www.findagrave.com/memorial/212950127/james-thompson-shannon
Shannon, Charlotte Waterman *Follett* **(1830-1860)**
https://www.findagrave.com/memorial/212951442/charlotte-waterman-shannon
Shannon, Ellen Wilcox (1841-   )
https://www.findagrave.com/memorial/212950825/ellen-adele-shannon

Shelby, David (1799-1872)
https://www.findagrave.com/memorial/214659280/david-shelby

Shreve, John Milton (1811-1886)
https://www.findagrave.com/memorial/54230823/john-milton-shreve

Singleton, Harold (1922-1978)
https://www.findagrave.com/memorial/42113210/harold-dean-singleton

Smith, Ruby Cumby (1880-1972)
https://www.findagrave.com/memorial/185129336/ruby-cumby-smith

Sulakowski, Valery (1825-1873)
https://www.findagrave.com/memorial/205849071/valery-sulakowski

Terán, José Manuel Rafael Simeón de Mier y
https://www.findagrave.com/memorial/221662175/manuel-mier_y_ter%C3%A1n

Thompson, Henry Livingston (unknown-1837)
https://www.findagrave.com/memorial/9766826/henry-livingston-thompson

Turner, Amasa (1800-1877)
https://www.findagrave.com/memorial/30591492/amasa-turner

Waller, Edwin Leonard (1800-1881)
https://www.findagrave.com/memorial/18182/edwin-leonard-waller

Wharton, William Harris (1802-1839)
https://www.findagrave.com/memorial/6064483/william-harris-wharton

Williams, Samuel May (1795-1858)
https://www.findagrave.com/memorial/33399038/samuel-may-williams

Wilson, Robert (1793-1856)
https://www.findagrave.com/memorial/18207/robert-wilson

Wisner, George Young (1841-1906)
https://www.findagrave.com/memorial/199636886/george-young-wisner

Appendix 4 – Duke 1999 Master Plan (Courtesy of Bob Duke)

- five pages showing five panels (portrait)
- five pages showing five panels plus explanatory text (landscape)

Panel **2**

EXISTING
SURFSIDE JETTY PARK

PROPOSED CAMPING
SHELTERS—ADDITION TO
SURFSIDE JETTY PARK

SURFSIDE JETTY PARK
EXPANSION
PHASE 2
(PANELS 1-5)

BRAZORIA COUNTY PARK COMMISSION

Design and Graphics by

DUKE
Landscape Architecture +Planning
1815 Avenue K
Galveston, Texas 77550-4920
409-762-5193   duke_lap@swbell.net

Overall Master Plan shown below
with panels numbered

1   2   3   4   5

209

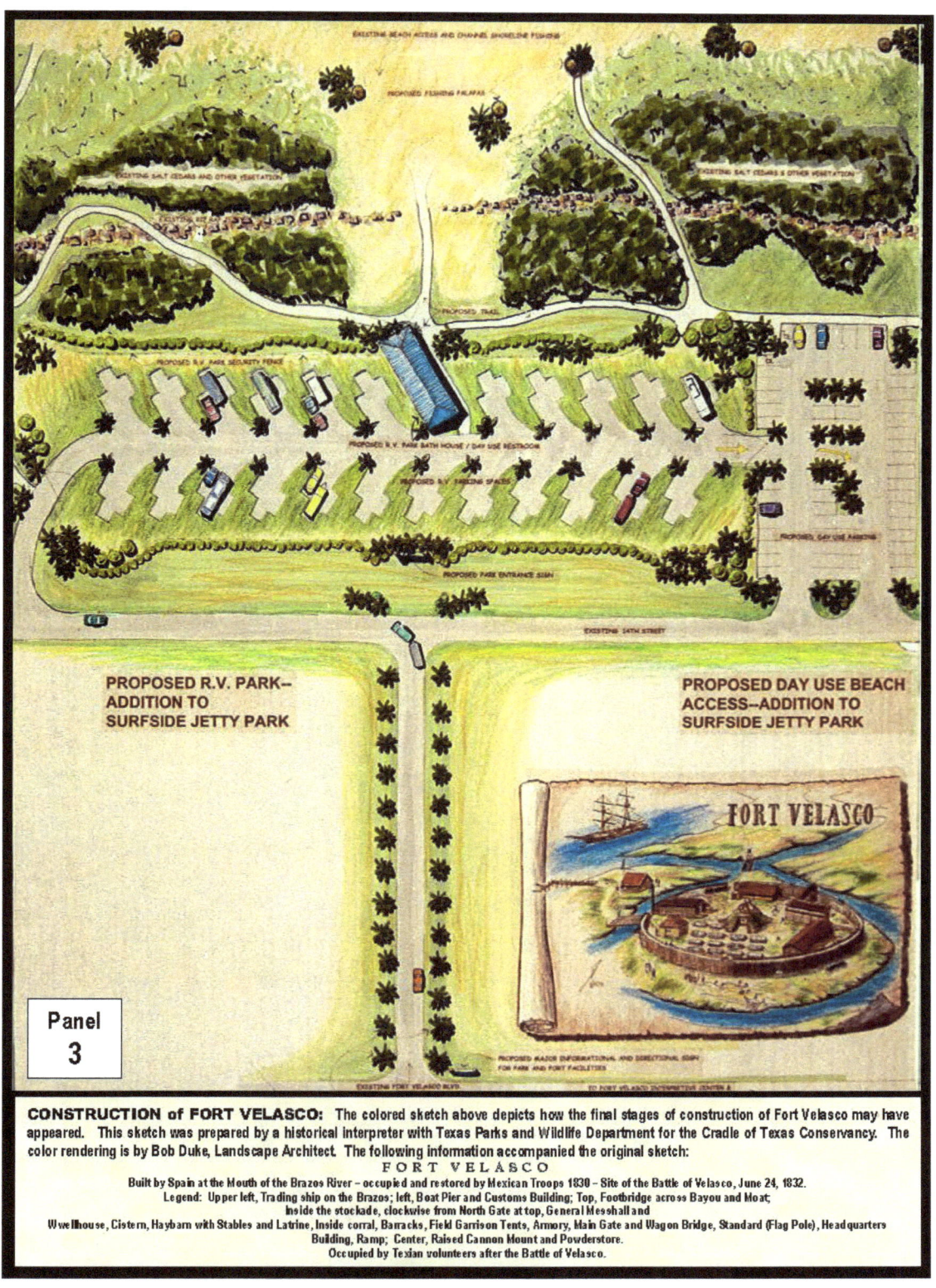

CONSTRUCTION of FORT VELASCO: The colored sketch above depicts how the final stages of construction of Fort Velasco may have appeared. This sketch was prepared by a historical interpreter with Texas Parks and Wildlife Department for the Cradle of Texas Conservancy. The color rendering is by Bob Duke, Landscape Architect. The following information accompanied the original sketch:

FORT VELASCO

Built by Spain at the Mouth of the Brazos River – occupied and restored by Mexican Troops 1830 – Site of the Battle of Velasco, June 24, 1832.

Legend: Upper left, Trading ship on the Brazos; left, Boat Pier and Customs Building; Top, Footbridge across Bayou and Moat; Inside the stockade, clockwise from North Gate at top, General Messhall and Wwellhouse, Cistern, Haybarn with Stables and Latrine, Inside corral, Barracks, Field Garrison Tents, Armory, Main Gate and Wagon Bridge, Standard (Flag Pole), Headquarters Building, Ramp; Center, Raised Cannon Mount and Powderstore.

Occupied by Texian volunteers after the Battle of Velasco.

PROPOSED HISTORIC FORT VELASCO RECONSTRUCTION

DUKE
Landscape Architecture +Planning
1815 Avenue K
Galveston, Texas 77550-4920
409-762-5193   duke_lap@swbell.net

Plaza Location
(Orientation of Large Drawing on following page is inverted)

PROPOSED VILLAGE OF SURFSIDE CITY HALL PARK

CONCEPT PLAN for FORT VELASCO: The current plan for Fort Velasco, shown above, is based on research by historical interpreters for Texas Parks and Wildlife Department and professional and amateur archaeologists who have worked on archeological digs near the original Fort Velasco site. While the location shown on this plan may not be the exact location of the original fortification, it will well serve the purposes of historical reconstruction—to bring to today's society a glimpse into our nation's past. Current plans are for the reconstructed fort to be a place that the visitor can experience from the inside out—camping & picnicking within the fort will be permitted and encouraged. Period tents—for campers--and historical reproductions of buildings will add to the realism of a visit to this facility.

PLAZA del AMIGOS de Mexico y Tejas The idea for the *Plaza of the Friends of Mexico and Texas* (illustrated to the left) came about during the early stages of planning and design work on the overall Master Plan. The story of Fort Velasco will by necessity be the story of both Mexico and Texas. The concept for the plaza is to provide a place for the citizens of Texas and Mexico to display special mementos of those who served valiantly on the frontier here at the mouth of the Brazos River. The plaza with its large map of Mexico and Texas will be easily viewed from the third story interpretive center, complementing the story that is both Texas' and Mexico's.

PROPOSED BOAT RAMP
&
PROPOSED WETLAND TRAIL

Panel
5

212

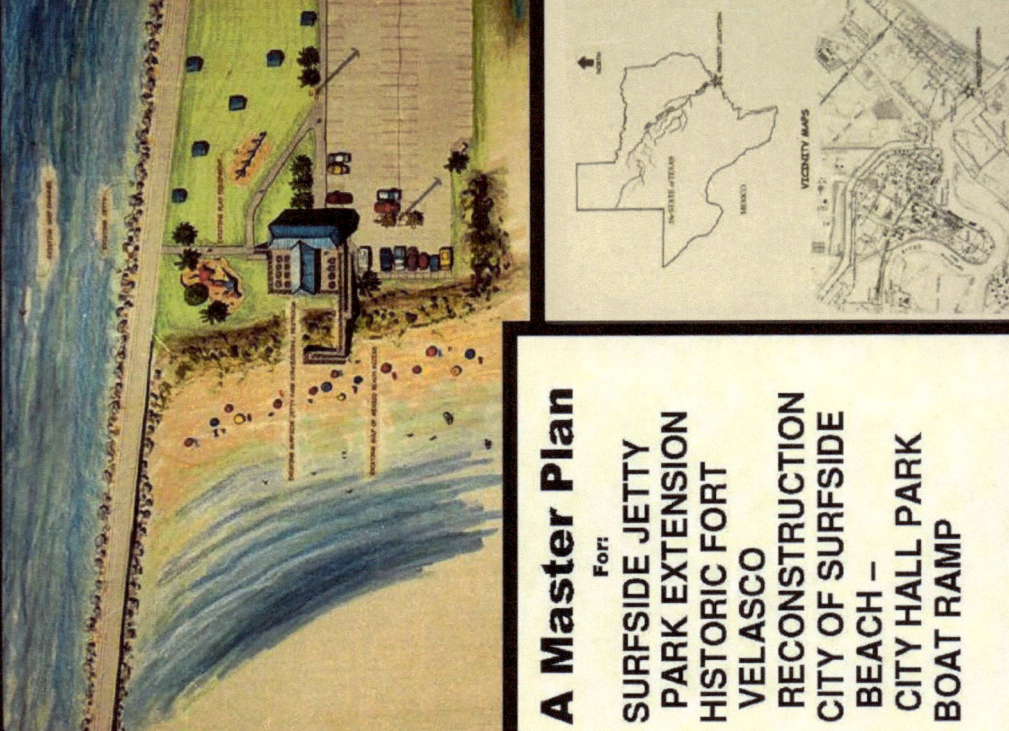

A Master Plan

For:

- **SURFSIDE JETTY PARK EXTENSION**
- **HISTORIC FORT VELASCO RECONSTRUCTION**
- **CITY OF SURFSIDE BEACH – CITY HALL PARK**
- **BOAT RAMP**

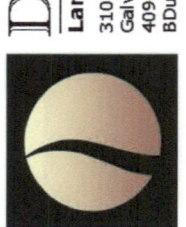

DUKE
Landscape Architecture + Planning

3108 Pine Street
Galveston, Texas 77551
409-356-3503
BDuke@DUKELandscapeArchitecture.com

Project Name: SURFSIDE JETTY PARK and HISTORIC FORT VELASCO

Location: Surfside Beach, Texas

Project Owner: Brazoria County Parks.

Project Description: Brazoria County and the Village of Surfside Beach jointly sought to connect the existing Surfside Jetty Park with the existing city hall (a historic Coast Guard station building) via development of County-owned land and acquisition and development of private and public land. The desired result is to be an expanded recreational palette, including more fishing areas, camping, and the re-creation of the look and feel of historic Fort Velasco, the probable location of the first conflict that resulted in independence from Mexico for Texas.

Scope: provide an illustrated master plan and estimates for continued development of existing beach park with addition of RV parking spaces, additional day use facilities and re-creation of historic fort

Image description: Existing Surfside Jetty Park

Status: awaiting funding

(Continued on following page)

Panel 1

DUKE
Landscape Architecture +Planning

1815 Avenue K
Galveston, Texas 77550-4920
409-762-5193   duke_lap@swbell.net

213

Panel 2

PROPOSED CAMPING SHELTERS–ADDITION TO SURFSIDE JETTY PARK

EXISTING SURFSIDE JETTY PARK

SURFSIDE JETTY PARK EXPANSION PHASE 2
(PANELS 1-5)
BRAZORIA COUNTY PARK COMMISSION

Landscape Architecture + Planning
1813 Avenue K
Galveston, Texas 77550-4920
409-762-5193   duke_lsp@swbell.net

Overall Master Plan shown below with panels numbered

DUKE
Landscape Architecture + Planning
3108 Pine Street
Galveston, Texas 77551
409-356-3503
BDuke@DUKELandscapeArchitecture.com

Project Name: SURFSIDE JETTY PARK and HISTORIC FORT VELASCO

Location: Surfside Beach, Texas

Project Owner: Brazoria County Parks.

Project Description: Brazoria County and the Village of Surfside Beach jointly sought to connect the existing Surfside Jetty Park with the existing city hall (a historic Coast Guard station building) via development of County-owned land and acquisition and development of private and public land. The desired result is to be an expanded recreational palette, including more fishing areas, camping, and the re-creation of the look and feel of historic Fort Velasco, the probable location of the first conflict that resulted in independence from Mexico for Texas.

Scope: provide an illustrated master plan and estimates for continued development of existing beach park with addition of RV parking spaces, additional day use facilities and re-creation of historic fort

Image description: Existing Surfside Jetty Park (left side of drawing) and proposed shelter camping area and new park office (right side of drawing), and new trail connections via existing bridge. At bottom is key to all sheets.

Status: awaiting funding

(Continued on following page)

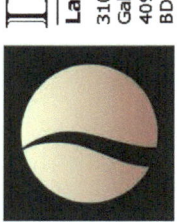

214

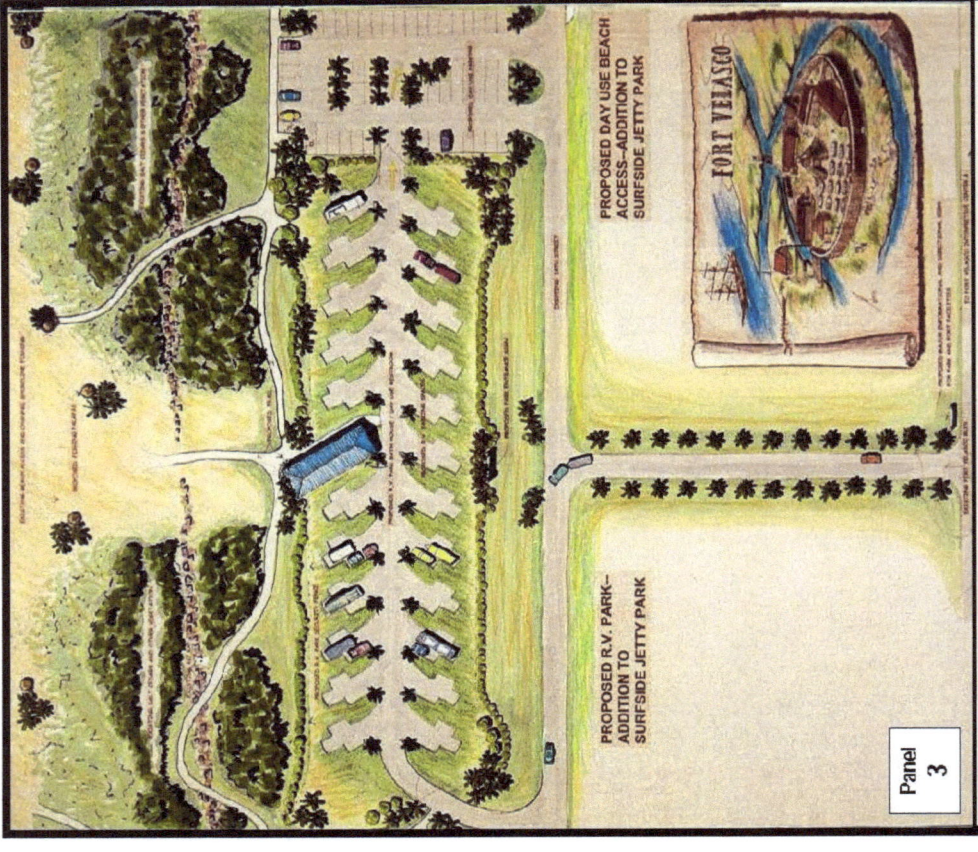

PROPOSED DAY USE BEACH ACCESS—ADDITION TO SURFSIDE JETTY PARK

PROPOSED R.V. PARK—ADDITION TO SURFSIDE JETTY PARK

Panel 3

FORT VELASCO

CONSTRUCTION of FORT VELASCO: The colored sketch above depicts how the final stages of construction of Fort Velasco may have appeared. This sketch was prepared by a historical interpreter with Texas Parks and Wildlife Department for the Cradle of Texas Conservancy. The color rendering is by Bob Duke, Landscape Architect. The following information accompanied the original sketch:

FORT VELASCO

Built by Scam at the Mouth of the Brazos River – occupied and restored by Mexican Troops 1830 – Site of the Battle of Velasco, June 24, 1832.

Legend: Upper left, Trading ship or the Brazos; Left, Boat Pier and Customs Building Top, Footbridge across Bayou and Moat

Inside the stockade, clockwise from North Gate at top, General Mess hall and

Wheelhouse, Cistern, Hay Barn with Stables and Latrine, Inside corra., Barracks, Field Garrison Tents, Armory, Main Gate and Wall, or Bridge, Standard Flag Pole, Headquarters Building, Shanty, Corral, Barabel Cannon Mount and Powder cans

Occupied by Texian volunteers after the Battle of Velasco.

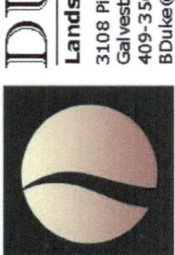

DUKE
Landscape Architecture + Planning

3108 Pine Street
Galveston, Texas 77551
409-356-3503
BDuke@DUKELandscapeArchitecture.com

Project Name: SURFSIDE JETTY PARK and HISTORIC FORT VELASCO

Location: Surfside Beach, Texas

Project Owner: Brazoria County Parks.

Project Description: Brazoria County and the Village of Surfside Beach jointly sought to connect the existing Surfside Jetty Park with the existing city hall (a historic Coast Guard station building) via development of County-owned land and acquisition and development of private and public land. The desired result is to be an expanded recreational palette, including more fishing areas, camping, and the re-creation of the look and feel of historic Fort Velasco, the probable location of the first conflict that resulted in independence from Mexico for Texas.

Scope: provide an illustrated master plan and estimates for continued development of existing beach park with addition of RV parking spaces, additional day use facilities and re-creation of historic fort

Image description: Proposed entrance, RV Park and fishing access into ship channel/former mouth of Brazos River.

Status: awaiting funding

(Continued on following page)

215

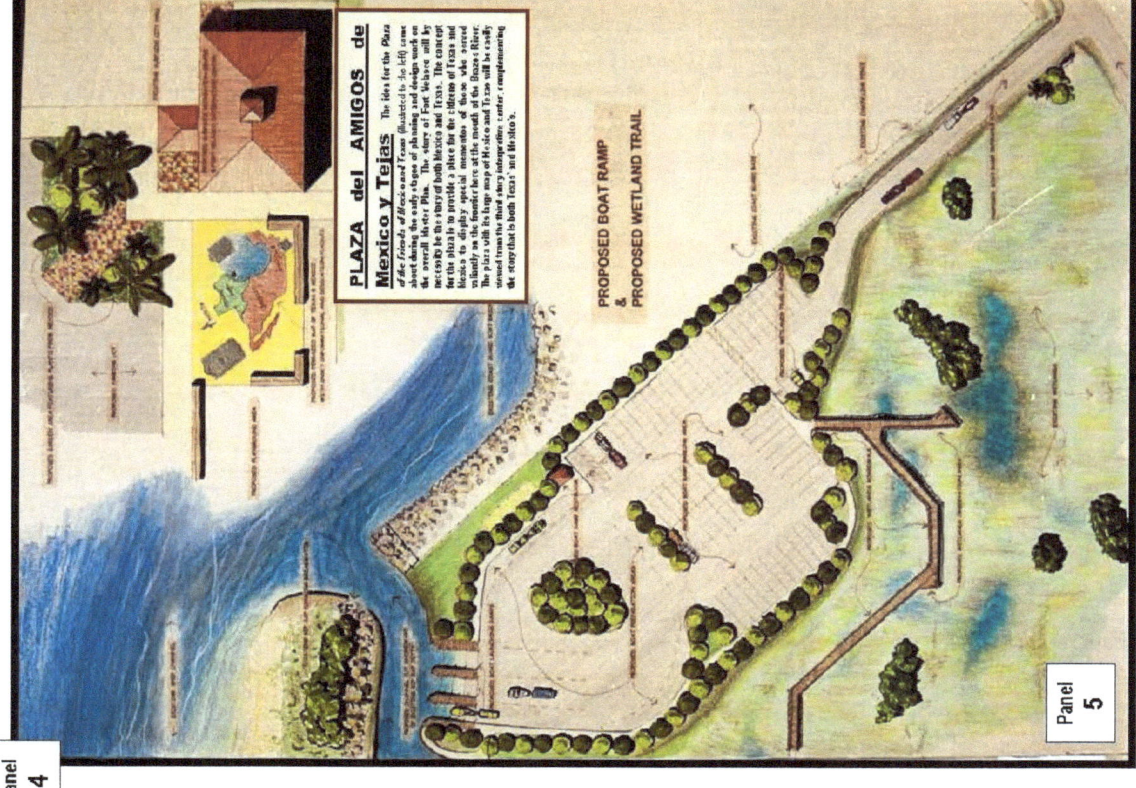

Panel 5

PLAZA del AMIGOS de Mexico y Tejas

PROPOSED BOAT RAMP
&
PROPOSED WETLAND TRAIL

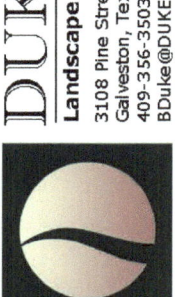

DUKE
Landscape Architecture + Planning

3108 Pine Street
Galveston, Texas 77551
409-356-3503
BDuke@DUKELandscapeArchitecture.com

Project Name: SURFSIDE JETTY PARK and
HISTORIC FORT VELASCO

Location: Surfside Beach, Texas

Project Owner: Brazoria County Parks.

Project Description: Brazoria County and the Village of Surfside Beach jointly sought to connect the existing Surfside Jetty Park with the existing city hall (a historic Coast Guard station building) via development of County-owned land and acquisition and development of private and public land. The desired result is to be an expanded recreational palette, including more fishing areas, camping, and the re-creation of the look and feel of historic Fort Velasco, the probable location of the first conflict that resulted in independence from Mexico for Texas.

Scope: provide an illustrated master plan and estimates for continued development of existing beach park with addition of RV parking spaces, additional day use facilities and re-creation of historic fort

Image description: Proposed boat ramp and wetlands boardwalk.

Status: awaiting funding

(Continued on following page)

216

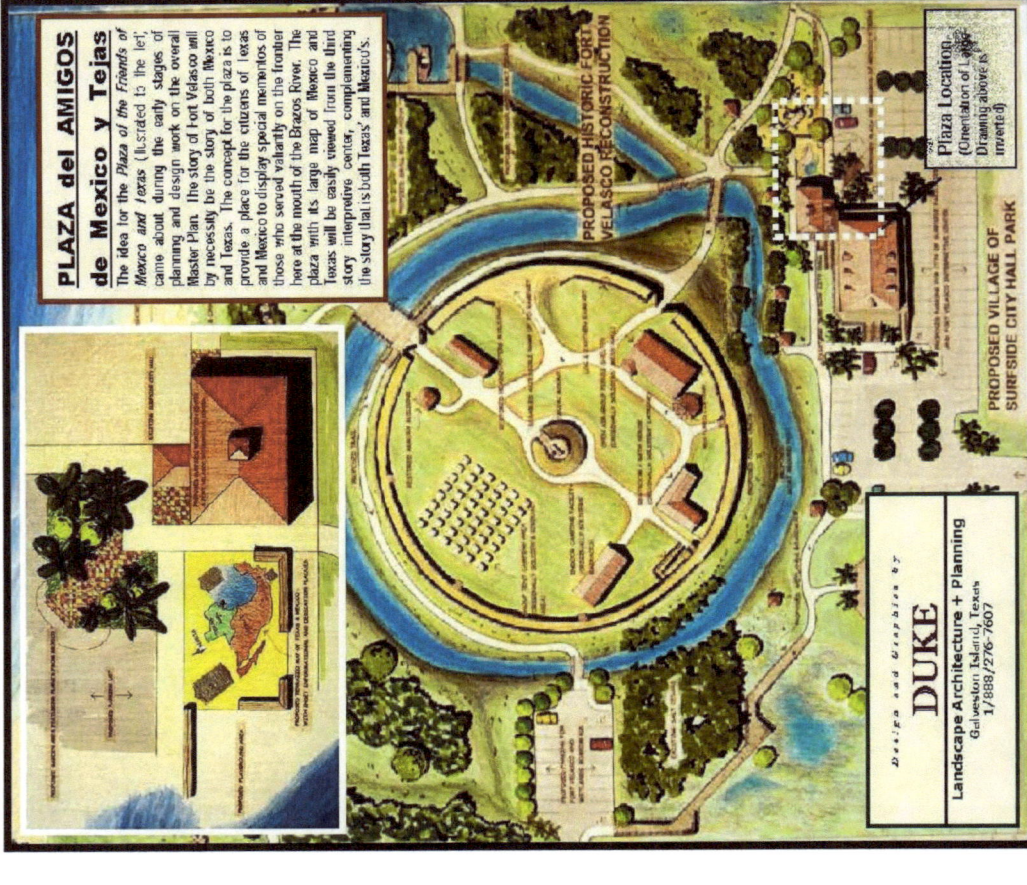

PLAZA del AMIGOS de Mexico y Tejas

The idea for the *Plaza of the Friends of Mexico and Texas* (illustrated to the left) came about during the early stages of planning and design work on the overall Master Plan. The story of Fort Velasco will by necessity be the story of both Mexico and Texas. The concept for the plaza is to provide a place for the citizens of Texas and Mexico to display special mementos of those who served valiantly on the frontier here at the mouth of the Brazos River. The plaza with its large map of Mexico and Texas will be easily viewed from the third story interpretive center, complementing the story that is both Texas and Mexico's.

PROPOSED HISTORIC FORT VELASCO RECONSTRUCTION

PROPOSED VILLAGE OF SURFSIDE CITY HALL PARK

Plaza Location (Orientation of Large Drawing above is inverted)

Design and Graphics by

DUKE
Landscape Architecture + Planning
Galveston Island, Texas
1/888/276-7607

CONCEPT PLAN for FORT VELASCO: The current plan for Fort Velasco, shown above, is based on research by historical interpreters for Texas Parks and Wildlife Department and professional and amateur archaeologists who have worked on archeological digs near the original Fort Velasco site. While the location shown on this plan may not be the exact location of the original fortification, it will well serve the purposes of historical reconstruction—to bring to today's society a glimpse into our nation's past. Current plans are for the reconstructed fort to be a place that the visitor can experience from the inside out - camping & picnicking within the fort will be permitted and encouraged. Period tents—for campers—and historical reproductions of buildings will add to the realism of a visit to this facility.

DUKE
Landscape Architecture + Planning

3108 Pine Street
Galveston, Texas 77551
409-356-3503
BDuke@DUKELandscapeArchitecture.com

Project Name: SURFSIDE JETTY PARK and HISTORIC FORT VELASCO

Location: Surfside Beach, Texas

Project Owner: Brazoria County Parks.

Project Description: Brazoria County and the Village of Surfside Beach jointly sought to connect the existing Surfside Jetty Park with the existing city hall (a historic Coast Guard station building) via development of County-owned land and acquisition and development of private and public land. The desired result is to be an expanded recreational palette, including more fishing areas, camping, and the re-creation of the look and feel of historic Fort Velasco, the probable location of the first conflict that resulted in independence from Mexico for Texas.

Scope: provide an illustrated master plan and estimates for continued development of existing beach park with addition of RV parking spaces, additional day use facilities and re-creation of historic fort

Image description: Proposed Fort Velasco re-construction, City Hall / Visitors' Center (bottom center and inset), and connection to small marina and boat ramp.

Status: awaiting funding

(Continued on following page)

INDEX

222

Topsail Schooner – a type favored in early Texas due to speed, agility and shallow draft

224

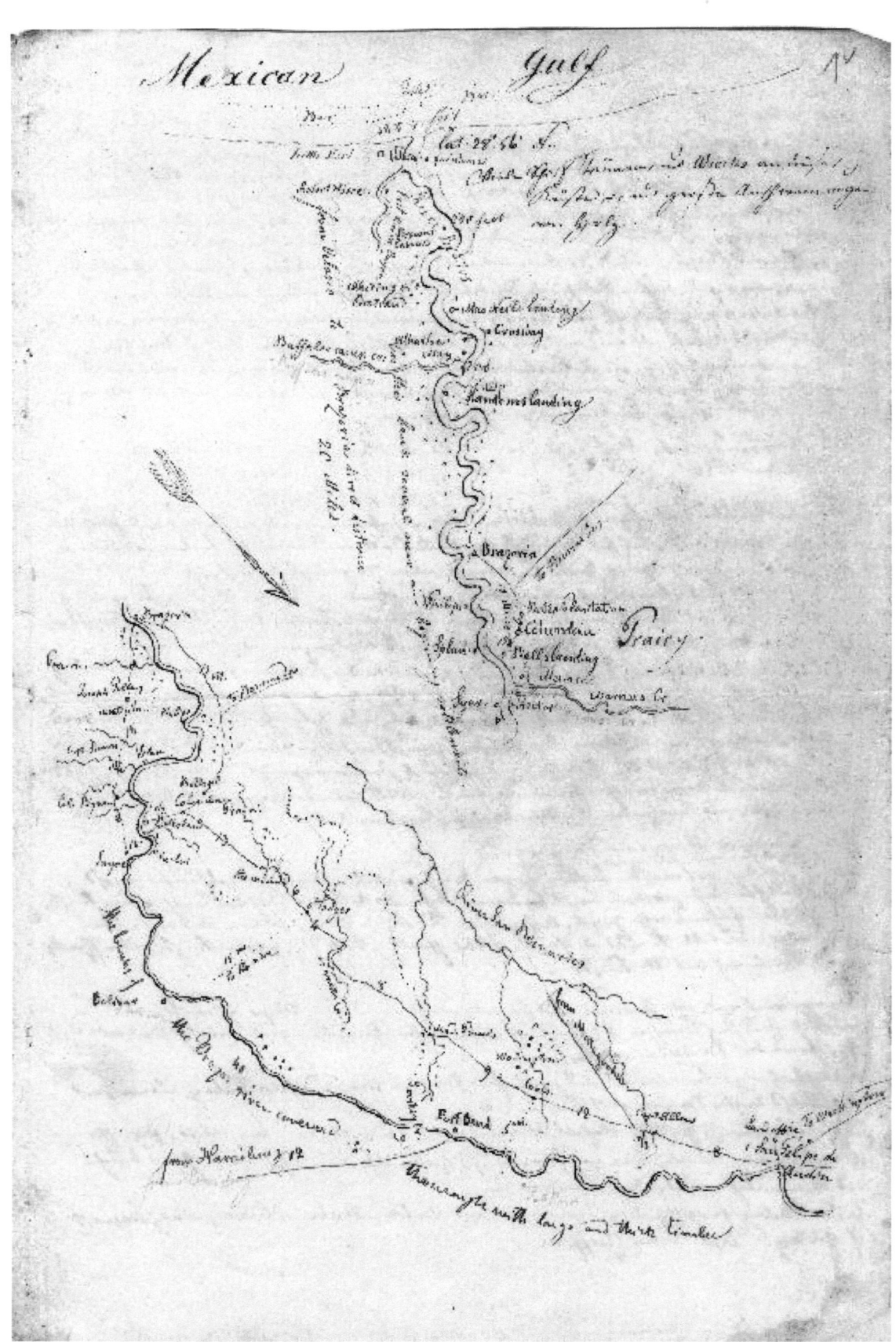

Eduard Harkort's Drawing No. 6 of the lower Brazos Valley – early 1836